The Kunar ADT and The Afghan COIN Fight

*How National Guard Agribusiness Development
Teams Support Battle Space Commander's
COunter INsurgency Operations*

LTC David M. Kelly

authorHOUSE®

AuthorHouse™
1663 Liberty Drive
Bloomington, IN 47403
www.authorhouse.com
Phone: 1-800-839-8640

First published by AuthorHouse   04/27/2011

ISBN: 978-1-4567-5303-0 (sc)
ISBN: 978-1-4567-5304-7 (hc)
ISBN: 978-1-4567-5302-3 (e)

Library of Congress Control Number: 2011906623

Printed in the United States of America

Cover photo © Janet Killeen, www.zonesofconflict.org
The game, Buzkashi, is played with a headless goat. Strong athletes and fierce horsemen, some of the riders are even professional wrestlers in the off season.

Edited by: Shelly Rosenberg

Dedicated to my Father and Family for the endless support they gave during my deployments and the soldiers of the Kunar ADT

TABLE OF CONTENTS

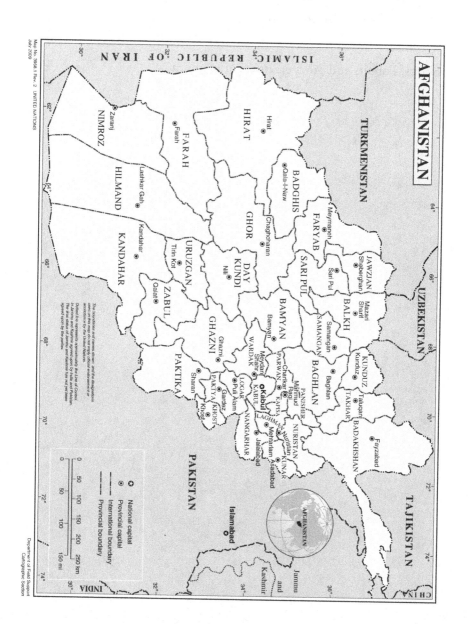

AFGHANISTAN

National capital
Provincial capital
International boundary
Provincial boundary

Map No. 3958.1 Rev. 2   UNITED NATIONS
July 2009

Department of Field Support
Cartographic Section

x

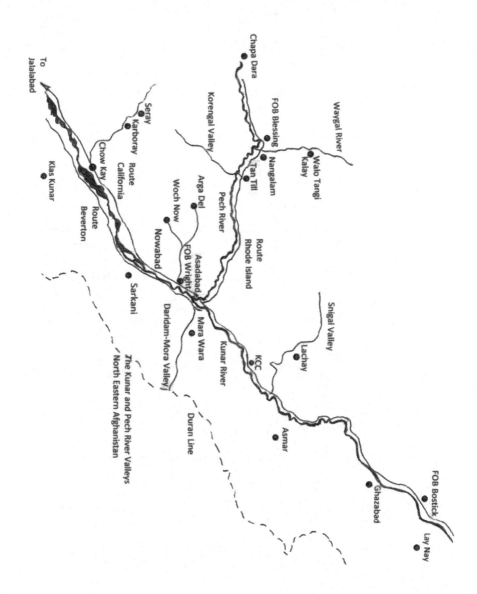

The Kunar and Pech River Valleys
North Eastern Afghanistan

PREFACE

The war in Afghanistan is a counter insurgency, which is referred to as COIN or the COIN fight. The difference between a COIN war and traditional warfare is the enemy doesn't always wear a uniform or fly a national flag. In an insurgency, there is an established government that is attempting to maintain the rule of law and provide for the general welfare of its nation while defending itself against an armed army that melts away into its own populace. In traditional warfare, established nations field their armies against each other in uniform flying the flag of their nation. In traditional warfare, there is a specific objective for going to war; this isn't always the case in an insurgency. Nations may find themselves fighting a proxy war, which is an insurgency funded and trained by another nation. The aggressor nation uses an insurgency to politically buffer itself, but still achieve the desired outcome. One desired outcome would be to make a country unstable so that its resources can't be exported in competition with the aggressor nation.

Insurgencies thrive in regions and nations that lack organizational and physical infrastructure to adequately defend themselves. Nations that have good transportation systems make it difficult for insurgents to be combat effective. A well-developed transportation system allows a country to rapidly move law enforcement personnel and troops to areas of conflict. Afghanistan's lack of infrastructure and governmental organization is what led to the Provincial Reconstruction Team (PRT) concept.

The United States has provided the majority of the PRTs to Afghanistan with a few more being provided by member nations of the International

Security Assistance Force (ISAF). A typical U.S. PRT is a joint organization of Army, Air Force and Navy to include both active duty and reserve personnel and other government agencies. Their main goal it to rebuild infrastructure and to support local government operations. PRT projects vary from the construction of new roads and bridges, to schools and medical clinics. The impact of the PRTs has been very successful in stabilizing local and regional economies and provincial governments. Road building, while expensive, hazardous and difficult, provided almost immediate results in reducing terrorism by both the Taliban and other insurgent forces.

The first PRTs in Afghanistan were established in 2001 using Civil Affairs units. Within a few years there was a need to address Afghanistan's floundering agriculture sector. Prior to the Soviet invasion, Afghanistan could feed its population and export agriculture products. Today, Afghanistan must import food to meet its domestic requirements. The cause for importation is due to the population surge and the underutilization of agriculture land. The Agribusiness Development Teams (ADT) were created in 2008 to address the provincial and village agricultural business needs.

The ADTs are special units, which only exist in Afghanistan. You will not find an ADT unit anywhere else. Since the active duty army didn't have soldiers with extensive farming and livestock experience to draw upon they turned to the minutemen, the National Guard, the citizen soldiers who for over 300 years have been both soldiers and tradesmen. Several states came forward and signed up to sponsor ADTs. They include Missouri, Kentucky, Illinois, Iowa, Kansas, Indiana, and California. Some states only fielded one ADT while others have fielded four or more teams to the same region.

This book is the chronicle of the Kunar ADT, with the vast majority of troops coming from the 40th Infantry Division and Task Force Warrior of the California National Guard and one from the Virginia National Guard. The Kunar ADT was known by several different names, but it was referred to as the Kunar ADT, just like the PRT at Camp Wright was called the Kunar PRT. The 40th ID ADT was deployed in September 2009 and called the Kunar ADT until it returned in August of 2010. I have made brief reference to combat experience of other units as they relate to the Kunar ADT, but didn't go into detail. I felt that these are stories that need to be told by people with firsthand experience as they relate to the soldiers and history of their unit. I wanted to illustrate those individual units even though they were located at different FOBs and COPs were all inter-related.

Chapter One

THE CALL

The creation of the Kunar ADT started by recruiting the talent required to support the mission. I received a phone call in February 2009 from Col Grimm, the division chief of staff, who would later command the Kunar ADT, telling me that I was going to Afghanistan and to report to Camp Roberts the following drill for SRP (Soldier Readiness Processing).

The SRP process includes a review of your life insurance, will, power of attorney, finances, and a physical. For my last deployment to Kosovo the Army gave me a full physical and learned that I was a type II diabetic. While they chastised me for being a diabetic, they deployed me anyway. When I returned home from Kosovo I wasn't allowed to go on any state active duty missions (where it was safe) because I was a diabetic. I was prepared to receive the same chastising for being a diabetic at the SRP site for this deployment to Afghanistan. I've prided myself for being in shape and trim - not your typical diabetic who is obese and out of shape.

When it came time for my medical review, I was honest and put down that I was a diabetic and taking Metformin for my diabetes. The state G-1 saw what I wrote and told me that there was no room in the Army for diabetics and he would proceed with a medical separation. I was smart enough to know the truth. In 2004, the American Diabetes poster boy was an infantry man serving in Iraq who used an insulin pump. I also knew a few doctors in Iraq who were taking insulin too. If they were allowed to stay, then I should be. The G-1 stated that there were new regulations that specifically stated that diabetics were to be medically separated. This concerned me because I didn't have my 20-year letter to retire yet. For some reason I could never get the National Guard to count my enlisted time so I was a few months short of a full twenty years even though I had served over 25 years and had two overseas deployments.

I was able to find the regulations about diabetics. At the bottom it said a diabetic could stay in the service if their A1c was below 7 and they were not taking any medication. My A1c was a 6.1, but I was on Metformin.

I went to my doctor, a retired Air Force major and told him what was going on. He shook his head in disgust while he read the forms the Army had given me. He gave me a full physical, then looked at how we could tackle the problem of the Metformin. My weight had been very steady and optimal for a diabetic. I was a long-distance runner and in very good shape. He said to try to lose ten to fifteen pounds, and start experimenting with food again. He would then check my blood sugar to see how it was affecting me. I was able to lose 20 pounds and didn't require any Metformin. The proof was my A1c, which came in at 6.2 without medication. He signed off all the Army's forms and I sent them off to the G-1 at the Joint Forces Headquarters. I didn't receive my official medical release from the G-1 until almost half way through the deployment.

My diabetes was just an example of the medical problems the troops had to clear before they were allowed to deploy. Many of the troops had old injuries from prior combat that had healed but required additional certification that they were fully mission capable from their private physician. The Army had no problems requesting National Guard soldiers to get medical tests and evaluations at the soldier's expense. By the end of the summer all of the troops who could be medically cleared, were.

Chapter Two

KEEPING A SECRET AND GETTING READY

I had to keep the possibility of a deployment secret for some time. Since I returned from Kosovo in 2006 I had been placed on one deployment list after another. Each time just before the unit deployed my name was removed from the list.

It was about this time my mom was diagnosed with breast cancer; this meant I really had to keep my mouth shut. When my mom's surgery was over I let my father know about the deployment. The two of us agreed that we shouldn't tell either my mother or sister for a while longer. Funny, neither my mother nor sister picked up on my studying Pashto, the language spoken in the region of Afghanistan where we were going or that my father had taken a big interest in events in Afghanistan. When I finally told my mom and sister I really wished I was having lunch with the Taliban. My sister just about killed me!

Our official unit's name was Kunar Agribusiness Development Team. We were stationed on Federal Avenue in West Los Angeles. We didn't exist as a unit; our troops came from all over California with one from Virginia, SGT Stevens who managed the orchards of Thomas Jefferson's Monticello estate. Our training started in April with combat life saving where we gave each other IVs and learned about the latest life saving innovations used on the battlefield. That took four days. Then we had a day of hand-to-hand combat training. I had ruptured a disk in my neck the year before while serving at a wildfire in Northern California, so my neck was giving me problems, mostly pain. By the end of the day I felt like a giant practice dummy with a few bruises.

In May we went up to Camp Roberts for more training on vehicles. It turns out the biggest cause of injury and death in Afghanistan is vehicle rollovers and accidents. The Army took a vehicle and mounded in on a mammoth rotisserie that spins the whole vehicle upside down. They had us get in it with our seatbelts on, then rotated the truck several times stopping either with us hanging upside down or on our side. We had two minutes to exit the vehicle. Two minutes is about the amount of time it takes for the fuel to catch on fire and cook everyone inside.

August was our biggest month for training. On the first day of the month, we had a big barbeque for the troops and their families. My mother and sister still didn't know that I was deploying to Afghanistan and the barbeque was just four days away. My dad had told me to leave it to him and he would break the news to my mother. I asked him on the Monday evening prior to the barbeque if he had told her. He said "Oh no, I haven't yet. Now is a good time for you to tell her while she is watching Walker Texas Ranger." I went out and told her and she seemed to take it well. I had planned to tell my sister in person the next night. The following morning I received a rather heated email from my sister. Turns out my mom didn't take it as well as I thought.

The Kunar ADT is a very small unit with only 62 people, who were all hand picked. The core of the unit, the Agriculture Section, (also known as the Ag Platoon) is made up of 15 agriculture specialists and animal experts. We are protected by a security platoon of 40 National Guard infantrymen and supported by a headquarters section and a small Intel group.

After the barbeque, the Ag Platoon went to a university located in southern California, which in its glory years specialized in agriculture and engineering, for a concentrated class on agriculture, which was a complete waste of time and taxpayers' money. The school's dean introduced himself and then proclaimed that they teach urban agriculture and specialized in how to maintain golf courses and city parks, not growing crops. The instructor had no experience in the real world or in agriculture! To the credit of the university they did have several experts come in and speak on the last day of the training. While we were at the university, our medics were at camp Williams Utah going through their certification. By the second week of August the Kunar ADT had reassembled at Camp Roberts for weapons training and certification.

The Kunar ADT was outfitted with all new weapons straight off the production line with the exception of our M-14s and 9mm pistols. The unit was fielded with 50-cal machine guns, MK-19s, 240s, and SAWs. Everyone would carry an M-4 and a 9mm pistol. The MK-19 is a machine gun that fires grenades; the 240 and the SAW (Squad Assault Weapon) are machine guns, which can be carried by one soldier. The M-4 is the carbine version of the M-16 rifle. A few select individuals had M-14s, an old rifle that the Army was bringing back for a short time until the new M1-10 could be fielded. Our M-14s came from the state's honor unit and were modified to hold the newer scopes. For a little unit we could give anyone a real hangover.

At Camp Roberts we went through several pallets of ammo in a few days. When we weren't shooting we were doing battle drills, how to react to ambushes, recover the wounded, call in helicopters etc.

After two weeks at Roberts we returned to West L.A. to pack. SGT Palacios had filled the armory floor with tri-walls ready to be packed. A tri-wall is a large box that fits inside a Container for Export (ConEx). Finally everything was loaded. Our advance team got on a plane for Camp Atterbury and our contracted truck (bonded carrier) arrived to haul our equipment to Camp Atterbury. One of our senior NCOs ran the forklift to load the truck while everyone else took care of last minute details. After the second tri-wall was loaded, the driver asked if we had any bolt seals because of the weapons. My first question was what is a bolt seal? He explained that a bolt seal is a rod that is inserted into a non-reversible plastic nut. In order to open the door you have to break the seal which can not be re-used. I hit the yellow pages and the Internet looking for bolt seals. You would think that in Los Angeles, bolt seals would exist in abundance. Finally after ninety minutes of calling all over southern California I found a place that had them. I raced across town only to learn the guy had no clue about what I was talking about and was going to sell me a master lock. I finally signed a waver on the bolt seals and SGT Palacios crimped on our standard metal seal on the doors of the trailer.

The truck pulled away. This signaled the start of our four-day pass. I still had plenty of things to do to secure my house while I was gone, and so did the others.

My parents were starting to track our progress in the newspaper trying to get a better understanding of just what we were going to be doing once we got to Afghanistan. They would call me each time they logged onto the Internet. I read about our deployment and all of the great things we are going to do. None of it was true but it made for a good story. The bottom line is we didn't really know what was waiting for us. We did know that we were going to try to help restore the agriculture industry, which could mean teaching or building facilities such as a forestry center or a chicken processing center. There was even the possibility of rebuilding some irrigation systems. We needed to be ready for whatever came our way. We did receive some clues during the summer from a U.S. Department of Agriculture employee who was working in the same region to where we were to deploy. He had sent us a set of translated notes from a conference he had attended.

Chapter 3

GOOD BYE CALIFORNIA

On August 30th, the Kunar ADT (Agribusiness Development Team) hosted a family day as a final send off for our deployment to Afghanistan. The families were told to arrive at eight o'clock for more briefings, which would be followed by a lunch.

When the day was over some of the troops took advantage of one last night out on the town at the Santa Monica pier while others spent one last evening with their families. I was in need of a ride to the armory in the morning so my father spent the night with me.

My father and I got up at five A.M. Monday morning August 31st, loaded up my two duffle bags into the car, disabled my truck, set the hot water heater to vacation, and turned the water to the toilets off. We left the house at 5:45 A.M., got on the 405 Freeway headed toward West L.A. and arrived at the armory on Federal Avenue at 6:05, a record for a Monday morning. My car died just as we approached the armory but it started right back up.

There were two troops already sitting in the parking lot, my platoon sergeant SFC Medina and SFC Hanlin, my construction supervisor. I said goodbye to my dad, took my bags over to the parking lot and waited for the others to arrive. At 6:30 the first of the troops started to arrive from the Holiday Inn Express on Santa Monica Blvd. There were two shuttle vans running back and forth. Anyone who lived more than 50 miles from the armory had to stay at the Holiday Inn; this included about 75% of the unit. The remainder of the unit arrived one at a time. The single soldiers like me had a parent drop them off. There was one little girl about four years old who just couldn't stop crying; she fully understood that her dad was going away for a very long time.

By 7:00 A.M., the unit was assembled and accounted for with plenty of time to kill before the buses arrived for LAX. So we made one last assault on the Seven Eleven on Wilshire for coffee and goodies. This would be a second breakfast for most folks. We had been giving the Seven Eleven a fair amount of business over the past two weeks when we were working out of the armory so this was just one last visit for old time sake.

At 9:00 A.M., the first bus arrived right on schedule. The bus driver said that the second bus was just a few blocks away. Our Security Platoon loaded up on the first bus and headed out for LAX, which gave them enough time for our 11:40 flight. At 10 o'clock, the second bus still hadn't arrived. We should have asked the first bus driver, "A few blocks from where?" Our commander started making phone calls trying to track down the bus while the rest of us just lined up in the shade of the armory. Finally at 10:45, our bus arrived. It took us all of five minutes to load the Ag Platoon and Headquarters up. Two of the full time soldiers went out onto Wilshire to stop traffic so the bus could back out of the parking lot, but the cars just went around them as the bus was backing out into the street. MSG Barcerra was standing at the cannon and gave us one last salute as we passed the armory.

We arrived at the LAX Delta terminal at 11:10. One of our sergeants was standing out in front handing out plane tickets. There were only a few people in line at the counter so it only took a few minutes for the 30 of us to check our bags. The next obstacle was security, but when we got up there, there were three lines open and just a couple of people ahead of us. We had enough time to swing by the news stand, woof down a third breakfast if desired and relax a few minutes.

The flight was packed. I think our 64 tickets helped make it a profitable trip. The stewardess made an announcement to the passengers that we were on our way to Afghanistan. All of the passengers gave us a round of applause. It was a standard flight with no meals so I bought a turkey cob salad and read my book on the history of the Northern Pacific Railroad, which was written back in 1883.

We arrived in Detroit at dusk and had about 45 minutes before our flight to Indianapolis. This was enough time to grab a turkey sandwich and a diet Pepsi for dinner. The flight to Indianapolis was a quick one with just enough time to get the wheels up. We landed in Indianapolis' new airport, which was opened in November of 2008. Down at the baggage claim area was our advance team waiting for us. Major Leeney was issuing room keys to the officers and women, along with two trash bags full of Camp Atterbury meals for dinner. Camp Atterbury had their own brand of rations packaged up, which included a bottle of water, a couple of cans of food and goodies in them. Behind the terminal was a van, a large bus and a panel truck waiting to take us to Camp Atterbury. As the troops were loading their bags into the truck we noticed that not all of the bags made it. Delta put the remaining bags on another plane but didn't tell anyone. The missing baggage started coming down the chute just as the troops started making lost baggage claims.

We got on the highway going south toward Evansville for the 45-minute ride to the camp. We arrived at the barracks at 11:30 Monday night and sorted out our bags. The advance team had been busy. Every bunk had a stack of linens and everyone had a brand new footlocker, which they could take with them to Afghanistan. The few women were taken over to the officer quarters. By midnight I was making hospital corners and putting my gear away.

We got up at 5:00 A.M. Tuesday and made our way to the mess hall, which wasn't easy. It was still dark and we didn't know the post yet. The mess hall was a huge clamshell tent with foam insulation on the inside. Breakfast was good– just about anything you could want just as long as it was scrambled. By 6 A.M. the sun was finally starting to make its way over the horizon and we had our first formation. We had about an hour to reassemble over at the SRP in-processing station. I still don't know what SRP stands for but it has something to do with shipping people out and sending them home.

Camp Atterbury was built in 1942 and named after the WWI general who was in command of all the U.S. railroads during the war. After the war he became the president of the Pennsylvania railroad. The post found an old observation car they thought was his and had it moved to the post. The car was a basket case ready for the scrap yard. After they got it all moved on post someone completed the research and found out the car was never Mr. Atterbury's private car. Now they have a big piece of junk displayed on a slab of concrete.

Most of the WWII buildings are gone now with the exception of the correctional barracks, which the state uses, and the post chapel. The barracks and orderly rooms they have today were built out of concrete blocks in the late 1950s, early 1960s. The newer buildings were built in the last 10 years to support the war effort. Indiana wanted to be the deployment center for the guard and reserve and they set their mind to do it. They took the business away from Ft. Lewis and Ft. Bliss.

Chapter Four

LIFE AND SRP AT CAMP ATTERBURY

Overall, life at Camp Atterbury was good including the weather and the food. Our first week was all in-processing, which included our records, medical, and the issuing of equipment and uniforms. Our second week was dominated with additional briefs and developing equipment lists. Since we were a new unit, we didn't have much in the way of organic equipment. The concept was for us to develop a list of equipment required to perform our mission and the 1st Army would purchase them.

The most time consuming problem the troops had to deal with was pay problems. Every state had an office of the United States Property and Fiscal Office (USPFO) responsible for processing the soldiers' pay. The California USPFO had received all of the required documents and orders to properly process the soldiers' pay prior to our mobilization, but several mistakes were made. The same mistake was replicated for every member of the unit.

At first the USPFO stated that we didn't fill out the required forms. The problem is all of the forms we signed were posted to our iperms, which is an electronic database that we have access to. After that, USPFO wanted all of the documents re-signed with a current date. We refused because they were going to use the new date to cover the fact that they made a mistake. The next tactic was to strike at the single people. Troops like me who are single changed their mailing address to their parents' or someone who would be taking care of their affairs while they were gone. USPFO stated that they were going to call CID (Criminal Investigations Division) because people were trying to get a higher housing allowance by falsifying their home of record. The troops had submitted their property tax records, mortgage agreements, mortgage payment slips, rental agreements and letters stating that they had changed their home of record so that all official mail would not go to a vacant house. It would take SFC Graham more than two months to resolve the pay problems. Pay is one of the last things a soldier needs to worry about when deploying for a combat mission.

After the first two weeks of in-processing and briefs (which were worthless) we finally went to the field to train. The post had built what looks like a forward operating base (FOB), which they refer to as a COL (Coalition Operating Location in Afghanistan; they are called FOBs, Forward Operating Bases). Even in the Army we must be politically correct. The COL was built using a bunch of the FEMA trailers that the people of New Orleans rejected because of the presence of formaldehyde. Formaldehyde is what the Army uses to preserve canvas, the same canvas that is used for our tents, and duffle bags. These trailers were constructed of the cheapest materials available. All of the trim molding was cardboard, the doors were one-inch thick press board. Basically they were just one big cardboard box. The post gutted most of the trailers and made barracks out of them. The best part was the beds, which had brand new mattress. The showers were in a converted ConEx built for very short people. The shower heads were about four and a half feet from the floor, which meant at 6'-3" I had to get on my knees to wash my head. The water heating system was somewhat of a challenge. I would turn the water on and it would be warm. I would jump in and soap up and the water would revert to ice water. I had no choice but to stay in and hose off the soap.

Our training at the COL was conducted by soldiers from Fort Gillian Georgia, which is located just south of Atlanta and is scheduled to be closed because it is so small. Everyone from Ft. Gillian was first rate and had their act together. The first day was classroom instruction about IEDs and a walk through in the motor pool. One drill was just like the old west where they circle the wagons when the Indians attack. The instructors had six 1151s in a box like circle where we practiced cross leveling ammo and treating the wounded. The instructor picked two privates to give IVs.

Then he asked them both to select a victim. They each picked a senior NCO. The instructor said "wise choice, go ahead and lie down. They will be giving you your IV."

The next day we spent outside practicing how to react to IEDs (Improvised Explosive Devices). They had a few miles of road where they planted IEDs for us to find while we were driving and a few simulators that would go bang! We also practiced emergency vehicle recovery and medivac of the wounded. The next day we went to a mock village and practiced our room clearing tactics and how to move around a village under fire. We ended the day by practicing for when things go wrong and how to *get out of Dodge*. The following day we when to the range and practiced a live fire defense with our machine guns shooting over the heads of the riflemen and our medics going out and bringing back the wounded. If you got tagged to be wounded that meant you received an IV; that was the big finale of the training.

A few of us wanted some more time with our weapons so we drew a range and some ammo and shot for the afternoon. We now had the army's new carbine rifle called the M-4, which is like the M-16 except shorter. The new rifle has a new sight on it that uses a laser. It looks like a four-inch long scope with a red dot in it. You have to adjust the sight just like the old fashioned iron sights. The difference is that with the old sights you usually closed one sight to aim; the new sight, called a CCO (Close Combat Optic), requires you to fire with both eyes open. Your mind merges the two images so you don't notice that you're looking through the sight.

After we came back from the field we had a lot of white space to deal with. White space is blank slots on the training schedule. The training brigade here is either overwhelmed or just doesn't have their act together. They told us to stand by because we were going back out to the field Friday morning. Ha! They were not going to work on the weekend so we stood at the ready with nowhere to go. Finally Saturday night they gave us an Operations Order that said go to the field and interview a local leader. We launched out of the motor pool at 6:00 A.M. not thinking that the instructors didn't have time to get things set up. When we got to the field the instructors scheduled another unit to use the same training site. Our training was cut short and we came back to the barracks. Then we were told that they would have a new Operations Order for us in 90 minutes and we were to be ready to go back out. Over all what training we received was good, but there is a lot of down time waiting for the 1ˢᵗ Army to train us.

We started putting our aircraft loads together the week of September 20th. The plan was to have a C-17 follow us into Afghanistan with our equipment while each of us carried one duffle bag and one ruck sack. Everything else would be loaded up into a tri-wall. A tri-wall is a large ¾ inch thick cardboard box, 42 inches tall and 4 feet by 4 feet with a plastic pallet bottom and top. Each aircraft pallet, which is aluminum and weights 400 pounds by itself, can hold eight of the tri-walls. We were able to pack up two aircraft pallets and take them up to the airfield, which is the back side of the Indianapolis airport.

On Wednesday September 23ʳᵈ I got a real scare. We were doing a two-mile run for section PT when I started having pain in my left kidney. The pain went away by the time I returned to my billets. After showering I went to relieve myself and urinated very dark blood. I was able to go to the troop medical clinic for treatment that same morning. I was received just like all of the other troops. The first thing was to have my temperature and blood pressure taken.

Timing of this little event was at both the best and worst of times. Our four-day pass was just days away and I had planned to meet my father in Chicago. The good news is it happened here in the states and not on an airplane. And it was after we completed our training. I was finally able to see a doctor who was very knowledgeable about kidneys and after doing a few simple test assured me that I would be fine.

That was good news to me and I kept my mouth shut about the problem to my family and decided to enjoy my pass. Turns out Doctor Evans was right. A week later I was back to running several miles a day with no problems and there was not even a hint of any kidney problems during the deployment.

Chapter Five

THE PASS

If you watched enough WWII movies, you would know that the privates are always excited about getting a pass. In our case, everyone was excited about getting one last look at freedom before shipping off. We had about two weeks notice that the pass dates would be set in stone and approved by the next higher. Pass is different from leave. The commander can authorize up to four days off without touching a soldier's leave, which is better known as vacation. Planning the pass for the unit fell on the shoulders of our Intel officer LT Ko who was serving as the adjutant. He arranged for the bus to and from the airport and tracked everyone's flight and travel plans. We had to submit our request for pass two weeks prior to the pass date for approval. The request was the easy part; then the Army wanted us to print out a strip map to where we were going, take an online class for travel safety and complete an online risk assessment.

The big day finally arrived and everyone was excited about the pass. Our commander had a little safety and common sense talk with all of the troops; this included "don't go home and get married!" Funny thing… That day, I was working with our Deputy Commander LTC Velte on tracking down some of our equipment that we were trying to buy. This happened to be one of our rainy days too so we were both soaked. LTC Velte looked up at me in the warehouse and said, "hey Dave do you got this covered?"

"Yep I can handle this."

"Great! There is something I need to do in town and it will take me about two hours."

I didn't think much about it. We were all trying to get things done before we went on pass. My plan was to take the bus with the troops to the airport, rent a car and drive to Chicago. I was going to take two of the NCOs, SFC Hanlin and SSG Lucas from my section with me and drop them off at their hotels in Chicago. The bus was set to leave at 3:30 P.M. I got a call from SFC Hanlin at 2:30 and he was just a little frantic to say the least. LTC Velte wanted to meet all of the NCOs who were under his command at Camp Roberts at the post chapel for a quick brief. SFC Hanlin was afraid that whatever brief he had to attend would prevent him from catching the bus and missing a free ride to Chicago. I grabbed SFC Hanlin's bag and told him I'd hold the bus and not to worry. The time was getting close at 3:25. Here came a small group of NCOs moving at a good clip to catch the bus. Right at 3:30 the bus pulled away from Building 202, our orderly room, and turned down Fairbanks Road where the post chapel was. SFC Hanlin yelled to the bus driver, "Hey honk the horn." We all did a quick look left and there was our deputy commander in a tux with his new bride walking hand in hand out of the chapel. He kept the whole thing secret, even from the NCOs he invited.

The bus pulled out on the county road to the town of Edinburgh, which is a nice sleepy little town, home of two veneer companies and not much else. From there we got on Interstate 65 headed up to the Indianapolis airport. The Army Blue Bird bus pulled up in front of the airport and the troops scattered like a bunch of cockroaches. Some found shelter at the USO where they would wait for their flights. Others had true faith in the Army and scheduled flights within minutes of our arrival time.

I went straight to the rental car counter with SFC Hanlin. We were dressed in our civilian clothes and there were maybe four other troops in their civvies. The rest were wearing the ACUs (Army Combat Uniform). This is a little trick for traveling. Sometimes the airline will bump a serviceman up to first class if they are in uniform.

While we were still in Indiana, my dad called and let me know he had arrived safely and to stop someplace and pick up some sandwiches he was a bit on the hungry side. After dropping SFC Hanlin off at the

Kinckerbaucker Hotel, which was an officer's club during WWII and Korea, I got on I-90 for the Chicago O' Hare Airport and made a quick stop at Wendy's for some cheeseburgers. The airport Hilton was easy to find; it is right in the terminal. You can walk straight to it from the baggage claim area. That was the good news. The bad news was, to park cost $45.00 even for just an hour. I played the poor combat veteran angle and got the price knocked down to $30.00, which was what the airport charged for parking. I checked in and went up to the room. My father's first words were "You saved the day," referring to the cheese burgers I had in hand. Turns out all of the food courts in the airport were on the far side of security and once you're on the outside you're not able to get back in without a ticket. The Hilton was robbing its patrons anyway it could and meals were no exception. They wanted $25.00 for a day old salad; my dad wasn't that hungry.

The next few days my father and I toured the sights. Our first objective was to find the Newbury library, which required us to take the red line. I never claimed to be the world's best pathfinder and my exploits in Chicago were a testimony to the sad truth that I couldn't find north to save my life. It was overcast so I couldn't see the sun and there were no trees with moss growing on them either. We had a map and still got twisted around.

It didn't take us long to find the library, which was nestled in a residential section of town. There was even a large French library in the neighborhood. When we got to the library we couldn't get past the security guard. I called the reference librarian who explained that the only way past the guard was to come up and apply for a reader's card. With that we went up and applied for a reader's card. My father and I had been researching our family history with the railroads in Mexico. The Newbury library is one of the main depositories of the Pullman Company records. These records include their Mexico operations starting from 1917. The Newbury's Pullman collection dates back to include all of the companies that Pullman purchased, which pre-dates the Pullman Company.

After doing some quick research at the Newbury Library we took in the Chicago History Museum then rode the "EL" back to downtown. We found a bakery café that was open for dinner, which was fortunate for us. There weren't many options for dinner on a Saturday night; most of the places were only open for lunch. After dinner we picked up the car and drove to the town of Union, the home of the Illinois Railway Museum.

Signs of the suburbs disappeared very quickly. It wasn't long before we were in the country. The museum exit showed up soon enough and we pulled off for a pit stop and asked about the availability of hotels in Union. I got a strange look from the clerk. The only motel in Union was at the truck stop where we were, the Super 8 motel co-located with super mix concrete.

The Illinois Railway Museum turned out to be massive. It took us several hours to tour the collection. We spent the night in Union then left early Monday morning for Chicago after breakfast at the truck stop. We wanted to get back to Chicago when the Museum of Science and Industry opened. We checked into the Hampton Inn, which provided a free shuttle via Thrifty Car Rental to the O'Hare CTA station. An hour later we were in downtown making a quick bus connection to the museum.

At the Chicago Museum of Science and Industry we toured the inside of the German U505, which the US captured during WWII. There was also an American Airlines pilot who gave us a tour of the 707 that had hung from the ceiling. The pilot had a remote control device that would operate every flap on the plane as he told us about how the plane worked. We spent a good four hours there and finished with a tour of the Burlington Zephyr.

Tuesday was our last day together and the Field Museum was our big send off ticket. This time we parked at the Rosemont station and took the blue line in. We made all of our connections just like we had lived there all of our lives. We stopped at our favorite Bakery Café for breakfast then it was back on the "EL" for the Roosevelt station. We spent four hours at the Field Museum; there was a lot to see and not enough time to take it all in.

After we left the Field Museum we made a quick stop at the Rosemont station where my dad got his bags and a book he bought my Mom about a doll house at the Museum of Science and Industry. I went back up to the platform with him to wait for the next train to the airport. The train arrived and we said our good byes. My Dad got on the train for O'Hare and I headed for the Indianapolis Airport.

The USO was our rally point for our troops at the Indianapolis airport. I arrived at the USO to find LT Ko and a few troops enjoying TV and surfing the Internet. The Indianapolis USO was a small room about 15 by 30 feet, run by one man sitting at a desk by the front and only door. Across from the reception desk was a set of shelves to put your ruck on. In the center of the room were two couches and two recliners facing two flat screen TV sets mounted on the wall. In the back of the room was a wet bar with all the free soda you could drink. There were bowls of candy, stacks of chips and a full display of mudpies. I decided to go into the airport and get dinner. The terminal was deserted with the exception of three of my troops eating by the Mexican café. There were only three out of the six food counters open. I selected a Japanese place and had a load of vegetables and a can of fruit for dinner.

The USO was filling up as our troops slowly arrived. At 8:45, LT Ko called for a bus to come pick us up. I decided to sit out in the concourse and read my book on the Canadian Pacific. About 9:30, several flights arrived and a stream of our troops arrived all at once. Some came out in the concourse to call home; others just wandered around. We had one last troop who had to make it in. SSG Carter was coming in from the bay area. He arrived at 10:30 and we loaded the Blue Bird for Camp Atterbury. Forty-five minutes later we were winding our way through Edinburgh. The whole town was dark except for a few street lights. It all gave the effect of driving through a still life diorama. In some of the homes there was a light on in the kitchen, which allowed us a peek into their homes. We turned the corner where the bait shop was and crossed over the creek where the hundred foot wide water fall was. The short waterfall picked up all the ambient light from the town just like a surreal black and white photo. About a mile farther the fence line of the camp appeared in the woods followed by the front gate. The bus dropped the troops off at their barracks and then the rest of us at the officer's quarters. I was able to get to bed just after midnight. Our commander called for a training meet at 6:30 A.M. so the morning would come early. At breakfast I learned that SFC Fulton, one of my troops, had gotten married during pass.

Chapter 6

THE FINAL PREP FOR DEPLOYMENT

As far as our movement to Afghanistan was going, it had become a daily guessing game. First, we were given a C-17 to transport all of our equipment; then it was a C-47; as of October 5th it was a FedEx MD-11 with a departure date still to be determined, which would not be any sooner than a week after we were to leave on Friday October 9th. We were approached by the Nevada ADT to bring their lost equipment with us. We said yes we had plenty of room. We thought it was just a pallet; it turned out to be 16 pallets. Nevada's equipment was shipped after they departed. When it arrived in Afghanistan no one at the Bagram air field knew what to do with it so they shipped it back to Nevada. Nevada moved quickly and sent the equipment back to Camp Atterbury so it could be shipped back to Afghanistan. We were not taking any chances with our equipment. We decided to send a four-man team with it, with SGT Palacios as the NCOIC. That turned out to be a very prudent move. We were one of the few units not to lose any equipment in transit.

I decided to attempt to buy a new pair of running shoes after striking out in California. So we loaded up the van and drove up to the Walmart in Columbus. We had received word from our advance party at Camp Wright that there was no laundry soap available at Camp Wright and no laundry service or power strips, so I purchased a large box of soap and a power strip along with a book for the flight. The Columbus Walmart's policy, which the community shared, was any troop in uniform went to the front of the line. They knew that we were all taking shuttle buses from the camp so they made sure that we were all out on time.

I could remember having staff duty during Thanksgiving at Fort Lewis and I was going to buy a magazine. I was in uniform and was thinking about going to the front of the line just like AAFES (Army Air Force Exchange Services) policy signs stated, when a woman next to me looked at my patch and said, "don't even think of going to the front of the line." Such love for the National Guard the active duty knows their patch.

After Walmart, we went up the road to Best Buy and a large sporting goods store. I should have known that there would be a very minimal selection at the sporting goods store. There was not one slim person anywhere in sight; everyone was a porker! Sure enough they had a very small selection and lower quality shoes. With that some of the guys went over to the Taco Bell and Rallies for a late dinner and then we headed back to the camp. On Monday we went to the camp's forestry center for a quick class on re-forestation. It was a good presentation, and pretty straight forward.

Most of our time since the four day pass had been spent packing and re-packing the pallets for the aircraft. I had been spending my free time reading a book on the Canadian Pacific, which I wanted to finish and send to my dad. Reading took up only a small part of my time. My main effort was learning Pashto, by memorizing over 300 flash cards for different sayings and words. The goal is to make a good first impression. The COIN (Counter Insurgency) center at Camp Atterbury is where I spent my free time online listening to Pashto either on the Defense Language Institute's field support site or the US Army Skill-port Rosetta Stone site. Both are very marginal compared to the old Berlitz courses, but Berlitz doesn't carry Pashto.

I thought things were going fairly well with the exception of our struggle with USPFO trying to get our pay fixed. I was taking comfort in the California law that allows a soldier who is deployed to Iraq or Afghanistan to defer his/her mortgage payments for six months. That was just the amount of time I thought it would take for USPFO to fix our pay. Otherwise I would have to dredge my savings to keep my mortgage payments current.

With billions of dollars of taxpayer bailouts paid to the financial institutions one would think they would honor the law. On Monday October 5th, I had to go to the JAG for a new Power of Attorney for my dad. Turns out Bank of America decided to not to honor the law and turned my letter requesting a deferment over to a collection company. All of my payments were automatic and on time with additional principal, but B of A had other plans. Soon my parents started receiving phone calls to the house reminding them that my mortgage payments were due. Bank of American refused to honor the Power of Attorney I gave to my dad. I wasn't having any luck with them on the phone, which burned up an hour plus of cell phone time each call. I had the JAG call Bank of America, who refused to talk to my attorney. When I was finally able to talk to them, they assured me that the calls were only for goodwill and my account was in good standing. The calls started after they received my letter asking them to defer my mortgage, which they signed for and also noted that they received on September 1st. They actually received it in August, which is the date on the registered return. It took ten months to get Bank of America with the aid of attorneys to resolve the issue. Had it not been for my Congressman Brad Sherman stepping in with a letter to the CEO of Bank of America, and his staff following up for several months with B of A, I would still be fighting B of A for the deferment that I was legally entitled to.

Life was changing at Camp Atterbury; the Marines took over our mess hall so we were sent across post for meals. Our old mess hall was about 200 yards away from the barracks. The new mess hall, King Hall, was just over one mile from the barrack. It really didn't matter to me; my quarters were halfway between them. The walk was not a problem; it was the time it takes to get there. So the troops were either skipping breakfast or they ate at their own expense at the all ranks club, which opened at 6:00 A.M.

Tuesday October 6th was a special day. We had to eat at 5:30 A.M. when King Hall opened. My platoon sergeant came by my billets with a van load of troops and picked up Spc Tanson and me for breakfast. After breakfast we turned in our laundry for the last time and dropped off our weapons at the supply room, which was looking very empty. At 6:30 an army Blue Bird bus arrived at our orderly room building 202. Mustering at our building was the Ag sections from three ADTs (Agribusiness Development Teams): ours, the Kunar ADT from California, one from Missouri and one from South Carolina. We were going to Purdue for a class on sheep and goats otherwise known as small ruminants.

23

We pulled out of Camp Atterbury at 6:40 A.M. while everything was still very dark. During the evening the clouds had rolled in blocking the light of the full moon and what stars that were bright enough to still reach the earth. We went through Edinburgh, which was still asleep except there was some life at one of the veneer factories. Other than that there wasn't a light on in any of the homes. By 7:30 the sun was able to provide enough light to see the sights along I-65; this was about when we reached the city of Indianapolis. I enjoyed looking at all of the old buildings and homes along the way. It was a shame that some of the more ornate architectural examples were boarded up void of any life or purpose.

Just outside of Indianapolis we stopped at a truck stop, then headed for the city of Lafayette, which is a beautifully preserved city with its prime just about the turn of the century. A few twist and turns later we were at the Purdue campus being escorted by Dr. Darryl Ragland, a veterinarian who was also our instructor for the day. We were forty minutes early, which was better than being forty minutes late. So we waited in the student café until the classroom was available.

The class was very good. It started off with what the proper vital signs were for goats and sheep. It included how to palpate their organs and what to look for, followed by the types of parasites that could be excepted in Afghanistan and how to treat them. Dr. Ragland went into great detail and answered a lot of questions. At noon we had to give up the classroom; there was a women's club that had the room for a large pizza party. We were given instructions about where to go for lunch. We walked about ¾ of a mile up the road to a small shopping center called West Purdue that had several cafés to choose from and enjoyed a simple lunch before returning to the university.

We re-grouped after lunch back at the veterinarian school and took some photos of the bronze statues they had out front. We then boarded our Blue Bird for the farm. Purdue has a very large demonstration farm about ten miles out of town. There we met Gerald Kelly the manager of the sheep unit. He taught us how to handle sheep, how to take blood samples and again answered many questions. The sheep unit had the one customary cat and three very large white sheep dogs all enjoying life asleep on the hay while the drizzle came down. The farm was surrounded by acres of feed corn all waiting to be harvested.

On the way back it was light enough to see the countryside. We got directly back on the interstate and bypassed the city of Lafayette. The nice thing about the interstate is it runs above the countryside. You could see the first signs of autumn appearing. The hillsides looked like a Christmas tree with a bunch of orange and red lights. Some of the individual trees just burst into a blaze of red yellow and orange while others stood fast and loyal to their dark green coats.

We arrived back at Camp Atterbury in time to have dinner as a unit. General Johnson arrived to wish us the best and to tell us about his meeting with General Petraeus and his goals for the ADT. I had dinner with General Johnson, who was my Brigade XO when I was the HHC engineer commander. I told him all of the positive things I could think of and how we overcame some of the negative shortfalls in the training.

General Johnson's visit meant that our departure was just around the corner.

Chapter Seven

GOOD BYE CAMP ATTERBURY

Friday October 9th was our day of departure for Afghanistan. On Thursday evening we all lined up to be checked for the flu. The Army had made its best attempt to give it to us by blowing the H1N1 vaccine up our noses a week earlier. It was now time to see if they were successful. We lined up in alphabetical order outside the orderly room until it started to rain. They then moved our line into what was left of the supply room. Our medics took our temperature, and to the Army's dismay none of us showed signs of the flu.

We held a quick leader's meeting for final coordination of Friday's departure. The troops were already headed to dinner either by driving over in the van or buying their own dinner at the all rank's club. I got a ride over to dinner with SGT Palacios, our supply sergeant, and LTC Velte. I paid one last visit to the USO to work on my Pashto flash cards and to indulge in the consumption of some of their free Diet Pepsi. That evening the post stationed a 40-foot tractor trailer at our barracks, which we would share with the Missouri ADT for our short trip to the Indianapolis Airport. Friday morning we finished packing, stripped our bunks of linen and loaded a van with our gear. Our billets were about three quarters of a mile from the barracks; none of us was looking forward to carrying 150 pounds of gear that far. We swept the floors in our rooms, then drove over to the orderly room to turn in our linen and stash our assault packs. An assault pack is the same size as a student's book bag. A few of us walked over to the all ranks club for breakfast. I had my usual canned fruit and bought a Diet Pepsi and a granola bar to go with it.

At 8:30 it was our turn to load the semi trailer with our equipment. Missouri was still not finished so when we were done they returned and kept loading their stuff. The weather was real soupy with a light amount of drizzle. The days prior had seen rain on and off so there was no shortage of mud in the area to walk through. We gathered for one last safety brief before loading three blue bird buses, which had arrived. Volunteers from the USO arrived to see us off. They gave us each a wooden nickel that said thanks for your service with a map of the state of Indiana on the back.

We arrived at the abandoned site of the old Indianapolis International Airport. The post chaplain greeted us at the door as we entered the terminal where all of the old customs counters still stood. There we waited for our Ryan air charter aircraft. Someone from the post brought a bunch of Atterbury training meals and hot water for soup. I came prepared with a can of fruit and some tuna for lunch. The Ryan air B575 finally showed up and our semi truck with all of our gear drove out to the plane. About nine guys from our unit and the Missouri ADT went out to load the gear onto the plane. They just packed it all in the belly of the plane the best they could. I took a moment to call my folks and sister before we got on the plane.

We saw the flight crew arriving. The pilot was a royal porker; he was so fat he couldn't even tuck in his shirt. Ryan Air was the lowest bidder. I still can't figure out just how that pilot was able to fit through the cabin door or even fit in the pilot's seat. The call finally came to load the plane. Missouri walked out first and took their seats on the left side of the plane. Then we followed filling in the other side. We lined up by sections inside the terminal and waited for the signal to exit the building. There was a light mist drifting in the air, which had soaked the tarmac and the stairs we climbed. I stopped to take some photos to document our trip while PFC McGee passed me with our guidon in its sheath. Funny how an age old tradition of carrying a guidon proclaiming what hamlet or village the unit arrived from has become second nature. I took just a minute to look the aircraft over; this B575 had seen better days. Ryan Air didn't even paint the outside of the plane; just took the logos off from whatever airline they purchased the plane from.

It took us a few minutes to get our weapons tucked away. They wouldn't easily fit under the seats. The sharpshooters' scopes were just too big and hung up on everything. The flight attendant kept telling us that we couldn't take off until all the aisles are cleared including the emergency exits. I felt like telling him, "Look Mac, it is not like we are in a hurry to start this 30-hour flight." But I kept my mouth shut. He was one of the two more disorientated male stewards on the flight. We finally got situated and took off for Nova Scotia, our first re-fueling stop, at 1:20 P.M.

In Nova Scotia we stayed on the plane for the 90-minute layover, then took off again. We were scheduled to make stops in Iceland and Romania but the pilot received a new flight plan while we were in Nova Scotia. We flew straight to Leipzig Germany, which is in the old Eastern Germany. A large articulated bus came out to get us. We were taken to a special terminal for U.S. troops. We were the first to arrive. I bought some postcards and some disposable razors, which were a bit pricey, then attempted to make a phone call.

None of my prepaid calling cards would work so I had to use my Visa card. The operator told me that a five-minute call would cost $30.00 I decided not to make the call fearing that the conversation just might be a long one about the family cats. So I went to the Internet. The cost was $6.00 for three minutes. I made several attempts to send an email and finally on the last attempt when the system displayed the "times up" my message "Safe in Germany" went through.

We landed at Manas Air Base in the Republic of Kyrgyz at 8:20 P.M. on Saturday night. A large flatbed semi truck drove up to the back of the plane and our baggage detail went to work unloading the plane. Three blue bird buses drove up. We loaded into them. The terminal looked like it was an old civilian terminal with the entire runway face of the building constructed of plate glass. We were not authorized to take photos on the air field. There was a big sign in some Cyrillic alphabet on top of the terminal building. We drove off the airfield through a small turnstile out on to the main access road to the airport.

The road was lined with old 40-foot high Mulberry trees with white washed trunks. After a hundred feet of mulberry trees, the street was lined with Birch trees. A 12-foot high wall of Hesco barriers appeared on our right side. I could see farther down the road to the base perimeter, which had a 20-foot high Hesco barrier. The Hesco barrier is a wire box lined with heavy felt and filled with crushed rock and dirt.

We made a right turn to a guard post where an armed U.S. Air Force NCO looked into our bus when the driver opened the door. He then waved to another guard who pushed a button that opened the railroad style crossing gate. We drove into the post while weaving through a bunch of red and white candy striped K-rails. (A K-rail looks like the concrete dividers on the freeway only they can be moved around by a forklift–the same ones they use for temporary work on the freeway.) We arrived at an elevated guard shack with a guard pointing an M-4 at the bus. The light was on in the shack so he really couldn't see much of anything. The crossing gate went up and we drove in. On our left was a small running track followed by several very large clamshell tents guarded by a row of black and white zebra K-rails standing on top of the curb. The Hesco wall on our right continued with a few openings alone the way. We followed the road into the post and drove through a gravel parking lot that was lined with black and yellow tiger stripped K-rails.

We stopped in front of a Quonset style tent and unloaded the bus. Inside the tent we received our first briefing–basically dos and don'ts. The main point of the brief was "Don't drink the water!" Sure enough there were pallets of water stationed all over the post for us to drink. We walked over to the billeting office and picked up our linens, which was a nice fluffy blanket, one pillow and two flat sheets. The Army usually issues the old 5-foot by 5 foot-wool blankets that just don't cover enough of you to keep you warm. Since I was a Lt. Colonel I was given a semi-private room. The room had two bunk beds; one was occupied by a senior sergeant from the Missouri ADT.

While we were getting our linens, the baggage truck had arrived and the baggage detail had moved all of our gear to a fenced in parking lot. They got a workout! Every person had at least 150 pounds of gear and there were 120 of us. We verified that our gear had made it and took out anything that we might need for the next couple of days, then stacked our gear on pallets. The pallets were the standard Air Force 400-pound aluminum cargo pallets that were located under what looked like a hay barn, basically a building that had only a roof.

After that we went to our quarters. The troops were sleeping in one of the clamshell tents numbered API 1. The women in our unit were across post in what they called a California tent. We passed the API tent on the way in. These clamshell tents were 50 feet wide and 200 feet long. The lights are kept low because at anytime there were troops sleeping. Heating in these tents is accomplished using six large heating units that connect to what looks like an 18-inch plastic straw with a bunch of holes in it. They hang limp from the ceiling of the tent until the heater kicks in; then all at once you hear a loud ripping sound as they inflate. The tents have two entrances. When you walk in, you pass three rows of bunk beds. Then you get to the center of the tent, which has several weapon racks running down the middle. Across on the other side are three more rows of bunk beds.

My quarters were built from ConEx boxes, the same type you see on ships and trains. These two-story buildings were made by stacking the boxes one on top of the other. So my room is eight feet wide by 20 feet long with an ice machine mounted in the back next to my bunk. I call it an ice machine because it just blows cold air. I finally turned it off and was much warmer. The drawback to the tents and our building is there are no windows so you have no idea what time of day it is.

I decided to get dinner and to met SFC Fair and SFC Fulton for dinner. We enjoyed a good midnight meal then asked where we could make a phone call. We were told about some free phones where we were allowed to make a 15-minute phone call. I decided midnight was the perfect time to call home. After all it was 11:00 A.M. Saturday in California. I talked to my mom who told me I just missed my dad who was in route to my sister's home. So I called my sister on her cell phone. Try doing that back during WWII when "V" mail was the fastest means available. She was at the Goodyear Tire store at the time. Turns out my dad was meeting her there so they could drive up to my house and inspect the place. So I got to talk to everyone. With that, I called it a night and went to bed.

I found myself wide awake at 5:30 A.M., so why fight it? I got dressed and went to breakfast where I found a fair amount of my troops suffering the same condition. After breakfast we decided to do some exploring. The sun was just coming out and the temperature dropped to the low 30s in just a few minutes. A few of us walked around the little AAFES. They had a bunch of little shops. If I wanted a tailored suit I was in luck but there was nothing else that I could use or take with me. The Manas AFB is located in a valley full of haze and tulle fog. We could see the mountains to the south of us covered in snow. They looked just like the Swiss Alps but there was no completely clear view to take a photo. I went back over to the MWR (Moral Welfare and Recreation) telephone and Internet office and checked my email, then decided to get back inside where it was warm.

I took advantage of the morning and did some laundry. My uniform had mud splattered on it from walking around Camp Atterbury the morning of our departure. I also wrote out a bunch of postcards that I picked up in Germany. Kyrgyzstan is not part of the free mail system but they do have a post office. I walked over to mail my postcards and found it closed. Turns out it was Sunday. "Yack Samba in Pashto." I decided to walk around the post just to have something to do. It was a very small post so it was a short walk. With nothing else to do I went in for an early lunch to find my troops once again doing the same thing I was doing.

The time change was finally getting to me. I decided a short nap was in order. After two hours I decided to write some letters, when my roommate came in and decided it was time for his nap. He turned off the lights and I decided *why not just another hour*. It couldn't hurt. I was dead to the world for the next four hours. I woke up at 7:00 P.M. and decided to go have a late dinner. Once again my troops were at the mess hall. They too had fallen prey to the sand man and were recovering from a long nap.

Later that evening Lt. Ko and SFC Graham went to a movement meeting. A movement meeting is one in which you are briefed on when flights are leaving. The Missouri ADT got notified that they would be leaving for Afghanistan on Monday. Their plan was to have their troops back over where all the gear was stacked up like a small mountain at noon and to load it on pallets for their flight. They would be locked down at 2:00 P.M. until their flight was ready. We got some different news. Since we are a new unit and had to bring all of our own equipment, we couldn't go down range until our equipment arrived. The next problem was there was no room at the Inn in Afghanistan for our equipment even if it did arrive. It turns out the Bagram AB is packed to the gills with aircraft and equipment. We were told that we would be leaving Manas no earlier than Tuesday at best.

The plan was to have some classes at Bagram AFB for two or three days then convoy north. Our advance team was only able to draw enough ammo for light security, not a fire fight. Another challenge–we couldn't leave the base without our 50 Cals, and MK-19s, which were still back at

Camp Atterbury. We received word Sunday night that the Army still hadn't found any MRAPs (Mine Resistance Ambush Protection vehicle) for us, but they did have the 1151s, which are HMWVVs with gunner's turrets. So we could move from Bagram to Camp Wright when our equipment arrived, but we couldn't do our mission. The theater commander's policy is no one leaves Camp Wright unless they are in an MRAP.

I got back to my quarters and told my roommate the news of his departure. I decided to take my computer over to the club and work on some letters. The club was very noisy with some game on the big screen at full blast and crowds of troops cheering for their team. I decided to work outside on the patio. By now it was near midnight and close to freezing, but I had the patio to myself.

After thirty to forty-five minutes I decided not to freeze any longer and went over to the mess hall for some chili. I shared the morning with SFC Hanlin and SFC Medina. I got to bed at about 1:00 A.M. and could hear the troops inside the club cheering for their favorite team for the next hour or so.

October 12th I got up at 5:45 and started the usual routine of walking down the hall and shaving. I then stepped into the chamber of transformation. There was a set of five of these chambers on either side of the room; each portal was covered with a plastic sheet to give it the resemblance of a standard RV shower. Once inside the chamber there was a set of controls, but no instructions. The left control knob transfigured the occupant into a red lobster. The one on the right, into frosty the snow man. It takes skill and a sober hand to tune the controls so that something that resembles a human form walks out. There are factors that are outside the operator's ability to control. Any vibration in the building can throw the unit out of calibration. If someone enters an adjacent chamber of transformation, it could spell disaster if the situation is not monitored closely.

After getting cleaned up I went to breakfast. Then I decided to get some photos of the mountains. The best time to see the mountains in autumn is in the morning, due to the fog and haze. I found the perimeter road and took a mile walk along it until I reached the kill box. The kill box was the area in which the MPs were allowed to shoot people. It is marked by a sign that says "run no farther." There is a guard tower but the fence is lined with sensors and cameras. The guards are not going to shoot. The real reason they don't want you going any farther is the tree line thins out and the locals can see us. The U.S. wants to keep a very low profile. Earlier in the year the Republic of Kyrgyz wanted the U.S. to pack up and leave. The U.S. finally paid them more money and we got to stay.

The perimeter road was a very inviting dirt road that started behind the AAFES town at the north eastern corner of the base and went all the way to the visitor's reception gate that is located on the main north south highway. On the south side of the perimeter road is a ten-foot high chain link fence with barbed wire strung on both sides crowned with razor wire. On the side opposite the perimeter road is triple strand concertina wire. Concertina wire looks like a large three-foot diameter spring made out of barbed wire. There are two rolls of the concertina wire on the ground and one roll on top stacked like three logs. Usually a strand of barbed wire is run through the center of each roll to prevent people from mashing them down, but these were basically just thrown against the fence. On the other side of the perimeter road is a forest of mixed trees. The Soviets planted the trees for two reasons: one, to obscure the view of the post and two, to absorb the noise. There was another row of trees between the fence and the airport road so it was a little difficult to see much. The main airport road was lined with tall Birch trees and was well maintained. The terminal is new and about the size of the Orange County Airport in California. They had another terminal under construction. I could see the airport parking lot as well as the vehicle traffic. All of the vehicles were late model cars and well cared for. The people were dressed a cut above Americans with the exception of the construction men. I didn't see a man who wasn't wearing a suit.

After walking the perimeter road, I found the fitness trail that goes out into the woods. The base cut about three miles of roads through the manmade forest for running. It is very obvious that it is a manmade forest. All of the trees are planted in straight rows, but it still was a peaceful setting. I walked about two miles of the road and decided to come back and run all of the roads when it got warmer. It was 33 degrees in the morning and I really wasn't dressed for it. While I was out there, I met a Russian woman who was collecting wild mushrooms; some of them were huge. We couldn't talk to each other but we did communicate. In the afternoon, I repeated my walks and saw a Russian man also collecting mushrooms in the forest.

The Manas Air Force base is located in an abandoned field that was once used by the Soviets. Manas is also the name of the civilian International Airport that the U.S. is working out of. Manas is located near the Capitol of the Kyrgyz Republic, which is the City of Bishkek. You can Google the airfield and see a satellite image of the area, but you can't zoom in like you can on streets in the U.S. The country is ringed by mountains. The closest ones were to our south and east. We couldn't see the range to the north or west. The view from the south side of the base is a prairie of gentle rolling hills. It looks very similar to looking at western Colorado from the Kansas state line.

Later in the day I found LTC Velte in the mess hall at dinner time. He had received a list of projects that Major Leeney, our XO (Executive Officer), developed after a painful three-hour meeting with the minister of agriculture. When we left the mess hall I could hear the sound of crows. I looked up and there was just a slight red glow left from the sunset and thousands of crows flying over head. I couldn't believe the sight. We went back over to the day room in officer's quarters to swap photos and review the minister of agriculture's wish list. It was truly a wish list. The first item was ten tractors, followed by a dairy, a fish farm and hatchery, a major check dam project and on and on. The projects are a walk in the park for me, but I have to sell the projects to USAID or the Army to get the funding. The first question they asked was "how are they going to maintain what we build." Short answer: they are not!

After our meeting, I headed over to the club, which had been converted to a Catholic BINGO parlor without the Father. Once again the noise was too much for me so I went out on the patio and started writing more letters. By 9:30 P.M. it was time to go over to where the troops were to see what Lt Ko had learned about us getting out of Manas. I had read on the out-house wall that Manas in English means "where is my bloody plane!"

Lt Ko came back with the news that we would be flying out the next night. It was going to be a three-hour and 10-minute flight to Bagram, which would take off at 23:30 (11:30 P.M.), and land at 1:10 local time. If you looked at my math you might think I made a mistake. Afghanistan is one hour, thirty minute difference from the Republic of Kyrgyz. How they came up with splitting an hour is beyond me. Our name for the flight would be Torque 88, not the Kunar ADT. This was all for security reasons. We are a high value target for the Taliban and all of the other nuts out there, so it was good to keep our arrival quiet. I'm sure that everyone in the providence knew the exact minute we would set foot at Camp Wright. We would not be flying on a comfortable charter flight this time. The Air Force was providing us with a standard C-130 and we would be packed! There would be a few days training at Bagram before flying in CH-47 helicopters up to Camp Wright.

Chapter Eight

THE MANAS EXPRESS TO WONDERFUL AFGHANISTAN

The next leg of our journey to Afghanistan started at 3:30 A.M. October 13th. That's when we all woke up to turn in our linens, just like we did on October 12th in the afternoon when we were told our plane was canceled. After turning in our laundry and room keys we picked up our weapons at the circus tent where the troops were staying. We then walked up to the PAX terminal. Our A-bags and rucks were all in storage at the PAX terminal. We pulled out our IBA (Improved Body Armor) and stuffed whatever we wanted back into our rucks. While we were digging through our gear, the Air Force stationed two pallets for us to load our equipment on. We loaded the A-bags on the bottom and the rucks on top of each pallet, then the Air Force strapped everything down with a big cargo net. This is where hurry up and wait started. The Air Force weighed the pallets and calculated the load for the aircraft. While the Air Force was working their magic with a stubby pencil and slide rule we posted a guard on our equipment, which was by the side of the road and went to breakfast.

At 8:30 A.M. we entered the PAX terminal and started our lock down. The lock down period is when we are confined to the PAX terminal so no one gets lost before the flight. The PAX terminal had a selection of goodies for us to eat, hot tea and coffee. An hour and half later the announcement came to load the plane and everyone started putting on their IBA and

Kevlars (Helmets) then once again we loaded a Blue Bird bus for the air field. As we were getting on the C-130, I noticed that is was equipped with several different flare systems. The primary system had 240 flares and there were two backup systems each with 120 flares. These flare systems are often called Angel flares because when fired they give the appearance of an angel flying behind the aircraft.

With two large pallets of gear and 52 troops there was absolutely no wiggle room on the plane. Our legs were interlocked with the person across from us. On C-130s passengers sit in four long rows running from the front to the back of the plane that face each other. I was lucky I was near a porthole window about eight inches in diameter. To look out I would reach across with my video camera, take a photo, then watch the video to see what was down below.

We took off at 10:20 A.M. and promptly made three complete circles in order to gain enough elevation to clear the mountains that ring the Manas airfield. Twenty minutes later we were flying over the most impressive series of mountain ranges you had ever seen. They were a combination of the Swiss Alps and the Washington Cascades and went on for miles. The mountains were capped with snow and there were hundreds of glaciers. You could see where the glaciers had carved out valleys and rivers of snow from our 24,000-foot elevation. At noon we crossed over the border to Afghanistan and the mountains suddenly changed. The snow and glaciers were gone and the mountains turned to a light coco brown. At the end of two hours of flying we could see the Bagram airfield as we made a stiff dive and a hard bank to the left and one more plunge onto the runway. We got off the plane at 11:00 A.M. The Bagram airfield is just like Manas ringed with mountains. The area looked very much like the Fort Bliss side of El Paso with lots of dust and smoke in the air.

Another Blue Bird bus arrived at the plane and took us to the PAX terminal where we were ushered into a briefing tent. The briefing was very simple:

1. There's a USO next door

2. Don't pet the cobras!

We grabbed our assault packs and headed out to the USO, which had nothing in it. We were greeted by Spc McCool, our weapons expert. I was relieved to see one of our more senior NCOs; the sight of him answered one very pressing question that was on my mind. The quality and quantity of food that he had access to over the past four weeks was first rate. I think he had even succeeded in gaining a few pounds.

There was a pallet of water in the parking lot that we helped ourselves to while we waited for our gear. Finally two mammoth forklifts arrived with our gear. The troops tore the pallets apart and loaded it all in a panel truck. We loaded two buses for a long trip around the base to the back side where our tent was waiting for us. The Missouri ADT, which had left Manas a few days ahead of us, had already taken up one side of the white tent. The tent was 50 feet wide by 100 feet long with a plywood floor. We were not the only troops in the transition tents. Poland had about two hundred troops in the tents next to us. We quickly laid claim to some cots, then went to lunch. We gained an hour and a half flying west from Manas. You may have caught the additional 30 minutes. Afghanistan is 30 minutes off from the rest of the world for some reason. There wasn't much left for us to do so we found the shuttle bus and headed for the PX. This shuttle bus was really a mini bus, but we were able to pack about 30 people in it for the ride back around the airfield to Spc. Jason Disney Blvd. where the PX was located. It is something of a tradition when arriving at a new post.

You always check out the PX and make sure it looks like all of the other PXs you have ever seen. This one looked a little sick to say the least. The PX was about the size of a Seven Eleven but was servicing several hundred troops. Spc McCool gave me the heads up about buying a cell phone while in Bagram, sage advice that would pay dividends many times over during my deployment. I purchased a cell phone from a shack in the PX area so I could call home on Fridays from a company owned by Iran and Pakistan. Then I decided to call home on one of the AT&T phones that didn't honor any of my calling cards. My one un-used AT&T card had expired. So I used my Master Card and placed a call home. My math was a little off. I thought it was 7:00 A.M.; my Dad was quick to point out that it was 5:30 A.M.

After about an hour of wandering around the shops at the PX and determining that there was nothing worth buying or seeing, we headed back to the tent. The Bagram Air Base was built by the Soviets when they invaded back in the 80s. The place looked like the junkyards of Sunland California, with stacks of ConEx containers everywhere and junk vehicles to boot. I don't think anyone was able to stay up past 7:00 P.M.; even the Missouri ADT hit the hay early.

The next morning we got up at 4:00 A.M. and the Missouri ADT loaded out to the airfield and flew out to their FOB (Forward Operating Base) Finley Shields named after two enlisted soldiers who were killed by a VIED in Nangarhar. Finley Shields is located across the street from FOB Fenty the main airfield in Jalalabad (J-bad for short). We went to breakfast, then attended a four-hour class on IEDs (Improvised Explosive Devices) and land mines. That brief was followed by another four hours of mandatory briefs about life on Bagram AB, which had no relevance to us at all.

The land that the main post of Bagram is built on was a mine field. It was cleared by occupation. That means we just started building stuff and nothing blew up so there were no mines. Land mines still show up every now and then. When the U.S. took over Bagram it was never intended to handle the massive amount of troops it was seeing. Back in March of 2009 Congress authorized 200 million dollars in permanent construction. The area selected for the new construction sits on several active mine fields. There is a local company clearing the mine fields. They mark the fields with concrete posts and white rocks where mines have been discovered. Turns out any fence marks a mine field, so don't take any shortcuts. When the Soviets left they mined the daylights out of the area, even set bobby traps in all of the bunkers. Throughout the day you'll hear announcements of a scheduled explosion to happen in the next ten minutes. These scheduled explosions occur when enough mines have been collected to be disposed of. The other announcement you'll hear is aerial gunnery range is now active. That occurs when a plane needs to get rid of a bomb. That usually happens at night. There are some very large adobe structures on the base. Some of these structures are the size of major shopping malls.

The same morning we said good bye to the Missouri ADT we also said good bye to about 200 Polish troops. That afternoon another 200 Polish troops arrived. Bagram is just one big revolving door.

I make it a point to sit with different people at each meal. This morning I sat with several engineers from Fluor and a Polish captain. He was telling us that his government put two of their officers in jail after a fire fight because two of the local nationals were killed. Poland has also prohibited any weapon systems on their aircraft, and they are not allowed to fire their mortars. They are as effective as a de-clawed alley cat in the harbor. The guys from Fluor were telling me what a mess the Bagram base is and so are many of the other facilities that KBR built. They were all electrical engineers who are accustomed to building power plants and designing power grids. At Bagram there is no centralized power grid. The only thing they can do for the expansion is to start from scratch. Most of the forward operating bases were wired by the local nationals and have lots of problems. They worked under the direction of KBR.

SPC McCool had been tasked with finding us some security ammo for our movement from Bagram to Wright. He wasn't having much luck until he came across an outgoing PRT that was going to turn in their ammo. SPC Mc Cool made them a deal he would take the ammo off their hands for them and they could enjoy the remainder of the time sweating away in Bagram. SPC McCool brought us all of the ammo he had rounded up on Friday morning October 16th. The security ammo is just for movement when you are nothing more than a passenger. The ammo was old and the casings were tarnished and some were a bit green. Our troops were busy all morning cleaning the ammo and loading magazines with ball rounds and tracers. The tracers are the last rounds in the magazine so you know when you are about out of ammo. Each of us carry 140 rounds of 5.56 (the ammo for our M-4 assault rifles) and 45 rounds of 9 mm (our pistols). The big stuff would be flown in to us whenever it arrived from the states. The machine gunners, grenadiers and sharpshooters only had ammo for their 9mm until we reached our new home. One problem with the old ammo was the oil we used in our weapons also penetrated the ammo. It is possible that when you pull the trigger the round will not make it out the barrel. U.S. troops are trained to shoot two rounds at a time so by the time you hear the sound of a round not making it out of the barrel it's too late; you have already squeezed off the second round and Bang!

After the troops finished loading magazines it was time to exchange our body armor for the latest and greatest. KBR (Kellogg Brown and Root) was in charge of exchanging the body armor. Typical KBR, they took a 30-minute job and stretched it into four hours. It really didn't matter. We didn't have anything else to do for the rest of the day.

Sergeant Stevens who is the grounds manager of Thomas Jefferson's Montello estate, and I started working up a five-year plan for re-forestation that took us a few hours. Some of the troops went to a local bizarre (aka swap meet) to look at all the junk the Afghanis were selling from India. Most of the handicrafts, which are sold in Afghanistan are made in India.

Friday night October 16th we received word to be ready to leave at 2:00 A.M. A few hours later we got another call and were told to be ready to leave at 5:00 A.M. Later in the evening we received another call that the flight was off. Just like we thought, it was Friday and people were starting to leave their posts early just like in the states!

Life on Bagram was dead. Saturday morning the troops started going back to the main post to the PX. Why, I don't know. There is nothing to buy there. If they do stock the shelves, the Poles have already grabbed it. Besides, it takes 45 minutes to an hour to get out of the place. Mud is another problem Bagram has. You can tell by the amount of crushed rock that has been placed on the ground and roads. Walking on it is a bit of a challenge, which means running is out of the question. There is one gym on post with treadmills but it is on the main post and is packed.

The earth at Bagram is a fine power, which imbeds itself in your uniforms, sleeping bag, and airway. October is very mild but the dust dries you out very quickly. Some of the guys have toilet paper shoved up their nose to stop the bleeding. I have to drink several bottles of water during the night, which means getting up about every two hours and walking across the crushed rock for relief. The crushed rock is really baby boulders a little bigger than what you will find on railroad tracks. There is no hot water here anymore so showers are very quick. The showers that do have hot water are usually drained by a contractor who decides he needs a 30-minute shower. We brush our teeth with bottled water but bath and shave with the non-potable water. Laundry is a challenge. There is a laundry that has a 24-hour turn around if you dare. We didn't know when our flight out would happen so the last thing we wanted to do, was leave behind a uniform and a supply of underwear. We were not allowed to do our own laundry but we could always wash something out in the sink and hang it the tent. The F-15 fighters took off and landed here every few hours. They fly cover just waiting for something to pounce on. I was then able to stick my fingers in my ears while asleep to block out the noise. This air base is just like living at an air show. There are freight haulers from all over the globe, a wide variety of helicopters and aircraft to watch as well. I noticed that the CH-47s (the big helicopters with two massive rotors on top, fly with the back ramp down with a machine gunner covering their rear.

October 17th would be my last day in Bagram before I moved on to Jalalabad. In the morning just before dawn there were two men on the rocks praying. That takes some dedications; it hurt my knees just looking at them.

Chapter Nine

BAGRAM TO JALALABAD

I had just returned from the barber shop at Bagram when SFC Medina, my platoon sergeant, asked me if I got the word on Jalalabad. I replied yes and that the plan was to leave sometime that night.

His reply was, "Oh no sir you're going now. I've got a truck in route to take you to the PAX terminal. You're allowed only your assault pack and your full battle rattle."

No sooner had I packed all my gear up, when one of our troops arrived with a Toyota pickup. I gave Sgt. Stevens some last minute instructions of locating some seedling supplies in the U.S. and Canada and handed him my A-bag (with my sleeping bag in it - big mistake) and my ruck.

We drove around the north end of the runway, which I had never seen before. The Russians had built a multitude of bunkers for their fighter aircraft, which were fenced off. In the distance I could see the construction of a new prison, which would open in May of 2010. The entire area north of the base was riddled with trenches, abandoned adobe structures, and washouts from flash floods. You could hide a lot of troops and equipment out there. It would be impossible for the base to sweep the outer perimeter on a daily basis.

We stopped at the commander's and LTC Velte's quarters to load up their gear; they were taking their A-bags. The flight coordinator told them that there would be room, but it was too late for me. Our commander and LTC Velte got in the truck with the flight coordinator and we followed them. I didn't think we were going to make it. First we got pulled over for a safety inspection. Then, we were faced with the traffic on Spc. Jason Disney Blvd. The flight coordinator already had this worked out. With one sharp left we were on the tarmac weaving through air cargo and aircraft. For the next mile we got the cook's tour of the airfield but I wasn't allowed to take photos. We passed by F-15 fighters, A-10s, a bunch of EW (Electronic Warfare) planes, and a 747 cargo air craft flown by "My Cargo." There were C-130s representing just about every state in the union, and Kiowa and civilian cargo helicopters. Before I knew it we passed the fixed wing PAX terminal and arrived at the rotary wing PAX terminal where the 101st was re-assembling their CH-47s. It was an impressive operation.

Once we arrived we put on our battle rattle. I didn't have enough ammo pouches for all of my 5.56s so I had to put two magazines in my cargo pocket then double check to make sure my weapons were on safe. The last thing I needed to do was shoot down the bird I was flying on. I asked what kind of chopper we were flying on and the flight coordinator told me a "Huey." I thought he was pulling my leg! Sure enough when I looked across the field I could see the silhouette of a Huey going over the eastern mountains. About that time a Polish Hind helicopter took off on an escort mission. About four minutes behind the first Huey was a second.

Most of the helicopters have landing gear so they land on the taxi strip, then taxi over to the terminal. The Hueys have skids so they fly right up to the terminal and drop. This was an opportunity flight for us. The two Hueys were bringing in six former Miss Americas to the base for a goodwill tour. These women were well protected with press crew and body armor. I'll admit they did catch my eye, but they didn't look anything like you see on TV. The body armor they wore also required some extensive amounts of imagination too. I noticed that none of them wore their Kevlar helmets. Their Hueys were scheduled to go back empty so we got to jump on for the flight back to Jalalabad. LTC Velte and I got on one bird and our commander got on the other. Just in case one of them got shot down we wouldn't lose the whole leadership team. We had a DOD civilian with us and our commander had a chaplain who had a lot of faith in God. He took out the plates from his body armor. The plates weigh a lot and after a short time your back can really feel the load.

The Hueys were painted in two tone blue and white with the name "Operated by Canadian Helicopter," on the side. Our bird took off first and hovered at the end of the runway for a few minutes then the commander's bird lifted off. We took off going across the runway and flew over the compound where we were living. I could see miles of adobe ruins that looked like a large late 1800s Mexican border town on the west side of the base and not much of anything else. The two Hueys spaced themselves apart while we were approaching the mountains. There was no reason to make us a two for one target.

The mountains were completely void of any vegetation and there was no signs of human habitation. Then after 15 to 20 minutes I spotted a small compound of white buildings with adobe walls. There was no hint of farming or other means of sustaining the community. After another 10 minutes of flying we overshot a large lake, and once again the banks were void of anything green. The mountains were very rugged but passable and covered with a light brown layer of dust. One peak and ridge line came and went and every now and then a compound would mysteriously materialize on the landscape.

Finally we came upon the Kabul River. The Kabul showed evidence of major flooding. Even the mountain sides were nothing more than flood deltas (alluvial fans) flowing down to the river. For the most part, the Kabul was a wide shallow slow moving river running through miles of parched earth. Soon a paved highway appeared with a fair amount of traffic going in both directions. Then I spotted a long stone arched two lane bridge. On one side was the abyss of the barren hills and desolate river bed and on the other lush green farms and multi-story buildings. It looked like a large puzzle piece taken from the fertile farms of the Midwest that was misplaced in the middle of the desert. From the air I could see green parks and soccer fields, homes with back yard gardens, schools etc. Jalalabad looked like a well run city.

We banked east. Then I could see the airfield. It was just one straight runway, no taxiway with a bunch of buildings on one side. The base was bordered by the Afghan Highway 1 on one side and the other three sides butted up against a bunch of small farms. The guard shacks were spaced about every 100 feet along the wall to watch the farms. These guard shacks were manned by the ASG (Asian Security Group), not by soldiers.

47

Another hard bank and we were at the tail end of the runway. A quick swing to the right and we landed behind some concrete blast walls next to another blue and white Huey, which was being worked on by a mechanic. We jumped off and the Huey flew away. I noticed there was a hangar behind the concrete blast wall with a UAV "predator" in it. We decided that just maybe we should get off the landing zone before the commander's bird came in. Just like our Huey, the second bird touched down long enough to kick out its passengers and took off over the mountains.

There was a mini bus behind the blast wall, which took us over to the main side of post where we got checked in for the night. Remember, I left my A-bag with my sleeping bag back in Bagram. As Forest Gump said, "stupid is, what stupid does!" Our quarters were just a few steps up from a dirt pile. The beds were made from untreated 2X4s and 2X6s with mattresses made in Afghanistan. The Afghan mattresses are not duel sided like ours where it doesn't matter what side is up. Afghan mattresses are bi-cultural with one side fit for a homeless bum and the other suitable for a Hindu who enjoys sleeping on a bed of nails. My back was a bit sore and the bed looked very inviting. I had already shed the protection of my body armor when I hit the mattress only to be speared by a bunch of loose springs that had popped through. Another interesting facet of Afghani beds is they don't use box springs; they place three or four bed slats under the mattress and call it good. So you have nothing solid supporting you. I was quick to notice that there was no linen.

My commander and LTC Velte got the word that there was room for all of their gear so they were prepared for the night. We shared the same room that had been partitioned off from a large bay. On one side of the wall was the major general (inspector general) and the other was an orderly room with a group of troops enjoying the game on TV. The room had a concrete floor and the ceiling was made of bricks laid on inverted "T" rails, which were supported by some wide flange beams spaced four feet apart. All I could think of is just one coming loose in the night and putting me out of my misery. I put on my PT shirt and shorts and placed my hand towel over my legs for warmth. I was doing okay for the first few hours until the temperature dropped to the low 40s. I found the remote to the AC unit, which was hanging near the ceiling and set it to "MAX." I quickly learned something about the remote. The snowflake symbol means cool as in chill! It worked great. I was an ice cube within minutes. I was able to correct the situation and roasted LTC Velte who was sleeping in the direct path of the blast. Most of the hot air flowed over the wall to the two star on the other side.

The morning was a treat. I walked down to the showers. The sky was crystal clear for the first time. There was no dust at all. The scene looked just like standing at the Santa Ana Army Air Base with Santiago Peak rising over the control tower. The far side of the air strip was lined with gum wood trees that really set the place off. I was feeling right at home.

The showers were of some unusual construction. Each stall was constructed of plywood and the shower head was directly overhead controlled by one level valve. You got whatever temperature water shot out so you better test first before jumping in. Against both walls was a long wooden bench with towel hooks so it was like what you would find at a 1940s boy scout camp. On one side of the shower building was two 18-inch open ducts, one belching out semi warm air and the other sucking the warm air back out. I finished up and went to breakfast while LTC Velte decided to go to the gym. Here is where the story gets good.

Our room is off the main alley in full view of two guard towers and a bunch of Afghani construction workers who were building a two-story barracks across from our room. Our room was secured with a standard master combination lock. I was the only guy who wrote down the combination. Both my commander and LTC Velte would ask for the combination each time they needed to get in. The walk to the showers covered large rocks and was very difficult for walking on.

LTC Velte walked to the shower wearing only his flipflops and PT shorts with his hand towel draped over his shoulders. After he stepped out of the shower he looked down the 18-inch suction duct and laughed that someone lost their flipflops to the heater. After he dried off he noticed his shorts were missing. Yes they were with the flipflops at the bottom of the intake duct well outside the range of his arms. Now he had a problem. His hand towel didn't quite make it around his waist. Let's say one good size hip was exposed to the world. He quickly made his way down the alley to our room hoping that no one noticed him. His big concern was the ASG guards in the guard towers just might think he was advertising for love and they would come knocking on our door in the evening. The next problem was that his towel required two hands to keep up; so how was he going to spin the knob on the lock? The bigger question was, "what was the combination? The moment of truth was at hand and God was smiling on LTC Velte. Our commander was in our room with the door unlocked. LTC Velte was still not sure how many people witnessed his 25-yard dash over the rocks, but he'll never hang his shorts by the intake duct again.

After breakfast we applied for our email accounts and had our security clearances verified. By mid morning Major Leeney and our USAID rep arrived. At first I thought the USAID rep was an Afghani. His breath could knock out a drunken goat at fifty yards. We compared notes for a while. I quickly learned that the USDA rep had never worked on a big project and was afraid of them.

The main reason we flew ahead of our main body was to attend a regional agricultural seminar / workshop. On Sunday evening several of the other ADTs (Agribusiness Development Teams) along with reps from USAID and USAMED gathered for a no host dinner at the DFAC (Dining Facility aka mess hall). A no host dinner means you stand in line just like every other night, but you get to eat in the VIP room. We met for about three hours and then said goodnight.

The next morning started early. The conference started off at 7:30 and this time we had some local guests: two regional agricultural ministers and one entrepreneur who was born in Afghanistan. He went to college at the University of Oklahoma then returned to Afghanistan after 9-11; his name was Wafi Jalali and he was sharp! He was getting outside private funds for business development in Afghanistan and making a bundle at it. We would discuss problems. One of the agricultural ministers would say the U.S. needs to train my people better. Then Wafi would fire back "why do they need to train your people? Your people don't even know who is farming in your area, and they don't use the training they have been given." The reason he wanted more training is the U.S. pays his staff to attend the training; ant they pay their per diem, and travel costs too. For the most part people were pretty open about the problems and possible solutions. Not everything took a lot of money. There was one sour bunch in the room. An NGO didn't want the U.S. military working directly with non-government agencies; they wanted to be the intermediary if there was to be any partnership. This group would not tell us what they could do to help the situation, what they accomplished, or what they were doing. Basically they were just soaking up the taxpayers' money and demanding power.

Monday evening I started typing a bunch of memos we needed to have signed for the troops coming in for training. I would type the memos on my computer, load them on an external hard drive then walk to the MWR to email them to myself. Due to U.S. Army information security restrictions we couldn't plug in any external storage device to a government computer, hence the reason for going to MWR and emailing myself the document. It would take about 30 minutes to log on, upload a document and send it to myself. The MWR allows 30 minutes of computer time per visit. I made a lot of visits. Later I would find someone willing to let me log onto their computer to print the document. This also took about 30 minutes.

All of these memos and training were to allow my troops to draw CERP (Commanders Emergency Response Program) and FOO (Field Ordering Officer) funds. The CERP funds were to be spent on Afghanistan the FOO funds were to be spent on U.S. troops / operational needs. Our mission would depend upon our ability to spend money efficiently and effectively.

While I was typing away LTC Velte went to sleep before his head hit the pillow, and my commander was answering emails on his Blackberry and did some light reading. By 8:00 P.M. I was shot and went to sleep. Later in the evening two other LTCs came in and went to sleep. At 11:30 P.M. we were all suddenly awoken by two loud bangs, more like loud cracks. Then we heard a moan. I turned on a flashlight only to find one of the other LTCs standing up on his mattress. He had selected the upper bunk of a bunk bed set, which had no lower bunk for his slumber. The bed slats had suddenly let loose and landed him on the concrete floor.

Back at the Bagram Air Base they heard a very different noise around 3:30 A.M. In the early hours of the morning the distinct sound of a mortar register was going off echoed by the sounds of impact at the north end of the airfield. The rounds were being rapidly fired from one tube using the northern PX and temporary lodging as a target. By the time the sixth mortar was in flight, a 7.62 mini gun had locked on the location of the mortar crew. The whizzing sounds of rounds going down range could be heard across the airfield followed by an eerie silence. A few minutes later a captain and a first sergeant required medical attention. Even though our troops were more than a mile away they were still robbed of their sleep for the remainder of the night. Our other troops were already at the PAX terminal waiting for their flight to Jalalabad.

We got up early on Tuesday October 20th so we could meet our troops at the airfield. The first C-130 arrived with only one troop on it and several pallets of ammo. I kept scanning the skies for another plane and the roof tops for snipers, but the air was so thick with dust I couldn't see more than five miles. Within a few weeks I would relax about snipers as my situational awareness improved.

I finally spotted a C-130 making a slow bank coming in on the southern approach of the runway. The pilot hit the brakes good and hard half way down the runway so he didn't have to do a reverse taxi. This runway was the equivalent of a very old country road that was paved during Eisenhower's administration, and was only one lane wide. Anyhow, the plane was able to slow down enough to make a sharp right to the tarmac that was in front of the old Nangarhar tower and terminal. Once the cargo was unloaded, our troops unloaded and followed us across the runway. This runway was very busy in the morning There was a plane or helicopter taking off or landing every five minutes. All you did to cross the runway was wait for the green light and stay inside the crosswalk. The predator had the right of way because he had no pilot. You just let him pass and keep walking.

Just minutes before our troops got on the plane, the load master said "hey we got room for your whole unit. Can you bring them over?" Our NCOs wished they had known, but even if they left the far side of Bagram at that moment it would have taken almost an hour to make the trip around the airfield and the plane was set to take off in 20 minutes. It wasn't much of a problem; there was a second flight scheduled for later that day to Jalalabad.

After our troops walked across the runway at Jalalabad (Jalalabad, Nangarhar, and FOB Fenty are the same place) a forklift dropped off a pallet with their gear on it. They tore the pallet apart, then learned that the billets were on the other side of the runway where they had just come from. Not a problem. The troops just loaded up like a bunch of pack mules and hit the road.

Our troops got settled in time for breakfast, which left the better part of the day to catch up on sleep and to take care of some required finance classes. I was still trying to get signatures on memos to set up our FOO and CERP accounts before the commander flew out. I was still sending documents by email from the MWR to any office that had a printer, which took about an hour each time I needed a new document. It didn't help that FOB Fenty ran like a bank. 9:00 A.M. to 3:30 P.M. and then the doors were locked. It turned out to be a very long day having to create different memos because of different sets of examples that were provided each time I attempted to submit all of our paper work. Part of the problem was the finance office was in the middle of a personnel change, and they were implementing new procedures at the same time. My troops would show up for a scheduled finance class only to be told there was no class. Then when we went back later for the next scheduled class, we were told the class was given in the morning. Oh boy!

Wafi Jalali told me a joke at the conference when I was trying to understand how Afghans think and why the country just stood still.

"A man dies and goes to hell. When he gets there he is shown many ditches where sinners are forced to toil for an eternity. The ditches were all guarded and anyone who tried to climb out of a ditch was jousted with a pitchfork. The man noticed one ditch that was marked Afghans only and there was no one guarding it. He asked why there are no guards on the Afghan ditch. His escort answered 'because anytime an Afghani tries to climb out of the ditch three other Afghanis will pull him back in.'"

At times I wonder if the same is not true for us.

Chapter Ten

CH-47 TO CAMP WRIGHT

I had planned to stay in Jalalabad for two more days taking contracting classes, which is one of the reasons I didn't fly out with the commander and LTC Velte on the morning of October 20th. Due to some miscommunication from the finance people, three of my people missed a class for which they showed up on time. There was a change of authority going on. The outgoing folks were giving me examples of memos, forms and instructions and the incoming folks had a completely different operating procedure. It was be almost two months before we could draw funds because of the TOA and because we didn't exist on anyone's books.

I was passing by the mess hall on one of my many runs back and forth between the MWR and Finance to print documents when I spotted two of our senior NCOs standing out front. Once again I heard the familiar phrase: "Sir did you get the word about our flight out of here?"

We were leaving a day early and I had about two hours to pack my junk, clear the room, eat and hump all of my gear across the airfield. My troops had brought my gear to me on the first flight in the morning so I was back to dragging around 150 pounds of gear. We were scheduled to fly out on two CH-47 helicopters at 7:20 P.M. I don't know what the reason was but our flights got moved to the right by a little over two hours. That left me with enough time to email a letter home at the MWR, and buy some sheets and a few other goodies I needed at the PX. Camp Wright doesn't have a PX so if you don't have it you're not going to get it any time soon.

Our troops had been placed in another circus tent on the far side of the airfield about 100 feet from the edge of the runway. The lighting on the far side of the airfield was indoors only no outside lighting. The best lighting was provided by the green traffic lights that signaled that it was safe to cross the runway. All of the CH-47s were parked 300 yards from our circus tent, which wasn't so bad except we had to make several trips to move all of our gear. The flight ops called and told us that one CH-47 wouldn't take all of us. This meant our unit would once again be broken into two sections for the move. One of our more enterprising troops found a five-ton truck that looked like it came out of a Mad Max movie with its fortified box cab that stuck out like a sore thumb. We loaded our gear on the back of the truck, then waited out on the side of the runway and listened to the ghost fly by. We could hear the aircraft and just make out their shadows as they passed in front of us. The predator came close enough to us that we could see all of its armament as it took off. A while later it came home after lightening its load. It was hunting something out there in the hills – what beast, and what hills, we'll never know.

The time finally came to move out to the CH-47. The headquarters, Ag sections and a squad from the SecFor (Security Force) put on their body armor, checked weapons and ammo then headed out single file to the flight line. It was not an easy walk. What earth that wasn't paved with asphalt was covered with large river rock, which was very difficult to walk on. We veered out onto the runway where we could keep a secure footing, then as we closed on the family of CH-47s we moved back onto the rocks. The CH-47s looked like they had been abandoned on a playground with the doors open and no lights. The only light came from the other side of the field until our five-ton arrived along with a crew chief who had been resting inside the bird. We quickly formed a fire line and loaded everything down the center of the aircraft. Then the crew chief put the tail gun back on the ramp. We still had a long time to wait for takeoff. SFC Hanlin started some word games while we stood out on the rocks. The first game was to name off the famous people who died in a plane crash. His games kept our minds off the wait and gave us something to think about instead of when are we going to get some sleep.

Finally at 9:30 the crew chief gathered us all together and gave us a flight briefing. Rule number one: *keep your weapons pointed toward the floor. Everything that keeps us flying is up so don't point your weapon that way.* He went on to tell us what we would do if the FOB was under attack when we arrived. Basically, do turn around and come back. There was no way we could unload that bird and know where to go so why bother.

We loaded up, pressing ourselves between the piles of gear that had been strapped down to the center of the floor with not much room to spare. Once we got seated there wasn't enough room for the last man at the end so we all attempted to slide over enough so he could get two cheeks on the seat. I didn't come out on the winning end of the deal. I found myself split between two benches and slowly sliding between them. The lights went off inside the bird and then the winding of the jet turbines started up. Both front side doors were open to accommodate the port and starboard gunners and the back ramp stayed down for the tail gunner. The exhaust fumes from the jets quickly filled the cabin as the bird started to rock back and forth. We sat there for five to ten minutes just waiting; then the front end lifted off and then the rear. Just like Dr. Doolittle's "Push-me Pull-you" the double ended goat has one end that must follow the other or it goes nowhere. We lifted straight up for a hundred feet then launched over the Afghan Highway 1 toward the northern mountains. Even though I was seated half way inside the bird I could still see out the back ramp. The FOB that looked so dark and void was now a brilliant beacon, all lit up. There were a few scattered lights in the city, but as a whole you would never know a city was there at night. Then again why waste power at night when the world is asleep.

I kept an eye on the FOB as it diminished in size and faded into the distance. It was difficult to see much of anything. I knew we were passing over the mountains. I could see their charcoal outlines against the night sky, which was a dark purple. We kept gaining altitude. Then suddenly we made a great drop. I could feel myself go weightless for an instant but the weight of my ruck, battle rattle and having my feet entangled in the cargo straps kept me in place. Then the port machine gunner let open a burst, which was echoed on the starboard side and followed up by the tail gunner. The cabin was filled with the smell of sulfur that was replaced with the same smell of dust we had been enduring since morning. That sudden drop took us into a box canyon where they could safely test fire their guns before we reached Camp Wright. We were expecting it so no one was surprised.

Thirty minutes later we sat down on the back side of Camp Wright where blackout conditions were enforced. The crew chief tapped the troops on the end of the bench to get off. We unloaded, ran out about 50 feet, grounded our gear, and then formed a fire line to unload the gear. The CH-47 didn't let up much of the thrust. As I returned to the bird I could feel the hot blast coming off the engines trying to knock me down. The crew chief started handing me gear and I passed it on to the next man. I jumped back on board along with SFC Fair as the fire line continued to stretch across the abyss. The fire line was working in perfect coordination. I felt like I was sentenced to hell and my punishment was to work out with a medicine ball for eternity. Some of the rucks and A-bags (an A-bag is a duffle bag loaded with a soldier's primary gear) weighted over 150 pounds, which is what my total gear weighed. I couldn't imagine just what they could have put in their bags. When the last bag was out the crew chief gave me the thumbs up and SFC Fair and I jumped off the back ramp onto the helipad covered with more river rock. We ran to the dog pile and added our bodies to the cause. All of the gear was heaped into one pile. Then we covered it with our bodies to prevent it from being redistributed all over Afghanistan by the down blast of the Chinook (CH-47). We could hear the turbines increase their whine, then a sudden blast of wind and it was all over. We gave a good cheer, stood up and dusted ourselves off.

The whole area was void of light except for light grey dirt roads leading up to the helipad. I looked up and the heavens were crystal clear. I could see the Milky Way and big and little dippers. I can't remember when the last time it was that I could see so much of the universe. Even when I drive out past Frazer Park on I-5 I can only see a few stars at best.

The next voice I heard was the SecFor platoon leader telling us to load up the 1151s with our gear. The 1151 is the new improved version of the HWMVV. It has armor doors and bullet resistant glass and a gunner's turret on it, and not much cargo space. We were led to where the enlisted troops would stay, which looked like a converted warehouse and loading dock. We formed another fire line and unload the trucks, then sorted out our gear. While the troops were occupying their quarters, the rest of us were led through the dark to our new home through a construction site and several back alleys. An 1151 showed up with some of our gear. Then the rest of us had to walk back and get our own.

By now our CH-47 had returned to Jalalabad for the remainder of our unit. We had two lost souls floating around in the nether land, Sgt Olson our forward observer and Sgt Flynn my forestry expert. They were to follow our equipment from Camp Atterbury to Camp Wright. However FedEx would only allow two of our soldiers to accompany the equipment so they got bumped. The two of them hitch hiked their way across the globe to Manas and then to Bagram. They lucked out and were able to strap hang on a flight to Jalalabad on the 20th. They were beat to say the least when they hit the PAX terminal at Jalalabad. The PAX manager was on his toes when they said they needed to get to Camp Wright. They were planning to spend the night in Jalalabad and then catching a bird to Camp Wright. The PAX manager decided to do them a favor and flagged down a UH-60 that landed near the PAX terminal just in time to flight follow the CH-47 to Camp Wright. Our Kunar ADT family was only short two members who were with our equipment somewhere in Manas.

The officer and senior NCO residence was a 32 by 16 foot wooden hut with one front door. The first 12 feet made up our orderly room. Then the remainder of the building was divided up into six rooms. The hallway was less than two feet wide, and ended in a point where the end two room doors came together. The walls were all constructed of 3/8 plywood. The floor had a springy feel to it where it was starting to rot out. The nails on the floor boards in my room had all popped up. I found a hammer and drove them all back in. When I struck the first nail there was nothing on the other side to hold it.

One of the rooms had been used as a mail holding room for all of the care packages that were sent long before we got there. Some of the senior NCOs and I took the task of cleaning out the room. The fire line system worked on the CH-47. Why not packages from home? One NCO would slide the packages from the back of the hall to me at the halfway point. I would hike the like a football center to the platoon sergeants who were sorting the mail. There was a bunch of boxes for SFC Teso who held the record from home. I was looking for my eye protection, which I sent to myself from Camp Atterbury, and another box of uniforms that still hadn't shown up after two weeks.

After playing postman, I didn't waste too much more time. I just unpacked what I needed and put my new sheets on my bed. This time I got a mattress cast out of concrete. It was 2:00 A.M. before I was able to go to sleep. I woke up at six o'clock and went outside to be welcomed by sunshine.

The place looked just liked the opening scene to MASH or the Santa Monica mountains. I looked up and saw Willey the whale, a large aerostat observation balloon overhead and could see the 800-year old adobe turret "Shiloh" on top of the highest peak directly above the FOB. Shiloh and Bull Run were the two main observation posts (OP), which provided security for the FOB. OP Bull Run was located farther back behind the FOB with its main duty to protect the FOB's back door. The hills had streaks of green grass on them so there was water in the area. I found a shower and got cleaned up, then headed back up the road to the mess hall for breakfast.

I took a few minutes to look around a bit, then went to work developing a five-year plan for citrus and apple production. I stuck my head out of the office in time for lunch and saw a good sized thunder head forming directly overhead. When I came back from lunch they were reeling Willie the Whale down for safety. I went by our USDA rep's office just to say hello. Turns out he lives in his office. The place looked like a freshman dorm room–a royal disaster area.

Chapter Eleven

THE FIRST WEEK AT FOB WRIGHT

By the end of our first week at Camp Wright the excitement of being in Afghanistan had started to die off a bit. Our equipment was still in route from Manas with SGT Palacios doing everything that he could to get a plane to fly it on. It seems that because our unit didn't exist on paper no one in the logistics arena bothered to schedule any military cargo flights to support us. It was the same problem I was having trying to set up our financial books. This meant that we were stuck on Camp Wright. We had some 1151s, thanks to the efforts of Major Leeney, but no crew served weapons to mount on them.

Most of us used the first week to get settled and to learn the ins and outs of the FOB and who was who. My first night, October 20th I was too wound up to sleep, so I walked around a bit to find the more important aspects of the FOB. The first priority was to find the latrine and showers. During my wanderings I met one of the two longest residing residents of the FOB, Tripod. Tripod was the mother of two kittens who lived on top of the hot water heater in the laundry room. She was caught in the crossfire one night and was rushed to the trauma center where the surgeons amputated her left front leg to save her life. For a three legged cat, Tripod gets around very well.

The nearest latrines were two outhouses next to our bunker, which were kept locked so the locals wouldn't use them. The bunker was just a few steps outside the door of our billets; it may or may not have been de-snaked. Afghanistan is noted for Cobras and they don't rattle before they bite.

By the end of Wednesday, October 21st , I had a good feel for the post. Camp Wright didn't have a PX (Post Exchange), but there really wasn't a need for one because Walmart had a mini store on the FOB. A small group of local merchants, who had stores on Camp Wright named their stores after major department and discount stores in the U.S. The difference is the local merchants basically sold junk from India and knock off electronics from Turkey and bootlegged CDs and movies. There were a few merchants who sold diamonds, rubies and other stones.

Up by the airfield were two 155 artillery pieces that would be fired when called upon. I didn't think much of them coming from an 8-inch artillery battalion. After all just how much noise could they make? I would find out on my second night when I was starting to feel the effects of the lack of sleep. I was dead to the world when the first gun fired. Our little hut shook back and forth. I woke up just after the shaking stopped not really coherent. Then the two guns fired for effect and the place really shook. About this time I realized nature was calling after all I was up. 'Might as well take care of business. I went outside with my double "A" LED flashlight with the blue lens on it so I wouldn't break my neck on the pallets we used as a sidewalk. I was able to look up to the hill and see the flashes from the artillery. I did what I needed to, then went back to bed. I never woke up again for the artillery, just rocked back and forth in my bed. The following day the artillery was shooting continually. A bunch of us went over to watch. The gun bunnies offered to let me pull tail, but I remembered if you pull tail you get to clean the tube later. The artillery fired all day long shaking our little hut. This answered the question, why all the nails had worked their way out of the floor in my room.

U.S. Army Spc. Seth Mulcahy (left) along with U.S. Army Spc. Robert Mason (right) and U.S. Army Spc. Richard McNulty (center), all from Charlie Battery, 1-321 Airborne Field Artillery Regiment, Ft. Bragg, N.C., load a 155mm towed howitzer at Camp Wright, Afghanistan, Sept. 23, 2009. The team fired the weapon as part of a registry exercise where targets are pre-marked to increase speed and accuracy. Photo by Tech. Sgt. Brian Boisvert

On the evening of October 22nd LTC Velte and I were eating dinner in the mess hall when the alarm went off. First there was the big buzz, then the verbal announcement "Incoming fire, Incoming fire." We just looked at each other because we really didn't know what to do. The only bunker we knew of was a 100 yards down the hill by our billets. We noticed that no one in the mess hall looked alarmed at all. I asked one of the SF guys if it was a drill, and he said no it's the real thing but not to worry. The insurgents usually miss the camp by 500 meters and never can lob anything over the Kunar River. He said a few weeks back they did get off a few rounds by climbing up from Pakistan, but the artillery platoon answered with 22 rounds of 155 fire just in case they had friends in the area. They found parts of Taliban and donkeys the next day.

It turns out we were pretty safe in the buildings. I noticed that all of the excess water and MREs (Meals Ready to Eat) were stored on the roofs. The troops also overloaded water and MREs on their vehicles for additional protection. The buildings are constructed of red brick, which absorbs impact. The concrete block construction reacts much the same way that glass does when struck by a small object. Glass will blow out a small conic shaped projectile. On the interior it just transfers the impact.

Concrete blocks will do the same throwing large chunks of concrete across a room.

That night we had a fair amount of artillery fire, but I just acknowledged the big boom, rolled over and continued sleeping. In the morning at breakfast someone asked me if I felt the earthquake. I asked what earthquake? It turns out we had a 6.2 earthquake up north somewhere.

The Camp Wright Trauma Center was located next to our quarters. The FOB mayor was in the process of moving them up on top of the hill next to the flight line in their building. The trauma center was a full operating room always ready for surgery. When the camp north of us was being overrun, all O+ blood donors assembled at the gym as walking blood banks. One Afghani troop was flown in and required several pints of blood. There were only two people in the camp with my blood type and LTC Velte was the only one with AB-. SPC Larson, one of our medics, was there that night to help with the wounded, but only the one Afghani was brought in. Another lost a leg because it took 14 hours to get him out of the fire zone and the tourniquet that saved his life cost him his leg.

Afghanistan was scheduled to have a presidential runoff election, which was expected to usher in a lot of violence. The U.S. position was to let the Afghans handle the election security and operations. U.S. troops would stay put and not interfere. The concern was that any action by the U.S. or ISAF could tilt the election in one direction or the other, and even if it didn't the locals would still accuse the U.S. of orchestrating the results. Over all the locals were very excited about the runoff election. Villages voted as a block and by tribe. Individuals would vote for whomever the village elder directed them to vote for. It shouldn't surprise anyone when the results are reviewed that whole villages and regions vote for one man. The people who live in Kunar didn't think that the first election was rigged. President Karazi was demanding more polling places to be open for the runoff election. The runoff elections never happened due to some behind the scenes agreements among the candidates.

Even though our crew served weapons were floating around in theater, we still had our individual weapons and we needed to verify that the sights were still zeroed. On Friday October 23rd we went to the range, which was located below the Observation Post Shiloh on a dirt road behind the camp. We were given a quick orientation to the range: basically don't shoot any cows or goats and don't point your weapons at the village. We were told that the village up the road is not a friendly village. they sell IED parts. The rumor was some troops raided the Woch Now Village six months prior to our arrival and found IED components. A few months later we learned all of the reports we received were false and the men of Woch Now became extremely Pro American.

We could only set up six firing positions so the rest of us spread about the range and waited our turn. SFC Fulton decided to take up a position to watch the village and the road just because he thought it was a good idea. I went over to see what he could see. The first village, Woch Now, had a two story building with an open door facing our direction. I noticed every now and then a flash of light from the door. I asked SFC Fair, who had a scope on his M-14, to take a look. It turns out we were the entertainment of the day. It was Friday, their holy day so everyone was home. There were three men sitting in the door with field glasses watching us, watching them. With an M-14 I'm sure SFC Fair could have reached out and touched them. If he couldn't the two observation posts could have rained down on them like there was no tomorrow. We were still getting acquainted with the area and the environment based upon poor or outdated information. In a few weeks we would know where all the hot spots were, and who was friendly, etc. For now it paid to keep a heightened sense of caution.

The locals like to wear light brown clothes. This makes them very difficult to see. My glasses are a weak prescription because of eye strain. The only reason I knew people were in the hills was movement. Sgt. Olson made a comment that the hills were bare. I told him, "no there are a bunch of people up there and there is one running down the side of the mountain now." Sure enough a young teenage boy named Tony came running down the hill with four radio batteries, which needed to be re-charged. Tony speaks Pashto, English and Spanish. Tony stopped in front of me, pulled out an American smoke, not one from India, then hauled out his cell phone and showed me his run time up and back, which was nine minutes. I looked down at Tony's feet and saw a good pair of running shoes. With that I knew Tony had money and electrical power at home. Tony and his friends gather around the range whenever it is hot to sell their wares to the troops and to pick up all of the brass. When the other boys passed in front of the firing line Tony was quick to chase them all back to the safe side. There wasn't a real danger of the boys getting shot, but it pays to be safe. Tony and his father have a contract with the post to deliver supplies to the observation posts. Each morning at 3:30 they load up their mules and Dad goes to Shiloh and Tony goes to Bull Run. Tony makes some extra money running up and down the mountain to swap out radio batteries. There was another younger boy there making bracelets out of 550 cord (550 cord is used for parachutes.). SFC Medina bought one from him for a buck. Another boy who didn't speak much English sold me four 1000 Afghani notes from the 1930s for a buck.

Major Leeney was still working his magic acquiring vehicles. He was able to get his hands on a few MRAPs, which were damaged, but still worked for us. All the good stuff was sitting down at Bagram, parked like a massive car lot not being used at all.

I can still remember my first deployment to Honduras back in the early 90s when we lived out by mosquito flats and rationed water. Showering was limited to a sponge bath and laundry was contracted out to a woman who washed it in the local river. Showering at Camp Wright was bit of a challenge but a major upgrade from my last two deployments. The shower near our quarters, which is in the same quad as the gym and Trauma Center, have a door that will swing open at just the wrong time. The shower heads are along one side of the room and spray on the bottles of potable water that we use for brushing our teeth. There is one sink in the corner with a broken mirror for shaving. If you're shaving at the sink you get hosed at the same time if all three shower heads are in service.

The laundry is next door. You can drop your laundry off in the morning and a local guy will do it for you. He is on the payroll but most people will tip him a dollar. There is also a tailor on the payroll and he likes his tips just as well. The average pay per day is $3.00; five bucks is out of sight. The barber who receives one dollar tips all day long is a millionaire compared to the town folks. If you're tired of the food there is a bakery and a café run by the locals. The bakery bakes flat bread, and the café serves hamburgers, but I've never seen anyone eating there. The locals usually have a pressure cooker pot they bring and it feeds about four people. I'd see them sitting around the pot at lunch all scooping out rice and carrots with their hands. Folks need to remember their left hand doubles as toilet paper. The same goes for the barber who will rub his hands all over your head before he starts cutting. Our barber cuts everyone's hair and beards, locals, nationals and U.S. They do not clean their tools so it is wise to bath after having your hair cut. The Russians lost a lot of troops from diseases. I've seen how the Russians live, which isn't much better than how the Afghanis live.

We made our first trip out of the wire on Sunday October 25th with some borrowed weapons, and the PRT as our escort. In the morning we met with the PRT (Provisional Reconstruction Team) who were running the mission. They gave us a brief on what to do in the convoy and when we got there. First thing: don't shoot at anything unless you know it is shooting at you and no big guns in the town. Once you get there don't pet the monkeys and stay away from the monkeys. They will steal everything.

We lined up the vehicles and rolled out the front gate and made a left turn onto Route California the main highway into Asadabad. A hundred yards north of our FOB the landscape turned green with corps. I didn't see one horse cart or make-shift powered wagon like I did in Kosovo. We passed two car dealerships. On the way in I was told that there were two more on the other side of town. There was a traffic circle where we veered to the right down a road toward the river. I saw a large school on the left hand side that looked very clean and well kept. Then we arrived at the governor's compound. It took us a few minutes to turn around all of our vehicles. Then we took off our battle rattle and went in the compound. Sure enough there were two monkeys tied to the trees to greet us. The troops started feeding them trail mix and giving them cans of "Red Bull" energy drinks. We were given a tour of the compound. The U.S. had a mini base right behind the compound. We could see the river from the back of the compound and an irrigation canal running at the base of the main conference building. All you would need to break in is a ladder and a screw driver. There was no security in the back of the compound. We met with a few folks who asked me for a job. Then it was time to meet with the governor. I made use of the bathroom first and wished I hadn't. What a mess!

We were each given a small radio receiver to listen to the interpreter while everyone spoke. The governor spoke fluent English, but spoke in Pashto during the meeting. He was a sharp man. I have to give him a lot of credit. He really knew what was going on in the world. He made a statement about getting projects completed by his public works. The work wasn't getting done because Kabul was stalling and holding back money earmarked for Kunar. He thought President Karazi was waiting until the elections were over before releasing any further money. He ended the meeting by stating "my people may not have much, but they all have a mouth and a pen and they use them both!" I took several pages of notes and then we loaded up for the trip home. We had lots of security for a trip that was only 1.5 miles from the base.

By the end of our first week in Afghanistan the region was more of a reflection of the drug wars in Mexico. What happened makes the press but it is exactly what is going on in Mexico. Some people might say Afghanistan is the U.S. Army's training ground for the next Mexican civil war. Afghanistan does have its local crime just like in the big cities in the U.S. Sex crimes are the biggest.

The greatest improvement the United States has made there is road construction. Where the roads go so does commerce and the Taliban flees. Once a road is paved the Taliban will not put an IED (Improvised Explosive Device) on it. If they destroy the road the locals will kill them. The only time the Taliban will destroy a road is to strike back at the locals. All of the little development projects we did are great, but because they have no local ownership they fall apart quickly. The roads however attract private investors who can access a new market. That is what is driving the recovery and stabilization. However the area will never become stable as long as there is a Pakistan. The last thing Pakistan wants is foreign investment in Afghanistan that would draw industry and revenue from Pakistan. Afghanistan is landlocked due to the provisions of the Duran line. The Duran line was the result of a treaty in 1895 that set the western limits of the British Indian Empire. Afghanistan's only means of export other than by air is through Pakistan or Iran.

Chapter Twelve

IT IS IN THE BOX

Things were going slowly during our second week at Camp Wright. The running joke is "It is in the box. Oh did you check the box?" The box is where all of our gear and equipment was, to do our mission. Our equipment was getting closer. All but one pallet made it to Jalalabad; the remaining pallet was further south in Bagram, which meant we might never have seen it again. Thievery is a major problem this that area. The PRT (Provincial Reconstruction Team) had many of their ConExs broken into in Pakistan. Only personnel items were stolen, which means they knew what to take. One unit found that their personnel items were all replaced with bricks. The logistics convoys get hit every now and then so our equipment would be flown up on Absolute Air, an old Soviet Block carrier.

Our mission depended upon us being able to pay for items and services in order to improve the agricultural economy. We decided to send two groups back to Jalalabad to get certified so they could draw the needed funds. I went with the first group so I could prime the pump with the paperwork and be available to sign any memos that needed signing, which I hadn't already created.

Four of us went up to the helipad just after lunch: SFC Natividad, SSG Lucas and SSG Tyner. The PRT rolled up on the pad with all of their vehicles and out stepped some high-ranking Afghani with his security detail and Col George, our Brigade commander. There were two UH-

60 black hawk helicopters waiting for him, getting warmed up. Then two Kiowas came in and refueled. They then took off circling the valley. Finally, our Molson Air UH-1 blue and white helicopter landed along with another two more Kiowas, which came in for refueling. The pilot waved us over. We worked our way through the gantlet of swirling blades. The black hawks took off first followed by the two Kiowas, and then we lifted off. What a view! We could see up into all of the little canyons. Every draw and spur had been terraced eons ago but for some reason the locals stopped farming them. We flew south along the Kunar for a few minutes. The west side of the river stayed green and farmed while the east side did not.

Soon the valley opened up into a giant basin as we flew over one abandon adobe compound after another. Each compound had its farm marked with a short mud wall, but there was no evidence of any life, not even squatters. FOB Joyce appeared like an oasis in the desert. It was huge compared to our little camp. They even had a full size basketball court. We landed there and picked up three more passengers, two civilians and one military. We lifted off, circled over the camp and continued going south following the Kunar. From Asadabad to the mouth of the Jalalabad valley there was no irrigation on the eastern side of the river. That changed abruptly when we flew into the Jalalabad valley, which resembled the central California valley; every patch of earth was farmed. When we flew out of Jalalabad a few weeks earlier it was at night so we couldn't see the valley. With one hard continuous bank to the right we set down at Molson Air's terminal.

Within a minute of landing at Molson Air terminal, a shuttle bus came by and picked us up. We travelled to the PAX terminal. I left my ruck with the troops and went to inquire about rooms. I knew we were not getting rooms, but I still needed to know where we could rack out for a few nights. The billeting folks offered me a VIP room, but my NCOs would have to sleep in the transition tents on the far side of the field. I believe what is good for the goose, is good for the gander.

With a tent assignment in hand, we loaded up our gear and walked to the runway. We waited for the light to turn green at the runway crossing and as usual the predator just happened to be passing by sounding like a sick lawnmower. The tent was 20 feet by 80 and had 40 troops inside. The first cot I noticed had a twin mattress on it. Turns out the guy paid fifty bucks for it. SSG Lucas wasted no time following his example and acquired a foam mattress for his cot, which he intended to roll up and take back to Camp Wright with him.

We went over to the finance office, checked in and then went to dinner. There are always the customary things to do whenever you visit another post, whether or not you need anything. And that of course is to buy something at the PX, go to MWR for free popcorn and watch people play pool. I lucked out at the PX and found two boxes of Christmas cards and a pad of paper. SSG Tyner invested in a new coffee pot, played the homeless card at the chapel and landed two pounds of coffee.

By seven o'clock there wasn't anything left for us country boys to do in this big city so we decided to hit the hay. Besides, there are no lights to read by and the tent was dark. Funny thing… when we were at Manas, the other troops we shared a tent with were always very inconsiderate and noisy. In this tent people went out of their way to keep quiet.

I was lying on the cot listening to the soft hum of the generators and the blower unit and sweltering. SSG Lucas decided he was going to do something about the environment in the tent and started looking for a thermostat. We went outside together in our drawers and found the thermostat, which was set for 65 degrees, but the tent was in the 90s. Another contractor, Hallmark, put the thermostat outside of the tent to control the temperature on the inside. We fixed that problem, went back in and attempted to get some sleep.

This same evening at the Marha Warha (also spelled Marawara) Afghan National Police (ANP) compound on the eastern side of the Kunar River across from Asadabad, which was protected by a group of ASG (Asian Security Group) was attached by 16 insurgents. Had it not been for the efforts of Major Eric Stevennson from Sweden, the attack could have progressed to include the Marha Warha district center. The ANP compound located in Marawara had three levels of security. The first level was the ANP gate guards, the second level was manned by Afghan National Army (ANA), and the final level of security was contracted with the ASG (Asian Security Group). The security guards provided by the ASG were a combination of retired Gurkhas and Afghan nationals. This was the same mix that was provided to FOB Fiaz located near the Asadabad government center.

A few weeks earlier, while LTC Velte was in Kabul, the U.N. guesthouse was attacked by insurgent. Major Stevennson had made it a point to befriend the ASG guards. One evening after the attack on the U.N. guesthouse he was talking to a Gurkha captain who was cleaning his AK-47. When he asked the captain about the support he was getting from the ASG or the U.N., the Captain complained that he had one magazine for every two guards. Half of the AK-47s they were given were non-functional and he couldn't even get cleaning supplies.

Major Stevennson wrote a letter to the U.N. security people about the situation and within two days the ASG guards at the Marha Warha district center and FOB Fiaz received all the supplies they needed. Major Stevennson was certain that the attack on the UN guesthouse was the only reason he got a response.

The tent we were assigned to is located 25 yards from the edge of the tarmac and 100 yards from the runway with no sound wall. The first noise to distract my heavenly slumber was the dying lawnmower engine of the predator warming up at the far end of the field. The predator took off and flew past our tent like a drunken mosquito. By the time the hum of the predators had faded into the hills the Chinooks started to wake up from their hibernation. Then just like a box of dominoes falling down the whine of turbines firing up from one end of the field to the other began. Soon the only sound was the beating of rotor blades coming from all sides. The CH-47s led the stampede by flying over our tent, followed by the Apaches and Kiowas. Later on, a Black Hawk would take off on the far side of the field where the Med-Evacs stood by. The next sound was a C-130 hitting the breaks and making a hard turn off the runway to the tarmac by slamming two props in full reverse behind our tent. It was there for a short while never cutting its engines while it unloaded. The prop roar increased and tent flaps puffed out from the wash as the C-130 rolled past us for takeoff. Living in a vinyl tent with a C-130 going by is like being on the inside of a beach ball as it is being inflated. What was taking place was a very rapid response to the insurgent attack on the Marha Warha ANP compound.

At 18:40 November 2nd the Marha Warha ANP compound was attacked by insurgents while all Afghan personnel fled the scene leaving the compound undefended. Within twenty minutes, the United States had two F-15s overhead from Bagram Air Base and two platoons of infantry in route. One platoon of U.S. troops rounded up all of the Afghan personnel while the other platoon retook the ANP compound and secured the surrounding terrain and the nearby the district center. The U.S. troops were supported with F-15s, Apaches and Kiowas helicopters from Jalalabad. Before the night was over, twelve of the sixteen insurgents lost their lives and the other four retreated through the Daridan-Mora Valley toward Pakistan.

SFC Fair and SFC Hanlin witnessed the counter attack from one of the guard towers at Camp Wright while the remaining four insurgents were being tracked. Their location was confirmed and relayed to the F-15s that were stationed to drop a GBU (Guided Bomb Unit). The detonation of the GBU bought the U.S. infantry enough time to capture the surviving insurgents. Shortly after the F-15s dropped their GBUs, two CH-47 Special Operations helicopters landed at the Camp Wright field and waiting for the battle to conclude.

The flight path from FOB Fenty (Jalalabad) where we were staying, is straight up the Kunar River, which flows in front of Camp Wright. From SFC Fair's and Hanlin's position they could see all of the aircraft activity. They could also see FOB Fiaz providing covering fire across the Kunar. They couldn't see the detonation of the GBU because they were dropped far back in the Daridan-Mora Valley, but they could hear the explosion. The next two nights were be filled by air patrols and 155 illumination rounds. The United Nation and NGO organizations lost their nerve and decided to evacuate FOB Fiaz and never return.

Then all was still again. The pilot-less predator came back from its rounds and took off again. About two hours later the whole show repeated itself. This time I just acknowledged the performers and returned to my coma.

Our first class wasn't until 8:30 so I had planned after being forced to critique the evening performance several times, to sleep in a bit. Only a fool makes plans in this world. More C-130s were coming in. The honey truck was making its rounds followed by the diesel delivery man, not to mention the convoy of jingle trucks delivering road base to the new runway. A jingle truck is a local national truck all decked out with bells hanging from every edge. They are usually painted brighter than a parrot.

Just by chance I met SGT Palacios, our supply sergeant and SGT Johanson at breakfast. They pointed out all of our equipment, which was sitting in the middle of the tarmac. The two of them had to re-pack everything at each stop. Whenever they changed airframes there was a different load plan. They were also chastised for being three months late at each stop. It wasn't their fault that "Big Army" decided that the only way to save the budget was to make us wait.

We parted and went our separate ways. My group went over to the finance office and attended a short class on contracting to be certified. The Sgt giving the class in English was so poor I couldn't understand a word he said. After that I went about coordinating how to get our money. Once again it is easier to have a camel walk through an eye of a needle than to get the Army to cough up some cash. The captain in charge was going on leave and the NCO who took his place was gone. Even if all of our people were trained and had the paper work to prove it, the system still required four days to process everything.

With that, I went to the PX and purchased an American Diet Pepsi, went to the mess hall with the Christmas cards I bought and started writing out my season's greetings. When the place started getting full I went over to the air terminal and finished them up. You can't really count on the mail service there. The post office is run through a joint effort of a private contractor and Army personnel. They are all of the same mentality; a postal clerk is the same wherever you go. The mail is hauled by a local contractor so you never know when or even if it will get out of the country into a legitimate mail service. Since Jalalabad had a post office I decided it was in my best interest to get all of the cards out while I was there. This meant that some people would get their card in time for Thanksgiving; other may have to wait until News Year's.

Later in the day I went over and saw our equipment stacked up on the tarmac awaiting delivery. The first four tri-walls were set aside for Absolute Air to deliver them. Absolute Air uses old Soviet Hip helicopters and very Russian pilots. Absolute Air's operation area was a swamp compared to the Canadian operation; everything was in the dirt!

I was feeling the effects of the lack of sleep from the night before, but I knew if I took a cat nap I wouldn't be able to sleep through the helicopter rodeo that was scheduled for the evening. So I continued my walk around the field. The old civilian airport had drawn my interest since my first arrival so I decided to take a long walk around to look at it.

I was able to find a path to the perimeter road and started my trek to the old terminal. The perimeter has a large number of local national military buildings on it between the base and Afghan Highway 1. As I worked my way down the perimeter road there was a small lime green mosque with a nice English looking garden to one side of it. This mosque had two towers. Each had a twin public address system hanging from the top. Fifty yards from the mosque was an abandoned curio store with a sign in English and a advertisement for a men's and women's tailor with an image of a couple in formal western attire as if they were going to attend a ball. This was an old place. I don't know why they had the sign in English back then maybe because English is an international language. Across from the curio shop was the entrance to the airport terminal, which was gated up with an Afghan security guard. So I kept walking to the next airport building, which had a pile of airplane parts, wings, and tail sections, all leftovers from poor landings. In the front was a large Soviet fighter-bomber that looked like it was of Korean War vintage.

There was a bakery between the two buildings and a sign to another store in English. The bakeries on post all made flatbread and nothing else. However there were other bakeries with more variety in town. I continued to follow the signs. There was a hardware store! This guy had it all stuffed six ways from Sunday. There was nothing I needed but it was nice to see new tools for sale.

It was starting to get dark and dinner time was approaching so I headed back. I could see the Afghan soldiers starting to walk over to the little mosque as I went by. When I got back into the tent city, I could hear the calls for prayer going off starting in the town. Soon the echo of the call was coming from all directions. If you have ever been in a back alley behind a Chinese restaurant during a full moon you would be able to appreciate the chorus of stray cats howling in unison. The sound had an uncanny similarly.

With dinner over and not much else to do I hit the rack in full anticipation of the evening orchestra selection of variations of the "Flight of the Valkaries" performed by the U.S. Army Air Corps. The Air Force was not to be out done this evening. Several C-130 started the evening's overture with short interludes preformed by the twin predators. SSG Lucas gave up at midnight, called home and took a shower only to be coated with a fine layer of dust when the CH-47 flew over. It was really for his own good; the mosquitoes prefer to bite on clean skin. He was eaten alive our first night. SFC Natividad didn't have that problem. Right next to his cot is the 18-inch ventilation duct, which blows in the hot or cold air. The wind keeps the little flyers away. If that is not enough the smokers take their breaks by the intake, which gasses them out.

Morning came soon enough with the sound of a cat howling due to some intestinal problems. By the time I was fully conscious I was able to discern that it wasn't a cat at all; it was the call for prayer on a second hand PA system. I quickly gave up on the idea of sleeping in, got my towel and shaving kit and walked over to the showers only to find the septic system had overflowed again. Yes, KBR built a real first rate post (junkyard / dump) here with our tax dollars. The rest of the day at Jalalabad went very slowly. I ordered some custom maps for a watershed project we had coming up.

Being shot at or hit by an IED was not our biggest worry. During October there had been 27 cases of malaria. Another problem this time of year is snakes. Usually when winter approaches snakes hibernate, but we have changed the environment. The bathrooms are heated to the point you can bake bread in them. The snakes like to crawl into the toilet bowl and work their way under the rim in one big loop. There are signs with photos in the latrines telling people to scan the bowl before sitting.

Chapter Thirteen

THE RETURN FROM JALALABAD

We finished up our training in Jalalabad on Wednesday November 4th for all of our finance classes. I checked with all of the offices one last time before we left to make sure that they had every document and memo they required to release our funds. I got the thumbs up from everyone and called it a night. Wednesday was also the day that our first group of six tri-walls were flown to Camp Wright. These boxes had all of our equipment and the rest of our personal items in them. There was no specific order in which the tri-walls would be shipped. The loadmaster just looked at the weight of each tri-wall and determined how many he could get into an old Soviet hip helicopter.

Thursday morning, November 5th SFC Natividad and I got up at 5:00 A.M. and loaded up our rucks then proceeded to the PAX terminal (PAX = Passenger). We observed the usual custom of waiting for the predator to take off before the light would turn green for us to cross the runway. We checked in with Molson Air to make sure we had seats. There was one pilot and a young woman running the desk. The two of them ended every remark with "A." I couldn't believe it. The Canadians really do speak that way. SGT Johanson had been waiting at Jalalabad for several days with our supply sergeant and wanted to get to Camp Wright just so he could call someplace home. He was able to get a standby seat on another bird leaving the same time but taking the scenic route. We dropped our equipment off at the PAX terminal and grabbed a quick bite to eat. A shuttle bus picked us up with a bunch of other government civilians and whisked us to the Molson Air pad.

We loaded up on the UH-1s and for the first time we got the standard safety brief to include that there was a floatation device under our seats. The pilot also pointed out that if we should crash on our side or the door is stuck, you could push the window out to escape. Good luck! With all of our battle rattle on we had enough trouble just getting in with the cargo door all the way open. With that, the pilot closed the door. The two helicopters started turning their rotors and in about two minutes were up to full speed. We took off first and backed up onto the runway, hovered for a minute or two, then the second helicopter lifted off. Both helicopters left together, one following the other along the Kunar River. The sky was still filled with dirt. It was all but impossible to see the mountains, which were only a few miles away. We landed at FOB Joyce and dropped off one passenger, then flew into Camp Wright.

When I entered our TOC (Tactical Operations Center) where my quarters were, I found my big green footlocker with all of my extra uniforms and other hardware waiting for me. It was a welcomed re-union to have some of my personnel items with me again.

A few hours later that day another Hip dropped off six more tri-walls. This one had my engineering library. The tri-walls also contained our crew serve weapons and more personnel items.

The Hip helicopters are very much a kin to the Wells Fargo wagon. Everyone keeps an eye out for the Hip. We never knew when they would arrive or if they would arrive. The pilots never called ahead.

All flights come up the Kunar River and land into the wind. In the morning the wind blows north to south and reverses itself in the afternoon. The morning flight path takes the helicopters right over our guns (the two 155 artillery pieces named contingency plan). Friday November 6th was the Muslim holy day of the week so everything was quiet. The insurgents seemed to have no compulsion to follow the tenants of Islam and were out causing problems as usual. We were expecting our Hip with another six tri-walls to arrive at 9:00 A.M., the usual delivery time.

Two of our senior NCOs were waiting at the airfield with the forklift at the ready, when all of a sudden the call for fire went out and the gun bunnies started running up the hill. The guns swung around pointing right down the Kunar River. Our one and only flight operations guy got on the radio and attempted to wave the Hip off. The Hip was in sight when the round chamber and the breach slammed shut. Then came the Hip. The chief yelled, "Clear, Fire," and a ball of flame shot out the end of the howitzer. The pilot saw it coming just in time, dropped the bird to the deck and made a hard bank across the Kunar as if there was no tomorrow. I'm sure that thought was going through his mind, not to mention that here was a high probability that father frost would also be canceled. The next command to the guns was *fire for effect* and the twin guns lobbed two more rounds down the Kunar in less than 30 seconds. The Hip came around and landed with the wind with all of our supplies intact.

Friday was also mail day and we received a ton of packages. We sorted them all out in our first aid room. There were more packages than letters. Some of the folks were having a large amount of home furnishings sent. Some of these people really weren't thinking. When it comes time to go home they will have to either leave it there or mail it home. The post office comes to Camp Wright every six weeks and accepts U.S. currency only. We did not have an ATM machine.

Along with all of the packages we received, there were several care packages sent by schools in Connecticut and California. We took these, sorted out the contents and placed them on the shelves in the MWR (Moral Welfare and Recreation) room where everyone had access to them. The cards and artwork from the kids were posted on the walls for everyone to look at. I wrote down all of the names and addresses, sent them thank you letters and told them a little bit about what life was like here. A little while later all of the expatriate translators came in and grabbed all of the goodies. These people make 120K a year, a whole lot more than a private makes, and they are the first in line.

Friday night Willie the Whale, our aerostat balloon was hauled down from the sky as the thunder clouds massed over the mountains. By night fall the moon was completely imprisoned by the clouds and not one glimmer of light escaped to the earth. I went up to where the main latrine was to have a look at the valley. There is a patio in front of the latrine with a small lawn and rose garden, which is neatly kept. The shrubs were not even a silhouette; it was so dark. I could feel the wind coming down from the north, which was different for the evening. It had been very warm during the day so the breeze had a caressing effect while I was gazing at the lights in Asadabad. There weren't many lights but there were enough to highlight some of the distant trees. The troops all carry flashlights with colored lens to navigate around the camp at night because of the white light restrictions. Everyone selects his own color; some use blue, others red or green. The result is a walking light show that resembles a bunch of multi-colored fireflies darting in and out of the woods. A few raindrops started to touch down, but nothing major. Then the sky lit up. The lightning went off and turned the night into day. This wasn't like a desert storm it which you watch the lightning cut its way through the night sky leaving a trail. This was just like turning on a light switch. Then there was the boom, not a long trailing crackle, but just one big boom! The rain continued to be just a light sprinkle so I decided it was enough and walked on back to my quarters. It continued to rain until Sunday night when it finally stopped. Only a few times did we have a solid rain; the rest of the time it was just a light sprinkle.

Sunday, I took part of the security platoon and a few of the Ag troops out and surveyed the wash behind our camp. We got a lot done and would have continued but another unit was firing over the wash and we had to stop. I did get enough data to start the engineering on the flood control solution. I spent the better part of Monday putting my notes together and drawing a profile of the wash on my computer. I was looking forward to getting out to some of the other FOBs to see what kind of projects we could get involved with so I wasted no time putting my notes together.

Chapter Fourteen

THE FIRST TIC

Tuesday November 10th was our big day to see the Pech River Valley. Another unit (Task Force Lethal) came down to give us a tour and show us the ropes. They arrived at 6:00 A.M., which meant they were up at about 3:00 A.M. We left at 6:45 and headed for FOB Blessing, which was located at the far end of the Pech River Valley. The trip took 90 minutes in the morning and up to three hours if traffic was heavy.

We passed through Asadabad and the whole town was up and ready for business. I could see some of the cafés open for breakfast. The other merchants were getting ready for business. We crossed the Pech River and went up the east side of the river on route California then followed Pech River on route Rhode Island. The Pech River Valley is quite picturesque. I couldn't get any good photos from inside the MRAP; the windows are small and have a green tint to them. Besides that they were dirty and had bars across them to prevent RPGs from penetrating the windows. There was one location that had banana trees. The rest of the valley was built on retaining walls creating massive steps in the mountains.

We passed by all of the COPs (Combat Out Post) starting with Honaker Miracle, Able Main, and Michigan, which is 1000 meters from a village called Tantil. I heard a boom and SGT Johanson said "did you hear that?" At first I thought it was the range at COP Michigan. Then, the second explosion went off. We were being attacked by RPGs. I twisted around to look out my window just in time to see the dust trail from the last RPG that skipped across the ground.

I followed the dust trail and there was the insurgent. I remarked, "Hey there they are!"

SFC Median yelled up to SGT DeGeorge, "Gunner three o'clock!" DeGeorge swung around and marked the insurgent with 240 fire, which was all that was required for the MK-19 gunner on the next vehicle to return him from the dust from which he came. The insurgent was able to fire three RPGs at our convoy; the third round struck the road between my vehicle and the following vehicle, then flew into the Pech. That little TIC (Troops In Contact) taught us that vehicle defense is a team effort. There are no passengers. We arrived at FOB Blessing at 8:30. FOB Blessing is a joint base with U.S. and Afghan troops. A flood had preceded our arrival and most of the base was covered in a half inch of mud. More than half of the buildings had mud floors that were being pressure washed at the time.

FOB / Camp Blessing looking east down the Pech River Valley. The wooden buildings are called sea huts. November 10th, 2009.

We had arrived early so we waited in the mess hall for our appointment with their operations folks. They gave us a briefing and gave us a long wish list of projects. Then it was time for us to go. While we were in the meeting, our troops were completing the transfer of another ASV (Armor Security Vehicle) thanks to the "Mo-Joe" of Major Leeney. This left two empty seats in our MRAP, which were soon filled with a Navy chief and his working dog, a monstrous German Shepherd named Zach. This was a special dog trained to track explosives and drugs. There are several of these dog and handler teams working in Afghanistan. His handler told me that a few weeks ago he was called out on an IED strike. When he arrived, he learned that a fellow handler who he had dined with just three hours prior was the victim. His dog was able to trace the scent from the command wire to a house where three insurgents were held up.

The MRAP was designed based upon a South African vehicle with a "V" shaped hull, which protects the occupants from explosions from mines and small arms. The sides are several inches thick to stop RPGs. There is a turret on top for the gunner–the vehicle's only defense–and the only person who has a full 360-degree view of the world. In order to accommodate the gunner's needs for freedom of movement, the other occupants in the vehicle are bunched up. The inside of the vehicle seats six people: a driver and TC (front passenger responsible for operating the Blue Force Tracker and the radio). In the back, where the other four passengers sit is the extra ammo (lots of it) the DUKES system that jams radio activated IEDs, the fire suppression system, and the hydraulic system for the back ramp. All seven people carry with them an assault pack with food, toilet paper, extra water, rain gear, their weapons and ammo, and full battle rattle. This means the four people in the back have to interlock their legs with the person across from them and place their gear on their laps. The seats have nice cushions that are Velcro-ed to the steel frame below. The Velcro on our seat cushions was shot! So the whole time we were sliding toward our buddy, which means everyone got wedgies. Every few minutes or so there would be a big bounce and I would have to rise up, re-adjust my pants back to their proper position and attempt to reassemble the seat.

Now add in one very big German Shepherd, and a 21-year old local national interpreter named Sam who had already seen the angry side of local dogs. Sam was strapped into his seat when the big German Shepherd came flying into the back of the MRAP thinking he had a bigger landing zone than what he was given. The dog used Sam as a padded backstop. The dog recovered very gracefully from his Olympic jump into the MRAP and quickly got all four feet on the deck. His Navy handler was right behind him and reassured Sam that his dog wouldn't bite. There wasn't enough room for the dog to lie down so he did his best to sit on the floor and added his front legs to our tangled web of interlocking limbs.

The MRAP is not the most comfortable vehicle to ride in. You give up a lot for protection. The whole vehicle is mounted on a semi-truck chassis so the slightest imperfection of the road is excessively magnified. Each bump usually lifted us up off our seats about six inches. The seats in the MRAP are designed to bounce as a means of protecting the occupants back and neck during an explosion. The seats are attached to the vehicle with a block and tackle assemble that acts like a shock absorber. We stopped at each of the COPs on the way back to introduce ourselves. I took the opportunity to rearrange things at the first stop to give the dog more room. We loaded back up and the road really got bad. We were bouncing up and down swinging side to side. I had left my hat on the one vacant seat we had. The dog just looked up at me with his big watery eyes that said, "I'm trying to hold it all in, honest." He then placed his nose in my hat and closed his eyes. That became his favorite position for the remainder of the trip home.

Our Navy work dog with SFC Mosqueda in the back of an MRAP at Camp Able Main November 10th, 2009.

We stopped at two more COPs on the way home. All of them were nothing but mud pits. The last one, Honker Miracle, had the best view. The storm we had had over the weekend dropped a blanket of snow on the northern mountains. We said our hellos and got on the road as the sun was setting. We arrived back at Camp Wright at dusk. I took the handler and his dog over to flight operations, which was closed for the evening. So we set him up with a vacant room we had so his dog could have some privacy.

It was a very long day. We missed lunch in the process and almost missed dinner too. The day wasn't over. We had to get ready for the next day, which was a trip to FOB Joyce.

Our November 11th trip to FOB Joyce was the same deal: up at the crack of dawn and get out the gate. This time we would be going south and over the other bridge to the Marha Warha side of the Kunar River. When we exited the camp, we immediately passed under an arched entrance, which is also an ANP checkpoint. From there on, the road is lined with trees and farms on the low side near the river and compounds above the road. On the western side of the river the mountains have halted their march to the river almost at the edge of the road leaving just enough room for some homes. On the eastern side of the Kunar the mountains are in continuous retreat as you go south. Crossing the Kunar is like crossing the border from the U.S. into Mexico. Within a few hundred yards you go from lush green fertile farmlands to desert waste. Just before the bridge was another little town named Nowabad, which is trying to consume the road. We were about to cross the bridge when the gunner noticed a car had broken down and a group of men were assembling to push it across. We waited for them to clear the bridge and our convoy went across.

Once on the other side, the structures were all built out of adobe not rock and mortar. There were rows of decayed adobe walls one after the other leading up to the base of the eastern mountains. We continued south at a fair speed until we hit a stretch of newly paved road. The road crews place rocks on newly paved roads to keep the traffic off it while it cures. The rocks didn't slow us down much; the entrance to FOB Joyce came up very quickly.

We lined up our trucks and went to the base TOC to check in. Turns out we had several hours to kill. The people with whom we were to meet, wouldn't be there for a while. Major Leeney went hunting for trailers and

85

truck parts, and we went to the mess hall just to have a place to sit. After one soda, I decided to look around the FOB. They had the standard issue Wal-Mart shops, but no bakery or café. I noticed that the whole post was under construction–new brick barracks, showers, maintenance facilities, you name it. This was a big FOB and the troops were sleeping in tents.

I met up with a USAID rep who told me about some other organizations that could help me pull off some of our missions. We had been watching the sky for helicopters hoping to see a Hip that just might have the rest of our gear on it. I was also looking for an Embassy Air UH-1 with our guests on it. We had been talking for about two hours when I looked up and saw a UH-1 coming up the Kunar. Sure enough it was the Embassy Air coming in. We walked over to the airfield and greeted the passengers, LTC Schauertdy from the Oklahoma National Guard and Major Meyer from the Air Force reserve. They both worked at the embassy. There was another gentleman, Ferenc Sandor, who worked for Roots of Peace, and two Afghans. I led the group back to the TOC while my USAID friend went to the front gate to escort in the local nationals. Mr. Sandor was from Hungary and lived in Ecuador; he said people call him Francisco. With that my section sergeant SFC Medina piped up and introduced himself as Poncho and the two of them started talking in Spanish. Ferenc had married an Ecuadorian woman. His last assignment was in Africa before going to Afghanistan. His first project was to plant 75,000 orange trees, which he had flown in from California.

By ten o'clock everyone had arrived in the conference room and the meeting started. There was no agenda for the meeting. The first topic was planting hay. The Afghans said they would plant hay if we paid them to grow it. We told them "no." They pointed out that the last group paid for everything. The meeting went downhill from there. Finally at three o'clock it was over and we got to go home.

Chapter Fifteen

THE CHARACTERS OF KUNAR

By the middle of November we had introduced ourselves to all of the Battle Space owners and told everyone that we were open for business. The Battle Space owner is the command responsible for a specific geographical area. Units traveling along the highway are required to check in with each Battle Space owners as they pass through their area of responsibility. This allows the Battle Space owner to know who is in their area in the event something goes wrong. It's a system similar to aircraft being handed off from one control tower to the next as they fly across a country. Our first six weeks in the country had been very busy, but we had little to show for our efforts.

Traveling takes up a lot of time in Afghanistan; you don't just jump in the car and go. You must plan every detail of the trip and rehearse for any possible outcome. The roads are very risky, not because of the insurgents but because of general safety. In some places the roads are very narrow with unstable shoulders that crumble into the river. Other places have very tight hairpin turns that make it difficult for larger trucks to maneuver. On route California North of Asmar there are tons of vehicles that have gone over the side into the Kunar, some the result of insurgents, but most due to the road giving way. Landslides, unstable shoulders, sudden erosion were the enemies. The vehicles were left on the riverbank where they fell because there was no way to set up a crane with its out riggers to safely recover them. The ANP (Afghan National Police) will not shut down the highway for safety only if they are shaking down a motorist.

Back home I traveled the I-5 grapevine a lot to attend my National Guard duty up in Sacramento. I usually got upset when the CHP closed down the grapevine for something stupid. I remember one night the grapevine was shut down for a truck load of cabbage that over turned. I decided that I would just pull into the truck stop and sleep for a few hours in the back of my pickup truck. I assumed that when the grapevine re-opened all the trucks would start up and I'd wake up. I made the wrong assumption. The trucks never turned off their engines and more and more trucks kept on arriving. I never got any sleep.

Living at Camp Wright is very much like living at the grapevine truck stop. We had massive generators located all over the place. In locations where they can't fit big generators they slipped in a few little ones. To add to the chorus of generators there are several dozen MRAPs and other assorted military vehicles that run off semi-truck engines, along with the aircraft, Oh yes, we can never forget the ever present artillery for a good roar of thunder, which shakes the fillings loose from one's teeth.

While a few of us were getting acquainted with Afghanistan, other members of our units were busy building our new TOC (Tactical Operations Center). The trauma center was finally moved to its new home up on top of the hill next to the air field. This opened up their old surgery center for us to start construction of the TOC. SPC Larson had the honor of supervising the KBR local nationals' work on the remodeling.

Things were finally starting to come together. The additional office space allowed us to move some of the senior NCOs off the hill down to where our TOC was. SFC Teso, our operations NCO, was one of the first to move off the hill. While he was setting up home in his new quarters, he was having some difficulty with a red CAT-5 cable that ran straight down the middle of his room. He was tripping over it and he just couldn't get his new carpet to lie flat. So he grabbed a pair of scissors and cut it. Just a few rooms down the hall, SFC Velasco, our Intel NCO, lost her connection on the SIPR-Net (Secret Internet), but SFC Teso's carpet would lie flat now.

Sergeant Palacios finally arrived from Jalalabad after pushing out tri-walls as fast as he could. We still had several more tri-walls trapped down at Bagram, which needed to come up. There was a National Guard sergeant major who was the guard LNO at Bagram who helped coordinate their travel up to us.

We received five local national interpreters, whom Lt. Ko and I started training. I gave them classes on agriculture, and engineering. SPC Larson trained them on basic first aid and how to use a tourniquet. Lt Ko instructed them on all of the rules of the FOB and what was expected of them. We had to pull our resources to equip them, because neither their companies of the Army supplied them with anything. SGT Palacios was able to make enough phone calls to get them squared away. SFC Hanlin even bought them all metal foot lockers.

Just when you think nothing could go wrong something does. The local national who serviced the port-a-potties was caught stealing fuel. That ended the service contract and the port-a-potties quickly filled to capacity. We had to lock all of the port-a-potties up because they were overflowing. This meant that any emergency in the middle of the night required a mad dash up the hill to the main latrine. This inconvenience lasted ten days until a new honey man could be hired.

Learning all of the characters Uncle Sam has sent to provide aid and guidance to the people of Afghanistan has become an interesting lesson in human behavior. Our USDA rep had several meetings at the governor's compound, which he had to attend so he invited LTC Velte to join him. The true motive was the PRT didn't have room for Pedro and he needed a ride. LTC Velte had taken several of my troops south for a Vet Cap (a Vet Cap is a health fair for animals) so I was asked to attend. The deal was we would follow the PRT to the governor's compound, then each of us would do our own thing. Once we arrived at the governor's compound the PRT dismounted and walked into town to tour some furniture shops and the nursery. We went into the governor's compound. I took half of my troops and our medic, SPC Larson, on a tour of the compound while our USDA rep checked on all of his meetings.

The reason for the tour was to make sure my security detachment knew where the danger zones were and how to get us out in the event something went wrong. November 12th was a Thursday and just like government offices in the U.S. on Friday not a soul showed up for work. We had the courtyard to ourselves. Our first stop was to see the monkeys. There were two monkeys tied to some trees on the route to the US TOC in the back of the compound. SFC Natividad stopped to look at one of the monkeys who immediately opened up his Velcro boot pocket and took out a granola bar wrapper. She examined it, threw it on the ground and waved the back of her hand at him as if she were giving him an obscene gesture for not having a granola bar in the wrapper.

We left the little miffed monkey and went to the PRT's TOC. This TOC is self contained, complete with gym and kitchen. The captain and his troops were a good team and knew what was going on. They took us around the back side on the roof and showed us some of the security improvements and the sleeping Afghan National Army troops on the other side of the irrigation canal. The next stop was the governor's kitchen to use the back door of the compound to the irrigation canal. The governor's kitchen had a three-burner wood fired stove. The stove was of adobe construction, which had several burning branches sticking out, and a pot stewing. There were a few bird cages with some game hens at the ready. The back door was just a few planks nailed together. We walked through the door to the irrigation canal and were greeted by some turkeys. On the other side of the canal was the Afghan National Army OP (Observation Post) with no sign of life. We looked over the erosion, studied the area and went back in.

The Kunar Governor's kitchen in Asadabad. In front is SFC Hanlin, SPC Larson our medic, SFC Natividad, and SFC Fair in the rear.

It was about this time, when our USDA rep found us and informed me that the first meeting was ready. I quickly showed everyone the layout of the building and the governor's conference room. I told SPC Larson if she needed to use the restroom to use the one upstairs because it all flows down hill and into the room below. We would post a guard for her if she needed to go. She could smell the restroom from the hall and was certain she wouldn't have to use the facilities during her visit. With that we parted with SFC Natividad, Hanlin and Fair and attended our meeting. SFC Natividad went back, grabbed a few more of the troops and started orientating them with the compound. SFC Fair provided roving security and SFC Hanlin held a quick reaction force where the trucks were parked.

The first meeting was with an Afghan group called Madera. In attendance from my section was SGT Stevens and SPC Larson. The Madera group was very well organized and had made considerable accomplishments with the farmers. They were very much against handouts to the farmers. We made several offers to them and they declined all of them. Instead they told us what they could do to help us. What a surprise! A few months later when we tried to verify their claims, we couldn't and even ran into some mild extortion from them concerning our VETCAPs.

We reached the mid point of the meeting with Madera when our USDA rep's second meeting was starting. The second meeting was a women's empowerment meeting and the reason for SPC Larson's presence. Just prior to our departure, SPC Larson was hunting around for a scarf to wear so she wouldn't offend anyone. She finally found one that was really a handkerchief so it didn't really do the job. This was a Thursday so I wasn't too concerned about offending anyone. With a Kevlar and IBA she looked just like any other soldier.

SPC Larson came away from the meeting disgusted! The topic of the meeting was women's poultry projects that would empower women. The whole thing failed due to lack of training, planning and follow through. The Camp Wright representatives from the State Department, USAID and USDA want to use it as a model for another project.

Our next meeting was with the Ag director who wanted poultry farms for widows. He wanted one poultry farm for every 25 to 30 widows so they could support themselves. His concept was women would work the farm during the day and some men from the village would sleep in them at night for security. He thought a poultry operation who could produce 1000 fryers a month would be sufficient. He didn't have any land to build the poultry farms, nor did he have a community signed up for the project, nor a location from where he was going to get the chicks, etc...You get the picture! A wonderful bright idea with no thought put into it. The main goal was for us to build a home for several of his friends and call it a chicken farm for widows.

About this time the call for prayer went off echoing all around the town. SFC Natividad decided he would walk back up to the entrance to the governor's compound just to have a look around and noticed that all of the governor's security had left! With that SFC Natividad posted himself as the first line of defense to the compound. He really was the first line of defense. The governor's compound is a hot target for the insurgences. The ANP (Afghan National Police) compound on the other side of the river was assaulted because there were no guards at the front gate while we were in Jalalabad a few weeks earlier.

The next meeting was with the three wise men from the Kunar bee keepers association. Their meeting was straight to the point. We want fifty, 50-pound sacks of sugar a month or our bees die! Then they boasted that the Kunar association produced 60 metric tons of honey that year for local consumption. I read up on bees before I left California. The first question I had was: why did you over harvest the honey and not leave the bees enough for the winter? They gave me a sob story about how there were no flowers in the winter etc. Then they said that USAID gave them sugar last year and they expected it again this year. I had another question for the wise men of Kunar. This year "Roots of Peace" planted 75,000 citrus trees and several thousand other fruit trees. How are you going to meet the pollination needs of these new orchards in the next three to four years? They looked at our USDA rep and got no response. Then they told me it wasn't a problem, they could have enough bees in just a few weeks and told me all about the process. There were some details they left out. First off in an earlier conversation they talked about a shortage of boxes for hives and about the expense. They also failed to understand that yes you can trick the bees into creating another queen, but that doesn't get you a few thousand bees over night. At that point I just shut my mouth and let our USDA rep talk. He promised them the sugar.

We didn't have any more meetings, but the PRT was still out on patrol. They patrolled over to a place called the "Cheese Burger" a restaurant adjacent to the governor's compound. I noticed a few of the PRT security team members in the courtyard just enjoying life; they were not invited to lunch either. Troops are always resourceful. Choice number one is to eat the MRE (Aka Meals Ready to Eat) or you hand a kid ten bucks and send him into town. For ten bucks the kid came back with a feast! This was my first attempt at eating the local cuisine. There was one sack of flat bread, which was still hot and two types of what they call kabobs. The first kabob was just some mystery meat. I think it was goat, cubed up and cooked in some red sauce, which didn't look very good. The second looked like a hamburger patty; it was some type of meatloaf with lots of vegetables in it. It was very soft and tasted great! For the rest of the day I wondered if I was going to get sick but never did.

We were still waiting for the PRT to finish up with their lunch and wondering what to do when SFC Hanlin noticed a memorial in the center of the courtyard. We got one of the locals who spoke perfect English to tell us about the memorial. It was erected for a large number of people who were massacred by the Soviets and buried in a mass grave; some were buried alive. It was unusual to see any monument since very few people had firsthand memories of the Soviet invasion. The memorial was only five years old, but it was rapidly decaying.

We wandered back to our vehicles and put our battle rattle back on just in time to see the PRT parade return from lunch. This was a State Department dog and pony show, which I got roped into later. There are far too many State Department and USAID / USDA people going over as tourist wanting full briefs and guided tours. These people do nothing to help the situation and demand all kinds of reports.

We finally got the signal to move out. We swung by another little COP (Company Operating Post), picked up some people and returned to Camp Wright. Once in the gate, our gunners cleared their crew serve weapons. Then we got out and cleared our personnel weapons, then loaded them again. The clearing process is to remove the round from the chamber, but you always keep a loaded clip in your weapon.

Chapter Sixteen

FOB BOSTICK

Every night, we had a planning meeting to go over the next 24 and 48 hours. Major Leeney stated the following people are confirmed to fly to Bostick: our commander, 1Lt Ko, and LTC Kelly. That was a surprise to me. I asked, "Is this up and back the same day?"

Major Leeney turned to me and said, "Plan on staying for three nights." I was down to one set of clean underwear so I wouldn't be going to bed early.

On the morning of November 13th the three of us were standing by at the air field for Molson Air. They arrived 30 minutes early, dropped off a bunch of people from Fluor and waved us over. This was my first flight north along the Kunar River. The Molson Air pilots like to hug the mountains for some reason. This gave me a great view of all of the villages tucked away up each one of the tributary valleys that fed the Kunar River Valley. I was amazed with all of the terracing and the places they built adobe housing.

The western side of the valley started gaining elevation while the eastern side maintained a gentle slope toward the river. We made a long "S" shaped bend and there standing above the Kunar was FOB Bostick. FOB Bostick was named after Major Thomas G. Bostick Jr. who was born on December 8th, 1969 and killed in action on July 27th 2007. He was a member of the 1st Squadron 91st Cavalry Airborne, 173rd Airborne Brigade combat team.

We were greeted by SGT Sneddon who had just returned to the service by joining the Army Reserves in Utah. He took us to our quarters. We came to a tent. 1LT Ko went in first. I just assumed we were all going to live there as 1Lt Ko started un-stacking the cots. Then Sgt Sneddon turned and told us to follow him. He took us around to another tent and pointed out a hardened structure in the event we should receive mortar fire during the night. Our tent was similar to the one where 1LT Ko was staying with the exterior sprayed with insulating foam. We opened the flimsy wooden door to find that the interior had been divided up into small rooms each with its own door. We dropped our stuff off and met up with 1Lt Ko for a tour of the FOB: the important things first, the latrine, the mess hall and the TOC in order of precedence.

Enough time had elapsed that lunch had crept up upon us. We met Captain Pittard who was sporting a red beard. He was one of four civil affairs people working the area. He gave us a very detailed rundown of the area and what was going on. Once again our press is so far out in left field they print nothing close to the truth. The captain didn't tell us anything secret so why doesn't our news media take the time to learn what is going on? (I know why. It requires work. And news about Britney Spears is easier to sell.)

Captain Pittard took us up on top of the original house, which started the FOB. From the roof top we had a beautiful view of the valley. We could see where the Kunar bent to the east and crossed over into Pakistan. The ridge line of mountains to the east of us was the Pakistan border also known as the Duran line. To the west of us was a mountainside, which sloped into the FOB. The farmer was paid not to grow crops so the insurgents couldn't use it for a sniper base.

The Kunar River valley looking north from FOB Bostick. The Pakistan border can be seen where the Kunar River turns east.

Our orientation of the FOB was over and we had the rest of the day to kill until the hosting unit held their evening planning meeting for the next day's conference. My commander decided to take an afternoon nap. I grabbed a book and headed to the little reading room they had. An hour or so had passed when I heard some kind of announcement over the PA system. I didn't pay much attention to it and went on reading. I turned the page and Boom! The building shook back and forth; then there was another salvo shot out of the howitzers. It didn't take long for me to realize that the gun bunnies had no intention of stopping. I climbed back up to the roof to watch the platoon fire. There was someone somewhere west of our location who wasn't having a good day. I came back off the roof when I was stopped by a Fluor employee who told me about the sniper problems they had. Standing on the roof was not beneficial to my safety.

I went back to the reading room and started reading again when my commander walked in. I asked him what happened to his nap. He pointed out that our tent was rather close to the artillery and not conducive to an afternoon nap.

After dinner we attended the conference planning meeting and were surprised to be asked to give a full presentation about flood control and what the Kunar ADT does for a living. We cranked out a presentation. I started drawing up slides showing how check dams worked while my commander worked his magic with PowerPoint. 1Lt Ko had been busy interviewing anyone he could about the area and taking lots of notes. You learn a whole lot more by talking to the people on the ground than you do by reading the "Official" intel reports. 1Lt Ko was also working on getting us home a day earlier.

The whole time we were working, there was a captain who just wouldn't shut up. All this kid could talk about was how he was going to move to Wyoming and live like a hermit while his wife supported him. He wasn't joking either. 1Lt Ko quickly picked up on his mental stability and found more reliable sources to interview. I was later told by some of the more level-headed people that this kid was swinging on the outer rings of Saturn most of the time and he wasn't even getting warmed up while we were there.

We retired to our tent. My boss asked to be woken up at 6:00 A.M. When we travelled, I was his time piece. He doesn't carry a watch. Imagine that, an artillery officer who doesn't carry a watch! He carries a Blackberry, which he left back at Camp Wright.

I got up at 4:30, showered and shaved and then returned to the tent for a short nap. I was surprised at all of the people up and about at 4:30. At Camp Wright I was the only one up at that hour. Six o'clock came around soon enough and my commander and I popped out of the tent with one thing in mind: Where was the closest latrine. I knew of one that was a straight shot for lower enlisted but with the morning urgency any latrine would do. We were moving with considerable haste when a sergeant in full battle rattle stopped us. "Sir, I don't mean to be disrespectful but you need to wear uniform three at this hour." (Uniform three is the full battle rattle.)

"Why?"

"This is the hour we get mortared."

"Oh, when was the last time you were mortared?"

"About six weeks ago they hit a HMWVV."

I thanked the sergeant for his concern and promised him that we would promptly return to our tent and put on our battle rattle but we really had more urgent needs at the moment.

The conference was scheduled for 9:00 A.M. but none of our guests had arrived at that time. A young kid showed up with plates full of raisins and almonds and two kettles of hot water for tea for our guest. He stood by at the ready. Finally at 10:30 a very senior man showed up and apologized about being late. He was asked to attend the meeting on behalf of the district sub-governor who had been delayed somewhere south of the FOB. His name was Abdul Jabar and he was the estate assistant of the Naray district. This man was sharp. We gave him our presentation. He asked some very good questions and took lots of notes. When we suggested doing a flood control / watershed project he countered with a proposal. During the short time we were together he developed a concept for doing such a project. He told us that he would call several villages together, discuss the project and would select four potential locations for us to evaluate. Then, he would organize the labor. He wanted one location to serve as a demonstration site for the rest of the district.

LTC Kelly discussing the use of check dams and other flood and erosion control systems with representatives from the Ghaziabad district. Location FOB Bostick November 14th, 2009. Photo 1Lt Ko collection

The Naray district had two telephone lines and a section of Route California that was paved. New construction on Route California had just recently connected their town with the government center in Asadabad. This man had some real organizational skills to be able to assemble village elders over 20 miles without telephones or the use of a motor vehicle. This was an accomplishment. He asked for copies of my drawing so he could explain everything to the village elders and parted our company. I was very impressed with him.

It turned out for the best that all of the conference attendees didn't show up at the same time. The others were stuck in traffic on Route California. One of the battalion's MRAPs went into the Kunar. There was no foul play; the road just let loose. The final outcome was to send a team of mechanics down to strip the vehicle and leave it where it lay.

We took a break for lunch hoping the next group would show up. We were not briefed on what to expect with each group so we just assumed the next meeting would be as productive as the first. Ha. The three amigos arrived from the Ghaziabad district. It took about two seconds to realize these guys were a bunch of thugs. We gave our presentation and every now and then they would start talking among themselves. Our interpreter wasn't doing much translation while this flurry of conversation was going on. I could pick out about every fourth of fifth word, but couldn't make much sense out of their conversation. I asked them a question through the interpreter. They responded and before the interpreter could translate I said I understood Pashto. One of them gave me a very strange look. The truth was I didn't understand a word, but I knew a song and dance in any language.

We finished our presentation and they presented us with a list of demands. They wanted 500 tons of wheat seed. This was the honey bee association all over again. Why didn't they didn't keep some of the seed from the harvest to re-plant? I asked that question several times but never got an answer. I told them that we would deliver their request to the governor who controlled the seed in Kunar. They didn't like that. Then they asked me for $35,000.00 to buy the seed in Pakistan. We told them we couldn't buy seed, but we would give the governor their request.

1Lt Ko came in just after the meeting was over and announced that he was able to get us on the first flight out in the morning. With that, our commander said, "Follow me; I want to show you something." He took us back up to the roof of the original house that started the FOB and pointed out different points on the river. He asked about their potential and what it would take to get water up the hill. 1Lt Ko and I had carefully crouched down behind some sand bags on the roof, while he decided to just saddle the sandbags while he pondered the potential of the valley.

After a minute or two he looked at the two of us and asked why we were slouching behind the sand bags. 1Lt Ko responded, "Well sir we're not really dressed for the occasion to be targets in a turkey shoot." With that our commander decided it was probably in his best interest if we finished up the conversation on the ground.

The morning of the 15th arrived with the usual fan fair. The tent next to ours was home to Chief Boy R' Dee and his band of renown. The tent was occupied by a group of local nationals who had their cook stoves in the tent. One could hear the clanging of all of their pots and cans.

We were all up at first light on our way to the shower when we heard an announcement from the PA system that the range was going hot. We looked up on the mountainside and saw the crew serve weapons test firing. Then we noticed the 155s rotating the guns from west to east. We just thought that was odd and kept on walking. The next sound was the mortars going off followed by the artillery. We looked to the mountains east of us but couldn't see any rounds hit. That meant the rounds were hitting something on the other side.

We quickly finished up what we needed to do, grabbed breakfast and jumped on the bird home. On the return trip I was treated to a view of the western mountains still capped with snow from the last storm.

Chapter Seventeen

HOME IMPROVEMENTS AND A VISIT TO ASMAR

Our return from FOB Bostick was pleasantly uneventful. When we arrived back at Camp Wright our troops and KBR's carpenters were busy building our offices. We had expected that LTC Velte and his team would have returned from their mission down in Baraki Rajan, but they had been bumped from their flight. SFC Medina gave SSG Lucas a call on his cell phone, which is operated by an Iranian company. He couldn't ask, "When are you coming home?" for security reasons so he asked him, "When are you going to feed this dog."

SSG Lucas responded, "The dog is fat. He can afford to wait two more days."

The Fluor Corporation won the service contract for service support in Afghanistan and started their inventory of all of the KBR equipment the week we returned from FOB Bostick. A Russian Hip from Absolute Air landed and unloaded a bunch of Fluor folks the day we returned from Bostick. These folks looked like a bunch of thugs, not the polished professionals I knew back in Irvine. Some of them were massively obese, others dressed like gang members. I met one woman from the team. She was an Albanian from Bosnia and a former KBR employee. I remember when we were in the Balkans, when there was a reduction in the force at

Camp Eagle the local national KBR employee put ground glass in the chili. I'm glad to see KBR go, but what Fluor has done is hire back all of the problem people. Part of that decision is due to a presidential order directing them to offer employment to all KBR employees. I had to do a lot of documentation on the activities of KBR in Kosovo and in the end it fell on deaf ears.

The nightly show in the heavens was still a treat to me as someone coming from the city. I noticed on the Internet that we were due for a meteor shower, something I was never able to witness at home due to all of the city lights. About an hour after sunset I went out looking north toward the night sky and waited for the show to start. The Milky Way was fully visible and the Giant Orion could be seen climbing up the mountains to the east of us from Pakistan. I gave up, went back inside and worked on a few other projects (cutting 2 X 4s for my shelves). I came out again about 1:00 A.M. Still no shooting stars, but Orion had crept un-noticed to the southern mountains. At 4:00 A.M. when I got up to shave, Orion was sliding down the mountains to our west but still there were no streaks in the sky.

The following morning, November 16th, the first Molson Air flight arrived with two of our troops from LTC Velte's expedition. A few more came in later in the afternoon. That left LTC Velte and SGT Bentley back at Jalalabad waiting for a ride home. It didn't look good for coming home soon so LTC Velte got a bright idea. The gal at Molson Air was a young single attractive Canadian and Sgt Bentley was also from Canada. LTC Velte told SGT Bentley to try his luck and see if he could win them two seats on the next bird to Camp Wright. As it turned out SGT Bentley and the dispatcher were from the same town! SGT Bentley came back all smiles and told LTC Velte "She is going on leave and will be brining me back some coffee."

"That's great. What about getting us two seats on the bird?"

"Oh Dan Rather has the next bird reserved but she got us the two empty seats on his flight."

For some reason Dan Rather selected Camp Wright as a place to look around. The Army put out its guidance and so did the State Department. The Army's guidance was very simple: Show the man what we have accomplished. The problem with that was there was no way to show him what things were like before. Where roads go, freedom and commerce follow. There are thousands of miles of unimproved dirt roads in Afghanistan, which take hours to travel just a few miles. When a paved road reaches a town, the community is instantly connected to the government. The next thing that happens is people start buying vehicles, which brings in gas stations, and auto mechanics. The cell phone companies are next to follow because now they can service their cell sites. Car dealerships and banks are next. People now have access to health care in the bigger towns and the insurgents are pushed back. Paved roads allow the government to move troops and resources quickly when there is trouble.

Mr. Rather attended a packed conference room full of Americans but didn't take the time to talk to the troops or the local nationals. He came with his agenda and was just looking for the right information and footage to tell his story. To me, Mr. Rather was just another TV newsreader, but the troops had a very low opinion of him. Mr. Rather ate in our mess hall surrounded by his own staff so he wasn't interested in meeting the troops, but at the same time most of the troops steered clear of him. When I was in the MWR computer lab I could hear the troops vent about his presence. I could understand the older troops who witnessed the Viet Nam era, but why were the younger troops repulsed by him? I guess if I watched more TV I would understand. I get most of my news from the L.A. Times and the Daily News by reading.

It had been several days since LTC Velte completed his Vet Cap and he was still charged and excited about the accomplishments. (A VetCAP Veterinary Civil Assistance Program.) They spent a few days down at the U.S. Embassy compound then flew down to Baraki Rajan in the Logar Province for the Vet Cap. They had to build all of their own cattle chutes and stalls for the event, which was held on a dusty high school soccer field. The locals climbed up on top of the walls and roofs overlooking the soccer field to watch the excitement. SSG Lucas was the hero of the event. A young boy all of eight years old was leading a cow on a rope when it spooked and broke loose. SSG Lucas ran after the cow and was about to grab it by the horns and flip it when the cow snapped her head and rammed his fingers with her horns. SSG Lucas got a sudden rush of energy, gave the cow a good twist to the horns and brought her back after she had run through the razor wire. SPC Tanson was working the livestock too and the old men thought it was great to see a woman working the herd. I'm sure they were thinking if she could do it so could their women and then the men could spend the whole day at the coffee house. The younger men didn't like the fact that SPC Tanson knew what she was doing. She even exchanged chewing tobacco samples with the old men as a gesture of friendship. Yes, she is one of the few women I know who chew. SSG Lucas continued to prove his worth during the whole event, coming from the farm country of Indiana, and knew how to handle livestock.

In one day LTC Velte, SFC Fulton, SSG Lucas, SGT Flynn, and SPC Tanson serviced over 300 animals, administering vaccines, de-worming them and supplied the farmers with an assortment of vitamins for their animals. A few months later our team would service over 3000 animals in one day.

My quarters were drastically reduced in size after all of my equipment showed up along with all of the provisions that my family had sent. I decided to build some shelves to accommodate all of my clothing and gear. I knew of a pile of 2 X 4s that had been salvaged and placed in a discrete location. I quietly asked around about them and it appeared they were free for the taking, but even with all of the green lights I received, it was best not to attract attention when shopping. I waited until after dinner when everything was dark. I went, selected a few sticks of wood, carried them back to our new office and cut them to length, then went back up for more. I was very careful to turn off my flashlight if I heard anyone coming and just walk on past the stash. I thought the coast was clear and started to select another 2 X 4 when I saw a shadow on the other side of the pile. Then I heard the soft whisper, "Colonel Kelly is that you?"

"Sergeant Palacios is that you?" We were two thieves in the night both going after the same trophy.

By the end of the evening I had all the pieces cut for my shelves, which I constructed once the TOC (Tactical Operations Center) moved out of our billets. There was no need to draw attention to my renovations. On the evening of November 18th we had a rehearsal for our trip to Asmar. I cleaned my rifle and pistol that evening, which included taking all the rounds out of my magazines and cleaning them too. It is amazing how much dust and crud gets into the magazines in that terrain.

On November 19th we were off to Asmar to meet with the district agriculture representatives. Asmar is 30 miles north of Asadabad on Route California. It took us one hour to make the drive. Route California stays on the western side of the Kunar River until a mile south of the town of Asmar. From the air the highway and river appear as if they just slowly meander their way through the valley. On the ground at 30 mph it is like a roller coaster ride. The road is smooth, but it is one dip and hairpin turn after another. There was only one hot spot on the route, hill 1311, and our commander arranged for artillery fire if we should encounter any problems. We passed by without incident. There are many details about life on the river you'll miss from the air. The suspension bridges and boatswain's chairs are incredible. There was also a lot of high quality brick construction going on–a clear sign of the prosperity a pave road brings to an area.

We finally passed by COP Monti, which was located off of Route California on the eastern side of the Kunar River near the Asmar District center. From the road it didn't look like much but a bunch of HESCO barriers. When we crossed the bridge over the Kunar we could see an ANA post that really looked like a defensive fortress sitting on top of a large granite out cropping rising up from the river.

There were several men walking their cattle about a quarter of a mile north of the bridge. They were doing everything in their power to get their cows to walk along the side of the road, with no luck at all. We finally cleared all of the cattle and came upon the town of Asmar. A quick left and we were in the government center plugged up on the road. We had been expecting a different layout to the compound, which would have been correct a few days prior. We arrived in the midst of a large wall construction project that didn't leave much room for our MRAPs to drive around. It took a few minutes to get everyone in and turned around.

We had been told all kinds of scary things about Asmar so everyone was very alert. The local U.S. Army garrison commander arrived and told us we could relax; the area was very safe.

The government center was comprised of an Afghan national police station with old U.S. Army HMWVVs and new Ford sport pick-ups, a medical clinic built by the U.S., a nursery and the government center. We met in the government center with the district police chief for Asmar and the agricultural director and agriculture extension manager from Dangum. They were all very reserved and candid about their problems. Once again the big problem was flood control and irrigation. This area would be no easy solution. I looked the hillsides over where an aqueduct would have to be cut and it was all granite. There were two possibilities for construction, drill and blast or install pre-cast concrete troughs. Both would be expensive. We were treated with tea and cake. I passed on the tea but tried a small piece of cake. They baked it using newspaper as a pan liner. I'd sampled the local food in several places and learned to identify what they use for cooking fuel by the after-taste. Things baked over wood charcoal taste the best; diesel and trash taste the worst. Meat cooked over wood tastes great, but not baked goods.

After the meeting we were given a tour of the nursery and the rest of the grounds. Our commander was invited in for another tea meeting. I was going to follow him into the small room but it was rather tight so I stayed outside with the security force. SFC Fair and I took the point on a trail leading to the health clinic.

We could hear a baby being born in the clinic while we were pulling guard. Several women walked past us, some wearing burkas, some wearing head scarves and others just in their good clothes. Some local boys came up to me and started asking for my phone number so they could program it into their phones. The last thing I wanted was to have some local kids calling me. I told them no; then they wanted my camera I told them no. SFC Fair was glad they found me to talk to. He had been entertaining them for over an hour.

Our commander finally finished up his third tea and it was time to hit the road. I noticed the entire time we were at the government compound our interpreter, Ralfi, kept his face fully covered. I knew he was scared but I didn't know from what. Later he told me that he was from Asmar and if people knew he worked for the U.S. they would kill him. Several months later his father met him at one of our VETCAPs and told him to take his scarf off because he had nothing to be ashamed of. His father was very proud of his son's accomplishments and the fact that he was working for the U.S. Army.

Small house at the Asmar government compound where our commander had tea with a rep from the medical clinic, November 2009

On Friday November 20th Major General Harrell gave us a visit. He could only stay a few hours; the 82nd Airborne really didn't want generals that far forward but he persisted and was able to get a flight out.

We held a formation and he awarded us our combat patches for being in a combat zone for over 30 days. PFC McGee and SFC Mead were called forward to receive the first patches. Private First Class McGee was the youngest member of our unit and Sergeant First Class Mead was the oldest. The patch we are authorized to wear, is the 4th Infantry Division now called the 4th Mountain Division. It is somewhat ironic to be wearing the 4th Division patch. The 4th Division was our sister division in the 1980s. Back then a large number of the guardsmen were combat veterans from Viet Nam and few if any of the 4th Division troops had seen combat. It was an adversarial relationship at best. It was one of the reasons I didn't want to go on active duty after I was commissioned. Then, there we were over 25 years later on the same footing.

The combat patch is deceiving. When I was in Honduras we got shot at by the drug lords each time counter drug destroyed their crops. We were not authorized a combat patch for that; we weren't allowed to shoot back either. There are troops who spent their entire tour in Kuwait, went to the city in their civilian clothes and received combat pay and a combat patch. The patch doesn't mean you saw combat.

We were starting to have problems with the USAID and USDA reps, two of the U.S. Government organizations that are responsible for agricultural development in Afghanistan. They hadn't been doing their job, which is why the Army created units like the Kunar ADT. One of the priorities for the area was flood and erosion control. We had been working on several flood control projects for several weeks, which included surveying and some engineering. The reps from USAID and USDA started speaking out at some regional meetings stating that what we proposed would fail. I wasn't going to just sit their while these two attempted to make names for themselves. I asked them what was the flow rate in the wash after the hillsides have been saturated during a ½ per hour rainstorm. No answer. Then I asked them "what is the pressure per square foot on a check dam structure with a five-foot weir?" Again no answer. I asked them several more questions, which they couldn't answer. Then I asked, "If you don't know the answer to any of these questions and you have not seen the engineering, how can you state the design will fail?" They responded that it would be better to just have the locals build rock dams by stacking rocks. I told them that the flow rate was 1000 cubic meters per minute and a pile of rocks would just end up in the Kunar.

That didn't stop the two of them. They had their agenda and sound engineering wasn't part of it.

The State Department was also demanding we attend their many meetings. These meeting had no purpose. They were just discussion groups about subjects that have no bearing on the mission. I've learned that our Federal Government people here only know how to hold meetings, not run a meeting with an agenda that includes a task, purpose and some basic goals. These people have no concept of how to build something or run a project.

Chapter Eighteen

THE FIRST HIKE

Thanksgiving was approaching and we finally had a few projects to start developing. The first was the Kala Kowchano flood control project to protect the Jalalabad Highway. The project started with a long survey mission in the Kala Kowchano dry river valley with headwaters coming from Argadel Khwar. We left the back gate of Camp Wright when there was just enough light to read a tape measure. There was only a marginal dirt road that ran up the valley and crisscrossed the dry river. There was no way we could drive all of our vehicles up the road, which meant everyone was dismounted. We did have two 1151 (HMWVVs) trailing us in support, but we easily out paced them on foot. We had dropped down into the dry riverbed shortly after exiting the back gate and started our survey. A few of the local kids came by to say hello, the same ones I purchased some old Afghan currency from. These kids were teenagers; one has been blind for over seven years and keeps his hand on his friend at all times. They are all fluent in English. The leader of the trio went by the name of Bruce Lee. He was part of one of two father and son teams that haul supplies up to our troops on the ridge lines. The blind boy is remarkable and so are his friends. The boys pride themselves on their ability to run up the hills to the O.Ps. Watching the three boys run up the hill together, you would never know that one is blind. After awhile the kids parted from us and went back to being kids.

Just prior to starting our hike, I scanned the valley with a pair of field glasses my dad had sent me. There wasn't a soul up in the hills, just a bunch of goats and two kids. We hadn't walked more than a few hundred feet and the hills were crawling with people. Soon there were jungle trucks driving up the hills balancing on three wheels. The jingle trucks hauled a crew of men up the mountainside to collect flat rocks for construction projects.

As we worked our way back into the valley, the hills turned from a dusty brown to a nice rich green and we could see some timber up on the ridgeline. Our survey team consisted of SGT Flynn a Forester and SGT Percival, a geology student who loved rocks. Together we took all the measurements that I would need to design the flood control systems for the valley.

Back at Camp Wright we were the prime time entertainment courtesy of Willie the Whale, the eye in the sky. The security force platoon leader was watching our every move using the camera from the eye in the sky. He was also listening to our radio traffic. This snooping can be either good or bad depending how you look at it. The view of our survey party from the air, which was broadcast to several different headquarters looked like an invasion force getting ready to move on the enemy. The task force who's area we were operating in, called up wanting to know if we had action because two people forgot to inform the rest of the world that I was out there. My end of the operation was squared away; every "T" crossed and "I" dotted.

I knew what was going on in the mountains above me at all times. If there was someone walking above us without a bunch of sheep I knew about it and so did the rest of the team. Back at in the states people wouldn't think twice about taking a nice walk around the park and the same held true there. The difference was there was no park so people walked on the mountainsides.

We were getting close to the end of our survey, but not the end of the valley. We had worked ourselves to a point at which the riverbed was no longer scattered rocks and sand to a transition of massive boulders, which could do far more for flood control than we could with any locally built structure. About this time a member of my near security spotted a man up on the ridge who wasn't attending any goats or sheep. His movement was picked up by several more members of the security team. Within a minute whoever it was up on the ridge had four M-14s with scopes pointed at him along with two crew served weapons. My near security noted that the man jumped behind a large rock and hadn't moved in over two minutes. About this time our SecFor platoon leader who was watching everything in the comfort of our TOC, called out on the radio for us to end the mission because the guy was up to no good. I relayed back that I wasn't worried about him. The SecFor platoon leader came back with, "Sir he is behind that rock for a reason and I can't see him with the eye in the sky."

"Yea I know the reason; he is doing the same thing I would be doing if four Yanks had their M-14s pointed at me. I would get behind the biggest rock I could find and hold tight in the fetal position until they found something of greater interest."

I would have liked to have just kept walking to view the rest of the valley, but we had no reason to go any farther. SFC Natividad brought up the rear with our two vehicles while SFC Fair stayed with me calling a halt every so often to let the vehicles catch up. I noticed that the NCO that SFC Natividad wanted to smoke in the hills was riding in one of the vehicles. This particular NCO receives 100% of his nutrition from coffee and cigarettes, and SFC Natividad wanted to prove to him that he was not mission capable unless you eat real food and drink water. I asked him why he didn't assign him to our left flank up on the hillside. He told me, "Sir, I thought about it real hard and decided there was no way I would be able to drag him off that mountain if he went down." When the mission was over the NCOs and I noted that for some reason only the trim and fit people were on this mission. The "Glory Hounds" were nowhere to be found. Within our unit we had a number of senior people who were overweight and out of shape. However, their mouths could run with the endurance of a gazelle, on any given subject. Our unit wasn't special; every unit has a glory hound or two.

The long walk home from the flood control survey in the Kala Kowchano valley. November 22, 2009

The survey was over; now the hard part, the engineering was to begin. I took all of the data and entered it in a database I created. Then, I started creating an elevation view using a CAD program I had. The flood control solution for this valley was going to take a lot of work, but it would be worth it.

Our commander wanted to do a watershed project on the land directly east of us on the other side of the Kunar River in Marah Warah. He selected six potential project sites for us to look at. By the time the guest list was complete we had three interpreters, two reporters, my small section and the whole SecFor platoon.

We arrived at the first site, which looked good for a watershed project except all of the land in the wash was in private hands. We met with a bunch of the locals who were very friendly and didn't ask for a thing. This meeting gave us a chance to try out our new interpreter from Dallas Texas. He is an older gentleman who can't seem to speak above a whisper. I gave up trying to hear him and grabbed one young man and started in with my broken Pashto. He responded, "I speak English. I'll tell you what you want to know." Within a few minutes I had more information than the commander did. The young man was very proud of his village and was excited that someone would be asking him about its history. We said our goodbyes and moved on to the next site. Our new interpreter later told me that Pashto was not one of his strong languages and he was a little hesitant when speaking. A few months later he became the golden key when dealing with women in the smaller villages because of his age and some of the other languages he spoke.

I took one look at the next site from the road and knew right off the bat there was nothing we could do. Our colonel thought it looked like a nice easy hike to take his guests on. The wash was a bit tricky on the knees and feet but not a major challenge. The change in elevation during our hike was about 150 meters. When we got up past the base of the mountains and back into the valley I noticed tire tracks. All I could think of was *how on earth did anyone get a vehicle up this far?* Sgt Flynn was with me and took a look farther into the valley with his field glasses and noted that there was some type of mining going on, which would justify the tire tracks.

On the way down, Janet Killeen, our lady reporter received a call from nature. There were no trees or big rocks, which would lend themselves for privacy. She finally found a spot on level ground and we all turned out backs to her. She remarked that she preferred to choose security over privacy.

As we came into sight of the road where our vehicles were parked, a delegation of three men all wearing brown approached us. They zeroed in on our colonel much to my pleasure. They were from a local school. The leader taught English and math, the second taught math and the third just remained silent. Their leader introduced himself and said he spotted us and decided to ask for help. This guy spoke so quickly and in complete circles it was hard to understand him. Bottom line: he wanted us to fully equip his school.

He was very aggressive about his needs. I asked him where all of his students were and he replied that it was Friday and there was no school. My colonel and I looked at each other with the expression, "it's Friday and we skipped right on past Thanksgiving." I took a quick look at my watch, which displayed the correct day as Tuesday. I told the teacher that today was Se Shamba. Then he recanted his statement and said there was no heat in the school. I had been hiking up and down the hills for several hours since the break of dawn and saw no need for heat.

The teacher then stated that there was no heat in the school for the children. That still didn't add up. Sure it was in the mid 60s, which was far from freezing. The leader went on to state that the governor had toured his school the day before and refused to help him so now we must help him. We told him that he needed to send his request through the education board and they would send it up to the PRT if they approved it. That wasn't good enough for him; he demanded that we come to his school. We told him no, but he wouldn't shut up. Then he saw Janet, our female reporter, and wanted his picture taken with her. His friend produced a new digital camera and took a few shots. If he had a digital camera that meant he had a computer and a means to print his photos. Technology in Afghanistan cost just as much as it does in the U.S. I was wondering why he didn't spend some of his money on the school like I did when I was teaching.

After meeting our teacher friend, I could detect the slight aroma of a rat drifting through the air, which reminded me of an old children's fables and one of my favorites. It is about a lion and a mouse (not a rat). One day a lion captured a little mouse with his mighty paws. The mouse asked the lion to spare his life. The lion replied, "why should I?" The mouse pointed out that eating him would not satisfy the lion's hunger and just maybe someday he just might be able to save the lion's life. The lion laughed at the joke and let the mouse go free. It wasn't long after that the mouse came upon the lion all tied up by some hunters who planned to sell him to a zoo. The mouse quickly went to work gnawing his way through all of the ropes and set the lion free. Sometimes your greatest friends are your smallest. I was still learning who my friends were in Afghanistan.

I had about as much as I could take of our teacher friend's show, motioned our commander and then started down the hill. There were three more teachers waiting near the commander's vehicle just in case he was able to escape the grasps of the first three. SFC Fair was with me and called in the dismounts, which bought the teachers a few more minutes while the dismounts came off the mountain. Just as it looked like we would be rolling again another teacher raced by on a motorcycle and stopped at the colonel's vehicle. By now just about every kid in the village had assembled on the road making it very difficult to maneuver.

We finally cut the anchor chains and moved to the third project site. This time our colonel was not inclined to spend an hour and forty-five minutes hiking up the mountainside. He just told me to look it over. I'm not sure what changed his mind. He made a comment on the way down the last mountain that this was why he didn't stay in the infantry. Then again being cornered like a rat by a gang of hungry alley cats may have also influenced his decision. He gave the same instructions for sites four and five. My little team moved pretty fast; within a few minutes we took soil samples, GPS readings and photos, and scurried up and down off the mountain.

When we arrived at the last possible project site the road attempted to strangle us. We turned off Route Beaverton onto a less than single lane dirt road. Our colonel's vehicle was the second in our convoy and since I was second in command my vehicle was second to last. The distance between the two vehicles was about half a mile. The convoy stopped, SFC Fair got out and hiked up to the head of the convoy, then came back and got me and the rest of the team. By the time we hiked up to the lead vehicle, our colonel and the reporters had dropped down to the bottom of the wash to look at a dry well. The change in elevation in the half mile walk was about 50 meters over a very rough road. The road surface was about the same as the bottom of the dry river beds we had been in.

We got to a place that gave us a beautiful view of the Karware Naw River valley. Then I noticed two boys. One kept his hand on the other at all times. I thought, *that was odd they look just like the boys over at Camp Wright.* I looked farther up the road to the village of Sangamy and saw a few men coming down from a large white compound with Bruce Lee. Bruce introduced himself to me, even though we already knew each other, and told me that this is where he lived. I couldn't believe it. These three boys walked several miles twice a day to work at the camp. Bruce acted as an interpreter for the men who came with him. They told me that they had weapons in their home but they were not bad men. They went on to point out a goat trail on the far hill across from their house. The trail was used by insurgents. I thanked them for the introduction and told them not to worry about us. We were there to look over the water situation. Bruce just disappeared and the men turned around and went back to their house. Bruce returned with his two friends in tow and told me that if any of us continued to walk up the valley past the house where the men lived we would be shot. I asked him if the men whom I just met were going to shoot us. He said no. He said bad people from Pakistan are up on that hill and he listed all of the weapons they had. Sure enough, a little mouse may have just saved my life.

Chapter Nineteen

THANKSGIVING

I remember as a Boy Scouts reading a story in the paper about the war in Afghanistan. An American reporter followed a small band of Afghans as they fought the Soviets. When the reporter asked the Afghan commander what he thought about Americans. He replied they can't hike or shoot, but they sure can eat! He was right; it is the one thing we do better than anyone else.

When it comes to holidays, I think Americans have forgotten the original intent. For example, "The Thanksgiving Feast" was meant to give thanks for what the Lord had blessed us with, not to gorge yourself to oblivion.

Thanksgiving was the first holiday we celebrated at Camp Wright as a unit. The tradition once was for the battalion to hold a formation. The chaplain would invite us to bow our heads and would give the blessing. Then the officers would take their positions in the serving line, serve the troops and then pull KP. That was years ago when a unit still had its own mess section.

The mess staff at Camp Wright put on a spectacular Thanksgiving spread. The evening before, the officers and senior NCOs on post signed up for serving duty in one-hour shifts. Thanksgiving breakfast was reduced to only serve your selves items that translated to no short orders, but everything else was still available. I walked past the mess hall several times before lunchtime and the whole place was ablaze with activity. The cooks were hauling out decorations and baking bread sticks in the shapes of letters to spell out "Happy Thanksgiving," and bringing in additional serving counters. We assembled in the kitchen ten minutes before serving time and things were still a whirl of activity with the floors receiving a last minute mopping and big blocks of ice being hollowed out for tons of shrimp. I watched one of the cooks bring out a huge side of beef for custom carving. Then they loaded up the serving line with prime rib, ham steaks, BBQ chicken, turkey, stuffing, vegetables, rolls and more.

We took our positions in the serving line. LTC Velte handled the prime rib and BBQ chicken. I had the ham, steak and turkey. Major Leeney was on stuffing detail, and across the way was our commander carving the side of beef. He looked like he was born for the job. When our shift was over, our colonel's hands were a bit the worse for wear. His plastic gloves were too tight and they cut the circulation off in his fingers. He lived to tell about it.

Every mess hall in Afghanistan was hosting a Thanksgiving feast twice: once at supper 12 o'clock to 3 o'clock and again for dinner from 5 o'clock to 8 o'clock. Helicopter pilots could land at any FOB they wanted for Thanksgiving but they selected ours. I have had the opportunity to visit many of the other FOBs and I'll have to admit if I was allowed to choose I would choose Camp Wright. The rest are nothing but mud holes and given we just had a few days of rain they were all about ankle deep in fresh mud.

While on serving duty I noticed something about the people coming through the line. Most of the civilian employees took a full serving of each meat (prime rib, BBQ chicken, ham steak, and turkey and then went over to get a piece carved off the side of beef). They took it all, plus the side dishes. These folks have never missed a meal. Some of them were exceptionally obese. The troops who were slim and trim selected only one main entry while the heavier troops had more than one. The mess hall served the same amount of food for both meals.

I saw our troops move through the line. Those who knew they were on a mission with me on Friday were very selective because they knew what they were in for. The troops who manned the crew served weapons were just a little bit more liberal with the servings.

Thanksgiving Day was a day off for us, so if we really wanted to attack the FOB this was the day to do it. I stopped by the "Barn," the name we gave our office, to grab a one over 25000 map and found my troops playing poker with real money. This was a real *no no* in the Army. SFC Hanlin came up with a fundraiser for a local orphanage. All of us had American coinage in our pockets that would not do us a bit of good while we were in Afghanistan. So why not gamble it away? His concept was: the winner would present the final pot to the Chaplain to be used as he saw fit. The final pot also included the Pogs that AAFES gives out as change but refused to take back in Europe or state side.

To finish off Thanksgiving evening I went running for half and hour after making sure there was water in the shower. Then I went up by the main latrine to get a look at Asadabad. I really enjoy the view from there with the roses and fruit trees even in the dark of night. It gave me a chance to pause and reflect for a moment about all that I was thankful for. Once again I knew the night wouldn't be long enough and the morning would be coming early.

At four A.M. my watch went off and I was up. I grabbed my shaving kit and went to our little shower only to find that the water supply was back to a dribble again. A few days prior during our little rain storm we lost power and water. It really was a very mild rain, only an inch at the most. That was Wednesday morning, the day before Thanksgiving. On Friday morning, we had another mission. I had arrived at the shower while SFC Hanlin and Medina were there trying to rinse the soap out of their eyes when the power went off. During the night the camp's water pump failed after a pipeline had broken. Our shower was the only one with a dribble left. There are three showers on post and ours is located on the bottom of the hill. What water was left in the system would sooner or later flow down hill. I turned my flashlight on and grabbed a bottle of water for shaving while SFC Hanlin and Medina continued to hope for more water. The three of us were the early risers around and usually first in line for breakfast at 5:30. As far as we were concerned we were the leadership and we would be the first ones up every day.

On mission days it was to our benefit to be early risers. Missions, even little ones in our backyards require a lot of prep and checks. Our vehicles, with their appropriate weapons, were lined up by the airfield in time for us to have breakfast without rushing ourselves. I stopped at the patio of the main latrine to enjoy the sunrise and look to see if Willie the Whale was in the air. The sun was still coming up from Pakistan; the sky was powder blue with red clouds. The old sailor's chant, "red skies at night, sailor's delight, red sky in morn, sailors take warn." I could feel the temperature dropping just standing there and the trees had started to wave back and forth. Thirty minutes later after breakfast there wasn't a patch of blue left; the whole sky was grey. I wasn't having a good feeling about how the day would turn out; it just stayed overcast.

I would be taking SFC Natividad and Hanlin with me while SFC Medina would stay behind and support the base defense drill, which was to take place while we were away.

During our last visit to the area across the Kunar River from us one of the village elders told us that there were three springs providing water to the village. Our commander wanted to have a closer look to see if we could build a pipe system from the springs. I had asked the same question in my broken Pashto and a kid told me the springs were "dey legly." In English that means "very small." Our commander's concept for the mission was to go back to the village elder, have tea with him and send me up the hill in search of the three springs. I was game, but there were a lot of mountains to search.

We lucked out. Upon arrival one of the local young men agreed to lead us up to the springs. Our commander distributed a bunch of hand crank radios to the folks who were with the young man, as a way of saying thank you. This turned out not to be one of his better moves, but hind sight is 20/20. Our colonel and his circle of friends walked with the young man up the wash and we trailed behind him with our two 1151s (HMWVV) until we got to a point where we could go no further. That point just happened to coincide with the draw that we would be walking up. We got out and followed our commander's party up the draw. Sergeant Percival measured the incline at 53%. That was a bit stiff while carrying 90 plus pounds of gear.

We hiked up a total of 238 feet over some very nasty rock formations. SFC Hanlin turned back to me and said this was a whole lot easier at 20 then it was at 45. The two of us had it easy. SFC Natividad had to bring up the rear and fell in with the SecFor. The SecFor went for the high ground to provide us cover. Poor SFC Natividad had to go up to come back down to the first spring. It just about killed him trying to get there the same time we did. Sgt Percival couldn't be happier. He was a rock hound. Just about every type of formation imaginable could be seen during our ascent.

SFC Hanlin working his way up a 53% grade, Par Kot Kandare valley November 27th, 2009.

The first spring was nothing exceptional and only enough to support one family at best. The young man told us that there was another spring even bigger, but he used the word "mer," which means dead. Our American ex-Afghan interpreter tends to leave out key words when translating. I could tell he got upset with me when I understood someone's answer.

Sure enough, the next spring was a dripping spring and only provided enough water to keep two pits the size of a pair of kettledrums full of water. It was a nice hike but a complete bust. The best part of the day's adventure was yet to come.

A few days prior to this little quest for the fountain of youth we were in the same area when we had been ambushed by an English speaking school teacher. Word had spread quickly about the American colonel who was giving away radios. Sure enough the bloodhound found us and zeroed in on our colonel. The next thing we know he and his party were invited for tea at the schoolhouse. This was not a social event at all. The teacher spoke non-stop issuing a list of demands. Our colonel remained hostage for the better part of an hour sipping tea. Finally when his bladder could take it no more he decided it was time to leave.

Unknown to our commander, while he was enjoying a midmorning tea with the mad hatter we had our hands full with his students. We selected Friday for this mission. Friday is their "Sunday" and there is no school on Friday. Soon we had adults arriving in hordes all demanding radios, pens, bubble gum and candy. This was not a friendly crowd. The villagers didn't ask "If you have another radio I would really appreciate having one." It was, "You give me radio now!" It took some doing to get everyone loaded up. The SecFor troops had to walk back to the main road where the rest of the vehicles were waiting. The people would not stand clear of the vehicles. I thought for sure we would run over a few toes on the way down.

Once we made it to Route Beaverton where the rest of the vehicles were and the SecFor was loaded up, the kids and adults started throwing rocks at the MRAPs because we ran out of radios. I compare this to the villagers up in Naray who took time off from their jobs, and cooked food for us to come help them. They were so grateful just to have us there. They didn't have the money for the materials, but they had heart, labor and food at the ready.

On the way back, one of our ASV (Armor Security Vehicles) stalled from a clogged fuel filter on the Nowabad Bridge over the Kunar River. The local police came running to the rescue thinking they could just push the ASV to the side of the road, about like pushing the rock of Gibraltar. The crew figured out what was wrong, switched fuel tanks and the beast started back up. We arrived at Camp Wright in time for lunch. The base defense drill had been pushed back for the afternoon because too many of the troops were off post on missions.

LTC Velte and I filled the afternoon planning for a Vet Cap, then it was time for dinner. I decided to have an early dinner; that way I could hit the gym early and sleep in until maybe 6:30. I just walked through the door of the mess hall when Lt Ko found me. "Sir we are invited to an 'Eid' celebration. Our interpreters are hosting a traditional Afghan dinner for us." Oh Boy, I could still taste my last Afghan meal every time they lit the dump on fire. The Muslims celebrate Abraham's attempted sacrifice of his son, twice a year: once after Ramadan and once in the fall. The celebration of "Eid" lasts for several days.

I followed Lt Ko to the base of the hill to a little Afghan café on post and met up with SFC Graham who was also invited. We walked in and were warmly greeted by several interpreters who pointed out the main course, a stewed lamb. It smelled great! They had bottled water and flat bread to go with it. I went to take a scoop and saw they had just chopped up the lamb bones and all. I took a healthy helping and choked it all down pulling out the bones from my mouth as I went. I enjoyed the taste of the stewed lamb. I wouldn't order it at home though because it was awfully greasy.

I asked about "Eid" and they told me. Soon we were having a religious conversation. If you had walked into the room you would have thought you walked in on an Old Testament bible study. Some of the men were what we would call C&E Christians (Christmas and Easter) the others were more devout. They were all keenly aware of what the Taliban and the Saudis were doing with their religion. These men could read and knew what the Koran said, and it was not what the Taliban and the Saudi's were putting out.

I asked them would happen when the U.S. leaves or they decided not to work for us any more. The response was, "we will all be killed if we stay in Afghanistan, once you start working directly for the Americans you are marked for death."

We finished up the evening. I came out with a greater understanding of what happened during the Soviet invasion and about the customs of Afghanistan. One of the men at the table saw the Soviets round up thirty members of his family and kill them all.

When we parted, my stomach was not doing so well. What smelled good and tasted good was starting to stir in my stomach. I tried eating some fruit to calm it down, and then I remembered I had packed a bunch of Rolaids somewhere in my gear. I made a beeline for my quarters and rifled through everything I had until I found them. I popped a pink one, a green one and even a blue one and soon my multi-colored roll was gone. Just a word of caution: Rolaids have no impact on the effects of Afghan lamb.

Chapter Twenty

TRAVELING AROUND JALALABAD WITH THE MISSOURI ADT

The at the end of November the President of the United States announced his pullout plan for Afghanistan, which wasn't much of a plan. Basically, he said, "We'll keep paying off Pakistan the true cause of the trouble and think about leaving in 18 months." By June of 2010 after a visit by Afghanistan's president it appeared ours had had enough and there was a press leak that we would all be out of Afghanistan by August of 2011. Even with this great revelation of a pullout plan things were not slowing down any, then again they were not speeding up either.

Mail was the biggest "E" ticket ride at Camp Wright. Folks may not have been able to hear the incoming alarm go off but they sure could hear the sound of a Russian Hip coming up the Kunar River Valley or a PA announcement, "Mail Call." Our mail was sent my Absolute Air, a Russia company that uses Hip helicopters and by truck with heavy security. Thursdays and Sundays were the scheduled mail days for Camp Wright. We had Christmas packages coming in from hundreds of organizations across the United States. Our unit of 64 troops received over 200 packages. Multiply that by all of the other units in Kunar and it could really overwhelm the system. Family and friends don't have to fear about the

Taliban intercepting the mail. The Army protects the mail at all costs. SFC Hanlin kept reminding us, *Mail means Jail. Don't touch it!*

With Thanksgiving behind us it was back to work, not that we ever stopped. I was still having trouble getting our commander to understand that it takes some time to engineer solutions and to type up all the reports he wanted. He believed that there is enough time to do everything between the evening we return from a trip and the following morning before we go out again. He promised the governor of Sarkani an irrigation project even though I warned him beforehand that the water would have to be pumped and it would take a lot of power. After "we" promised the Sarkani governor that we would do the project, I showed our commander the calculations for the pumping requirements. To meet the minimum flow rate for a wheat crop we would need four 500 Hp centrifugal pumps, which would require 1500 kilowatts of power. He asked how many square feet of solar panels would that be. I responded "Sir we usually don't measure acres in square feet."

"Oh, looks like you have a problem, Dave," was the response. For the life of me I can't understand how we made a promise and my lips didn't move and now I have a problem. My saving grace was USAID's opposition to the project and the landowner's inability to agree on the right of way for the canal.

After six weeks in the country things were slowly starting to improve; we finally received some IP addresses for our computers so we could plug them into the network. That was the good news. The bad news was the bandwidth was so limited the computers were next to worthless on the Internet. Bandwidth and network security continued to inhibit us from doing our job. I was required to post photos of all the people I talked to and site recons on the military's Internet systems. The problem was the security system would not allow me to upload photos from my camera or a thumb drive. I was forced to create my report on my personnel laptop, save it to my external hard drive, go to the MWR computer lab and email it to myself, then walk back to the Army computer, burn a CD with everything on it, and transfer it to the secret computer. This takes a few hours.

On Saturday November 29th, we went to the Sarkani District Center to meet with USAID and a few other government agencies. We arrived with plenty of time to spare, and as usual the folks at the district center were not

128

expecting us. The Afghan national police chief for the district greeted us. (This guy is on Santa's naughty list; the U.S. would like to see him retire very soon.) The district center had the feel and appearance of tombstone Arizona: not a soul around except a few cops and a bunch of kids. After 30 minutes the district's principal of villages arrived and opened his office to us. We had our interpreter with us, Janet Killeen a blog reporter, our commander, and assorted security. The principal of villages is what we would call a public works director. He is responsible for 53 large villages and over 100 small villages. A big village would have a population of about 500 people. Within a few minutes his son arrived with a cell phone. He introduced his son and told us that he had eight children, four boys and four girls. His son spoke some English and wasted no time in asking for antibiotics because he is plagued with ear infections. Later during our visit he asked me to bring him a gift in my next visit.

The police chief returned with tea, a plate of sugar and some candies. He would scoop up sugar in his hand, dump it into our teacups and stir it with his pen. About this time the governor arrived and introduced himself. Our commander told him about our unit and the type of service we provided. Then the subject of water and the need for irrigation canals in the area came up. The governor said, "We have a canal; would you like to see it?" We all thought it would be another road trip, but the governor told us that it was right behind the district center. He led us out the back of the compound through a flimsy three-foot wide gate to the irrigation canal. It was an earth canal and serviced the farms that were not more than 100 yards from the Kunar River.

While we were discussing the finer points of irrigation the incoming alarms were going off at FOB Joyce. FOB Joyce was 1200 feet from the district center. One of the staff members of the governor's group turned to us and said "don't worry; that's the college." Directly adjacent to the governor's compound sharing the back wall is what we would call a high school, but they call it a college. Funny thing, I only saw a bunch of middle school aged kids around the place.

We finished looking at the canal and walked back into the governor's compound when the first round hit FOB Joyce. Janet, our reporter, turned to SGT Clemens and said, "What was that?"

Sgt Clemens replied, "A big boom." I pointed out the location of the insurgent's mortars up on the hill to Janet. She tried to snap a photo of them going off but only got a bunch of smoke. There were some people injured at FOB Joyce–how many and to what extent was unknown to us at the time. There wasn't anyone in the governor's compound who seemed alarmed about the mortar attack. We just went back to the principal of village's office and finished our tea.

The folks from USAID and USDA still hadn't arrived and we had stalled for several hours waiting for them. We loaded up in the trucks and started to drive away when the USAID and USDA reps arrived. They had nothing to say; they just wanted to stop by and round out their day. We finally left with our commander promising them a completely engineered irrigation system that would provide water to the upper section of their district. I told our commander that it was a 100-meter lift, not a gravity feed from the river and to accomplish the lift I would need a lot of power. (There is no power.)

The next day, Sunday November 30th, was another field trip. This time it was to a trade school up the Kunar River. We didn't have a need to go there; it had no real relevance to what we were doing. The real mission was to be a taxi service to USAID and USDA. We were told by Mr. USAID and Mr. USDA that the school site had the potential to be an experimental farm and the reason we were going was to test the soil and design an irrigation system. I had already been briefed about the school (KCC Kunar Construction College) and knew it wasn't suitable. A few years back the U.S. contracted with an Indian construction company to build a road from Asadabad to Naray. The Indian company's base camp where they dumped all of their chemicals and serviced their trucks was converted into the KCC. When we arrived there were still large oil spills visible and a fair amount of the soil had been dug up and used to build a road on the other side of the KCC. Basically the potential farm was a toxic waste dump that was being eradicated by being used as a borrow pit for local road construction.

We looked the school over. The level of education there was on a par with the 10th grade in the U.S. All of the students are required to sample every subject taught at the school, then select one to major in. The school is comprised of two large halls that were built by the PRT, which included a materials testing lab, administrative offices, dorms, and one art studio. Inside the first hall is a concrete skills lab where students are taught how to build forms and rebar cages. They have the basic concept, but know nothing about where to place stirrups or tying corners together. In the back of the hall are pipe fitting, plumbing and electrical shops. The other hall is dedicated to cabinetry and masonry.

I was taking photos of the landscape of the notorious hill 1311 where attacks on convoys were executed. I noticed a large number of white rocks all around the mountain. Then I wondered just how people got up there. The white rocks mark the location of land mines. We thanked everyone for the tour, loaded up and came home. We would be back to KCC at the strong request of USAID, but it would also be a wasted trip.

We arrived back at Camp Wright from KCC in time for me to do my laundry, re-pack my ruck and clean my rifle. There were nights that just weren't long enough especially when the morning arrived at 3:30. Tuesday December 1st was just such a morning. After getting cleaned up, the NCOs got four vehicles lined up at the airfield, and tested the radios. Our schedule didn't allow for breakfast so I had one of my emergency cans of fruit and raced back up the hill for the convoy brief. Very simple brief: "We are going to Jalalabad to see our ADT cousins from Missouri. Leave the front gate, turn right, stay on the highway for about two hours, cross a big bridge over the Kunar River, go left at the traffic circle, watch for our air field and turn in at the first open gate." It was about this time when LTC Velte decided that delaying our departure 30 minutes for breakfast was in order. We had been at it for almost three hours and were getting hungry.

The drive along the Kunar River was very scenic–something different with every turn. The kids would give us either the thumbs up or hang loose sign as we rolled through each village. After a long two hours of rolling and twisting down Route California we arrived at Jalalabad. This city is one massive farmers' market! The economy is booming with one convoy of jingle trucks after another coming over the border from Pakistan.

Getting through the city streets was easier than we anticipated. The next thing we knew the traffic circle was behind us and we were at the gate to FOB Fenty the Jalalabad airfield. This is the same airfield the Russians used, and the last commercial airport Osama Bin Laden landed at. The hotel at FOB Fenty doesn't take advance reservations due to the poor credit rating of the troops. Can you imagine troops would call up, make reservations and fail to show up? They would give the cheapest excuses such as: we were attacked; our helicopter got re-routed due to a firefight. We arrived at the front lobby of the Grand FOB Fenty Hotel and made sure we didn't track in any dust on their highly polished plywood floors. I asked the clerk for seventeen rooms with private bath accommodations. He responded with, "There is no room in the inn." This was in keeping with the Christmas spirit. There was no manager either.

We thanked the man for his honesty, then ruled out sleeping at the Afghan Veterinary Association's hospital, which was the closest thing we could think of. There was no sense worrying about being homeless; we all had our field gear with us. The only thing left to do was eat. We had lunch at the FOB Fenty mess hall, then loaded back up in the trucks and went back out to FOB Finley-Shields, which was named after two enlisted soldiers who were killed in June of 2008 when a vehicle loaded with explosives detonated outside the FOB on Afghan Highway 1 in the middle of a convoy. FOB Finley-Shields is unique compared to other FOBs; it was once a Russian officers' retreat complete with a swimming pool. To enter the FOB you pass through an Afghan Army post, then through a public park.

Once at FOB Finley-Shields we coordinated for the next day's activities. The USAID rep didn't even know that his organization has built a poultry feed mill capable of producing 200 tons of feed a day, a seed cleaning mill, a honey processing plant, or that there was even a veterinarian school just up the road, which was doing things that the NGOs and the Afghan government failed at. (NGO is a Non Government Agency. Most NGOs contract with either the United Nations or the U.S. Government). We inquired about staying at Finley-Shields, but they had even less to offer. So we headed back to FOB Fenty in hopes that at least 17 troops vacated their bunks. There are no private rooms at FOB Fenty and no one had checked out either. It was starting to get dark when Sgt Palacios, our supply sergeant, showed up to say hello and ask for a ride home to Camp Wright. We told him the situation. He suggested, "Why not sleep in the classroom tent right by the PAX terminal?"

"Why not?" We quickly went to work moving all of the tables and chairs outside to make room for sleeping. The classroom tent had a plywood floor, which I thought was just fine. It beat the marsh by the runway. Sgt Bentley, our medic, had admired the trauma center's screened-in porch earlier in the afternoon. He noted that the porch was screened in with litters, and litters could be used as cots! He quickly organized a raiding party and I followed along at a distance.

Bentley and crew were in the process of acquiring a bunch of litters when the door of the trauma office opened. I heard Sgt Bentley say, "Oh Nuts!" (He said something else but I'm trying to keep it clean.)

The night duty NCO started to come outside when I stepped into the light as he asked, "May I help you?"

I responded, "I just came by to say thank you for all the support you gave us the other day; it was really appreciated."

"Hey no problem that's what we're here for." That was all the extra time that Bentley and crew needed as they raced down the darker alleys of the FOB to our tent.

Janet Killeen and LTC Kelly discussing honey processing Jalalabad Dec 2nd, 2009. 1Lt Ko collection

As I was walking back I came across Sgt Palacios again. He told me that he was working on getting us some cots. By then it was after dinner and dark. FOB Fenty works banker hours. I didn't give the idea much hope. I stopped at the PX to buy a new watch and more batteries before returning to the tent. Just as I arrived there was Sgt Palacios with a truck load of new cots. The next challenge was how to quietly put 17 litters back where they belonged without getting caught.

It took some doing but we finally got all of our gear into the tent. In some places our cots were bumped up against each other so it was a bit tight. SFC Hanlin gave us all a warning that if he was talking or fighting in his sleep to leave him be. He just might be winning. He was across from me and next to him was LTC Velte. On my side I had 1LT Ko who was between me and Spc Tropeano. 1Lt Ko is a young six-foot-three Korean. There is no way I could imagine him in life's senior years wearing a horse hair hat. I think his parents forced him into the Army because they couldn't afford to feed him any longer. He had arms that rival those of a full-grown orangutan.

Sleep didn't elude us for long. We didn't even hear any of the aircraft landing on the runway, which was just 300 feet away. I was dead to the world when I heard SFC Hanlin yell out, "Sir, Sir Sir!"

I sat up and said, "I'm up; what's wrong?" I got no response. SFC Hanlin was talking in his sleep and LTC Velte who was next to him slept right through the whole show. I lay back down when I heard 1Lt Ko start to stir. I heard a *Ka Wallop* followed by *oooooh*. 1Lt Ko had successfully flipped over swinging his left arm like a sledge hammer and plastering his paw square in the center of Spc Tropeano's chest.

It was an interesting night. The cots made a considerable amount of noise every time we adjusted our position. It sounded just like the rigging of a tall masted ship creaking in the wind. All would be quiet then one person would roll over then the next in a cascading sequence. Then there was the sudden in-cadence adjustment when the tent would roar from the sounds of the cots and not one eyelid would flinch.

Wednesday morning came soon enough. We were all awake at 5:30 when an NCO came in and said they needed the tent for a class that was starting at 6:30. We knew that 6:30 was a make believe time, because no one at FOR Fenty started work before 9:00. Nevertheless we wasted no time converting the tent back to a classroom, grabbing breakfast and loading up on the trucks.

Our first stop was the local honey grower association's honey plant. We drove down several residential streets (dirt roads) and through a few markets in order to get to the honey plant. Dr. Sofi was waiting for us inside. This little plant was set up for show! I asked about the market and the manager said he didn't have the proper health permits to export so everything was for local consumption.

They had a table set up in the quad with honey jars ready for sale all labeled in English. I looked their plant over and for a small operation they were doing pretty well. It was very easy to see why they didn't have their health permits. If they would make just a few changes in their operation they would meet the packaging requirements. I think what was holding them back was the limited amount of space they had to work with.

Due to security reasons, not everyone could go in at the same time. I walked Janet, our reporter, back to the vehicles to be greeted by a herd of kids all wanting their picture taken. I swapped out with Sgt Flynn in the turret and SFC Medina switched places with our driver Sgt Stevens. They each took a quick tour of the plant. The longer we waiting the more kids showed up. The kids were well behaved and didn't demand candy or anything else. There were just a lot of kids.

Once we recovered everyone, we slowly tied up traffic working our way through the kids and were off to the seed cleaning plant. The seed cleaning plant was build by USAID but only partly constructed. I fully understand that the Afghans must take on some financial responsibility at some point in the project cycle, but if you're going to give someone a gift give them a complete gift. The seed-cleaning mill is set up for local farmers to bring in their seed, have it cleaned and returned to them. The plant was equipped with machinery from Pakistan. Everything is from Pakistan, but there was no provision for storage or bagging.

When we arrived at the plant site some teenagers were throwing large rocks and bricks at our vehicles. One of the local elders went over and got the kids to knock it off. With all of the problems Afghanistan faces they still respect their elders. The area outside the seed cleaning plant was used to store farm equipment. The State of Missouri purchased just about every type of farm equipment imaginable. The only problem was terrace farms couldn't use the equipment. Here was another example of how big hearted Americans shoot the local capitalistic economy in the foot. The seed cleaning mill and the equipment yard is managed by the Agriculture Ministry. Just down the street is a private company that rents farm equipment. The private company must recover the capital expense of the equipment the Agriculture Ministry doesn't because the U.S. gave them the equipment. Both organizations rent the equipment.

Wednesday night was almost a repeat of Tuesday night except we had rested enough to really appreciate the location of our tent. The tent was located 300 feet from the runway, five feet from the perimeter road that all of the convoys used. It was at the intersection at the runway crossing so all of the trucks came to a full and complete stop next to our tent. A few of our troops decided that it would be more peaceful to sleep out in the vehicles that were parked just 50 feet from the runway.

About 2:00 A.M. SFC Hanlin managed to wake up the whole tent. He was speaking in tongues to someone. When the morning came someone commented about the event. SFC Hanlin said, "Oh I was probably fighting with my ex-wife again. I was married to her for six years. Thank God five of those years I was deployed."

One of the other guys piped up, "SFC Hanlin this was 2:00 A.M. in the morning."

"Yep that's about the time she shows up."

We busted camp again, had breakfast, worked over the vehicles then headed out to the Afghanistan Veterinary Association (AVA). It was just down the road from the FOB really easy to get to, but very difficult to get in. It reminded me of driving to Home Depot in my truck. I followed the signs that said contractor parking only to find all of the spaces were for compact cars. The same was true at the AVA. This is a facility for people to bring their large animals to for treatment. You would think that meant folks would drive them in a truck and trailer. Nope, not there; they are walked to the doc. There wasn't much room for our vehicles; the MRAPs are the size of a semi truck.

Dr. Sofi gave us a complete tour starting with the first building the Soviets built, which was now a feed mill. He showed us his cold storage, the surgery building, and finally his new building with classrooms, dorm, pharmacy and wall-to-wall carpet. He hosted us to tea and talked about all of the services he could provide or coordinate for us. The man has incredible organizational skills. He is also very honest. Every place we have visited people spoke very highly of him and what he has accomplished.

When we finished our tea he suggested we tour the USAID feed mill on the other side of town, the same feed mill that we were told by USAID was shut down. Dr. Sofi said it wasn't shut down. They just don't export due to poor management and bad QA/QC. The mill had a daily output of 200 tons, which could support 6000 farms. The main failure of the USAID project was no qualified plant manager. Another problem was once they started operations Pakistan undercut their prices. Dr. Sofi led us out to the mill in a white Toyota pickup. As we passed through town to an industrial area the people's attitude toward us changed from friendly to well let's say less than hospitable.

The mill was located outside of town in an area that was being developed for industry. SGT Stevens and I were remarking that the area was prime for opportunity sniper attacks due to all of the low walls and construction. We felt pretty safe from organized complex ambushes because no one would have expected us.

We pulled up to the plant at approximately 11:45, set up security and found the plant was in full operations. Trucks were leaving loaded to the gills. The Sec For went into the mill to set up security. Dr. Sofie was talking to the plant manager when three shots hit the northern MRAP at 12:00 hrs. SPC Tropeano had just scanned his sector, which included a large multi structure under construction, when he saw the muzzle flash in the building. He returned fire at the gunman who was dressed in black. Spc Tropeano fired six shots while the gunman got up from his firing position on the second floor and fled the scene. He called out the direction of the gunman and 1Lt Ko relayed the information on the radio. SFC Fulton's 1151, which was parked next to the engaged MRAP, couldn't see the gunman's location due to the position of the MRAP. SFC Fulton instructed SGT Stevens to pull forward ten feet so that our gunner could provide supporting fire if needed.

An ANP pickup truck arrived from the direction of the gunman at 12:02 and took up a position at the first intersection north of the feed mill. SFC Mead notified LTC Velte, the mission commander, of the situation. LTC Velte made the decision to leave the area. The first vehicle to leave was Dr. Sofie's. He had been stopped by the ANP. The convoy moved out in a slow pace with no further engagements at 12:12. Our convoy had to stop and wait for the ANP to finish talking to Dr. Sofie because the ANP and Dr. Sofie's vehicles blocked the intersection.

Even though our Sec For was in the mill for just a few minutes they saw a lot. SFC Mead reported that the mill was in full operation. The main grain mill was six stories tall and there were 30 to 40 employees. During the TIC one large Jingle truck left the area loaded with sacks of grain. The local people came out and stood in the line of fire and other civilian vehicles drove the roads between the gunman and our convoy.

A review of the MRAP showed that one bullet impacted the driver's side rear passenger window, a second round was in line with the center of the turret at the same level as the bullet strike in the window and a third strike was in the lower toolbox hinge.

The Jalalabad feed mill. Dr Sofie's truck parked in front. Photo taken about two minutes before we had a small problem. December 2009

Friday was the Muslim holy day so not too much was going on. Even FOB Fenty observed the holy day. I went in the S-4 shop to see about our money only to learn they lost the documents. We went over to FOB Finley-Shields to coordinate for a joint tour with the Missouri ADT and to look over their contracts, then met with USAID and Idea New, an NGO, about projects.

We got plenty of sleep as we adjusted to SFC Hanlin's nocturnal habits. SPC Tropeano learned to move his cot out of 1LT Ko's striking range for his own safety. Saturday was an early start. We loaded up and went over to FOB Finley-Shields, linked up with the Missouri ADT, grabbed a bite to eat and hit the road. We had two stops to make. The first was a town that wasn't on the map, which wasn't surprising.

We drove up Afghan Highway 1 past FOB Fenty and passed through an area that looked like Santa Ana California in the 1950s. The highway was lined with eucalyptus trees. The same trees were used as wind breaks between the farms. We could see snow capped mountains in the distance that looked just like home with foothills in the foreground. Then we came upon a traffic jam. Yes everything was just like home. The bridge had been washed out so vehicles had to take turns driving down into the riverbed. We continued on, heading toward Pakistan, the same route that the Taliban took when they fled Afghanistan. Funny thing: Pakistan didn't set up a dragnet to capture them. All of the Taliban were welcomed back with open arms. They just went home to Mama.

The landscape started to resemble El Paso back where the old Spanish mission was. We finally arrived at Spin Gar to tour their new slaughter house, vet center and cold storage unit. We were unexpected guests, but it didn't take long for the community elders and veterinarian to arrive and show us around. They were very proud of what they had accomplished. The slaughter house was clean and ready to go. They bought their stainless steel from Pakistan, which was Re-bar powder coated in silver. Then one of the locals let it slip that they used the facility for the Eid celebration. The community slaughtered up a feast for the village and you would have never known it; the place was so clean.

The next stop was to conduct a pre job walk for an irrigation project. As we drove, the landscape became void of any life, plant or animal. The convoy stopped on the road. We all dismounted and started walking. I just followed because I didn't have a clue where we were going. We popped over a hill, which overlooked a lush green valley. The Missouri ADT discussed the project with the village elder and inspected a storage area for the project concrete, then called it a day. But we still had a long drive back to Jalalabad.

We were starting to call FOB Fenty home. Lunch was on the road so a hot dinner was the treat for the day. Most of the day was spent in the vehicles wearing our body armor. The weight of the body armor coupled with the other gear really drains the energy out of you. By now we had become experts in setting up our bunk house. LTC Velte said, "Let's have lights out at 9:30 tonight guys. We have an early day tomorrow." Our lights were out before 9:00, but no one had the strength to get up to flip the switch off.

Sunday Morning December the 6th was the same drill: up before the roosters, breakfast at FOB Finley-Shields and on the road again. This time the Missouri ADT was going to inspect four wells that a contractor was asking for final payment on. The contract stated that each well would have a casing, an above ground reservoir, and a solar powered pump. We arrived at the first site that looked like the surface of Mars, void of any water. It was also void of any well too. There was a herd of cattle walking through the area, but we couldn't see what they were grazing on.

The Missouri and Kunar ADTs looking for a water well that the contractor stated was completed. The well was never dug December 2009.

We loaded back up and set out for the next well. The Afghan police led the way through every narrow alley they could find. At one point we could see the grooves carved by other trucks in the walls of the buildings on either side of the road. We managed to knock off both mirrors as we worked our way through one small town. We also passed by a funeral in route. It looked like the entire town had turned out to pay their respects. When we passed by, everyone was on their knees; then they all stood up in unison.

It took us about two hours to reach the second well site, because we had to drive over open country and through many little villages. The next well was located in a graveyard. All I could think of was they may have drilled through Uncle Albert to get to water. This well was further along than the first. The well had been drilled, cased, and a reservoir had been constructed, but it was not in service.

It took the Missouri ADT some detective work but they finally found the first well. The locals were in the process of drilling it next to a mosque. Missouri was firm with the contractor and the elder that the well is drilled where the contract stated or the Army was not paying for. Everyone got the point and decided to drill the well where the contract specified.

We parted with the Missouri ADT and headed home, with a quick stop at Jalalabad to grab our gear and to inhale our dinner. It was dark by the time we drove through the front gate at Camp Wright. The trip was very worthwhile especially the tour of the Afghan Veterinary Association and the friendship we established with Dr. Sofi. This friendship would soon become the hallmark of our deployment. I hit the rack at 2200 with a sore back.

Chapter Twenty-One

ALL CREATURES GREAT AND SMALL

Back in 1980 we took a family vacation to England. My mom took along a book titled "All Things Bright and Beautiful." At the opening of the book was a poem by Cecil F. Alexander that started with, "All things bright and beautiful, All creatures great and small, All things wise and wonderful The Lord God created them all." The same poem is also a church hymn. The book was about a veterinarian who traveled around the countryside attending to farm animals. The wealth of rural Afghanistan is in its farm animals. People may not own any land and live in a tent, but they can be wealthy in animals. If disease strikes these animals a family could not only be poverty stricken over night they can also starve. So we decided to go out into the country just like Dr. James Herriot and provide medical care to the farm animals up in Naray.

We had met with the estate manager of Naray a few weeks earlier while LTC Velte was in Kabul learning about how to put on a VETCAP (Veterinary Civil Assistance Program). The process was very simple except for the money part. We needed money to buy the pharmaceuticals for the operations. Getting money out of the Army has been like dragging an elephant through a knothole without any peanuts, to put it mildly. LTC Velte and I made a deal with the PRT to use their money and we would do the rest.

We coordinated with Dr. Sofi, the president of the AVA (Afghan Veterinary Association) down in Kabul for all of the required pharmaceuticals, which he delivered. Another unit that we supported down south sent us all of their leftover supplies. We still needed cattle chutes. SFC Medina ordered some lumber and SSG Lucas went to work on the chutes like a beaver on a caffeine high. We had to borrow trucks, which were missing parts. SGT Martinez and SGT Percival went to work on the trucks, which required some extensive repairs. If it wasn't one thing it was ten dozen others getting in the way. Spc Tanson rounded up all of the candy she could find and bagged in up to be handed out to the kids. We got 400 radios from the civil affairs team to hand out as well.

SSG Lucas and SFC Hanlin construct animal chutes for the VET CAP

SSG Lucas works on a chute door.

Finally, everything was ready. LTC Velte and I along with our commander had one meeting to attend on Sunday December 14th, at the Sarkani District Center with the governor about the proposed irrigation project. We arrived as scheduled and met with the governor who had invited his brother, a schooled hydrologist to attend. I was sitting next to his brother with my notebook open when he started asking me questions about where I got different factors for my design. I asked him if he knew what my equations were for and he did! I think he was there to check and see if I knew what I was doing, and not just a good idea fairy. The governor invited me to present my proposal. I displayed the map on the wall behind his desk, where I stood like a Redwood holding it against the wall for all to see.

The first thing the governor asked was how the water would get up the hill. I told him it would have to be pumped. He was quick to say, "No thank you," to the use of electrical pumps. His counter proposal was to include Marah Warah in the project so that the irrigation canal could be gravity fed. (Just like I told my boss) I agreed to develop another plan and present it to the Kunar governor and we parted. When we stepped outside there was a line of people waiting to see the governor and the usual mortar fire going off. One of the ground units located the site of the mortar fire and called in an air strike.

When we returned, the troops were still working on all of the vehicles we borrowed. The biggest problem was the radios. Several of the vehicles had electrical problems that would cause the radios to cut in and out. This was a problem that we couldn't solve.

The stars were standing ready to welcome the morning when we loaded up in the trucks for Naray (FOB Bostick). We waited for another convoy to clear route California. They came on Camp Wright as if their pants were on fire. Once they cleared the front of our convoy we pulled out onto route California and headed north through Asadabad. The first thing that happen was an oncoming car blinded our LMTV driver with its high beams. The result was we hit the Jersey barrier that was filled with water. The water blasted into the air and the barrier ended up under the front of the LMTV bending the front step. We stopped, did a quick inspection and hit the road again. The LMTV is a big cargo truck onto which we loaded all of the live stock chutes and hooked a trailer up behind it with even more barnyard goodies. We affectionately named it the rolling barn.

The first hour of the drive was on paved road. We made one planned rest stop at COP Monti, which is located near the Asmar district center. We pulled in, did what we needed to do and SFC Hanlin, our convoy commander, asked for directions on how to get back on Route California. He got a funny look from a Spc 4 and jumped back into the truck. Note we asked for directions, and we had several maps and a GPS mapping systems. We pulled out of COP Monti, went down a hill to a bridge and realized we made a wrong turn. It took us more than a few minutes to turn around. Lucky for us the gunners saw the "Y" in the road that led to route California. The road was obscured by dirt; you would have never known it was a paved highway.

The pavement ended in about a mile. The next five hours were over semi-improved and unimproved roads. It took us five hours to safely travel 30 miles. At first the road was ready to be paved, then it transitioned to an active quarry where men were excavating boulders by hand. Farther up, the road narrowed to the point where both I and our gunner up top had to guide the driver SPC Lopez so he wouldn't end up in the river. Our biggest threat was not being attacked, it was going over the edge of the road. We made another stop for nature along the way and I really needed it. My back and lower end had been taking a beating with the road. It was great to just walk around for a few minutes. Finally we hit paved road again, the gateway to FOB Bostick and Naray. FOB Bostick was just three miles north of the pavement and a welcomed site. We had left Camp Wright at 5:30 A.M. and arrived at FOB Bostick at 12:30 just in time for lunch.

Vehicle that had been ambushed on Route California.

After lunch we loaded our gear into a tent that was shared by another unit passing through. Every cot touched the cot next to it and there were cots side by side running down the center of the tent. There was about 12 inches of walkway between the cots.

LTC Velte linked up with Captain Pittard, and I located a platoon of infantry to act as my security for a survey. We had brought along two reporters: one from a blog site and one from a major west coast newspaper. The newspaper reporter was nothing more than a lead brick. Just before we left for FOB Bostick he asked me what the sleeping accommodations were like. I told him that we may be sleeping on the truck. I said, "Don't expect too much; the area is very kinetic and a lot of troops pass through the area."

His response was, "I need to call and check on my flight out." I would have thought a news paper reporter would have lots of questions to ask, but not this guy. We sat down with him and told him what was going on in great detail. We even arranged to give him a special briefing on the area. His questions of me were: Where did you go to school? Where is home? How old are you? All I could think of was *Look buddy, I've given you tons of information about the real problems here and you're not interested.* There was one thing he was interested in and that was flying out as quickly as possible. I invited him along for the watershed survey, but he backed out once he understood we were walking with full gear and rucks. For this guy walking to the mess hall was effort enough. I do have to give him credit. He did make the journey to Afghanistan and far away from Kabul, which is where most reporters stay.

Janet Killeen, on the other hand, lit up with excitement about all of the stories that were up in Naray that hadn't been discovered. After seeing the single sampling of newspaper reporters' stories I think I know why the printed press is going down hill. It's not the lack of readership; it's the lack of energy and foresight. However when I surf the Internet I notice very few hits on stories about Afghanistan. The American public is just not interested in the war.

Wednesday morning came. I grabbed my survey team and LTC Velte stood his crew up. My departure was delayed for a while because we needed the Afghan Army to escort us up to the town of Lay Nay. The Afghan Army unit assigned to FOB Bostick was one of the newest units in the field and built from people who have very poor family connections, which is why they were assigned to Naray.

We waited at the airfield for a while then finally moved to the north gate where the ANA (Afghan National Army) linked up with us. We were going to cross a swinging vehicle and foot bridge at Naray Kelay (Village of Naray). Crossing bridges is a dangerous event. There is nothing to hide behind and you can be seen from every direction. The agreement was the ANA would secure the far side of the bridge then my team, which included a survey team and three personal security from the ADT, would advance across and take up our positions while the infantry platoon secured the nearside of the bridge. As we approached the bridge we could see that there were some traffic problems. Too many cars wanted to cross over the swinging bridge all at the same time. The ANA moved forward to deal with the traffic issue. We got the signal to cross thinking the ANA was on the far side. Sgt Flynn and I gave each other a quick nod and ran like the wind over the 100 yard bridge. We got to the other side, and I said "where is the far side security?" (We were suppose to leap frog past them and take up the next key location for security.)

Sgt Flynn shouted back, "Sir we're it!" Within the same minute the rest of the ADT troops flew across the bridge and secured the gateway to the Naray village. Then came the infantry. The platoon leader told me to wait for the ANA to pass through and follow them.

Soon we were working our way through the village. My interpreter was very scared. He was certain this was going to be his day to meet Allah. The artillery had gone off at 5:30 in the morning firing into the area where we were going. He had learned form the other locals who worked at the FOB that the insurgents were in the hills with mortars. He never left my side. While we were in town he pointed out a little girl who was afraid of me because I would say hello to everyone in town and ask them questions.

We worked our way out of the village back to the bank of the Kunar River on a narrow dirt road that led up to the village of Lay Nay. Lay Nay had just received a new school from the PRT and was working on improving the area around it.

Going south on the eastern side of the Kunar River passing through the Village of Naray. December 16th, 2009

When we reached Lay Nay, all we could see was a deep valley with no possible chance of building any type of flood control or water retention system. I told the guys we need to go farther back and just validate there is nothing we can do. We set out to go deeper into the valley by walking along an irrigation trench that clung to the mountain wall. We slowly worked our way around a distant spur and noticed a sudden rise in the valley floor. The whole dynamics of the valley had changed. We slid down into the valley and started walking up the river bed to witness some major erosion along the way. While we were working our way up the river the village elder caught up to us, filled us in on the history of the area and showed us the village piping system that was out of service. Turns out they only use the pipe system when the water table is low. Just ahead of the pipe system was a granite faced water fall that stood ten feet above us. We thought it would be a good place for a retention dam.

Looking from the Village of Lay Nay into the river valley. Our survey team would hike along the terraces for another 500 meters before dropping down into the river bed.

After touring around in the river we returned to the village of Lay Nay and talked to the elder a little more, then looked at a few more projects that needed to be addressed.

We got back to FOB Bostick in time for a late lunch. The other half of our team had spent their morning meeting with the local battalion commander and some more village elders, so they hadn't had time to set the VET CAP site up yet. The battalion backed out of supplying a tent for the operation. Basically the local battalion washed their hands of the operations and decided it was a Civil Affairs and Ag mission not their's. It was the battalion that invited us up to provide the service because it was beyond their capability.

By the evening, my team had recovered from our little hike and I had put all of my notes in order. The other unit, which we had shared the tent with, had left at 3:30 in the morning and didn't return so we had the whole tent to ourselves. The newspaper reporter started interviewing members of our team. His side comment was we were all naively optimistic about our success in Afghanistan and the dangers. LTC Velte started playing chess with the interpreters and losing as usual. I found a good place to read and the troop played cards for the evening.

Mornings at FOB Bostick started with a call for prayer at 5:30. If you were in the transition tent you couldn't miss the call for prayer. The PA system is 25 feet from the tent. I could hear the noon time call for prayer up in the village of Lay Nay the day before. It was so loud. Getting up at 5:30 doesn't buy you much at FOB Bostick; their mess hall doesn't open until 6:30. It is only open during meals not 24 hours like all of the other mess halls. This is a commander's policy. No one lets the mess hall dictate terms. What it tells you is that they don't do anything before breakfast or late at night. This reminded me of a pitched battle in Texas, where a bunch of renegades open fired with six pound canons on a group of well drilled Mexican Army troops before breakfast. Those who fail to read history are doomed to repeat it. By the time this book is published several units will have rotated through FOB Bostick.

Shortly after breakfast, LTC Velte took the troops out to the VET CAP site and I waited with Lt Ko at the air field for our commander and most importantly our money man SFC Fair. They arrived on Molson Air with no fanfare and we walked out the south gate to a farmer's field where the troops were setting up. My job was to man the give-a-way table (Humanitarian Assistance) with Amann our interpreter from Dallas, Texas. Once people finished having their animals examined and treated they stopped by my table for some diet supplements for their animal, candy and a radio.

When you pass through an Afghan village you notice lots of men doing nothing. This is a status symbol for men. Your family can be starving, but you have succeeded in life if you can stand around in town and discuss the greater things in life. Knowing that animals are a key indicator of a man's wealth one would think that the men of the village would round up their families and their flocks and show up together at the VET CAP. There were a few men, but this was an event for children between the ages of five and eleven. The kids started arriving with their animals right on schedule. Their first stop was the security gate, then a holding yard while they waited their turn to see the vet.

It didn't take long for the kids to realize that they could just circle back around and come to my table again and again. I caught on to the trick very quickly. I would just hand them a sucker and tell them to hit the road. The kids were just kids, but the adults were a different story. There were the men who were very appreciative. They just stopped by to say thank you and passed up on the give-a-ways. Then there were the rich folks who were demanding supplies and services for their herds of 100 or more. I had my hands full with a few of them.

Overall things were going very smoothly. Every now and then I would hear a big crashing sound and see a bull bust through one of our cattle chutes. The next sound would be the voice of SFC Hanlin, "Colonel Kelly I need a dollar." We had a sheet of plywood and each time we needed a new chute door cut it cost a dollar. Bull and cow chasing was one of the major events of the day. I had to play rodeo clown a few times chasing after a hostile cow here and there. SSG Bentley thought he would just flip a bull that got away. He grabbed the bull by the horns and the bull shook his head and SSG Bentley lost his grip on one horn and held tightly on the other. The result was the bull used SSG Bentley as a plow as he raced across the field. SPC Lopez who we call short round had better luck. He was standing at the chute when a calf broke through the door. He grabbed the calf by the ears as his feet swung out from under him, which was all it took to take the calf to the ground.

As the day grew older the Afghan ODA really started pitching in. The ANP (police) looked like they would be more comfortable at a donut shop. SFC Hanlin had problems with one young man whom the ANP finally zipped up and hauled away. I don't think the kid was going to have a good night. Sexual perversion is quite prevalent in Afghanistan among the men. I saw several public displays of affection between members of the police force. From a western perspective we would call their affection homosexuality, but the Afghan men will tell you it is not because they don't love the other man, it is all for pleasure.

When the event was finally over that's when the fun began. People started stealing everything. I was chasing a three-year old who had one of our shovels; SFC Lucas was chasing the vet techs who were in training and were stealing our supplies and equipment. Dr. Sofi's men were professional and on our side. The civil affairs folks from the FOB just left. We got loaded up in record time, but what a challenge it was.

We provided dismounted security to our trucks as they moved back to the FOB. Once all the trucks were parked, LTC Velte ordered everyone to shower and do laundry as protection against infection.

One by one everyone got cleaned up, but we were short on uniforms. We usually only packed two for a week because of the lack of space, and our uniforms were filthy, so a few of the troops including LTC Velte wore their PT (physical training) uniforms to the mess hall. When I arrived at the mess hall I was behind three female NCOs who all noticeably had a chip on their shoulder. The cooks had just put out several trays of chicken in the serve yourself line. These women picked up every piece of chicken and selected the piece they wanted leaving the rest in a pile for everyone else. I sat next to LTC Velte. Then I saw SPC Tanson come in and one of the three female NCO snapped at her and kicked her out of the mess hall for wearing her PT uniform. It was obvious that SPC Tanson was either a private or a specialist and an easy target for a bully. I ran out, got SPC Tanson and told her to dine in the mess hall. I went to address the NCO who kicked her out only to find her equally disrespectful to me. I reminded her of my rank and she changed her attack to being Ms. Nice polite and respectful. She left and I knew it was just a matter of time before we would have problems so I waited. SFC Natividad was next to arrived in his PTs, and then it was SSG Bentley who took the cake. He had a green tee shirt, back shorts and boots– the furthest thing from a PT uniform you could get. Just as soon as SSG Bentley sat down the post sergeant major came busting in and went straight for SSG Bentley. I told the sergeant major these were my men and they were going to dine in the mess hall. He attempted to use his position as the post sergeant major to dictate terms to me. I asked him to step outside and we settled thing, by me listening to his threats. I thanked him and let him know I would take it up with his commander, which I did.

I gave the evening about 30 minutes to cool down and paid a visit to the battalion commander and the sergeant major. These two were not the brightest bulbs on the string. It was starting to dawn on the battalion commander that I was coming from a higher command that was the main effort and it would be very embarrassing for him for things to go south because of his sergeant major. We parted friends, but his sergeant major started posting policy signs all over the mess hall. What a way for the 4th ID to say thank you. On my way out I noticed the battalion commander's and sergeant major's battle rattle on display. Both sets looked like they came off the showroom floor–not the slightest hint of use. You can not only administer from behind a desk, you must command in the field. Six months later when this unit would TOA (go home) we learned they stopped ordering critical supplies and almost went black on water. The Army uses colors to indicate the level of supplies. Green, amber, red and black. Black indicated non-mission capable.

Friday, I had another survey to do and the rest of the troops were going to service the weapons and vehicles. One of the platoons drove my survey team and Janet, our reporter, down to OP Pirtle King where we linked up with our security platoon. OP Pirtle King is smaller than a road side rest stop on an abandon highway, but the morale was very high. We talked over how we were going to conduct the survey, then loaded up and drove down to Ghazabad.

We reached the ANP station by a small bridge on route California, parked the vehicles and dismounted. We linked up with some ANP troops and crossed over another foot and light vehicle bridge. This time we didn't run, but we didn't waste any time either. We worked our way through several old graveyards that still had the ancient Nuristani grave markers. These grave markers are almost from a pagan era; they are pre-Islam and carved out of wood. We passed the graveyards and came up upon the village elder's house and agreed to have tea with him on our way back. On the north side of his house was a trail that overlooked the Kacagal River valley where it met the Kunar. It was quite a drop from where we were standing. The SecFor LT said, "There it is; how much do you want to see?"

I turned to him and said we need to survey a mile or so from inside the riverbed. "What? You mean you need to go down in there to do your job?" The next thing we heard was the LT on the radio calling out FRAGO, FRAGO, which means a change in the mission.

We dropped down into the riverbed and started our survey. At first the riverbed was nothing more than a sea of boulders. Within 500 meters there was a dramatic change in the geology and we found ourselves scaling granite walls. A cat is given whiskers to check if an opening is big enough to crawl through. Humans don't have such appendages. We are supposed to rely upon common sense and judgment. I would look at a small ledge and think *sure I could make that* and get halfway out there and remember *I'm wearing body armor which adds another eight inched to my size.*

The Kacagal River Valley runs from Afghanistan to Pakistan. Water is not the only thing that flows through the Kacagal valley. The SecFor LT called out 155 incoming up top. We could hear the echo of the impact as if it were only a few hundred yards away, but it was really several miles away. Whoever it was up in the mountains was just too quick for artillery. Soon there was a pair of Kiowas flying figure eights along the ridge line. A team of insurgents had been spotted with RPGs. They were far away from us so we really weren't worried.

Our survey was finally over and the SecFor LT needed to visit a mosque that was under construction; it was one of his projects. We could see the mosque as we worked our way up the valley. There wasn't a soul near it. Wouldn't you know it… just as we arrived the whole village was working on the mosque. They were making a good show of it just for us.

We left the mosque and returned to Ghazabad by walking along irrigation canals and terraces, which was a welcomed relief from all of the rock climbing we had been doing. We had about a mile to go when I slipped on a tennis ball size rock, went flying down hill and cracked both knees and chins. I recovered as gracefully as I could and kept going as if nothing was wrong. I knew I had to keep moving or I wouldn't be moving. For the next mile I was doing really well, then it was tea time. Oh nuts! Tea time means you have to sit cross legged for a long time.

Lucky for me the village elder had a bunch of plastic chairs on his patio for us. I had two cups of tea and several walnuts and explained what the next step would be for the flood control project. Then some of the police who were with us started talking about the Taliban. One officer was told to quit his job or be killed. The other came home to learn that the Taliban had stolen all of his animals. The village elder finally bid us farewell as the evening shadows were getting long and the temperature was dropping.

We got back in the trucks and headed north toward OP Pirtle King when the MRAP we were in started having problems. We reached OP Pirtle

King, switched vehicles on the road and kept going in the dark. Another convoy was coming south to meet us at the half way point from FOB Bostick. Once again we got out on the road and switched vehicles. We arrived back at FOB Bostick in time for dinner as they locked the doors.

Lights were out at 2100 and I was exhausted but really couldn't sleep so I just lay there on my cot. At 4:00 watch alarms were going off and everyone got up without saying a word. By 5:15 we were fully loaded and ready to roll but were told we had to stay put. The battalion operations officer at FOB Bostick forgot to coordinate our movement with the brigade. A little over an hour later we were on the road. We wanted to get an early start because historically the insurgents didn't attack convoys before 8:00. We wanted to be through all of the hot spots by 8:00 A.M.

We stopped on the road in front of OP Pirtle King, checked our weapons, answered nature's call and got back in the trucks. We passed Ghazabad and had a line of seven or eight cars behind us. The radio and intercom system in our truck was not working well. I was in the back running the radios. We had two stacks of FM radios that I would switch over to the appropriate frequency as we moved along Route California and a TAC SAT that I called in our checkpoints on. Every now and then the intercom system would ground out and let loose an ear piercing noise. It was all I could do to rip the head set off, the noise hurt so much. I tried switching to different jacks but it really didn't work any better.

We had just passed over a bridge on a hairpin turn when our trailing truck announced that all of the civilian vehicles had stopped. Janet said, "You know what that means?" I never like to get people worked up or worried especially when there is nothing they can do about the situation.

I told her "Yep we're going to get hit, but not here. There are too many people in this village; it will come later."

Sure enough at 9:00 A.M. we came around a spur and SFC Hanlin called out "there is a man standing up in a cave at my 3 o'clock." The next thing we heard was radio traffic. We were taking fire from nine o'clock. SSG Bentley dropped down out of the hatch after having one round ping off the top of his helmet and returned fire. I immediately jumped forward to start handing him ammo only to have my head snap back by the cable to my head set. Because I was having problems I plugged into a jack on the other side of the vehicle. Janet was my angel and un-tangled me. I got a can of 50 cal. ammo ready to shove up to SSG Bentley. SPC Lopez, who was driving, called out, "They are in the draw 9 o'clock."

SSG Bentley called out "Colonel Kelly where are you?"

"I'm right here at your feet ready to give you ammo."

"I don't need no stinken ammo; I need fucking targets."

Oh. Silly me what was I thinking? Of course you need targets first. I went to see if I could find any. Janet was already looking out the side window, but we had passed the draw and they were hidden by the crest of the hill. Our truck was out of the kill zone but we had two more coming around the spur that still had to pass through the kill zone.

Sgt Carter, the gunner on our fifth vehicle, cracked the radio and told SFC Natividad that his driver's side front tire was flat. SFC Natividad called back, "I also have a hole in my windshield."

SFC Hanlin then called for a status report. Victor 2 Green over Green, Victor 3 Green over Green, and it continued to Victor 6. I had patted SSG Bentley down looking for blood and he seemed okay. Everyone was okay. (We use the word victor for vehicle, so Victor 1 is the first vehicle in the convoy.)

This is the location on Route California where the 40th ADT was ambushed on December 19th going south. This photo was taken on December 15th traveling north.

Farther down the road we met a patrol going north and told them what happened. They were quite excited. They were hunters and then the hunters would be hunted. We had only stopped for three or four minutes, just enough time to pass on grids (locations of the bad guys) and kept going. The patrol moved about 500 meters north and we could hear contact and artillery raining down.

We pulled into COP Monti to check our vehicles and swap out the tire on SFC Natividad's MRAP. The boys at the shop were more than happy to help us with their wrecker. The wheel had to be beaten off with a sludge hammer because of the intense heat that had been generated from running on the rim flat. (A rim flat is a heavy plastic wheel which is inside the tire that allows you to keep driving at a good clip.) We asked if we could have lunch at Monti and their cooks put some more burgers on the grill for us. I noticed that their mess hall was 100% heat and serve. Once again I Club Med.

We found a few bullet holes in our vehicles. The odd thing was our rolling barn only had two rounds in it. With all of the machine gun fire we received they couldn't hit the broad side of a barn. We counted six rounds that struck our vehicles. That was pretty poor shooting for some folks who had all the time in the world to set up an ambush. They even had a road guard at the bridge to stop the civilian traffic.

Our final hour on the road was uneventful, but we still had to unload all of the equipment before we could call it a day. Upon arrival our first sergeant, bless his heart, had assigned guard duty to four of the troops who were on the mission. The guard shifts were six hours long starting at midnight. LTC Velte, SFC Hanlin and SFC Fulton, and I each took two hours so the troops could get their needed rest.

I came on shift at 2:00 A.M. and pulled duty with SGT Eden. The first thing he told me was he heard what I did for the troops in the mess hall back at FOB Bostick. I told him I had handled it outside where no one could see us. He said "I know. I was there. Here is what you said..."

I responded, "Just where were you?"

"Oh I was back in the shadows. I had your six just in case something when wrong. I may be a bit old but I can still throw a punch or two if needed. You did good sir. You know that sergeant major stays in his quarters all the time working on real estate courses. His troops hate him."

Chapter Twenty-Two

CHRISTMAS

Just before Christmas, we went into Asadabad to conduct a market survey. I went to a furniture shop to see about having some Lincoln logs made while the rest of my section along with the commander walked the produce market. You would be very surprised at the amount of importation that goes on. For example they buy their flour from Russia, vegetables from Pakistan, honey from India and China, dried peas from the United States, spices from Iran, and electronics from Western Europe.

We were constantly told by the representatives from the State Department and non-governmental agencies that these people are so poor they have nothing. When I walked the streets of Asadabad I noticed several cell phone shops selling the top of the line phones, other stores selling personal electronics (no computers), hardware stores, motor shops, and fabric store after fabric store. There were many shops that catered to women's desires such as bath and beauty products, jewelry–you name it. Hmmm we are told that women are beneath the male society, so why are there stores that cater to women?

Even though many of us saw Christmas just as a milestone to the deployment there were several Christmas events going on. The chaplain hosted a choral event at the motor pool, we decorated the inside of the chapel, the mess hall was all decked out with cards sent by school children from across the states, and we even decorated our briefing room. (It was about time too.)

We started receiving care packages for Christmas in late October by the boat load. I started writing thank you letters to every organization that sent us a package. SFC Mead and I were talking about the overwhelming amount of support that was arriving. It was remarkable that after eight years of war people were still sending us care packages. These care packages are nothing cheap! The postage starts at $17.00; some were as much as $30.00. Churches and community clubs sent the best quality of any item they selected and tons of candy. We had surplus war candy from Thanksgiving, Halloween and the Fourth of July. We sorted the care packages after Christmas and ended up with half a pallet of candy.

Christmas Eve day Spc Larson and I started the project of decorating our briefing room. The first chore was to round up over 300 Christmas care packages. I started opening them up by removing all of the address labels, which meant cutting off the box tops. Once that job was over I got the hint that I was more in the way than part of the solution. So I took all of the box tops and custom forms up the hill to the burn barrel and lit them up. We have to destroy all of the address labels for operational security and to protect people at home from extortion.

Life on Camp Wright is very simple: work until you drop from exhaustion. So troops really don't have a need for anything from Santa. The best gift you can give them is a little extra sleep. After LTC Velte and I pulled guard duty one night after a very long mission word got around of our support for the troops. With our example, the officers of the ADT decided to pull guard duty starting Christmas Eve and ending at midnight Christmas Day. LTC Velte and I got the ECP tower (Entry Control Point). We got up in the tower and Sgt Stevens and Sgt Carter briefed us on the requirements, we then departed. Guard duty isn't that bad if you have someone to share it with. Things were very peaceful. I was expecting an attack or at the very least a few RPGs shot our way but nothing. Then it came. At 4:00 o'clock two out-of-tune Christmas carolers came up to the tower. SFC Hanlin and SFC Fulton arrived to relieve us of guard duty. We told them we wanted to do this and they refused to leave. We finally agreed to leave. Then SFC Hanlin said, "Sirs what happens in the ECP tower stays in the ECP tower. Be back here at 5:30 in time for shift change. The commander and Major Leeney are at the blue gate, which means cut through the airfield and go around back."

We returned at 5:30 to find SFC Fair and Natividad pulling guard. The real shift change occurred at 6:00 o'clock and no one was the wiser. When Sgt Carter arrived he asked, "Aren't you guys cold up here? Why don't you turn on the heater?" I looked down and saw that we did have an electric space heater. I pressed the "on" button.

I noted that something smelled funny. LTC Velte said, "Fire."

"What?"

"Fire, look behind you." Sure enough the wall socket was on fire.

I hit the off switch and LTC Velte said, "Pull the plug." SGT Carter pulled the heater plug out of the socket by the cord only to find the plug was nothing more than a molten ball of burning plastic. A quick stomp and the fire was history.

Christmas day was very quiet. I walked into our briefing room to find most of the SecFor just sitting in the chairs as if they were waiting for a briefing; they were surrounded by tons of goodies to eat. Spc Larson and I loaded up a wheelbarrow full of gifts from the city of La Habra Heights. SFC Velasco (Our intel NCOIC) hooked up her puppy to the front of the wheelbarrow to act as a reindeer as we delivered the gifts with our commander playing Santa to the troops in the barracks.

Christmas evening LTC Velte and I had the blue gate for our final guard shift. Christmas night was just like Christmas eve: temperatures in the low 30s and brilliant moon light. SFC Hanlin came out to wish us the best for the evening and pointed out the constellation Orion. LTC Velte remarked how much his foster dad loved stargazing. I could also remember going to Alvin meadows with my dad and he would point out all of the different constellations, but I couldn't tell one star from another there were so many of them then. Nowadays I can't think of any place in California where you can see all of the stars due to the pollution.

We had a steady stream of troops coming back in from the field that night as I watched the stars circle around us. The moon slowly meandered across the sky to the western mountains. An hour before midnight the moon was casting shadows across the road and the western slope of the eastern mountains started to reflect the moon's glow. Finally at midnight the moon set behind the western mountains bathing the eastern mountains in a silver hue. The hours of Christmas were finally over and our relief arrived.

The next few days we spent getting ready for our next Vet Cap and developing drawings for crib walls and concrete molds. We had four days of missions coming up, which would wipe us out. SGT Stevens went on all of the missions because they were centered on crop development. I went out on two watershed / flood control missions. If my name was called for a mission it means we are going to do a lot of hiking or were going someplace that isn't tourist friendly.

December 29th we went up to FOB Blessing, which is about an hour up the Pech River. Our mission was to test the water quality in a bunch of wells, to conduct a market survey and to assess an erosion problem. We arrived just after breakfast, met up with three captains, a civilian veterinarian and the same US USAID who had announced a few months earlier that they were going to establish an office at FOB Blessing without consulting us. I had very little confidence in the USAID rep.

We departed the FOB on foot out the eastern gate and followed the irrigation ditches across several farms to a small village, the home of the first well site. SGTs Stevens and Flynn took water and soil samples while SFC Hanlin and I supported security. Our commander was making himself a big target with the civilians and the three captains all standing in a tight huddle. We got our samples and moved up the Waygal River (also known as the Walo Tang River) to another small village. The village had one public well that had gone dry and a flour mill that was powered from the irrigation canal. From there we followed the banks of the Waygal River to the Village of Nagalam to do our market assessment. Once again they imported things from around the world. We were somewhat concerned about a snatch and grab so SFC Hanlin and I stayed close together and kept a sharp eye on SGT Flynn and Stevens. SGT Stevens and Flynn with the aid of our interpreters interviewed the local vendors. The town had just about every store a homebody would need to survive on their National Guard retirement if they decided to retire in Nagalam. Along the way Sgt Stevens and Flynn sampled the wells in town.

SGT Stevens and Percival take soil samples at Mr. Mohamad Yosuf farm near the Waygal River. Soil testing is very expensive in Afghanistan because all samples must be sent to Pakistan for evaluation.

A micro hydro power plant over a side canal of the Waygal River. Corn stalks are stored in the trees so that the animals don't eat them. SFC Hanlin provides security during movement to the village of Nagalam December 29th 2009

Our commander had once again collected a large crowd while he was examining some chickens. Spc Larson and our medic answering questions from the children. One little boy asked her for a pen, she said no, then he asked her for some candy, again she said no. Then the boy vulgarly demanded that she display a private part of her anatomy to the public. The boy knew what he was saying. The sad part is an American service men had to have taught him the words he used. Then again what America exports in music these days in not Rodgers and Hammerstein. I had to grin and bear the gangster rap the troops listen to, which is all lewd vulgarity.

We finally worked our way to the end of town to the spot where if we were going to get shot at it would be there. SFC Hanlin and I took a quick look around for a place to defend from and decided on a nice dugout section with a tall building wall to our backs. We took a pee and started scanning our sectors when SFC Hanlin said, "Hey Sir do you smell something?"

"Yes I think we are in the men's central urinal."

"Yes sir and judging by the smell there are a lot of men in this town." With that we found a new place to perch for a while. As we took up our new position SFC Hanlin ripped the crotch out of his pants.

"Oh no Sir can you see anything? How far did I rip my pants?" When you have you body armor on you can't see what's going on down below.

I told him, "You're fine. It's a small rip; no one should notice. That is no one who is 6'-3". SGTs Stevens and Flynn had finished collecting their water samples and it was time to move on. We walked through a few back alleyways then finally back out on the main street to avoid any possible contact. No sooner did we hit the street a little boy pointed out the rip in SFC Hanlin's pants, and so did just about every little kid back through town.

As we cleared the town, SFC Hanlin said, "You know Sir being in the Army is a lot like being in a motorcycle gang except your parents are so proud of you." This was in response to our taking over the streets like a bunch of bikers.

We walked through town down on route Rhode Island to a spot on the Pech River. My commander and the USAID rep said this is where we want to dam the Pech and build a micro hydro power plant. I asked USAID's finest how much power they need and where they need it. "Oh we want to power the whole town." Seeing my boss standing behind beaming with support for the idea I really had to bite my tongue. I asked a few questions and received the anticipated answers accompanied with the deer in the headlights look from Mr. USAID. My first question was about designing and building the power grid for the town. You don't install a generator and tell people to plug in. Mr. USAID came up with this idea when the river was at its low point of the year. The Pech at the point where we were standing was 100 feet wide and three feet deep. During the spring thaw it rises another 10 feet and increases its width by another 25 to 50 feet. This would be no backyard micro hydro power plant. The problem is, even with a solid design the craftsmanship and quality control of construction in Afghanistan is so poor the dam would fail causing major down stream destruction. We stopped at another well on the west side of the FOB and returned for a late lunch.

The Pech and Waygal River valleys are really nice. During lunch the guys started talking about their fly-fishing trips and how their fathers taught them to fly fish. They compared the area to a movie Robert Redford made about a preacher's family up in Montana who taught his two sons how to fly fish. The movie was based on the real life of the author who grew up on the Big Blackfoot River in Missoula Montana. The title of the movie came from one line in a poem, "And a river runs through it." The poem was about how all life's events eventually come together for some significant meaning. Like any other fish story they soon confessed that they were never really any good at fly fishing. The rivers there are highly contaminated, but they run crystal clear.

In the morning while we were hiking up the Waygal River I noticed a convoy driving down the other side with two Kiowas in support. The Kiowas stayed with them all the way back to the FOB Blessing. It was a platoon that was directed to go up into the Taliban's territory. There had been an unwritten agreement that the Taliban would stay up north and the U.S. would stay down south. This agreement was brokered by the villages in the middle. They wanted to just stay out of the fight. A few years back there was a US FOB up there that got overrun. After that the US started looking over the area and decided that there just wasn't enough population up in the north to justify maintaining FOB. With that the U.S. decided to close the smaller FOBs. I've seen the locations of these FOBs; they were very isolated and difficult to support due to the lack of roads. It was the right move to close the FOBs up there. It is prudent to just wait until there is a road structure to support the smaller FOBs. Then again I don't know how you would justify building roads up there with the sparse amount of population.

Sgt Steven, Flynn, and a team of our own SecFor and I loaded up in the 4th ID's MRAPS and took off to look at an erosion problem. The last five times this platoon went to the erosion location they had contact (were shot at). We arrived at Walo Tangi Kaley (Kaley means village in English) the 4th ID Platoon leader waved us forward and we followed him through the village as fast as we could, almost at a dead run. The village was about 150 feet above the Waygal River, which meant it was a steep drop to the river. There was one muddy alleyway that sloped at about 60 degrees with steps made out of river boulders. Each step was a drop of 18 inches to two feet. We reached the bottom of the alley in time to see the Platoon leader with the Wonder boy from the USAID race down some irrigation canals. These irrigation canals are just trenches dug in the earth with a slippery curb on either side. On one side you had a muddy wheat field and the other was a 20-foot drop. You don't want to walk in the wheat fields because the mud will cake itself on your boots.

I kept looking back to check if the rest of the troops were with us. All I could see were two 4th ID troops and assumed our SecFor was not far behind. Sgt Flynn was the first to reach the river. Sgt Stevens and I were right on his heels. We found the river okay, but the 4th ID Platoon leader was nowhere to be found. "Sgt Stevens said I don't like this Sir." I responded that I didn't either. I snapped a few shots with my camera when our two trailing 4th ID troops found their platoon leader. He had doubled back around and let us be the bait for the insurgents.

The platoon leader showed us the erosion problem and asked, "Well what do we do?" Sgt Stevens and I told him to just build a wall. We'd seen enough. Turns out without my knowing it the platoon leader ordered my SecFor to stay with the trucks. I don't mind sticking my neck out, but when people are not on the up and up with you from the get go why risk it?

When we got back to FOB Blessing I told SFC Natividad what had happened. His response was "Oh this is just like fly fishing except using American service men for bait." Yep and a river runs through it.

It was dark when we departed FOB Blessing. The PRT convoy that had moved out two hours ahead of us had an engagement along the way. At first we thought we were going to get tied up with the same Pech River Valley love affair. That's when another one of SFC Hanlin's proverbs came to mind, "Never marry the same woman twice." The same logic holds true for attaching convoys. I got to thinking, *the insurgents get paid based upon the videos they sell in Pakistan. We were moving at night, and unless you have some very expensive equipment you're not doing any night filming.* The insurgents also know we can see in the dark just like the light of day so why make it easy for us? Small arms fire against the insurgents is very effective even more so than artillery. You use artillery for a few things; first it gives them a headache from the noise; second after the big boom they jump up and run just like playing Marco Polo in the pool. Coming home to FOB Wright was dark and uneventful.

The next morning came early as usual, which I like because we could cut through Asadabad and most of the other little towns quickly. Also the insurgents are just like gang members; they like to sleep in. We arrived at COP Able Main just after breakfast and met up with LT. Harris, who would be our escort for the day. He laid out the plan for the day and we loaded up in the trucks to tour the local farms. This was a different experience for us. Usually when we are in a village the locals cluster around us and beg for pens and candy and attempt to pick our pockets. This time SGTs Stevens and Percival were treated like old college professors. When they would take their soil samples the kids and farmers would gather around and ask questions. They were all very interested in the process and just what the two NCOs could learn from looking at their soil. We stopped at villages with names like Gobay, Shekasay, Bardog, Danda and Passman Nagi.

The village of Passman Nagi was the reason I was on the mission; they had a water problem. We had returned to the COP for lunch and a bunch of the Able Main troops had the spicy sausage. Our troops resisted the temptation because they didn't know what effect it might have during the ride home. We really didn't know what we were in for next. We did know that we were walking over to Passman Nagi village and it was right up the road across from the COP. I should have been more in tune with what was going on. The 4th ID Mountain Boys were making this sound far too easy.

We walked out the front gate, crossed Route Rhode Island and started up a dirt road. Sure it was steep but nothing really taxing. Then we made a sharp diversion straight up the side of the mountain. The 4th Mountain boys were going to attempt to smoke us on their mountain. In the course of 30 minutes, we climbed 748 feet according to my GPS and about 1500 meters inward. We were able to stay with them all the way to the top, thanks to the spicy sausage. Seems the sausage was kicking them like a mule. I noticed the troops that recovered the quickest from the climb were the same troops I saw in the gym every night.

The start of a 600 foot climb to Passman Nagi village.

When we got to the top there was a school under construction. At the construction site they were casting their own concrete bricks and doing a good job at it too. Sgt Stevens interviewed the village elder. Then we went over to a lemon orchard by way of a 14-inch wide plank bridge that crossed a 60-foot crevice. We took turns crossing the bridge that was designed for a half starved Afghani not a 6'-3" American soldier with 90 pounds of gear. I could feel a nice spring in my step as I moved across. We finished up the visit to the orchard and then it was off to our water problem.

I had seen what I thought was an electrical conduit running across the ground. I didn't think much of it since they did have power coming up the mountain on utility poles. That conduit turned out to be the new water line. The water line was a conflict resolution project. A water line was built so that two villages would stop fighting. The village on the receiving end claimed that the other village was holding back water. The problem was the line was too small. The contractor had ripped the Army off by installing ½ EMT conduit for the 1200-foot run. I told the LT that I would get him some pipe.

New Year's Eve and day were very quiet and uneventful, which is the way I like it. I had a chance to read the paper about healthcare reform in America and just shake my head in disbelief when I saw what the rest of the world has for basic emergency medical treatment.

A few days earlier on December 28th a young boy up in Naray found a piece of unexploded ordnance and brought it home to his older ten-year-old brother. When his brother went to throw it away, it detonated blowing off three fingers on his right hand and putting shrapnel into his left foot. The family had their oldest son bring him to the Afghanistan hospital at Camp Wright. It was a three-day journey that started with a bus ride followed by a taxi trip to the front gate of the camp.

We don't think twice about calling 9-1-1 for the smallest medical emergency then watch the minute hand counting the seconds until the paramedics arrive.

Coming to a U.S. installation places the lives of the whole family at risk. The insurgent will either kill the head of the household or chop off the right hand of everyone in the family or village. This family was willing to risk their lives for medical treatment for their son.

We have many things to be thankful for.

Chapter Twenty-Three

KCC AND THE WITCHES TETON

The Kunar and Nuristan regions of Afghanistan received their hundred-year storm in 2008 according to many village elders we interviewed. A hundred year storm is not a scheduled event in the all famous "Farmer's Almanac." The term comes from the probability of a storm of a certain magnitude occurring once every 100 years, or there is a one in one-hundred chance of the same severe storm occurring every year. Water is a major part of our mission statement. The word "water" means water for livestock, irrigation canals, drinking water, wells, irrigation systems, and flood and erosion control. (Oddly enough damming the Pech River and building a one megawatt hydroelectric plant with substations and power grid is not. There are a few wandering idiots who still think it is.) Fall and winter is the best time to work on flood and erosion control before the snow melts and the rains return.

The ADT had been busting a gut surveying the countryside and assembling all of the data to get designs off the drawing board. It was no small effort. For what we accomplished my troops had a lot to be proud of. The engineering for the flood and erosion control systems required the use of new technology for our area of Afghanistan. Our plans required the introduction of crib walls constructed of interlocking concrete Lincoln logs and cable block. Cable block is a bunch of concrete blocks that are linked together with cable; they are used for roads, dry river crossings, and other places where erosion is a problem. Both of these systems require the ability to cast concrete in molds. The molds do not exist in Afghanistan or Pakistan, so we needed to build them. After several failed attempts with the locals we decided to go to the KCC (Kunar Construction Collage). After all, they had trained instructors there with a complete woodshop and the ability to bend re-bar.

We loaded up the wagons on Sunday January 3rd and headed up to the KCC with our CAD drawings in Pashto in hand. Getting to the KCC can be a surprise trip with hill 1311. Hill 1311 is where the insurgents like to shoot at convoys. The nice thing is they shoot from the same two places every time. So Sgt Olson just had the big guns lay on the targets as we approached Hill 1311 just in case someone needed to have an etiquette lesson. Once you're inside the KCC you are safe. You can have a picnic in the center of the school and take a nap in the sunshine. No one will harm you. The commander of the local insurgency has many family members who work at the school or attend it. The KCC is known as the Taliban retirement program.

The Taliban retirement system works like this. Once insurgents are off the payroll they show up at an outreach office with a firearm. The cost to enter the retirement system is one firearm. Unlike admission to Disneyland where each person is required to purchase their own ticket one firearm will buy admission for all of the people who can fit into the courtyard ceremony. The deal is: you (the insurgent) show up at the outreach office with your firearm and sign a pact that you will reform from your wandering ways and live like a good member of the community. The administrator then leads you into the courtyard and places your firearm on an old engine block and hands you a sludge hammer. You strike the weapon several times rendering it useless. The concept is to beat your sword into a plowshare. Usually three to five men will show up with a pistol that isn't worth its weight in scrap to enter the program. They never present a fully functional AK-47. God forbid they just might need it again if the insurgent pay increases. There are several reasons the men show up at these centers. First their sponsor hasn't been paying their bills, or they were injured and can't fight the Americans like they did before. These men are given a full ride at U.S. taxpayers' expense to the KCC. Anyone else must pay their own tuition and board. Attendance usually increases in the winter months and drops off in the summer months. This corresponds with the fighting. The winter months see a lull in the fighting while the fighting peaks in the summer months.

That should give you an idea of what the KCC is all about. The students are ex-insurgents; the teachers and staff are family members of the area insurgent commander. (I use the term insurgent commander for lack of a more descriptive term. Shadow militia commander or tribal warlord might be more descriptive.) We still thought they would be the best bet to have some forms made. Notice I didn't use the word Taliban. That's because not all of the insurgents are members of the Taliban. Some insurgent commanders are the true governing officials in an area. They assume the role of protecting and administering the area. Some do a very good job and do not want outsiders to dictate terms to them.

Upon arrival at KCC, we met with the master of instruction. Then we met with their business manager about the project. They were all for it they could see the fat little dollars rolling in the door. The next step was to meet with the instructors who would oversee the fabrication of the forms and re-bar cages. I let SSG Lucas take the reins since he knew more about concrete than I did. Soon I was giving little side classes to the instructors on how to read a ruler. SSG Lucas and I were very careful to make everything come out in full inches. The only thing that required fractions was the re-bar. We had checked out the local re-bar and the re-bar in other villages. They were all using the American standard re-bar, which meant it was measured in 8ths of an inch. If you're asked for a number three rebar you would receive a piece that was 3/8 of an inch in diameter. We didn't find anyone who sold metric re-bar. If you did ask for 10mm re-bar you received #3. After two hours of going over three drawings we realized that we needed to build a set of molds for the instructors and team teach with them when they built their molds.

1SSG Lucas going over plans for concrete molds and re-bar with the instructors at the KCC January 3rd 2010. The location is inside the cabinet shop of the KCC.

On New Year's Day LTC Velte and I set out to meet with the village elder of Woch Now. Woch Now is located in the Arga Del valley behind the FOB. It had been years since anyone from the FOB had paid them a visit. This village guarded the back door to the FOB so it made sense to make friends with them. Before dawn I sent a four-man team up on the Yargul Gharah ridge. Our commander accompanied us to provide security for our trip up the valley.

Our unit was a little different from other ADTs, PRTs and sadly most of the infantry units we worked with. Their motto is if you can't drive there you don't go there. We did a lot of dismounted patrols and surveys. The Ag section started the dismounted missions and word quickly spread about the positive experience. At first folks thought dismounted was more risky than driving in an MRAP. Turns out you're much safer on foot, but you need to have a fair amount of self confidence.

When my dad and I went to Chicago, I took him on a hike to several bookstores. I was looking for two books about the Soviet experience in Afghanistan. The first was <u>The Bear Went Over the Mountain</u> written from the Russian viewpoint and the companion book <u>The Other Side of the Mountain</u> written from the Afghan viewpoint. There is a proverb that states a fool learns from his own mistakes, but a wise man learns from the mistakes of others. The one thing the Russians didn't do was get out of their vehicles or make good use of their infantry. When they did use their infantry the Afghans would retreat in a route. The Afghan's quickly learned that a few well placed shots at dismounted Russians would turn them away. The Russians' artillery was ineffective and their air support had its limits as well. The most effective weapon the Russians had was dismounted infantry and they were very reluctant to use them. The Kunar ADT quickly learned that small arms fire was very effective against the insurgents.

The Russians were reluctant to send their infantry up into the mountains because they feared the Afghans. The Afghans were born in the mountains and they knew every cave and water hole. Oddly the same viewpoint is held by many American commanders I met. Our unit's mission is centered on agriculture and water. Food grows where water flows. Water flows from the mountains to the villages in the valleys below. There is only one way to inspect a pipe system, a spring or a retention dam; that is to hike back into the mountains and look at it. One reason U.S. commanders are reluctant to send troops dismounted into the countryside, is the lack of troops at their disposal. Bottom line: there are not enough U.S. combat troops in the region to effectively combat the insurgents.

Our mission was to inspect the springs that fed Woch Now village. This would require a lot a walking. LTC Velte had nothing against walking, but after our little hike up to Passman Nagi he was of the mindset, "Why walk any more than you have to." He was in for a surprise that day.

When we reached the back gate of the FOB there were two ANA Toyota pickups waiting for us. One team of SecFor loaded up into the first truck with Sgt Johanson hanging on the back like a fireman with his AT-4 slung over his back, and off they went. We gave them a five-minute head start then loaded up in the second truck. The old joke of how many people can you fit into a Jingle truck holds true for ANA Toyota pickups too: always one more! Oh, guess what, a 6'-3" American soldier with full battle rattle doesn't fit inside the cab of a Toyota. It took some effort for the remainder of us to load up, but we did. We had traveled less than a quarter of a mile when we saw our SecFor taking up positions along the side of the road. LTC Velte asked "Am I wrong or are those our troops?" Yep they were ours. We stopped, wiggled out of the cab and joined the SecFor on the road. SSG Arnold decided that the risk of having Sgt Johanson doing a back flip off the back of the pickup wasn't worth the comfort of the luxury ride to the village.

When the day was over LTC Velte stated, "That little quarter mile ride in the morning made all the difference in the world."

It was a good little walk up the road to Woch Now Village where we met the village elder at the mosque. The village of Woch Now is home to twenty families with a population of about 60 people. Their main crop is rock.

Laj Bar, the village elder, stated that the insurgents had destroyed the pipe system from the spring and they were thinking of abandoning the village. LTC Velte asked Laj Bar where the spring was. He pointed up the side on the mountains as if it were just a quick short walk. I had seen this trick before and knew that it was going to be no short walk in the park. LTC Velte asked Laj Bar if could guide us up to the spring without the 30 little kids who had gathered around us. Laj Bar agreed and we were off to the Witch's Teton. The Witch's Teton was a tall conic peak that stood out like a castle turret from the ridge. This was the first major obstacle in route to the springs.

Looking south from the mosque at Woch Now Village; the Witch's Teton is the second peak from the right in the background. January 4th 2010.

There were several reasons to look at the spring. First of all, the village elder stated that the "Taliban" destroyed his water pipe system because it was paid for by Americans. I didn't believe it because he had running water from the spring in the village. Second, when our FOB got mortared some of the positions were from back in the valley. That can't be observed by either of our two O.P.s or Willie the Whale, our eye in the sky. So we decided to have a little look around. Last of all we needed to learn our mountains. The one thing the insurgents didn't want is Americans who know how to get around in their mountains.

We followed the water pipe from the village to the spring because there was no established trail. I would stop every so often and take GPS readings and a few photos of the condition of the pipe. Whoever purchased the pipe was able to buy some high quality material.

On the ridge above us were our commander, SFC Fair, SSG Tyner, and our medic SGT Bentley. We had moved about 200 yards when the spurs of the ridge line obscured their vision of us and they had to re-position. They were concerned that any movement would attract attention and their presences would be known. The concern was soon voided when women were walking back and forth without their burqas on tending their cow patties. The locals use cow patties to cook on so they collect them and put them in an area with lots of sun to dry out.

We finally made it to the base of the Witches Teton and once again out of sight of our over watch. Sgt Bentley was able to use the scope on his rifle to snap a few photos of us working the granite face before we disappeared. Our over watch was wondering just how we were going to scale up the turret.

SecFor team members starting up Lucifer's stair case the rock face of the Witch's Teton.

Lucky for us we found an old "Gujer's" trail that had long since been abandoned. The Gujers are one of the many tribes that live in the hills and are not accepted by the Pashtos. What I have titled a trail was nothing more than a pile of rocks supported by a rotting stick that later gave way on our decent. We finally arrived at the summit of the Witches Teton where I could see the water pipe again. How on earth they were able to snake that pipe around the cliff was beyond me. I got out on the ledge as far as I could go and took some photos of the pipe, then I realized that we were living a Wile E. Coyote cartoon. What we thought was the summit was nothing more than a granite out cropping that cantilevered out over the canyon ready to let go. Laj Bar told us that the spring was just 100 feet away. This wonderful elder couldn't tell the truth even if his soul depended upon it.

Lucifer's staircase well behind us still climbing to the top. SFC Natividad far left, rear detachment of SecFor below.

We still needed to cross over the peak of the Witch's Teton to get to the springs. We had to hug the face of the turret while working our way up a granite staircase.

We popped up on top of the peak to the surprise of our over watch who joked that there must have been an elevator hidden on the other side due to our speed. It didn't feel like we were moving all that fast, but slow is smooth and smooth is fast. We had anticipated that we would be going down the backside of the Witch's Teton, but once again we were deceived by the terrain. The turret had masked over several other rock formations that were not visible from the base. We worked our way into a draw and found several abandoned rock buildings and a perfect location for a mortar pit. I GPSed their locations and took some photos. Our SecFor had cleared the buildings as we approached them. I took a careful look at the footprints inside and noted that there were many made by tennis shoes.

It was hard to say if the other foot prints were those of insurgents who had spent the night and stashed their supplies or just locals who had used the place as a refuge. I couldn't enter the buildings with my gear on. The door was too low and narrow. I pulled off my battle rattle and turned sideways to enter. There was evidence of indoor cooking or heating from the soot that covered the ceiling and the support columns for the roof. There was also an outdoor kitchen and what looked like a root cellar. This structure had two rooms that had a small pass-through window. To access each room you had to go outside, which led me to think that there were two families who shared the dwelling.

We also noted bloodstains on the rocks in several places, but without any way of testing it we didn't know if it was from goats or people. The draw that we entered fed into a large canyon that was ribbed with several spurs. We worked our way around anther spur to find the drippings of the spring and the return of the pipe line. It was another hundred yards of climbing over rocks to the spring. If we had elected we could have continued up to the ridge line and worked our way back over the Yargul Gharah ridge to O.P. Shiloh.

The spring was well developed. It was covered to protect it from rockslides and animals, with an overflow spout. Buried a few inches below the overflow spout was a one-inch galvanized pipe that wrapped around the rock face of the canyon held in place only by the occasional rock out cropping. The pipe had been damaged and repaired several times using PVC pipe, plastic bags secured with tape, and rubber garden hoses. Laj Bar said he needed 400 meters of new pipe. I paced out a total of 100 feet and that included a 20% fudge factor. We agreed to provide him with the repair materials and headed back to the village. We had climbed a total of 1200 feet to look at a pipe, and now it was time to go back down.

Going down would be a little more difficult than going up. The rocks and soil on the mountainside were very unstable. There were a few times I found myself standing upright and sliding five to ten feet as the ground gave way. Large rocks that looked fully embedded in the earth would suddenly break free from their slumber and roll down the hill when stepped upon. You would hear the crash and echo as they ricocheted off the canyon walls.

Our over watch radioed us that they would link up with us at the village and started their decent the same time we did. They had stayed in the shadow of the mountain until they came across some young girls tending goats on the mountainside. They stepped out of the shade and startled the kids. They had no clue that there were troops in the mountains. Usually the kids are the first to know of any changes in the mountains. SFC Fair asked them what direction was to the village, in Pashto, and a little girl pointed to a goat trail. He thanked her with some candy.

LTC Velte and I had tea with the village elder in the back of the mosque, discussed his needs and drew some pictures on how to repair the pipe. The concept wasn't getting through, so we told him that we would bring him an example. About this time the troops found a two-year-old boy whose hand injury had turned into gangrene. The SecFor medic was working on him while SGT Bentley was patching up another kid. The SecFor medic realized that his patient needed more help than he could give. We arranged to take him on post to have our doctors look him over. His older brother carried him for about ¾ of a mile. LTC Velte escorted them in through the entry control point while the rest of the troops just walked through the truck gate.

The doctor looked the hand over and told the older brother that the infection had advanced and the hand might have to be amputated if they couldn't get the infection under control. The older brother allowed the doctor to clean up the boy's hand and agreed to administer the antibiotics the doctor gave him. He promised to come back the following day with their father. I doubted we'd ever see the kid or the father again. The last thing you want to do is grow up missing a hand in this country even though they no longer cut hands off for crimes.

Chapter Twenty-Four

WE NEED BLOOD

We were in the process of getting ready for several Vet Caps in the Pech River Valley. As a goodwill gesture we decided to host a Vet Cap at our range for the villages around Camp Wright. We expected about 1000 animals judging by what we could count up in the hills. In the book, "Three Cups of Tea," the author describes how friendships are built over the course of meeting for tea three times. The first tea is just an introduction, the second you get to know one another and the third tea you're friends. This was a very true observation of the culture. We had already had tea with Laj Bar and this Vet Cap would be the first time we would work together for the betterment of the local communities. What I couldn't see at the time was how much our friendship would develop and what role Woch Now would play in the introduction of new construction technology to Kunar.

The Afghan know how to make two types of structures for flood and erosion control, gabion baskets and rock retaining walls. USAID prefers us to use gabions as a cure all for all erosion and flood control problems. The Afghans prefer rock retaining walls from rock they dig out of the hillside and a poor grade of cement. They do not use reinforcing steel in their walls, which is why they have a tendency to fall over. Their concrete dissolves too because they insist on using the sand and rock from the river, which is all nice and round. Both gabions and rock walls have their place, but they are just one tool in the toolbox and have specific purposes. Crib walls could solve many other problems that rock walls and gabions couldn't.

I spent the first half of Tuesday January 5th developing a bill of materials for crib wall forms, re-bar and what it would take to build several crib walls at different locations. While I was working, one of my troops stationed at the Blue gate stated possible indirect fire. While he was transmitting, the indirect fire alarm went off. I put on my battle rattle and headed to the bunker. Having one round impact is like having the neighbor's dog bark once in the wee hours of the morning. It wakes you up and you just lie there waiting for the dog to bark again. The same holds true for indirect fire; you just wait for the next round. The insurgents do not use the same approach on indirect fire as the modern world does, where one round is fired then it is adjusted until the target is destroyed. The usual method is to fire one round short, one long, then split the distance and place the last one on target. The insurgents just drop a round in the tube and hope it lands somewhere close to the target then run like hell before the 155s counter fire, or a Kiowa sees them. After a few minutes the all clear was given and life returned to normal again.

Just before dinner the call went out on the radio that the ANA (Afghan National Army) had an engagement. The trauma center declared a mass casualty and called for all medics. Our medics were standing by as the first Black Hawk landed. They only dropped one of the casualties off; he was the most critical. The rest were flown to Jalalabad. Sgt Bentley, the Ag platoon medic, saw that the man was bleeding to death and went to grab some Hextens but the cabinet was empty. Turns out the majority of the supplies were kept at the battalion aid station not the trauma center. Sgt Bentley called out on the radio and Sgt Percival and SFC Natividad raced from the top of the hill down to the senior NCO quarters to grab all of the Hextends they could get their hands on and back up to the trauma center. They were a bit winded to say the least. Hextends is an expander that is given in I.V. form to make up for massive blood loss. This ANA soldier took a round through his neck that lodged in his shoulder and arrived in hypovolemic shock per Spc Larson.

The trauma team pumped 10 units of AB+ blood into him, and then called out on the PA for all AB blood donors to report to the trauma center. I was in the mess hall with LTC Velte at the time. He heard the call and was about to skip his dinner when a second call came over our radio stating they needed AB+. SPC Derouen was on guard duty and ran all the way to the trauma center with his full battle rattle when his relief arrived. When SPC Derouen arrived there were twelve other donors standing by ready to give blood. SPC Derouen's heart rate was well above 110 so they had him lie down and rest. In the mean time one of the medics started double checking blood types and getting people ready to each donate a pint. A call came out from the operating room, "How much longer until we get more blood?"

The response was, "Fifteen minutes."

"He doesn't have fifteen minutes; we're flying him out of here in fifteen minutes. Anyone you haven't stuck, leave alone," said the voice from the operating room. There was a Black Hawk and an Apache standing by just for this ANA soldier with their blades turning ready to launch the moment they loaded him on.

Everyone knew this was an ANA soldier and no one hesitated to give aid or blood. While all of the U.S. blood donors were running up to the trauma center our TOC personnel checked the interpreter's blood types. Sure enough Sarief had AB+ blood. Sarief was already getting his shoes on to run up the hill when asked to donate. Sarief had never given blood before and was white as a ghost when he arrived at the trauma center.

By the time Sarief arrived the doctors decided the patient was stable enough to be flown to a more advanced surgical center. All this activity took place inside of twenty minutes during the dinner hour. During the twenty minutes, medics and blood donors who were on guard duty were replaced within minutes and supplies were being run up the hill. SGT Gonsalves, one of our SecFor medics, was on duty in the ECP tower and ran to the trauma center with his full battle rattle when his relief came.

I was outside when the two helicopters took off taking the ANA soldier to another surgery center. It was very dark out; the moon still hadn't risen over the mountains and the stars were not giving off much light.

Later that evening I went to the MWR to transfer some documents from my hard drive to the government computers. We still couldn't plug in a thumb drive. Everything had to be emailed from a non government computer. I had just sat down when I heard an RPG go off. *Nuts!* Both the indirect and direct fire alarms were going off, "Back to the bunker."

The bunker serves two purposes: first it is protection, second, it is the rally point for some of our troops. We have one MRAP parked next to it with a 50 cal and all of the required communication equipment to run operations. SGT Fry, our communication NCO, hopped in and fired up everything while SFC Fair and I counted heads. SFC Natividad ran to all of the locations on post, for which we were responsible. They couldn't hear the alarms go off to tell people to get into a harden shelter. We support the towers from the bunker. If they need ammo, our TOC would call us on the radio and we'd run it to the towers. We also served and aided and litter teams.

A few days earlier J.W., one of our interpreters, took leave to Jalalabad for an engagement party. I could hear one of the guys in the bunker ask Sam, another interpreter, to call JW on his phone. "J.W. stop shooting at us."

"I'm not shooting at you. I'm in Jalalabad." J.W.'s wedding would become the center of amusement by June when he asked for two weeks off and borrowed $10,000.00 to show all of his friends that he was rich.

This was a drive-by shooting Afghan style. Someone shot an RPG from route California after passing an ANP (Afghan National Police) checkpoint over our blue gate. The round hit between our camp and the village of Yargul Gharah. There were no civilian causalities and no one on the post was injured either. This all happened in the dark of night so checking the area out took a little longer than usual. There are two ANP check points located a quarter mile apart from each other with CP Wright in the middle. You would think the receiving checkpoint would have stopped each vehicle after hearing the launch of the RPG and checked for the launcher, but they didn't.

The all clear was given and once again life at the camp returned to normal. Sgt Bentley had stayed with the wounded ANA soldier until he passed away. He then returned to the barracks at 2200. SGT Bentley was pretty well done in after that. The surgeons and the troops at Camp Wright gave it everything they had to save the ANA soldier.

On Wednesday January 6th our colonel decided to go back out to Woch Now Village to check on the toddler who didn't return for treatment. Turns out the child's hand was not burned but crushed and it still looked like the only option was to amputate. Sgt Bentley went up to the trauma center to do some quick coordination and came back with some bad news. Yes, the doctors could amputate the hand either in the U.S. or Afghan surgery rooms, but if the Taliban found out the village would be punished.

There is a difference between the Taliban and the insurgents. The Taliban follow the Wahabi sect of Islam and forbid anyone from taking aid from infidels. They will destroy anything that the U.S. builds or punish anyone who has received medical treatment. There have been cases in which the Taliban has come into a village and chopped off everyone's hand, or just chopped off the heads of the parents who had their children treated.

The reason the child had not returned to the hospital was not out of fear of the Taliban, but his father worked in Jalalabad cleaning streets. His father was returning that night and would take his son into our camp in the morning. There is nothing in the Koran that states a Muslim can't receive service from an infidel.

While all of this was going on, I was trying to find vendors for lumber and re-bar. This took the better part of the day to find vendors in the local area. Asadabad doesn't have a Yellow Pages for all of the local business so you have to go door to door to get their phone numbers. We handed out one list after another of what materials we wanted a bid on and received a bunch of puzzling looks. After dinner I started receiving emails from prospective vendors all wanting my business.

Thursday morning came with the father from Woch Now Village carrying his son up to our trauma center for surgery. The boy was very lucky; there were two surgeons there on a 90-day rotation who were the specialists needed to save his hand. He had a very severe infection and was treated with an I.V. antibiotics and given some powerful antibiotics to take at home. The father was able to take his son home the same day.

I thought that was good news for the day. I finished up writing several contracts and drawings and decided to treat myself to a run at the gym. I was walking to the gym the moment the call for prayer was going off when I saw a stampede of Afghanis running down the road jumping over walls and climbing up ladders. At first I thought we had a nut on post with an AK, then I heard the snarl of a large dog. I ran up to the road to save the local populace from the vicious dog, which was no taller than my knee. The dog had turned around and started chasing the remaining Afghanis up the hill, then turned around to finish off the ones on the bottom of the hill. I saw a dozen or more Afghanis jump over the fence at the mosque for protection. I patted my knee and the dog ran right up to me, rolled over on his back and wanted his tummy rubbed. I rubbed his tummy for a few minutes allowing the Afghanis time to seek sanctuary. After about a minute the dog had enough and it was back to work chasing Afghanis. I couldn't stop him. He managed to round up all of the stragglers for prayer in about 15 seconds.

The dogs on post hate Afghan men because they throw rocks at them or beat them with sticks. We have been ordered to protect the locals from any dog on post even if that means shooting the dog.

Chapter Twenty-Five

THE KORENGAL VALLEY

January was taking its time navigating across the calendar. The heavy rains and snowfall that are typical of this time of year hadn't materialized. The farmers who planted their winter wheat crop would lose it because they are dependent upon rain, not irrigation, for their crops. The mild winter would have a residual effect in the summer when there is no snow melt to feed the rivers. There is another side effect of the mild winter and that is the continued insurgency. The typical Afghani wears garments comparable to pajamas, which have minimal thermal capabilities. Few Afghanis will venture out in the cold for a lengthy duration to fight an infidel. The snow that we saw on the mountaintops a few months earlier had vanished and the morning temperatures had rarely dropped below forty. In other words it was good fighting weather for an insurgent. The summer looked like it would be an active insurgency because of the pending drought. The lack of water means there would be less income generated by farming. Men would need to find another means to supplement their income.

The Korengal Valley heated up again. There is one COP (Company Operating Post) in the Korengal valley that is 100% supplied by air. The Korengal Valley is 20 kilometers to the west of Camp Wright and feeds into the Pech River Valley. One of the units there was going through their TOA (Transfer Of Authority) right then. Their relief unit conducted their first patrol up the Korengal and got hit hard. They lost one soldier, another lost a leg and a third had a round stuck in his ankle.

Our PA system called out for all medics to report to the trauma center, which is how I knew about some of the causalities. The same unit went back out again a few days later and lost another soldier. This time they brought the corpse to CP Wright. When someone is pronounced dead at a FOB or COP the Internet is shut down so the Army can notify the family before anyone else does. Troops think that the news should come from a friend first, but this makes the friend the bad news messenger. It is more advantageous for the Army to deliver the bad news and let the friend be there for the family.

On January 20th another U.S. soldier shot himself at one of the O.P.s in the Korengal. With all of the suicide prevention classes we are given there is just no way to know what is going through a kid's mind. The ability to send information home instantly or talk on the phone any time, day or night, doesn't allow time for problems at home to cool off before they get back to the soldier.

On January 7th in Jalalabad there was a rocket attack on some of the Afghan government offices. One of the rockets hit the home of our youngest interpreter, Waydot. The rocket destroyed part of his house, killed his youngest son badly, and burned his older son and daughter. His wife has suffered a broken back, and multiple fractures in her arms and legs. Because this was an Afghan on Afghan attack there were no reports posted on our system. The ANP (Afghan National Police) stated that it was a random attack and just bad luck for the family. I have my doubts about random bad luck. How could one rocket just happen to strike a house belonging to an interpreter who works for the U.S.? We took up a collection of $500.00 for Waydot, which is almost half a year's pay for most Afghanis.

One January 15th we hosted a Vet Cap for the villages around Camp Wright. With the exception of the two Gujer villages, Woch Now and Arga Del, the rest were Pashtu. We put word out that there would be jobs the night before, and to show up at the back gate at daybreak if anyone wanted work. We hired 16 boys and one old man. The boys helped set up the fencing and the chutes and the old man, well he knew how to pace himself. The Vet Cap was a junior NCO show from start to finish. SSG Lucas showed the kids how to set up the chutes. SGT Flynn set up the receiving and grading lanes. SGT Bentley handled the pharmaceutical supplies. SPC Tanson set up the small ruminants unit and trained one local boy how to treat the animals. We had two SECFOR troops, SGT Fry and Carter also handling animals. Our SECFOR was up in the hills, around the VetCap site and at the receiving lane providing security. This was our show so we were responsible for the outer and inner cordon for security.

The Gujers came in an orderly manner with Laj Bar, the village elder, arriving during setup and assisting in the operation. Kunar's Governor Wahaidi arrived when we shut down for lunch bringing with him his own press corps, his horse and cattle and a large security detail. I would be hard pressed to tell the difference between the governor of Kunar and a governor of any state back in the U.S. He didn't stay very long, which was good for us because we had a long line of Pasthus lining up for service. Later, local people would run up to us and tell us that they saw us on TV. This VetCap more than paid for itself with the messages and good will it provided to the local community, which ultimately increased our security.

Governor Wahaidi with his horse and LTC Velte, January 15th 2010

I was working the herds and the crowds for the day. When I gave the signal to the Pashtu villagers to come forward after lunch it was like the running of the bulls in Spain! Our SECFOR were standing at the entry like a set of bowling pins and the bulls were about to score a strike. We all moved quickly and got everything under control. So we thought. Just as I handed off a herd of goats to Sgt Flynn, I saw two boys running away with a pile of my ropes. I yelled at the boys in Pashtu to come back and they did. While I was recovering my ropes another boy was stuffing our leather gloves down his pants. Then the Pashtu village teenage thugs showed up demanding jobs. They didn't want to work; they wanted to case the site to see what was worthwhile stealing.

During the event, one man, Taj Mohammad, introduced himself to LTC Velte speaking perfect English. He had spent four years in GITMO as a prisoner. During the four years he learned seven languages including Spanish. Turns out, typical U.S. stupidity, he was involved in a family dispute and his cousin told the U.S. that he was Taliban and had been firing RPGs at our troops. The Gujers are a tight community that don't fight nor do they serve with the Taliban. If I could figure that out why couldn't our gifted CIA figure it out? He turned out to be a great guy, and we gave him a job. In the months ahead Taj's talents and ability to work with different villagers was priceless.

SFC Medina had taken his two weeks leave in December leaving on December 14th and returning on January 15th. Sure he enjoyed his two weeks at home, but paid for it by sitting in one PAX terminal after another trying to get back. He had heard all of the stories of what happened while he was away, but was having a hard time understanding the changes. I told him that I no longer required a platoon sergeant, I needed a production manager.

Somehow during the month of December our unit managed to promise just about everyone a solution to their flood control and erosion problems. Most of these promises were made for us by other well meaning USDA and USAID personnel. The battalion up at FOB Bostick said they couldn't wait for forms to be made for the cast concrete crib walls. I sent them the drawings so they could make their own molds. After all they were very simple. The first email I received was, "These drawing are very difficult for us to understand because we don't have an engineer on site. Can you send us an example?"

We created the drawings for junior high school students because we had planned to have the KCC (Kunar Construction College) manufacture them. I can't believe troops today didn't play with Lincoln logs when they were growing up or take wood shop in the 7th grade. The only difference in what we drew up and Lincoln logs is the size and the big ones are made out of concrete. I knew that God had me teach middle school wood shop for a reason; this was it. I taught wood shop fifteen years ago. Many of the active Army troops are old enough to have been my students. If I compare the average age of an active Army unit to ours, there is about a ten-year difference. The average age of the Ag section is 40.

My troops were overtaxed with the upcoming VETCAPs and I needed someone to fabricate some prototype wood forms for the crib walls. I went to Flour's carpenter shop for help. I decided I could just send them the wood and a cut list and SSG Lucas could assemble them later. I created some drawings simple enough that a middle school student could understand them. The problem was we were not dealing with American middle school students. The Afghan carpenters didn't know how to use a tape measure or understand drawings. Each drawing had an isometric view of the finished part for clarity. That didn't help matters.

SSG Lucas saw my plight and took over shepherding the carpenters. Soon they were knocking out forms left and right. SSG Lucas was teaching them every trick in the book on how to work smarter, not harder. He did finally admit defeat when it came to teaching them how to use a tape measure. The Afghanis' boss would joke with the carpenters and ask when they were going to come back to work for Fluor? The Afghanis responded, "Oh we can't, we're working on the big job now." SSG Lucas was now center stage at CP Wright. The carpenters brought all of their friends over to show them the forms and even brought all of the Flour supervisors over to see their accomplishments. I'll admit what they produced under the guidance of SSG Lucas was something to be proud of. Fluor was more than thankful to have the carpenters working for us; their lumber shipment for a long list of projects hadn't come in so they needed something productive for their carpenters to do. We have been fortunate with the KBR/Fluor team; they have been very supportive and honest. I can't say that about KBR in other locations. It is odd that in the more dangerous and less desirable locations you find the better quality people.

On Wednesday the 20th I was asked to join the Civil Affairs team for an erosion control survey. This was an interesting project. Kunar is planning to build a university next to the Kunar River just south of Asadabad. Construction of a large high school was already underway near the same site. The goal of this erosion control project is to protect the university site. During the winter months, Kunar River is at its lowest point. It is at its highest point in August with a change in water level of 20 feet. I took along Sgt Percival, my geologist, and Sgt Flynn, my forester, to look the site over. Together we walked a thousand meters of the western bank of the Kunar examining damage from past floods.

The location had some interesting attributes to it. There is a large island in the river that is forested, but prone to flooding in the later summer. The island is ideal for the construction of two suspension bridges linking Mara Warah and Asadabad together and doubling as a park. After looking the whole area over we decided it would be a two-year project starting with a coffer dam. The coffer dam would be placed between the western bank of the Kunar and the north point of the island. This would leave the western channel of the river dry so we could construct retaining walls with solid foundations. The other aspect of the project was to build a low level dam at the southern end of the channel that could be used as a hydro plant to power the university.

After I presented our initial engineering and construction estimate a war broke out between the PRT, USAID, the State Department, and Civil Affairs. The State Department wanted the entire project completed using manual labor and no heavy equipment. USAID wanted the project constructed using gabion baskets. The PRT was against the project, and Civil Affairs was trying to be the voice of reason agreeing with my cost estimate of three million dollars. My cost estimate fired off the next heated debate. The State Department wanted the project completed for under $200,000.00, the magic amount that could be approved by the division commander. Then USAID announced that they had a lot of money for erosion control projects that they just had to commit. This announcement led to another interesting development with the governor's office that would be caught by an alert first lieutenant.

The western fork of the Kunar River in Asadabad looking south toward the new high school. During summer floods the water will crest where the troops are standing on the bank.

Chapter Twenty-Six

THE THREE-HOUR TIC

The Army started issuing a piece of equipment called a boomerang. It's not the type you throw; this boomerang will tell the vehicle crew from what direction they are being fired upon. It works using a series of microphones and it measures the difference in time it takes each microphone to receive the sound. It then triangulates to give the direction. This system is similar to one featured in Popular Mechanics for helmets for $8000. This vehicle-mounted system is particularly susceptible to trees and low hanging utility wires that break off the microphones. In the coming months the system would prove itself time and time again.

On Thursday afternoon, January 21st, my Ag section rolled out of Camp Wright with LTC Velte to COP Monti. COP Monti was to serve as their Motel 6 for a VetCap mission up in Nishigam. Nishigam is the area where we were ambushed on the way back from FOB Bostick in mid December 2009. It is a traditional ambush site that we (we as in the U.S. military) haven't done anything about–just like the Russians. To properly deal with the ambush site you have to dismount and wait a long time. When SFC Natividad saw the location of the VetCap on the map he quickly pointed out all of the firing positions of the insurgents that were near the site where they would be working. I was a little disappointed that I wasn't going, but I had a lot of work to complete if we were going to attempt to build some flood control structures.

LTC David M. Kelly

With the next day being Friday and with the majority of the troops in the field, I was looking forward to sleeping in. I took the liberty of looking through some old family photos and stories I had on my computer. I came across an amusing story from my great grandfather Harrison Baker about a hunting trip. He had a grand buck in his sights and was about ready to pull the trigger when he heard a shot ring out of the woods. The buck made a big leap in the air and ran off. Someone else shot his prized buck.

I stayed up until eleven or so finishing a railroad magazine since I was planning to sleep in. Fridays are a bit slow anyway because the majority of the local nationals don't work on the FOB on Fridays. Just when I started to nod off to sleep I heard the artillery go off. Okay, no big deal; just roll over and go back to sleep. The sandman was fast at work when another single round went off followed by another single round a little later. By then I was awake and couldn't get back to sleep. So I went out, checked on my gate guards at the blue gate and got them some hot cocoa and coffee. We watched the illumination flares drift down from the sky over Marah Ware. Just as the flare would drift out of sight the artillery would fire another one up into the sky.

I went back in and attempted to go back to sleep, but the cyclic pattern from the artillery kept me up until well past 3:00 A.M. Five o'clock came around and I was wide awake, so the heck with it, I just got up and started the day.

LTC Velte and the rest of my Ag section got up in the predawn darkness and rolled out to the VetCap site. Setup and operations went very smoothly. The AVA vets and their Vet Tech students did most of the work. The new metal chutes SSG Lucas and Sgt Flynn had made were making the job of setup and vaccination easy. Lunchtime rolled around and everyone took a break, then they heard a machine gun firing in the distance. No one thought much of it because it was well outside its maximum effective range. Then the locals started getting up and moving away. The firing of the SKS was a signal to the villagers to leave. At that point, LTC Velte sent word back to us that there might be a problem, as they geared up with their battle rattle. A short period of time went by and no more shots were heard. The locals stopped showing up with their animals around 1 o'clock so LTC Velte and the AVA decided to close everything down.

Back at Camp Wright we were juggling the guard schedule and SSG Tyner

200

was trying to get old number 20 fixed. Number 20 is one of our MRAPs, which constantly has electrical problems. SSG Tyner was on a quest to find out what was wrong with his truck and decided to use the morning working on the truck instead of sleeping. SFC Fair and I were still trying to get the Army to cough up $50,000., which was proving to be as simple as mating elephants.

By 1400, LTC Velte and the Ag section were on the road to COP Monti doing a whopping 6 MPH. I had just read a history magazine about a U.S. Army in 1919 making a cross country trip and their average speed was 6 MPH driving model Ts. We have bigger trucks, same road conditions and the same speed.

Lt Ko was telling me about some problems we were having at our observation posts. Someone was cutting the wires to the claymores mines. The OP commander decided to send the Afghan Security Guard (ASG) somewhere else to see if it would stop the problem, and it did.

We were constantly getting threat reports about attacks on the FOB. These reports meant nothing. What was important was watching the trend of the attacks, the cycle and the frequency. The trend is what they are attacking with, small arms, RPG, mortars, etc. The cycle is basically the pattern of who gets hit. For example a cop knows that if a bank on the corner of Elm and Main is robbed on Monday the next bank to be robbed is on Oak and Main because the same bank robbers rob the banks and follow the same route. The same is true for the insurgents. We are on two routes, the Pech River route and the Kunar River route. Camp Wright was about due for another attack. It could be either an RPG or mortar attack and it would happen when I was either in the shower or the outhouse. These attacks usually fell short of hitting the camp.

At about 1440 SSG Lucas, who was riding in the back of ADT 17, called out over the intercom, "We're taking fire." ADT 17 was tail end Charlie in the six-vehicle convoy. SGT Diaz who was in the vehicle. TC looked out and saw sparks come off the vehicle; then their MRAP came to a dead halt. Once again the ADT was in a complex ambush. (A complex ambush is when you're being shot at from both sides.) The boomerang system went off calling out, "fire coming from the 3, 5, and 7 o'clock positions." SGT Diaz PIDed (positive identification) one of the fighting positions and had the gunner return fire.

PFC Mc Gee, their driver, was doing everything he could to get their MRAP moving again. Their engine would roar but the MRAP wouldn't budge; the brakes had locked up. Sgt Diaz jumped out to guide the MRAP in front of them back for a quick tow. SGTs Carter and Johanson were in the LMTV, our traveling barn, towing a large trailer full of metal chutes and other barnyard goodies. Johanson was the TC and called out to Carter who was driving "They need cover; Victor 5 is backing up to get them."

Sgt Carter yelled out, "Hang on," as he popped up over a three-foot berm, into a farmer's field dragging the trailer through a field of sprouting winter wheat, and back over the berm. The two of them and their gunner, Sgt Contreras, positioned themselves between the insurgents and Sgt Diaz and gave covering fire with the aid of Sgt Contreras. SSG Lucas and Sgt Steven provided additional security. There was a Predator in the air at the time that fired off one shot at the insurgents and then returned to base.

The tow bars for an MRAP are extremely heavy and require two to three men to carry them. SGTs Carter and Johanson jumped out of their vehicle leaving Sgt Contreras on the gun to provide covering fire at the same time someone lobbed a smoke grenade. The insurgents knew what smoke meant. They focused their fire on the smoke where the troops would be. Carter, Johanson, and Diaz just waited until the shooting stopped and hooked up the tow bar. This took about five minutes and then the signal was given to let her rip. Both MRAPs hit the gas and, nothing. The troops grabbed another MRAP and tried to push while the other pulled. Just like a stubborn mule it was staying put.

The insurgents didn't have a lot of ammo so they fired every two to three minutes and then moved around. This is what is known as harassing fire and it continued. LTC Velte couldn't see what was going on so he twisted around on his back so he could look up out of the windows to call in air support. SFC Mead was his gunner and spotted one of the insurgents who decided he had enough fighting. LTC Velte radioed the Kiowa scouts the man's position. They raced in and found he had ditched his weapon and was now carrying a piece of wood. He was now off limits as he casually walked across the battle field. There were more tracer rounds going over SFC Mead's head; one struck the antenna, twanged like a guitar string and bounced back and forth.

About this time the convoy was running low on ammo and called out for a speedball. A speedball is an emergency re-supply of ammo. Radio is great! The call went out and everyone heard it, except us. Because of the mountainous terrain and the distance we were only getting sporadic reports. As soon as we got word about the TIC (Troops In Contact) Spc Larson went up to the trauma center in case any of our troops were injured. We were dependent upon the TOC at COP Monti for any information.

Meanwhile Sgt Diaz and the troops found the problem. It was a one in a million shot, which had ricocheted off the road and severed the airline causing the brakes to fail in the closed position. With all of the tools and supplies that were packed, there was nothing that could be used to fix the airline. The one socket they needed to unlock the breaks was the one they didn't have.

The first of six speedballs started to arrive. Blackhawks and Kiowas were landing off the side of the road near the edge of the Kunar River and kicked ammo out the door. Sgt Bentley and Sgt Percival moved out to pick up the ammo. Sgt Bentley managed to rip the crotch out of his pants clear down to his knees so he was fairly well ventilated. Sgt Percival on the other hand had decided to wear his thermal underwear because it was near freezing that morning; he was then sweating to death while running the ammo.

At 1530, the first QRF call sign, "Battle 16" commanded by Lt Nguyen arrived with a mechanic, but no wrecker. There was a lull in the shooting for the moment. The mechanic just strolled back to the MRAP when the tracers started up again. SFC Natividad pointed out to him that those tracers are not ours. Sometimes it takes just a little rub like that to flip the right switch on in one's brain. The mechanic knew what to do and went right to work.

LTC Velte's truck was still attracting fire. SFC Mead could see the tracers fly over his head but the insurgent just wouldn't show himself. Then he moved just a little from behind a rock and SFC Mead lined up a shot with his M-14. Just as he was about to pull the trigger LTC Velte called out, "Hey Wes do you have PID?" SFM Mead shouted down the gunner's hatch the distance and direction then went back to set up his shot again. Just as he was getting ready to pull the trigger the zipping sound of a 50 cal went off followed by the whoosh of a rocket as a Kiowa flew overhead. LTC Velte shot his buck using a Kiowa he had called in. "Hey Wes where's your target?"

"It's gone now sir."

"Bummer Wes."

The intensity of fire increased just after the first QRF arrived. The insurgents opened up with PKM and AK fire shortly after the QRF mechanic and their LT dismounted. The QRF was able to respond with a solid punch because they are allotted more ammo than an ADT. This is because they are combat arms, which meant our troops were dependent on speedballs. The amount of cover fire to protect aviation assets on the ground consumed a large amount of ammo. Lt Nguyen was the only one wounded during the TIC. He was either grazed by a round or a round ricocheted off a rock into his cheek. In either case he got walloped but good. Sgt Gonsalves, our medic, attended to him and he didn't require medivac.

The insurgents' fire died off once again just as the second QRF call sign Battle 26 commanded by Captain Nagy arrived with their wrecker. Captain Nagy walked down route California just as the insurgents' fire resumed pinning Captain Nagy for a considerable amount of time. Sgt Wareham was gunning a MK-19 in an MRAP that SGT Bentley was in. SGT Wareham would have been selected as a B-17 ball turret gunner because of his size. When it came time to reload his MK-19 a round jammed and he couldn't reach well enough to clear it. Tried as he might his arms just couldn't stretch the extra two feet required to set everything straight. Sgt Wareham is a seasoned vet and was wounded three time during the Gulf War. He knew what to do, but just couldn't reach. SGT Bentley popped the roof hatch in the back, climbed up on top and cleared the weapon. It was about this time SGT Bentley realized he was standing on top of the MRAP like the Statue of Liberty in the middle of no man's land. Hmmm not really the best place to be. He jumped back in the hatch like Bugs Bunny when Elmer Fud was hunting him and called it good.

The speedballs continued to arrive at the ambush site. SPC Coffman and SPC Derouen ran ammo from the LZs (landing zones) to the lead trucks. Our interpreters, all local nationals, were breaking open the ammo cans and passing the ammo up to the gunners. Unlike the ANP and the ANA (Afghan National Police and the Afghan National Army) they didn't pack up and run away. They became part of the crew. It was the rear vehicles in the convoy that were receiving the lion's share of the insurgents' fire due to their location. They were right in the punch bowl.

We were monitoring the sporadic radio traffic when Chief Fuller (US Navy) came into our TOC gasping for breath. "Your guys have requested a speed ball." He took another breath. "We've got two birds inbound now. Do you have any ammo?" With that SGT Brumley grabbed the keys to the 1151 that we kept loaded ready to go, while I ran to the top of the hill to coordinate the load. I got there just after two Kiowas landed, and ran up to the first crew chief who wore a California Flag (C Troop 3-17 CAV) on his helmet and asked which bird for the ammo. He pointed to the first bird. I radioed back to SGT Brumley and told him which bird to go to. Just then, two troops came up to the flight line in a gator loaded with crated ammo. I helped carry the boxes over to the first Kiowa. I thought it was our gator being driven by SFC Mosqueda but it was the PRT answering the call for ammo. I looked up and saw our 1151 coming across the airfield. SGT Brumley, SGT Fry and SPC Tropeano got out and we started carrying the ammo from the 1151 to the Kiowa. We had it all: MK-19, 50 Cal, 5.56, 7.64, SAW. While we were staging the ammo the ground crews were refueling the birds, loading more missiles, reloading the machine guns and servicing the weapons. The crew chief filled every nook and cranny of space with extra ammo then pointed to the next bird for all the ammo we brought. (A NASCAR pit crew has nothing on these guys).We each picked up several boxes and ran across the rocks to the next Kiowa past the tail rotor of the first bird. Tail rotors are nothing more than a king-size "La Machine" if you should happen to get too close. We got everything to the next Kiowa and the ground crew started loading everything up. We backed out of the way. About two minutes later the second Kiowa lifted off, moved over to another pad and did a 180 pointing north. It held there for less than a minute until the pilot of the other Kiowa closed his door, lifted off, did a 180 and hovered while the second Kiowa took off over our heads. The first Kiowa waited until the lead Kiowa got a good head start, then followed.

I turned around and my commander was standing behind me. He stated, "I'm taking LT Ko with me; we've got a QRF going up there."

I looked back at the pad and saw all of our ammo still there. OOPS! I called SGT Brumley back with the 1151 and we loaded it all back up. We got overwhelming support from the other units on post; there was plenty of ammo on those birds. We even had PyOps (Psychological Operations) offering to send a team and an MRAP with our QRF. Kunar is the Wild, Wild West and the settlers stick together. We gave our QRF all of the loaded 5.56 magazines we had so they could cross level our troops for their final trip home.

COP Monti was responding with 105 fire on one of the insurgents' known locations. SGT Flynn observed the rounds hit and called for a 300 meter adjustment because the insurgents had moved. COP Monti couldn't fire the adjusted mission because it would put the rounds near the village that the insurgents were moving to. SFC Mead spotted the crack in the mountain where the bulk of the insurgents (he counted ten) had moved to. They were coming out during the lull in the fighting to recover their brass. Brass brings in big money in town. A thrifty insurgent can't afford to leave his brass behind. (One hundred 50 cal shell casing buys a live chicken.) SFC Mead marked their location with his 50 cal while LTC Velte vectored in a swarm of six Kiowas; they moved the mountains over two feet fully exposing the insurgents. The harassing fire that our troops were taking on the road had stopped.

SFC Fair, SFC Teso, SFC Graham and I had a quick meeting back at Camp Wright and came up with a game plan for base defense based upon what we had left. The PRT is responsible for the overall defense of the FOB, but we still had our section that we were responsible for. First thing was to get some more magazines and re-load them. We sat on the floor of the TOC with a production line going with the additional help of our USDA rep. We started rotating troops off the guard towers for dinner with SGT Olson being the roving switch hitter for guard. We still had Spc Larson up at the Trauma center just in case.

After the Kiowas made their big run on the crack in the mountain one of the two that we loaded with ammo landed on route California and transferred ammo directly to SGT Carter and Sgt Johanson's LMTV. They had the ammo stuffed in the electrical compartment of their bird. The LMTV was the biggest target out there and it was never struck by an insurgent bullet. SGT Carter had managed to position it so the rocks made it next to impossible for the near side insurgents to hit. However the insurgents on the far side of the river didn't have that excuse for missing our rolling barn.

Just before 1800, our convoy, with the help of the mechanic from COP Monti, was able to get the breaks released and hooked our MRAP to Monti's wrecker. Our QRF arrived at COP Monti at the same time. Forty-five minutes later the last two Kiowas that were escorting the convoy reported that they were low on fuel and had to depart. A few minutes after that our convoy rolled into COP Monti. SFC Natividad sent a one word text message to Spc Larson "Alive." We received word that everyone was okay; we could relax a bit.

We each went up to the mess hall and grabbed two dinners for the QRF. And, I fed Tripod the colonel's cat.

Tripod enjoying some tuna on the back side of the ADT TOC building

Saturday started early as usual. The first word we received was the second VetCap didn't have a place to set up. When LTC Velte arrived at the proposed VetCap site the land owner wanted a hundred thousand Afghanis for the use of his land. (That is $50,000.00) LTC Velte said, "Let's go." And he found another location. The same man who wanted $50,000.00 for the use of his land arrived with all of his animals at the VetCap.

LTC Velte and the Ag team treated nearly 900 animals during the two days. Our commander called the brigade commander about our ammo allotment so we could carry more in our trucks. We were also trying to find a part to fix our wounded vehicle. SGT Martinez, our maintenance chief, called around to every base he could think of with no luck. We couldn't even find a hanger queen to strip one off of.

I listened to the troop's recount the events so I could document what happened. With the exception of one who made it sound like the assault on the Remagen Bridge on the Rhine River, all gave a very conservative account of the events. I captured the highlights during the course of three hours. The insurgents were not hitting the entire convoy with heavy fire for the total three hours it took to recover the MRAP. The tow bar was connected and disconnected twice as different approaches of moving the MRAP were tried. Each time a different group of troops was involved. Our troops were not running all over the road like a bunch of scattered ants;, most just sat and waited until they were needed. Conservation of force and ammo are important during an engagement. This was strictly a small arms encounter so troops were better off staying in the MRAPs.

The insurgents had a limited amount of ammo, basically what they could carry. The last time we were ambushed in the same location there were seven insurgents spotted. The troops believe there were five insurgents when the ambush started and more joined in later leaving when they fired all of their ammo. They didn't have RPGs; if they did they would have initiated the ambush with an RPG. SFC Velasco, our Intel NCOIC, noticed this after reading many reports that the insurgents don't save their RPGs for later. If they have them they use them first. Our troops used most of their ammo giving suppressive fire when helicopters were landing and to the people who were moving up and down the convoy. There were long durations between insurgent fires with most of their shots being taken at our last two vehicles.

Sunday morning all was back to normal. I got up to take a shower by way of the all American outhouse when I spotted our Navy decky sneaking into the woman's shower with his bag of seven different hair shampoos. This guy had been a problem. He would lock himself in the men's shower and wouldn't let anyone in. I took off the locks on the inside and installed a closet closer to counter that tactic. There are four showers in the room; he didn't need the place to himself. After that he would barricade the door with the bench. One night we came in and he wouldn't reduce the amount of water he was using, which meant the rest of us couldn't shower.

This kid would spend 30 to 45 minutes taking a shower, and water is very limited. It is obvious that he never crewed on a sub. I had a heart to heart talk with him. After that night he started using the woman's shower and locking himself in. So I took my shower, went back and changed and then waited for him to come out. My commander was passing by to brush his teeth while I pounded on the door telling our sea cadet to come out; he had been showering for 30 minutes. No response. My commander said, "Just turn off the lights," as he flipped the switch. Then I heard a voice; it was SFC Velasco. Our sea cadet slipped out and SFC Velasco went in prior to my return. We got a kick out of it, but SFC Velasco didn't see any humor in it.

Our USDA rep along with his counterpart in Klas Kunar came up with another bright idea to convert wheat fields to vineyards. We rolled out in the morning going down route Beaverton when SSG Tyner said his battery wasn't charging. Once again our electrical problems were raising their ugly heads in ADT 20. We arrived at the Klas Kunar district center with the battery bleeding dry so we shut down most of the electrical system in the MRAP just to conserve what we had.

Klas Kunar is about 30 miles south of our camp on the eastern side of the Kunar River. The district center was under construction, and was going to be a show place. The contractor who won the job knew what he is doing. I took a moment to look over his formwork and re-bar cages. He was using all metal forms, and his re-bar stirrups were all hydraulically bent. He was using number 8s (one-inch diameter rebar) with the stirrups properly spaced, which was unusual for Afghanistan. We waited around for 45 minutes to an hour for the battle space owner's Civil Affairs Team to show up, then finally went ahead and met with the agriculture people. The battle space owner's COP was within walking distance of the district center. Our visit just wasn't important enough for the Civil Affairs Team to go to work before 9:00 A.M.

LTC Kelly meeting with Klas Kunar Agricultural Ministry Officials.

We met with the Klas Kunar forestry minister, forestry protection manager, their agricultural extension manager and a few others who didn't identify themselves. When we asked about planting vineyards they responded that no one wanted to plant grapes. The Ag minister just put some names on a list to get the USDA rep off his back.

Then they asked for a long list of things. I told them no to everything except making some cattle chutes for their new vet center and helping them with a VetCap. At 9:15 the battle space owner showed up and was upset that we started the meeting without him. I just about sent the young E-6 to the moon for disrespect to a field grade officer, but decided the public forum was not the place. He quickly disappeared when there was an appropriate place to discuss his conduct and lack of performance. I had other creative ways of dealing with such individuals, but in his case he was on a course of self destruction. He had no knowledge of his area of operations, what major contracts were underway or why agriculture was important to his mission. Life can be tough, even tougher if you're a knot head.

We jumped back into the trucks only to find that our truck had decided to shut down most of our systems, which included radios, and other fancy gadgetry. We rolled out and made it about a third of the way home when the battery died. We hooked up to the MRAP in front of us and basically became a wagon with a big gun on top.

Tuesday January 26th was going to be a fun day of building forms and re-bar cages for our contractor's day. Once again we had one little emergency after another. (Little emergencies such as load this, inventory that, write a report, etc.) I decided the only way we were going to get our re-bar cages made was to pay one of the contractors on post to make the stirrups. I found one who had a re-bar bender on site and gave him some templates to follow.

I went back to where SSG Lucas was working and he had fashioned one cage using the re-bar and some stiff wire. We talked about using the jig we had made to bend some stirrups and have everything ready. I told him that the jig was good for a number #3 but not the number 4 that we had. He tried a piece and it bent a little, then he went back to his stiff wire. I left him to see about using the table saw. I had just rounded the corner of the building when he felt a surge of super human strength and decided to bend the number 4 re-bar. He gave it one solid pull and Ka-Wapp! He was out like a light looking at stars. I was coming down the hill when LTC Velte asked, "How's Lucas? There's blood all over the place?"

We went up to the trauma center to find him lying on a table with a collar being fitted to his neck. The surgeon said, "We're flying him to Bagram for a scan. He has all the symptoms of a head injury." I saw a big drop of blood on the bridge of his nose and knew his nose was broken. I asked him if he wanted me to take some photos for his baby book. He agreed. Then I took his pistol from him and SFC Medina sent someone to go get his IBA and Kevlar for his trip to Bagram. SSG Lucas called us that evening and confirmed that he had broken his nose and his noggin was okay. He hitched a ride home on the red rim flight at midnight and was back at work the following morning.

The following morning was contractor's day for our crib wall projects. We had sent the interpreters to every manufacturer in town asking them to come to the camp and bid on making cast concrete pieces for our crib walls. What showed up were contractors thinking they were going to build a rock wall. We showed them photos and I brought out my Toys 'R Us Lincoln Logs to illustrate what we wanted. We weren't getting very far. I turned around and found the contractors building a log cabin out of the Lincoln Logs. Our word of mouth advertisement brought in 30 contractors and every one of them had an email address. They all brought a portfolio of their companies that listed all of the heavy equipment they had with photos of the jobs they had completed.

We were currently on the hook to built 3000 meters of crib walls in Asadabad for the new university. This was a project that just wouldn't go away and would soon be the center of a major scam. The task of building 3000 meters of crib wall was too big for us so we were teaming with several NGOs to run the project. Our attempt to work with NGOs who were in competition with one another for State Department and USAID contracts turned out to be a mistake.

By late afternoon we had storm clouds rolling in, and a convoy returning from Jalalabad. We sent them down on a supply run to replenish our ammo and other items. Jalalabad was receiving heavy rain during the day. At twilight it was sprinkling on Camp Wright, which meant our Thursday soil-sampling mission in Narang would be cut short. This mission was part of the USDA's vineyard project, another flash in the pan. The project required soil sampling at each proposed vineyard site.

We arrive at COP Fortress on our way to Narang on Thursday morning in a steady rain, which was wonderful. Rain meant that the pajama-men wouldn't be waiting on the hill sides to fire RPGs at us. I met with 1LT Eidemiller and his platoon sergeant and was very impressed with their attention to detail for the mission. The three of us had a quick huddle about what was going to happen, at least what we thought was going to happen. This was a meeting set up by the USDA, but they declined to participate. I was to give two specific messages to the sub-governor. First he needed to start working with the people in the small villages and second we would not be helping him unless he did something about the security. Out of the three southern districts, this sub governor was the best. That isn't saying much because he keeps his hands in both honey pots. The honey pots are the government and the insurgents.

We arrived at the Narang district center and I was greeted at the gate by two ANP officers. I addressed them and introduced myself in Pashto. One officer told me I should learn to speak Pashto because I was in Afghanistan.

I agreed and continued on to the main court yard. Mind you, we had that conversation in Pashto and I thought I did pretty well.

Lieutenant Eidemiller and I met with the sub governor who was very hospitable. During the conversation, I worked in my commander's two main points. His replay was "Terrorism is a worldwide problem; you need to learn to deal with it." I'm learning that fighting terrorists and insurgents is like swatting flies at a picnic. You expend a large amount of energy but you never get rid of the pests.

The sub-governor took us to the main conference room where 42 farmers filled in behind us. The sub-governor gave us a very nice introduction and then handed the meeting over to me.

"Sama-da (OK) what is my next step?"

Who wants to grow grapes? (No one) Think quick Dave you need a good transition out of this hole. Ah, yes tell us what are your concerns? (I opened myself up for a royal ambush with that line.)

The first gentleman stood up and said, "Sir, there have been many organizations that have come here to help us and we have been very grateful but each time it all ends in failure." I listened and started to really understand just how incompetent our State Department, USAID and the USDA people have been. Incompetent is a big word. You don't have to be stupid to be incompetent, just apathetic. Perhaps apathetic is a more descriptive word for what occurred. A few years ago a USDA rep with an individual from the State Department convinced the farmers to establish orchards and vineyards. The deal was several NGOs who would front for our government; they would provide the seedlings, the training and soil amendments. The seedlings were planted; the farmers cut back on their other crops and waited for the training. The training never came and the soil amendments were delivered to a high ranking government official who sold them. The irrigation improvements never happened either. The end result was the seedlings died and the farmers lost income because they didn't farm all of their fields.

The farmers told me, if "we" wanted them to try to re-establish an orchard or vineyard the training comes first, followed by soil testing and treatment, then the seedlings. In other words fool me once, shame on you. Fool me twice, shame on me. They were not about to fall for the same trick twice.

We had a very good conversation about the problems they were facing. They knew the solutions and were only able to go so far. They didn't ask for any major projects just training on a few subjects and support for their VetCap. Narang has an unusual problem called Gypsies. During the winter months they bring their animals up to Narang to graze, then return back to Kabul in the summer. Each time they return they re-infect the local herds. What these men wanted was for us to run a VetCap for the Gypsies either before they left or before they returned. The locals had been staying vigilant with their animals, which has kept two private practice veterinarians employed. At the end of the meeting one of the men introduced himself as a retired Afghan Army colonel who learned English 35 years ago. He encouraged me to continue my Pashto stating the only way I'd master it was to keep using it.

Lieutenant Eidemiller and I compared notes about what we agreed to, which wasn't much because they didn't ask for much. Lieutenant Eidemiller was new on the ground and he already had a firm grasp of the problems the villagers had and a good repose with the government officials. He was rapidly learning where all of the hidden resources are.

Chapter Twenty-Seven

THE GUJERS

The battle space owners were starting to receive some very positive feedback from the VetCaps we conducted. It didn't take long for word to spread around the brigade that Kunar ADT's VetCaps were the biggest bang for the buck going. We started receiving requests from other battle space owners. I started meeting with more and more battle space owners to brief them on how we could support them. Lieutenant Eidemiller of COP Fortress quickly understood how we could support him and the amount of positive gain he would have with the locals. He wasted no time getting the local Noor Gul district agricultural line director to send up a request for a VetCap. He was also very interested in assisting the farmers with establishing vineyards and orchards. His timing was perfect. USAID had just awarded a contract to Roots of Peace to establish vineyards and orchards in the Pech and Kunar River valleys. The deal was the farmer must pay half of the cost for trellising their vineyard. This forced the farmer to buy into the project. Otherwise they just let everything die.

There were some aspects of the project that were taken for granted such as soils and education. Sgts Percival and Flynn assisted me in writing up a series of contracts for soil testing and education. We decided to go ahead with the soil testing, but hold off on the training class until we knew the scope of the Roots of Peace contract. That contact was a closely guarded secret; we were never allowed to read it, so we didn't know how to support it.

The district level projects could reach out and touch many families, but there was no personal connection like with our friends, the Gujers, up in Woch Now Village. We could see how our friendship was developing by the amount of trust Laj Bar was giving us. During the previous several years Laj Bar would never have approached the ECP gate due to fear of the Americans. More recently he felt very comfortable stopping by and giving us reports about what was going on up in the hills.

Laj Bar stopped by during the first week of February and asked us for more pipe to complete the reconstruction of their pipe system from the spring on the far side of Witch's Teton. LTC Velte ordered more pipe, and had it delivered. The delivery driver couldn't make it past the range because of the poor road so he dropped everything off as close as he could to Woch Now Village. Our Gitmo employee, Taj, saw the pipe and told his fellow villagers that he had just returned from Jalalabad with the pipe he purchased with his own money. The next morning Laj Bar returned again wanting to talk to LTC Velte. I was busy across the room working the books, trying to get money for everything we were doing and listening to the conversation at the same time. He asked for a pipe threading die set so they could use the coupling and unions we gave them. I looked up from my work and told him to use the rubber hose and the hose clamps to splice the broken pipes together. Sensing that I was the bad guy, he turned to LTC Velte and asked us to come build his pipe system for him because his villagers didn't have the skills to do it on their own. I spoke up again in Pashto and said, I trained you! Then in English, I said, "I've got photos to prove it!"

Hmmm, you could see in his eyes that his tactic didn't work as he tried the puppy dog look. He took another breath and tried LTC Velte again. I'm sure he was thinking that one of us must have a soft spot.

"Sir the truck driver didn't deliver the pipe to the village; he dropped it off by the range. We need the driver to deliver it to the village."

I could see LTC Velte holding back a grin and trying to keep a straight face with this little ping pong match going on. LTC Velte explained about the road and that there were plenty of strong able-bodied young Gujer men who could carry the pipe to the village. The expression of the elder's face said *I'm not wining at this game.*

Then LTC Velte broke forth with compassion for Laj Bar and volunteered my services at the spring. "I'll tell you what, Dave here will go up and help you install your pipe system, but you and your men need to carry the pipe up to the spring. If any of the pipe is stolen I'm not replacing it ok?" Then Laj Bar reluctantly agreed realizing that we were going to hold him to his part of the bargain. I gave him a big smile and told him that I was looking forward to providing him with more training up at the spring. I'm sure he was thinking, *Oh great I get the guy who expects me to work.*

I didn't mind at all going back up to the Witch's Teton. We had to go anyway to check on the job to make sure they did it correctly and to document it so no one in the future pays for it again. It's a 1000-foot climb that my survey team and SSG Arnold's security team can make like a mad bunch of Billy goats. It's a beautiful climb.

After Laj Bar left, SFC Hanlin pointed out that when SPC Lopez trained them on using the pipe cutter he had them cut off six inches of pipe at a time, then used the pieces to demonstrate the use of the couplings, unions and other splicing techniques. "Sir you just might find a pile of six inch nipples on top of the spring when you get there." I didn't think of that, but SFC Hanlin just might have been right.

SPC Lopez on the right instructing, Laj Bar the Woch Now village elder on the far left and his friend with Sam our interpreter in the middle, how to use different splicing techniques and tools to rebuild their pipe system. The truck in the background is Afghan Army. The insurgents destroyed the village drinking water pipe system because the people of Woch Now were friendly to U.S. forces.

LTC Velte and I were also working on a flood control project with SFC Eaddy from Civil Affairs. SFC Eddie was ready to fund the project, but he needed all of the landowners' signatures and he also wanted to see the project.

We went out one afternoon and met with the man who said he owned all of the land. LTC Velte talked to him about the greater things in life while Sam, our interpreter, and I staked out the spillway and retaining walls with SFC Eaddy. The old man who owned the land was in the Afghan Army and fought the Soviets back in the early 80s, but didn't give any details of his ordeal.

When we were done staking out the project we went over to LTC Velte and the land owner. I told him that we would need his permission to proceed with the project. Then the land owner told me that he wasn't the sole land owner. He shared title with five brothers. Okay no problem; we'll just need all of them to sign off on the project. Well, they each have an extended family so there are about 150 owners involved. Not a problem; just have all of them come by on January 27th to sign the master blue print for the project.

On January 27th only two men arrived to sign the blue prints. The first man came up from Kabul and the second elderly man who had an "S" shaped nose lived on the property. The man from Kabul was very excited about the project and saw a major benefit in the value to his property. The older gentleman thought he could get something more out of the deal if he played hardball. His property was right on the bank of the Kunar River; the floodwall that we were going to build would protect his property and increase the amount of usable land.

He first responded that he wanted to build a house there. I told him that once the wall is built the land would be ready for construction. He told me that he wanted to build where I proposed to put the structure. I told him he couldn't build a house there because it would wash away and besides it was all sand at that moment. Then he suddenly had a heart for the safety of the local children who play near the river. They might fall off the structure and into the river. I told him that the structure would include a guard rail made out of pipe. "Oh no the animals wouldn't be able to get to the river to drink."

"How about I add in a ramp to the project?"

"Oh I don't know…"

With that, I pulled out a pen and crossed out the structure guarding his property. "Please sign here that you don't want it."

Once again I heard, "I don't know."

"Sir, here is the problem. If I get killed the contractor might build the wall because he doesn't know you don't want it." In this case "I don't know" meant I can't write. SFC Media took out a felt tip pen inked his thumb and had him place his thumb print on the drawing.

The other man asked if I had a photo of what I planned to build. I pulled one up on the Internet to show him. Then the old man's eyes lit up, "Who's in charge?" It was obvious that he suddenly changed his mind.

LTC Velte said, "We are all in charge; we work together on these projects." The old man was trying to get back into the game, as LTC Velte said, "Sir I want to thank you for sharing some of your valuable time with us today," while keeping one hand in the center of the old man's back pointing him to the door. In the end we didn't proceed with the project because not enough landowners would sign off and because of a twenty-nine million dollar scam, which we wanted to stay clear of.

SFC Media walked the two men to the gate when the old man asked if he could have a bottle of water. "Oh sure, help yourself" SFC Media replied. The next thing SFC Media saw was the old man carrying a case of water on his shoulder. They had a quick lesson about what "a" bottle of water was and what "a" case was.

The old proverb, *give a man a fish, he eats for a day; teach him to fish, he'll eat for a lifetime*, leaves out the rod and reel. Most Afghans would just prefer that you hand them a fish cleaned and cooked. They have no intention of learning how to fish, or gut, clean and cook it. There are some who are eager to learn all there is about fishing. The U.S. State Department believes in make work projects and would just buy everyone a fishing rod and reel. What we need to do is set up someone in the business of making the rod and reels, then create a demand by teaching people to fish.

We studied many of the past projects that were attempted and why they failed. Some failed for very apparent reasons such as the bright idea fairy flew by and didn't plan a thing. Other projects succeed at their purpose but cause destruction to the community. One reoccurring example is a village well. The village men will ask for a well because their women are forced to walk a long way to the river to carry water back. The U.S. builds the village a well and it is a success and the women no longer have a reason to leave the village. It was the trip to the river that allowed the women to communicate with women in other villages. OOPS! Too late now we can't go back and fill in the well.

We decided to focus on two projects: animal health and poultry production. In this case the rod and reel manufacturer would be Para-Vets and backyard poultry farms.

We had discussed providing scholarships to people to training them as Vet Techs. We met with Dr. Sofi from the Afghan Veterinary Association (AVA) about the project after I researched the money issue for the project. Dr. Sofi gave us a proposal to train 12 people as Para-Vets (Vet Techs). The training would be an intense five-month course taught at their new facility, which we toured a few months earlier in Jalalabad. The program would include lodging, books, meals, transportation to field sites, and a reference library upon graduation. This project later met stiff opposition from USAID and the Nagalam University, which was sponsored by USAID.

I adopted the Vet Tech curriculum from Columbus Community College in Ohio for the program. The total cost was going to be $77,000.00 and the AVA would do all of the work. We would just need to stop by for a visit from time to time. Best of all we would have Afghans to run the VetCaps. There was another reason behind our desire to train Para-Vets, and that was the women's poultry program.

A few months earlier Spc Larson was asked to sit on a board about women's empowerment. She was furious about what was going on. The State Department, with the help of the U.S. Agricultural Department, came up with a women's and widows' empowerment poultry project. The idea was women would become self sufficient by raising chickens. The chickens were imported from Pakistan and dropped off around the providence to women who qualified for the program. The chicken's died! There was no training, no follow-up inspections, no feed, (They needed 90 days of feed for the market cycle to become self-sustaining) no chicken coops, nothing just *here are your birds lady*!

That same day I met with the agriculture minister who wanted to attempt the program again. I didn't know at the time that the program had been tried and failed. The Ag minister's concept was to build a central village chicken coop and a man would live in it. The women would walk to the central chicken coops during the day to service the chickens, the man would take them to market and sell them. I had asked questions about training, feed and some other details, for which he had no answers. The whole plan smelled fishy.

Over the next few weeks the ADT's Ag section's junior NCOs developed a plan for a poultry project and what it would take to make it successful. By now we had enough experience in the field with small villages to have a good understanding of the challenges the people face when it comes to raising poultry and livestock.

The junior NCOs (Sgt Flynn, SSG Lucas, Sgt Stevens, Sgt Percival, Sgt

Bentley, and Spc Tanson) met with Dr. Sofi and presented him with their plan. They discussed it for an hour or more with LTC Velte who was sure I could find the money. The final plan, which was developed with Dr. Sofi's help listed 350 villages in the Pech River Valley with a goal of supporting 50 families in each village.

One of the cost-saving measures my NCOs came up with was why build a chicken coop when all we needed is a fence. We had been using a nylon mesh fence at the VetCap to keep the animals in and the children out, and it worked well. Why not use it for a chicken pen? The other change was to build a small nesting house for ten chickens to sit on their eggs. Some of the chicken coop structures that were built in the past became living quarters for people. Good luck living in the little chicken houses that we were going to build. The other novel idea was to let the chicken hatch the chicks like God intended and not install expensive solar-powered hatcheries that were quickly used to power the family TV set.

Dr. Sofi came back with a proposal for $55,000.00 which included, training, chicks, the fence material, the chicken house, and site visits by Para-vets. What we were doing was integrating the projects so they become self reliant.

The ADT wasn't the only organization that developed project ideas; the local government came up with projects too. We were presented with three fencing projects by the agricultural minister. The first was to rebuild the front wall of the agricultural ministry and the other two were to build a rock and concrete wall around two government agricultural sites, the Salar Bagh tea farm and the Asadabad nursery. We changed his request from ten-foot high rock and concrete walls that would have blocked the sun, to chain link fencing.

Our first project site was the Salar Bagh tea farm just up the road from us. The Ag minister agreed to meet us there and signed off on the drawings. Due to the location of the tea farm we couldn't drive. I was thankful because the MRAPs are not comfortable. The hike to the tea farm has some nice scenery, but is a bit risky due to the way the locals and the ANP drive. More than once we flipped the lever on our M-4s from safe to semi when drivers didn't understand "slow down" and appeared to be aiming at us. They understood several soldiers looking through their sights at them very quickly. The locals and the ANP don't give running over an American a second thought. I had SSG Arnold's team for security and they are quite levelheaded when it comes to the use of force.

When we arrived, I met with the Ag minister while SSG Tyner measured the property with the help of SFC Graham who documented the property with photos. SSG Tyner told me that his real desire was to be in the community, building something that would last. So I decided to put him in charge of all of our construction contracts.

While we were there, the Ag minister didn't hesitate to ask for other projects. I was prepared with blank request forms. "Here, just fill this out and have the governor sign it. I know he has money." (He has a heaping hand full of my tax dollars.) The behind the scenes deal is: the governor gets 20% and the Ag minister get 10% of the contractor's contract. That's thirty percent right off the top.

SSG Tyner and I were able to tag along on another mission. That was going up to Asadabad to look at the Ag Ministry wall project. We looked it over and decided we put it on the back burner for awhile. What the Ag minister didn't tell me was he was building a miniature orchard in his parking lot. He was going to great lengths to build a solid foundation for a planter wall, but left the concrete slab untouched. He planned to put in 12 inches of topsoil over the concrete and plant fruit trees. Somehow I don't think he has a degree in Agricultural Science. SSG Tyner and I found the old entrance gate that was replaced because it was shot full of holes. The existing perimeter wall was once the structural wall for a large warehouse. The old window and door openings were filled in with rock and concrete. The remaining was coming down on its own; one good push and it would all fall over.

On February 6th, SSG Tyner and I were at it again with contractors. This time we needed to teach them about crib wall construction. I invited only five contractors for the job walk just to keep things under control. A few weeks earlier I tried to find a cabinet shop to make me a load of Lincoln Logs. They wanted $1700.00 U.S. and the samples they made didn't even fit together. So I got out my credit card and ordered a box from Toys R Us. The box of Lincoln Logs was made in China shipped to the U.S. then shipped to Afghanistan all for $40.00. SSG Tyner took one of the pieces up to Fluor's table saw and made some additional pieces to demonstrate crib walls. When the contractors arrived he was ready. After 30 minutes of demonstration only one contractor understood the concept. When it was all over SFC Hanlin reminded me, "Sir, there's a reason these people don't have a space shuttle." He's right these contractors didn't even bring a tape measure to the job walk.

Chapter Twenty-Eight

SGT BENTLEY VS THE MRAP

Our perfect weather vanished on February 5th with snow fall in the mountains. Up along the Pakistan border all of the mountain passes had frozen over leaving just a few of the improved roads open where there are customs checkpoints. Nature had brought a halt to the trafficking of weapons and other smuggling operations. In the mornings you could see the diurnal winds draw the clouds over the mountains and into the valleys as the sun warmed the valley floors. The rivers keep the valleys from freezing, but the mountain ridges stayed below freezing so as the warm air rises from the valley it pulls the cold air down over the mountains bringing the clouds with it. It's a very pleasant sight to watch in the morning.

We continued to receive steady rain for the next few days filling up every trash can and wheel barrow that was left out in the open. Walking by one can full of water reminded me of what one of my colleagues at work remarked about two rather arrogant individuals in management who thought they were irreplaceable. He said, "When you pull your fist out of a bucket of water there is no hole."

I looked at the talent that we had in the Ag section as the water in the bucket. We have a small bucket and every drop of water is priceless. I noticed something else about the bucket of water. If an individual cups his hand at the bottom of the bucket and suddenly pulls his hand out he takes out a large amount of water, reducing the available talent.

We scheduled two weeks of leave for every soldier throughout the deployment. Their two weeks start when they touch ground at their leave destination and stops when they sign back in. For some the process of getting to and from leave has taken a full month. The reason is usually being bumped off flights, or flights being cancelled or diverted. The scheduled leaves we are prepared for; it's the emergency or urgent leave that puts us in a bind. We are very blessed to have a mature and stable group of soldiers, which minimizes the majority of the problems troops face when they are deployed. Still there are the unexpected problems. So far the problems our troops have had to face revolve around deaths in the family or extreme medical problems of a spouse or child. At first when people receive word via email, it's no problem. The problem is back home twelve times zones away. By the time the Red Cross message arrives the individual is coming out of shock. The distance that buffered them from the problem was blocking them from rendering aid. Bottom line you're here not there.

SSG Lucas received word from his family that he was needed home rather urgently. SFC Teso and SFC Graham worked their magic and were able to fly him as far as Jalalabad on Saturday February 6th. The weather turned sour so he became a reluctant resident of FOB Fenty along with SFC Fair who went down to clear his books for the month. We still had SFC Fulton and SSG Palacios stuck down in Bagram due to weather and shortage of flights, and Sgt Stevens enjoying some well-deserved leave. One fourth of our Ag section was missing, and we had another VetCap scheduled for Sunday the 7th.

Sgt Bentley, our medic and another multi talented individual would have to do double duty taking on the additional responsibilities at the VetCap. Fortunately the SecFor section had a few good NCOs, Sgts Carter and Fry who knew how to handle animals and enjoyed working on the VetCaps.

The troops were set to roll out the gate at 6:45 Sunday morning, which meant wake up at 4:30, put the trucks online at 5:00 A.M., then eat breakfast, followed by convoy briefs, final checks of weapons and latrine call.

The moon was supposed to be shining Sunday morning, but with the rain clouds above there wasn't even the smallest glimmer of light seeping through. There was a light rain that made the road slick. I had to use my flashlight as usual to navigate the roads of the FOB so I wouldn't fall into one of the drainage ditches. Even with a flashlight it was difficult to make out anything other than the road three feet ahead. Only the focal point of the light illuminated the road. The light's halo was swallowed up whole by the darkness. I wouldn't see a vehicle parked along the road until I was right next to it. When I reached our barracks area, the troops were busy loading up the guns and other last minute equipment on the MRAPs. One by one a ground guide would step forward with a small flash light and guide them up to the flight line. I went as far as the last of the big guns to see what was going on, then turned around and went back to our office to work on contracts before the convoy departed. Even if I was not on the mission I liked to attend the convoy brief and see everyone off. If my troops were up at 4:30 then I was up at 4:30.

Just as I reached our office, SFC Medina came down the stairs and told me that SGT Bentley had just crushed his foot under an MRAP. The other troops had pulled a stretcher off one of the vehicles and carried him to the trauma center. I arrived at the trauma center just as they were cutting off his pants and taking his boot off. Sgt Bentley had a firm hold on the bed rails trying not to move his leg while they pulled his boot off. He had the attention of the full surgical team so I left and went to collect his personal gear from the MRAP. I found his rifle and his bag and took them back to my quarters. Then I went back to the trauma center. One of the medics who answered the call gave me his IBA (Improved Body Armor) which by then was in pieces and a big plastic bag of what was left of his clothes. I placed everything in my quarters so it would dry out. We were having a steady rain since 11 o'clock the night before so all of his clothing and equipment were soaked.

We went back up to the trauma center and met Chaplain Schobrt who had also been summoned. By then the morphine was starting to take effect. I thought morphine took effect almost immediately but it didn't. The surgeon told me that Sgt Bentley is a big guy and the bigger you are the longer it takes. It is true, Sgt Bentley is a big guy. His boots are the size of a battleship. I asked Sgt Bentley if he wanted a photo for his baby book and he said "yes" and gave the thumbs up to the camera. I asked if there was anything he wanted and he said "no." I walked out and the chaplain stayed behind for a minute. I gave a progress report to everyone in our TOC. The doctors planned to fly him out to Jalalabad, then Bagram and finally to Germany. The chaplain walked in and gave us a list of things

SGT Bentley wanted to take with him. One item was still in the MRAP and the other items were in his room.

The chaplain and I went up to the flight line just as the convoy was moving out. ADT 17, the vehicle that SGT Bentley was gunning was being left behind. We just didn't have enough people because we had two missions going out that day. SFC Media the Ag NCOIC and SFC Mosqueda the SecFor NCOIC decided to leave ADT 17 behind and move the rest of the folks around. They were taking several civilians including one reporter from one of the three major TV networks. We were able to get the keys to ADT 17 and didn't find what we were looking for. The chaplain parted from me and went back to the trauma center to be with Sgt Bentley, while I went to Sgt Bentley's quarters. Just as luck would have it the medivac flight flew over with its escort and I had the wrong combination to the lock on his quarters. I went around to the other side and contemplated boosting Sgt Olson who had just come off guard duty and was out like a light. Hastling with Sgt Olson over the participation was easy enough. The trick was how would I recover him with the goods? Then he woke up and told me the combination. I found everything Sgt Bentley had asked for and was out the door. It was an uphill run to the helicopters. I reached the flight line, could see the door of the helicopter being closed and the litter team moving out of the way. Chaplain Schobrt saw me and waved to the pilot then grabbed one of the bags I was carrying. The crew chief opened a window, reached out and grabbed each bag then shut the window. The medivac and its escort Black Hawk took off. Our commander had arrived as the chaplain and I cleared the helipad. The weather had turned sour and that medivac flight was the last flight of the day.

We had two of our NCOs marooned at Jalalabad: SFC Fair and SSG Lucas because of bad weather. They greeted SGT Bentley and gave us progress reports. By evening SGT Bentley was off the morphine and parked in front of a TV set. The doctors said he had four broken bones in his foot and two broken toes. They couldn't operate for at least two weeks until the swelling went down. The doctor told SFC Fair that the mountain boots Sgt Bentley was wearing saved his foot otherwise he most likely would have lost his foot. The footprint of each tire on the MRAP is 85 pounds per square inch, but when you reduce the contact area and concentrate all the weight of one tire on a person's foot, the pressure almost triples.

The winter storm, which had pelted us with snow and rain had also dropped enough snow in Bagram to close down the runway. SGT Bentley would remain in Jalalabad for another night. The doctors said that there was a possibility that he might be able to return to Camp Wright on limited duty, but only if they could operate on him in Bagram. We weren't going to be holding our breath. At his request we put together a suitcase and a care package for him that we hoped to get on Molson Air to Jalalabad where SFC Fair and SSG Lucas could deliver it. We struck out with that plan when all flights were cancelled.

In the mean time, LTC Velte and my Ag section were busy setting up a VetCap in the rain. The village elder greeted them and told them that no one was coming due to the rain, and then asked "Why did you come in the rain?" LTC Velte was not about to turn around and go back. He laid a guilt trip on the village elder and told him to tell his people to come the VetCap.

This time there wasn't anything close to an ideal location to host a VetCap so LTC Velte and the Civil Affairs LT from COP Michigan set up inside the village using the village as part of the security. Zormanday Village is located at the mouth of the Korengal Valley a real hot spot for the insurgents. To get to the village you have to cross the Pech River leaving Route Rhode Island behind. Before the day was over LTC Velte and the Ag section with the help of the AVA vaccinated over 500 animals. Amazing, the village elder thought no one would show up due to the rain. The rain was our friend because the insurgents do not like to fight in the rain; they stayed home where it was warm, just like a bunch of street thugs.

On Monday the 8th SGT Bentley was flown to Bagram. As luck would have it Sgt Johanson was going on leave and flying out that night to Bagram so we handed him Sgt Bentley's suitcase and care package to take with him. We knew that Sgt Bentley wouldn't be walking around at the bazaar with a crushed foot and wearing only his shorts, so it wouldn't be a difficult task to track Sgt Bentley down at the hospital.

By midday Tuesday we received word that Sgt Bentley wouldn't be coming back and to prepare his belongings for shipment home. SFC Graham, 1LT Ko and I spent a good five hours inventorying his property and packing it. Medics have a lot of equipment especially this one.

The good news for Tuesday was the return of SFC Fulton, and SFC Fair with our cash draw. We finished the day with a rehearsal for the next

VetCap. Then Sgt Johanson called back and said they flew Sgt Bentley out a few hours before. He arrived and was sending his stuff back with the PRT.

The rehearsal brief for the February 10th VetCap had just started when I heard the direct fire siren going off. It sounds like a WWII air raid siren. We piled into the bunker, and the SecFor NCOs prepared to respond. We had the QRF (Quick Reaction Force) duty for the week. Chaplain Schobrt just happened to be in the trauma center when a local national walked in. All the local nationals knew was he fell by the fuel point and his back hurt. Turns out he didn't fall, he was knocked over when he was shot and his back hurt because there was a bullet in it. The insurgent who shot him couldn't have had worse timing. A Black Hawk gunship was flying by when the shooter was spotted. He was running for his life several kilometers back to his village knowing full well what the Black Hawk could do to his future. There wasn't any word on the outcome.

We rolled out on the morning of February 10th just as the sun was making its way over the mountains. When we entered the Pech River valley we could see snow capped mountains at both ends of the valley. This time we were taking along several visitors from the embassy, and a new State Department rep by the name of Jim who was very astute about the situation in Afghanistan, Haiti and Mexico. Jim is part of the civilian surge to Afghanistan. He was given two weeks' notice to be in Kabul. There was a major civilian surge going on in both Afghanistan and Iraq. The State Department was gearing up for a major effort in Iraq. When the president said he was pulling out the combat troops, he didn't mean that he was pulling out. Combat troops are now security forces; all others are non-combat troops like us. I think that the pajama men of the insurgency understand that there is no difference between attacking an active Army infantry unit or a bunch of citizen soldiers who just happen to be farmers. Either way you're going to get your clock cleaned.

What we had been able to accomplish with these VetCaps was amazing and word made it past the division level up to the higher command and the embassy. We also took along the same reporter from a major TV news channel who witnessed SGT Bentley crush his foot. She was a bit snippy to put it mildly. Jim made a comment that she is not your friend and to be careful. That much I knew having talked to her a few days earlier. I had asked her what types of stories she was interested in covering. She took a long time to respond, then said she was focusing on veterinary stories. I told her about Dr. Sofi and the remarkable things he had achieved with the AVA, and what the animals meant to the villages. Then I realized she wasn't there to cover VetCaps. She started asking questions that had no relevance to animal health. The following day when I was outside the wire with Sgt Arnold and his security team I saw her drive by in the back of one of EODs MRAPs. She made a point to wave as they drove by. Her fame spread quickly around the FOB with each contact she made. At the VetCap she decided to interview a man with his horse. The man was well off; his horse was sporting a new English saddle that wasn't made in western Asia. As God's timing would have it one of the locals brought in a large water buffalo. The buffalo wouldn't move so one of the kids we hired swatted it with a branch. That's all it took to drag five of our troops with it. We told the reporter to move, they had a buffalo coming through. She snapped back ,"I'm doing an interview!" Tell it to the buffalo Toots. The horse had the sense to move out of the way. She really expected us to watch her camera equipment and tend to her needs as if we were sent by the American taxpayer to support her.

I am becoming more and more jaded when it comes to reporters. Most come with an agenda and are just looking for footage to support their agenda. They fail to report what is going on. One reporter from a major California newspaper referred to the residences as mud huts. This gives the reader a very different mental image of the structure. A more accurate description would be walled adobe compounds. Thus far I had found the Associate Press presented the best information. The stars and stripes feature many of their articles and I was able to verify the contents very easily.

When the day was over we serviced 908 animals. I worked with the village elder handing out dietary supplements for cattle, and radios. I just kept the supply coming and he marked their hands and kept the kids in line. We developed a good system in dealing with the unruly kids. If a kid pushed past him to the table he would point to the road with his thumb, and I would tell him to go home (in Pashto) in a stern voice then refer to the elder.

Our up and coming TV reporter left the following morning. Many people were quite relieved to see her go. She had the ability to put people on the defensive very quickly. You could almost see the hair on the backs of people's neck stand up as she approached them. The rest of the day was spent writing contracts and closing out the mid month books with SFC Fair.

The last event of the day was when Sgt Bentley emailed Sgt Flynn and let him know that the count was up to seven broken bones in his foot and that he was being flown to Texas for the surgery in the morning and that SSG Lucas was stuck in Bagram. SFC Fair and I called it a night after spending 12 hours working on finances and contracts.

Chapter Twenty-Nine

THE DEATH OF WILLIE
THE WHALE

Laj Bar, the village elder from Woch Now Village came down and told us his cousin was killed repairing the pipe system from the spring. We were wondering why all of the men had gathered at the mosque the day before. He didn't have much more to say just wanted to share the news with us. He came back a few days later and told us that while he was out gathering wood he spotted an RPG team up on the ridge line. Once again a little friendship goes a long way. We planned to have his village make re-bar cages for us as a means of seeding a new crib wall enterprise soon. We also thought it would be a good way to strengthen the relationship between the village and the camp.

The last of our old artillery unit left by mid February and the new unit was conducting registration firing for their first few days. It's a lot of fun to watch the rounds hit the mountains to the east of us. First you see the flash, then the smoke followed by an explosion of rock blasting out from the mountain. The rock formations are unstable. At first glance the rock formations look like grey granite, but they act more like slate. The locals can split the rock with a few well placed strikes leaving two flat edges. Just the over pressuring of an artillery blast will cause these rock formations to crumble.

We had another good snowstorm on Sunday February 14th. The snow level dropped down to the 500-foot level, but still there was no ice on the valley floor. The Kunar River is fed by glaciers so it is not a warm river, but it is the only thing I can think of that keeps the valley floor from freezing. The freezing and thawing up in the mountains also causes the rocks to break apart and fall to the canyon floors, which is what I think happened to our friend up by the Witch's Teton. He was working up there during the period when we had ice and snow on top of the ridge line. We were told he was killed when a large rock struck his head. We hiked up there in December and January when the weather was warm and there were rocks falling down from above, then.

All of the mountain passes to Pakistan froze over on Sunday preventing the insurgents from moving supplies into Afghanistan. The only routes from Pakistan to Afghanistan left open pass through customs checkpoints. The customs officials could still be bribed, but the insurgents would have to pay a healthy bribe to get their supplies across.

On Monday morning the storm front lifted and we had clear skies again, something we needed. The concrete forms SSG Lucas made were soaked and needed to dry out so we could paint them. SSG Tyner took over the task of building foreman and put the Fluor crew to work making mini forms and assembling re-bar cages. By lunchtime most of the snow had melted. Later in the afternoon only the distant peaks and ridgelines still had snow. The daily high was averaging 65 degrees, not the 45 degrees we enjoyed for the week prior.

With the storm front past and the skies clear it was safe for Willie the Whale to climb back up into the sky. Willie was our eye in the sky and is controlled out of a small ConEx office on the ground. Our concrete forms were all laid out getting a suntan so we could get them painted before the next storm front rolled in. The marines were having their big offensive down south so the weather was supporting everyone.

In the mornings, I'd check the net to see what was going on down south. If the papers didn't tell me that there was a major offensive going on I never would have known; it looked like business as usual. The offensive is like repairing an old garden hose. Just as soon as you repair one leak another one springs forth.

When the storm front lifted and the temperatures increased the mountain passes thawed out. The insurgents were smart enough not to attempt to smuggle supplies through the south because of the Marines. The Marines were fighting foreign fighters from Pakistan and the Middle East. The Afghan insurgents had enough brains to either lay low or go back to Pakistan the mother ship of the insurgency.

On Tuesday afternoon I heard the sound of a lawn mower engine flying over the valley. I knew by the sound it was the Predator, but I couldn't see it. The Army uses the Predator to patrol the MSR (Main Supply Routes) and other hot spots. What I didn't know was a few miles north east of us was a large caravan of mules loaded full of supplies intended to support the insurgency being led by a hundred or so insurgents and their leaders. What insurgents didn't know as they left Pakistan through the Kaga pass was there were more than one set of eyes on them. Since the weather cleared there was a ton of flights that were backed up for shuttling troops and government folks back and forth. There were helicopters six ways from Sunday up in the sky. There were troops in the field catching up on patrols, and an F-15s cruising the area. If it wasn't one person it was ten dozen others observing the Kaga pass. It was just the wrong day to try to sneak through someone's back door.

Just about everyone and their brother was keeping an eye on them letting them get just a little closer. The closer they came the longer the run home to Pakistan was. The pass also gets very steep in some areas. The caravan finally stopped at a cave complex for one reason of another, just when an F-15 was flying past. The F-15 was given the ten digit grid of where to drop the first GBU by someone who had a good set of eyes on the target. The F-15 dropped its GBU 12 on the caravan and departed. Then F-16s and F-15s joined in dropping an assortment of GBUs. The GBU 12 and 38s are 500-pound bombs while the GBU 31 is a 2000-pound bomb. All of the GBUs are GPS guided with some additional back up systems. The GBUs sealed up most of the caves and caused an avalanche. There were twenty insurgents known to have been killed by the initial GBU blast and one was spotted being buried under the ensuing avalanche. The big guns at Camp Wright were given the honor of the grand finale.

At 1900, the big guns went off blowing my window open. You could hear a split second delay between the guns as their tails were pulled. I went outside after a few minutes and the guns were still firing. I heard a funny sound after two rounds went over head. I didn't hear any explosion so I just ignored it. About that time Lt. Ko noticed the feed from Willie was going haywire. Down below at the eye in the sky control room, it was "Huston we have a problem. Willie's been harpooned! Quick reel him in," called out Captain Ahab. The crew scrambled out of their control room to the winch and gave it all they had just as if Fedallah's body was still beckoning them on. It was a fight between man and beast. Willie crashed in the farmer's field 500 yards from the post right on the crest of the Kunar River.

Willie the Whale the Lockheed Martin Aerostat balloon in the background. Kunar ADT troops participating in the June 4th first ever Camp Wright 5K run.

Sgt Gonsalves and Spc Coffman, in the Entry Control Point Tower saw Willie hit the ground. They called it in to the PRT TOC, and then quickly built two magazines of tracers in the event local scavengers decided to grab a souvenir.

The ANA rolled out within a few minutes to secure the road in both directions. Willie's tether was stretched across Route California; any vehicle that hit that cable would be in a world of hurt.

I went over to the eye in the sky boys to see what they needed from us. SFC Mosqueda was already spinning up the QRF. What the eye in the sky boys needed was a five-ton flat bed truck to haul the balloon's payload back

236

to camp. We didn't have a flatbed, but we did have a large trailer, which had been transformed into a drying rack for our concrete forms. I gave a call on the radio to SFC Mosqueda to come get the trailer on his way out the gate. Sgt Fry met me at the trailer and we readied it for "Operation Salvage Willie." Spc Mc Cool came over from the blue gate and the three of us hauled the trailer down past the blue gate and waited for one of our 1151s to come get it. Within ten minutes we had the eye in the sky boys out with their wounded toy and the area fully secured. SFC Mosqueda ran the operations staying with the eye in the sky boys while Sgt Arnold had the responsibility of securing the site, leaving SSG Valenzuela with the responsibility of safety and catching the balloon once the payload was cut free. SSG Valenzuela had no intention of chasing the balloon; he just parked an MRAP on its tether and called it good.

Just after the QRF picked up our trailer, the remaining blue gate guard was having a difficult time with a group of interpreters who lived across from the blue gate. I walked up to see what was going on. All of the interpreters had their cell phones out telling their friends what was going on, leaving the building door open washing the gate in white light. I approached them and asked, "Didn't my sentry just tell you to go inside and close the door?" Their leader responded saying that they were going to a meeting at the PRT and the group started walking down the hill. "Gentlemen the PRT is uphill."

"Oh the meeting is over."

"Then go inside and shut the door." All of a sudden none of them understood English and kept walking down the hill. I raised my voice and told them to go inside. They reluctantly obeyed, then I doubled up the guard on the gate.

Having taught middle school for a few years I knew what to expect next. I went over and leaned up against the threshold of their doorway. I could hear all of the shouting going on inside when it suddenly got quiet as the door opened. I asked "Why are you coming out?"

"Oh my friend wants to know if he can go home. He lives off post."

"Tell your friend that he is staying here for the night and don't come out again."

They knew something was going on worth telling the world about. I'm certain that when they attempted to come out they saw six troops standing at the gate. I left the blue gate and went up to the Entry Control Tower to tell the troops, "Job well done," for spotting the landing site of the balloon. Without them we would have had to follow the tether cable.

Within 90 minutes the payload was cut loose and loaded on the trailer. I could hear SSG Arnold moving his troops back away from the cable just in case the balloon decided to make a run for it. Our troops stayed and watched the balloon until 1:00 A.M. Then the PRT came out and took over. We swapped positions again in the morning.

I was up early as usual. I had some unfinished business to do with the interpreters. I went up to their boss and told him about what happened during the night. We went down together and rousted them all out of bed. We lined them up outside to read them the riot act. We almost fired one of them, but the problem was all seven of them together were the problem. While their boss was drilling away they sadly couldn't understand English. That was the wrong tactic to pull. Their boss reminded them that they all understood English otherwise they wouldn't be interpreters. Then it was my turn at bat. I don't believe either speech made an impact, but getting them out of bed in the morning I'm sure upset them.

I went up the hill for breakfast and passed SFC Eaddy who was on his way to talk to the farmer about the damage our balloon did to his floundering winter wheat. The farmer demanded that the United States pay $1200.00 for the wheat crop that would fully recover. The Afghan farmers must have learned this trick from the Germans!

When I reached the mess hall there was a sign on the door for all to read. On the left side was a photo of Willie the Whale with the caption, "Good." On the right was a photo of Osama Ben Laden with the caption "Bad."

Kunar (40th) ADT troops unrolling a new balloon on Friday morning February 19th

Willie the Whale is a Aerostat balloon who's design is very similar to the WWI and WWII balloons that were used to protect ships from aircraft. Willie was 30 years old, is a veteran of the War on Drugs and flew over the Gulf of Mexico monitoring drug trafficking during the 1980s.

The first step in the resurrection process of Willie was to strip down the cradle and place the pallet containing the new balloon on top of the cradle. With the help of some local nationals several large tarps were laid on the ground to protect the new balloon from sharp rocks. Having a new balloon in flight was extremely important to the defense of the FOBs in the area. The insurgents knew that the balloon was a vital part of the defense. If they knew it was disabled they might mount a hasty attack against one of the FOBs.

On Friday morning 12 of our troops went over to the balloon yard to help six Lockheed Martin folks unroll a new balloon. Willie would be inflated at midnight when the air temperature was its coldest and the winds had died down. The goal was to have Willie in the air by Saturday morning or at least make the insurgents believe he could fly by morning.

Willie's nose and main body were unrolled on the cradle and his lower body and tail fins rested on the tarps below. After the skin was rolled out the Lockheed Martin crew install all of the ornaments such as infra-red marker lights, gas valves, cables and ropes.

The following morning Saturday February 20th at 1:00 A.M. the ADT arrived back at the balloon yard to assist with the inflation process. We had a quick safety brief, then the fun began.

Inflating an Aerostat balloon is similar to ballasting a ship in the water; it must be balanced. Ballasting a balloon requires different gas mixtures in specific parts of the balloon. The two lower tailfins are filled with outside air, which is the heaviest mixture. The heavier air causes the lower fins to hang down and act as a twin rudder. The team's favorite tool for inflating the lower tailfins is a leaf blower and a shopvac for the starboard and port tailfins.

The belly of the balloon is filled with a mixture of air and helium. This makes the belly heavier, which keeps the balloon upright. The backbone of the balloon and dorsal tailfin are filled with pure helium. While all of this was going on the crew was up on the cradle slowly winching the nose of the balloon into the nose cone of the cradle. The rest of the team worked under the cradle making sure that the balloon fabric didn't catch on anything.

We were having a slight breeze at the time, which was causing the balloon to thrash back and forth. The helium is filled from the main body to the tail and the dorsal fin. As the volume of gas increased the body started to rise off the cradle. Just as luck would have it the wind also picked up. We had several people pulling on the lines trying to keep the tail straight so it would fill properly. The wind was so strong that it twisted the tail shutting off the flow of helium. Finally there was a lull in the wind just as we pulled on the ropes and the tail righted itself. Almost instantaneously the gas surged from the main body to the tail and the tail lifted off the ground. We raced around securing the lines while the crew on top of the cradle started securing the balloon to the cradle. The gas was shut off at the same time.

By first light, the new Willie was securely moored in his new home. He still wasn't ready to fly, but the insurgents had no way of knowing. The Lockheed Martin crews continued to mount all of the equipment on

Willie's belly and started the calibration process. It was non-stop until Willie started making his first test flights. The crew would send him up a ways and check his balance then readjust the payload and try again. The high winds we were having weren't helping the process, but they weren't stopping it either. It took a team effort of manpower and logistic support to get Willie back up in the air; it was the hallmark of an American community.

Chapter Thirty

WELCOME TO THE CHOWKAY VALLEY

The week of February 14th had been interesting. Besides big guns shooting down Willie the Whale, Mr. USAID cried wolf again. A while back he wanted us to work with the Kunar Construction College on a crib wall project. He was going to pay for it all if we engineered it. He wanted us to come up with a solution for the entry road, which was rapidly being eaten away by erosion. I pulled up a crib wall design from the Cal Trans web page and then designed the forms to cast the concrete parts. After we coordinated everything with the KCC, Mr. USAID told us he couldn't pay for it and that the KCC had no means to accept money from us to do the job.

His next caper was, "I'll pay for the Kala Kowchano Valley flood control project; call off the contractors. I have a group in Asadabad that will do it." Then he started making conditions, "USAID will only pay for the project if gabions are used and they must be made by local women. USAID will only pay for what can be seen from Route California. USAID will not pay for the project because it is too close to Camp Wright."

I called the contractors back and submitted the funding request again. I lost a full month because of Mr. USAID.

Mr. USAID wasn't finished. He told our commander that, "USAID will pay for flood control projects in two other valleys just south of the camp if the ADT will do the engineering." Our commander agreed, called me in and gave me my marching orders for two surveys. The first location was just south of the Nowabad bridge the resting village for the insurgents. The second location was the Chowkay Valley by FOB Fortress. I asked him where the Chowkay Valley was since one Chawkey sounds like another Chowkay. Ah yes that Chowkay Valley where the AAF (Anti Afghan Forces) invited us to the surprise RPG Fest at Kandaray (also spelled Karboray) Village.

Fortunately for me that day (December 12th, 2009) I was entertaining a sniper with the rest of the Ag section, which turned out to be another unremarkable event. We sent a team to the Kandaray Village for a KLE. (Key Leader Engagement - the Afghans call the meeting a shurah when they include the village elders.) Attending the KLE was the village elder selected ANA (Afghan National Army) troops and some boys from the 10th Mountain Division. While the meeting was going on Spc Larson attended to some of the children in the village who were in need of medical attention, at the battle space owner's request. Soon the old toothless men started crowding around her wanting her to feel their foreheads just like she did for the children. The old men got an endless amount of joy from the experience. While the shurah was going on SSG Valenzuela took to the task of turning the vehicles around and setting up a defense. Just as our team was coming out of the Shurah a group of AAF fighters who were hiding across the valley behind a spur opened fire with RPGs on our troops. The AAF troops were not that familiar with their weapons. They fired their RPGs beyond their maximum effective range so the rounds fell short into the valley below. With each RPG round that was fired the position of an AAF warrior was revealed. The ADT and 10th Mountain responded with 50 cal, MK 19 fire at the AAF positions. The gallant ANA was nowhere to be seen. SSG Valenzuela jumped into an abandoned truck and fired up its 50 cal then joined SFC Fair who had his EBR. They grabbed SSG Arnold and went to a spur where SPC Rivera and Robledo had set up a position to guard against any flanking movement by the AAF. There was a report on the radio that AAF had been seen crossing the valley to the ADT's south.

After forty-five minutes, the whole event was over. The ADT and 10th Mountain started loading up in their trucks when the ANA suddenly reappeared. "ISAF!" (Aka - I Saw Americans Fight.) The ANA started firing their RPGs up the mountainside and spraying the mountains with lead. Our troops yelled at them to cease fire, because there were people up on the hills, but the ANA didn't care; it was then safe to come out and shoot.

The Chowkay Valley is several miles long with a wide mouth and a steep narrow road. The headwaters for the Chowkay Valley originate on the Kugal Ghar (Mount Kugal) ridge line, which is also the origin of the Korengal Valley. Both the Chowkay and Korengal Valleys are major insurgent locations. The mouth of the Chowkay Valley opens up directly across from several mountain passes that lead directly into Pakistan. This is almost a super highway for smuggling and insurgent movement.

Battle space owners rotate out every year plus or minus a few months. It wouldn't be long until the Kunar ADT escorted a new unit up into the Chowkay Valley. The Kunar ADT is by no means a ranger battalion. We are blessed to have some very seasoned NCOs and plenty of good soldiers. You never know just how good you are until you work with a new unit.

On Tuesday February 23rd we moved out before dawn to meet with the new company commander who owned the battle space in the Chowkay Valley. We were going up the Chowkay Valley together to meet with the village elders, survey the river and inspect a small hydro plant. The battle space owner wanted us at his FOB early so we could meet with the village elders at 0900. When we arrived the company commander was in the process of getting dressed. He told us that things were pushed back an hour. The reason was the government officials were not going to be ready until later. He knew this the morning before and didn't bother telling us.

We waited an hour, then finally moved out to the district government center to pick up the officials. The government officials had no intention of getting into one of our vehicles let alone go up into the Chowkay Valley. The convoy started up again, then turned off Route California up the Chowkay Valley. We passed an infant funeral along the way. There was one man, carrying the child with a tapestry draped over the corpse, leading a procession of men out of the mosque to the cemetery. The cemetery was the usual design void of any green vegetation. All of the graves were marked with a large piece of slate protruding out of the ground like a large crystal growth. The slate grave markers have no marking on them at all. Large markers are for adults and smaller ones for children. A woman's grave is indicated by a squared off slate while a man's is pointed. From the road it appeared that the graves were just dug in a random pattern.

Kunar ADT movement from Karboray Village to Seray Village February 23rd 2010

We arrived at Karboray Village at 11:00, dismounted and walked up to the clinic at the Seray Village. We passed a large amount of timber, all cedar. Some of it was hued square with an ax, some had band saw markings on it. We were certain that all of it was smuggled into the country due to the small size of the timbers. When we arrived we learned that the village elders were not expecting us. The village elders work during the day; they do not wait around for visitors. The battle space owner told us that they had scheduled a meeting at the community clinic. When dealing with Afghanis you never know what is going to happen when it comes to meetings. After waiting in front of the clinic for an hour, a group of elders from the Karboray Village arrived and escorted us down to their community center. Our commander went in to attend the meeting while LTC Velte and I stayed outside and added to the security.

SFC Fair on the right with an M-14, LTC Kelly on the left with an M-4. In the background is the Seray Medical clinic under construction.

I took up a position with SGT Percival, which gave us good fields of fire and visibility of the road, with a fair amount of protection. Then the battle space owner moved one of his 1151 behind us. This is also called an RPG magnet.

The KLE wasn't going well. The battle space owner was telling the elders about all of the detailed processing they had to go through to get projects. The elders complained that the district government only helps people down below, never their villages. Finally our commander piped in and told them they need to go to the district government and tell them what they want. The elders responded, "You never help us. You never come visit us. You are never at the district center." This wasn't the case. There was a new school under construction by the PRT in the next village. There were new well pumps installed by the PRT and new retaining walls. Even the paved road that linked their villages to the district center was a PRT project. The U.S. tax payer has spent a lot of money on these two villages. Our commander ended the meeting but asked if we could walk down to the river and check out erosion problems and the micro-hydro power plant. He told them that what was causing them problems with erosion was also causing major problems downstream. If they would work with the villages downstream they could solve both of their problems.

While this was going on, SGT Percival and I noticed a herd of four cows coming up the road, but only one passed us. The other three had been secured back in the draw, which was obscured from our sight.

The KLE with the village elders was over. The tone of the meeting was, *we want to be your friends and we want to help you.* We could hear traffic on the radio that the artillery from the local FOB was going to fire some registration rounds. We also heard traffic from the Kiowa scouts overhead asking the FOB FDC (Fire Direction Control), "Are you sure you want to do that now?"

We assembled on the road and pushed back up the hill past Seray Village to a point where we could walk down to the river. Both villages were deserted and we couldn't see anyone working around their homes or out in their yards. We were expecting to be attacked when we were loading up the trucks to go home. The imminent attack was confirmed by the absence of villagers and the securing of livestock.

We moved off the paved road walking across some barren earth to the first wheat field. The fields were overwatered as usual, which made the soil stick to our boots if we stepped off the irrigation canals. We would walk the canal, then there would be a three to four foot drop to the next terrace. About halfway between the road and the river was a flour mill. The mill stone was in good shape, but there was no evidence that it had been used in recent history.

Once in the Chowkay River we took a moment to see where the high water marks were. The sunlight was just right to see the change in the rock's color indicating where the high water marks were. The Chowkay River had risen up over thirty feet, more than once, in its lifetime. Sgt Percival and I started a hasty survey of the river taking photos and GPS readings but no tape measurements. The canyon walls were interfering with the accuracy of the GPS elevation readings. We concluded that any improvement project would be a major undertaking, which the security of the valley wouldn't support.

Further down the river was a set of retaining walls on either side that prevented us from walking along the river banks. The retaining walls started at the headwater of a concrete lined canal that fed the micro-hydro power plant, which our commander and LTC Velte were going to inspect. LTC Velte was an electrician by trade. We climbed on top of the canal wall and walked to a point where our two patrols would have to split up. Our commander and LTC Velte, 1SGT, SFC Fair, SGT Arnold's security team and our USDA rep followed the aqueduct and I took SGT Percival and Corporal Derouen's security team back down into the river for some more GPS points and photos. Corporal Derouen's team included SPC Clements, Spc Rivera, and Spc Arechiga.

Location where the ADT's commander and LTC Kelly's patrols took separate routes. The poppy fields were discovered behind the first spur on the right. The RPG firing location is overhead. The green grass is winter wheat.

A few minutes after we dropped down into the river, we heard the 105 rounds impacting in the mountains above Seray Village. I noticed a man sitting by the river relaxing and reading a book. We kept right on going. We had moved about another 500 feet when SGT Percival found a beautiful muscovite rock. He cleaned it off and I put it in his backpack for him. I had just zipped up his backpack when two 105 rounds struck the ridge line. Then we heard the sound of an RPG go off. We looked up toward the road and saw the black smoke from the impact. The next sound we heard was a PKM machine gun going off. We stopped for a second to attempt to determine where the rounds were coming from. Knowing from which direction the rounds are coming determines which side of a rock you hid behind.

At the same time, over at the micro-hydro plant our commander's team came across two poppy fields. Our USDA rep took a few cuttings to bring back to verify they were poppies. This crop hadn't bulbed yet so the discovery needed to be verified back at the office. LTC Velte noticed a man securing his cow to a tree, then disappear. LTC Velte observed some of the first PKM rounds fired hit about 20 feet from their group.

By then the ADT was returning fire to the mountain above us. The host unit still didn't know that they were taking fire; they just assumed it was the registration rounds. Once they got the word from us they flooded the radio net making it difficult for our gunners and drivers to communicate over the intercoms. Fortunately we had our own LMR (Land Mobile Radio), but the canyon walls were also interfering with our LMRs. We could hear the rounds flying over our heads and we went for improved cover. SGT Percival and I agreed that the targets were the trucks not us. I tried calling our other patrol on the LMR to see if they needed me to set up near side security on the river, but couldn't make contact. We took an extra minute or two to scope out the situation. SGT Percival was able to see a crevice that had been carved out by storm water leading down between two farmers fields. Corporal Derouen waved the two of us forward with SPC Rivera leading the way. We vaulted over several stone walls. I got stuck straddling one wall. My foot sunk in the mud so I didn't have enough oomph to get over in one jump. I received a friendly push from below and promptly stuck the other foot into the mud on the other side. I think I know why these farmers are having problems with their wheat crops. They are watering for rice.

We hopped a few more rock walls until we reached the crevice. Corporal Derouen saw where the RPG gunner was and laid down some suppressive fire while we worked our way up the crevice. I gave SGT Percival a boost up one rock face then threw him my M-4 and was able to pull myself up. I turned and gave a hand up to Spc Clements who assisted Spc Arechiga. I looked up in time to see an RPG go haywire from its projectory and burst in the air in front of an approaching Kiowa. The Kiowa's response was instantaneous as we could see the 2.75" rocket's impact on the mountain and hear their 50 cal burst.

The Kiowas would fly over us firing at the insurgents and peel off then the ADT would lay down more MK-19 and 50 cal fire. We couldn't hear any returning fire from the other unit. Then we heard one of the pilots announce that he saw one insurgent chuck his AK-47 at the mouth of a cave, which had a pile of RPGs in it. The second Kiowa swooped in and fired several 2.75" rockets into the cave. The resulting explosion looked like the 4th of July. Whatever was in that cave blew a hail storm of rocks down into the canyon.

We continued our climb homing in on the sound of the 50 cal on the road. Just as we reached an exposed landing, Corporal Derouen and Spc Arechiga spotted the PKM gunner across the valley. They laid down some suppressive fire and then caught up to the rest of us about 30 seconds later. We rallied at a house after climbing 80 meters just before we reached the road. The house was all closed up with no indication of activity, not even chickens in the yard. We met a sergeant and two soldiers from the battle space owner who told us that one of our vehicles had been struck by an RPG. I asked which way the vehicles went since they had moved. The sergeant told me they moved down the road. They had to reposition the convoy because his unit's vehicles couldn't target the insurgents from their locations. I told Corporal Derouen's when we get there we'd either pull security or aid and litter. We still had another 30 meters to go until we reached the road.

We reached the crest of the road a bit winded. Our vehicles had moved a good 300 meters down the road to meet up with our other team. We spotted the rear vehicle, made a quick check for security and made a run for it. Fortunately, it was all downhill. As we approached the vehicles I noticed a large hole that had been blasted in the road.

An RPG had struck the mountainside above Spc McCool's MRAP. That was the hint he needed to back up to throw off the aim of the insurgents. Just as he backed up, one RPG flew over the gunner's head and cratered in the road. Mc Cool put the MRAP into drive and parked over the impact. When asked why he was parking there, Mc Cool replied, "RPGs are like lightning; they never strike the same place twice." This was why the sergeant we met thought one of our vehicles was struck by an RPG.

Our commander's team was farther down the river when the attack started. They had the pleasure of moving across the terracing. Each terrace was a ten-foot drop. Our commander managed to perform a face plant into the soft mud below one of them and injured his ankle pretty badly. Our convoy spotted his team moving across the farms and moved farther down the road to be closer to him. This movement is what required us to run the extra 500 meters down the hill and why I spotted the crater in the road.

Our other team still had to cross the river before they could rally at a small village then work their way up to the road where the MRAPs were waiting for them. Since they were farther down the river when the attack started, they didn't have the steep climb to make.

We had a guest from the Pentagon named LTC Owens who turned out to be very astute about what was going on in Afghanistan and Washington and how the ADTs were having a positive impact. During the attack she observed the ANA (Afghan National Army) troops who were with us continue to sleep, eat, or just sit and talk during all of the fighting.

The attack had stopped the moment the Kiowas hit the weapons cache but things weren't over yet. The Kiowas spotted a group of men by a culvert that ran inside a structure when the Kiowas approached. The convoy would have to pass over the culvert to get back to Route California. We waited until the route clearance team came and cleared the road back to Route California. They had to clear it twice: once on the way up and once leading back to Route California. The route clearance teams are equipped with some special equipment that is much faster than having us dismount and do it ourselves. They didn't find any IEDs, and we arrived at Camp Wright in time for dinner.

Chapter Thirty-One

GOOD BYE PRT FRIENDS

We have a group of people from a prominent east coast university, who were doing research on how the Army can share data with other organizations. They told me that they were focusing on systems and software integration. I told them the software is fine. What we needed is for the State Department to order all of the other government agencies and non-government agencies that were contracted by the State Department to share the information that the U.S. tax payer paid for. I had many phone calls and sent emails to several companies. I received no response or just spoke to a belligerent individual who hates the military. The first thing this study group asked for was access to our ARCGIS database. I explained to them the several reasons that we do not have our ARCGIS up and running. The first reason was that Camp Atterbury didn't send the ownership documentation with the software so we are forced to go through a lengthy process to prove to the supplier that we didn't pirate the software. Our other problem was the Internet times out when we attempt to register the software. The study group responded by telling me to work with the software company. Then they asked for copies of all of our soil samples, which was what they were really after. Turns out they had a bunch of students in Afghanistan taking soil samples. They wanted us to enter all the data on ARCGIS so they could complete another study unrelated to sharing information.

There is a problem with sharing information here in Afghanistan. You can ask a thousand times for information and receive nothing but blank stares when it comes to dealing with the State Department, USAID, USDA and the NGOs they contract with. Then when you spend the resources to conduct a dismounted patrol to get the information, the same organizations step forward and tell you, "Oh if you had only asked we could have told you that." Hence, that is the reason we purchased rubber hip waders.

Another good example of this occurred on March 3rd when MR. USAID wanted to do a flood control project within sight of Route California, also known as the Jalalabad Highway, so he could get some photos. We asked the battle space owner for a fitting location for Mr. USAID's request and they suggested the Chow Kay Valley. On Wednesday March third, I took my team down to the lower Chowkay Valley with a group of Sec For. We dismounted two kilometers above Route California and moved toward the Kunar River while the trucks along another segment of our team went to the Chow Kay district center.

This is an abandoned adobe compound in the lower Chow Kay River Valley 2 km West of Route California. Photo taken March 3rd 2010

Before dropping down into the riverbed we looked over several of the irrigation projects. The canal and spillway both had dedication plaques dating 2006 and 2009. I took a few photos then we dropped down into the Chow Kay River and started a hasty survey. We could see several tractors and wagons in the river just a hundred yards from us. I went over to the driver of the first tractor and asked what he was doing, with the aid of Sarif, my interpreter. He said he was building retaining walls on both sides of the river as part of a PRT contract. I asked how far the project extended. He pointed to the Route California Bridge. We thanked him for the information and continued to photograph the project. The community was using the riverbed as a public toilet; the whole area was littered with human excrement.

When we passed under the Route California Bridge, we could see more construction going on. We stopped where a large spillway was under construction to take some photos and a man approached us. I greeted him and asked some questions. Sarif came to my rescue in translating Pashto. The man told us about the major flooding that occurred in 2008. He pointed to his farm and said that the flood washed away most of his soil and he needed help rebuilding his farm. Then I heard the Afghan national motto, "Please help me; no one helps me, my government will not help me." I explained that the whole reason we were there was to help the farmers in the area. I walked over to the foreman who was running the job and asked him who he was working for. He told me that he was working for Idea New and was responsible for building 14 miles of retaining walls, spillways, and irrigation intakes. He pointed out where they were building walls and I could see the foundations being excavated right on the property line of the other man's farm. I thanked the foreman for the information and continued down the river.

Our next stop was a group of men shoveling up silt and top soil into trucks. I asked them what they were using the dirt for. They told me that they were putting the soil back in the farms along the river. They even pointed to our friend's farm who was getting all the help he needed. He was just trying to get something extra.

By this point the Kunar River was in our sight so we pressed on to finish up our photo survey. We decided that since the project was already underway we would just do Idea New and the PRT a favor. We would document the progress and send them a disk with the photos.

The spillway under construction was at the end of the water flow in the

Chow Kay River. All of the water had been diverted to irrigation canals along the way. The dry sandy riverbed made of an excellent playground.

We found the only enduring evidence that the British had been in Afghanistan. "Cricket!" There was one hot cricket match taking place on the north bank of the river while practice was occurring on the south bank. This was the first time that kids didn't rush upon us for candy. Cricket was far too important to stop to beg for candy.

We finally made it to the Kunar River. Sgt Percival took the last of the GPS readings and we headed back to the district center. One of Sgt Arnold's men spotted a man video taping us as we approached the Kunar River. He continued to video tape us as we started to move to the district center. The insurgents like to video tape their attacks so they can sell the tape to their sponsors. We were a surprise to the locals so the only thing they could respond with would have been a sniper. We knew why we were being videotaped since no one fired upon us.

The river levy turned into a dirt road that led to the Chow Kay district center where our commander and our convoy was. Our commander needed a few minutes to complete a meeting with the district Ag director so we just piled back into the trucks. The few minutes turned into an hour and nature was calling.

SFC Hanlin, Sgt Percival and I ex-filled from our MRAP and went to the discreet side of the vehicle only to find an old woman standing there. She gave us the look of death and stood her ground. We waited for her to continue on, but she just stood there and glared at us. Nature waits for no one so we hustled over to the other side of the MRAP. Then we spotted another old woman. She walked up behind an ANP (Afghan National Police) officer and walloped him across the back with her walking stick. He turned around and she started screaming at him. He just stood there and took it. Then he finally pointed down the road and the old woman walked away. The officer turned back around to talk to his buddy when the old woman came back and whacked him behind the legs then continued on with her business. We think it may have been his mother.

The next few days were filled with a lot of changes. The PRT was conducting their right seat left seat ride with their replacements. There was a short period of time when the old PRT members had to take up residence in the newly completed interpreter quarters while the new folks filtered in.

On Friday March 5th the first of two CH-47s arrived and loaded up 35 members of the outgoing PRT. The second group left on March 10th. I went up and said good-bye to the friends I had made. The old PRT was a mix of active duty and reserve Navy and Air Force so some were going home hoping that their jobs would still be there and the others knew the service would take care of them. The remaining members of the PRT included the commander and a hand full of others, enough to fill one HU-1 Huey flown by Molson Air, who stayed behind for the TOA ceremony.

On Thursday March 11th LTC Velte and I went back to Woch Now Village to check on a few things. March 11th was also the Transfer of Authority ceremony for the PRT. To commemorate the event the PRT cancelled mail delivery that day for the FOB. We missed the TOA ceremony due to our mission; by the time we returned the remaining old PRT members had been flown to Bagram.

Our trip to Woch Now started at 9:00 o'clock when we left the back gate with the usual kids hanging around. We didn't think much of them as they followed us up the road. We were greeted by Laj Bar Khan, the village elder, who led us to the mosque for tea. He asked us if the kids were ours. We told him no, they were not our kids, and we didn't invite them along. His father promptly got up and chased the kids away. Laj Bar Khan was worried that the kids would report to the insurgent what they had seen or heard. The village of Woch Now received two mortar rounds the night before. We could understand his concern because the insurgents' activities were increasing in the area. Laj Bar Khan was up by the village spring the week before when the insurgents called for him to come to them. He refused and they pelted him with rocks from above the ridge line. His cousin was killed up by the spring when a large rock struck his head. It still is hard to determine if someone threw the rock or of it came loose on its own. The mountainsides are very unstable.

This is a KLE with Laj Bar the Elder of Woch Now village and his father Hakeem along with LTC Velte and Kelly. Photo from Willie the Whale courtesy of Lockheed Martin

We continued with our tea. I pulled out some Lincoln Logs and built a model of the crib wall that would protect their access road, while LTC Velte pulled out a pile of children's shoes from his ruck. LTC Velte was working with a group called the Spirit of America and LTC Owens to get shoes for women and children. These were the first of the shoes to arrive. LTC Velte helped a few kids put the shoes on while the other kids struggled to put theirs on by themselves. The concept of a tongue in the shoe was something they didn't know how to contend with. Finally between LTC Velte and Laj Bar Khan all the kids were fitted with shoes.

I presented a proposal to Laj Bar Khan about building a series of crib walls and manufacturing the concrete pieces. He was receptive to the idea so I handed the discussion over to SSG Tyner who pulled out a small re-bar cage and some pieces and demonstrated how to assemble the cage. Laj Bar Khan said his village would do it but his men would need training. We told him to bring ten men down on Sunday and we would train them all. With that I started gathering my team together to climb the mountain, which included Spc Larson our medic. We were just about to leave when a young man brought his younger brother over for Spc Larson to look at. He had been treated at our trauma center and received a number of stitches across his scalp. Spc Larson looked him over, saw no signs of infection and reminded them to keep their appointment with the trauma center to have the stitches removed.

With that we left LTC Velte at the mosque with some security and we followed the water pipe to the cisterns. This was part of our QA/QC for the repair of the village pipe system to the spring. The first cistern was empty, but was connected to the one located higher on the mountain. Once the upper cistern reached capacity the overflow pipe sends water to the lower cistern. On the way up to the upper cistern we decided to check out a cave that had Sgt Arnold's attention.

Sgt Percival and I got down on all fours and crawled inside. The cave looked rather large from below, but the inside could only accommodate a pair of goats. The cave was not carved by people; it was the work of nature. These mountains are very porous. The snow melts, penetrates the mountain and the hydraulic pressure forces the water out the weakest path. The weakest path becomes a cavern that humans expand. News of extensive cave networks, are not carved out by humans, but by nature and are modified to meet the needs of humans.

Chapter Thirty-Two

SLIDING DOWN THE
WITCH'S BACKSIDE

March was moving along very quickly, and our VetCaps had become the biggest game in town, in some cases too big. We had been focusing on the central Kunar River Valley, which is south of the Pech River and north of Jalalabad. When we first started VetCaps, the average turnout was 500 animals. Eventually, we were servicing an average of 1500 animals per VetCap. The central Kunar and Pech River Valleys have cell phone coverage and TV reception. The locals communicate very quickly about the VetCaps and they have also seen us on TV. The battle space owners have witnessed us in action servicing over 1500 animals. When we brief a battle space owner's civil affairs team about VetCap operations and the number we plan to serve we hope they listen. When we conducted our first solo VetCap at FOB Bostick we told Captain Pittard that we were prepared to service 700 animals. He quietly announced to only a few villages to make sure that the population didn't overwhelm our capacity. The battle space owner's CA team of Khas Kunar had seen us service over 1500 animals in one day and decided the sky was the limit. The VetCap was announced far and wide. "Bring all you've got!"

On March 13th our Ag team rolled out of Camp Wright before dawn for Khas Kunar loaded with enough supplies for 2000 animals since we briefed the civil affairs team that we would service 1500 animals. I stayed

261

back at Camp Wright working on some engineering and contract projects. Just before lunch LTC Velte called Sgt Palacios and said we needed an emergency re-supply of meds or we were going to have a riot! I just happen to be behind Sgt Palacios when the call came in. He handed me the phone. Sgt Flynn gave me his list and where to find everything. SFC Teso called SSG Valenzuela to spin up our QRF while I started packing meds in boxes. I grabbed Sgt Olson and told him to climb up on top of our ConEx and throw down a thousand ropes. SFC Natividad and SPC Lopez drove our new MATV down and loaded up the supplies while I grabbed my battle rattle. Then Sgt Flynn called again, increased the quantity and asked for 20 cases of water. We had supplies loaded six ways from Sunday in the MATV. It was a wonder that nothing flew out the back. We met SSG Valenzuela and the QRF at the ECP (Entry Control Point) and hit the road.

It had been a few weeks since our last trip down to Khas Kunar at which time Route Beaverton was under heavy construction. The locals were busy building "California Crossings" at every dry stream location along Route Beaverton. When we passed through this time all of the crossings had been completed and most of the road had been compacted ready for paving. There was a mile stretch of road construction approaching Khas Kunar about five miles from the town that had just received mounds of crushed road base. It was all piled up on the western side of the road and under guard by men with RPGs. Once we passed the mountains of road base we spotted people walking their animals in procession toward the VetCap site. We were still a good four miles out and people were still coming.

It took us just over an hour to make the trip. That same hour LTC Velte announced to the crowd that they were taking a one-hour lunch break to stall for time. He had just restarted operations when we arrived. The whole area was packed with people. It took us fifteen minutes to drive the last 100 yards through the crowd.

Khas Kunar VETCAP after lunch with about 500 people waiting with their animals for service.

We pulled up to the LMTV, our rolling barn and transferred all of the supplies and 20 cases of water. I took a few minutes to take some photos before we got back on the road. Sgt Flynn told me that the first customer had a herd (flock) of 600 sheep. The crowd was observing the boundary lines of the ropes we had strung up, but it was obvious the situation was stressed. Our SecFor were being put to the test dealing with a mob that was ready to explode. The battle space owner had the responsibility of the outer cordon while our SecFor was responsible for the inner cordon. The outer cordon was some distance away from the VetCap and they kept an eye on the mountains for trouble. I did notice a bunch of the battle space owner's troops relaxing in the shade of our LMTV and another bunch sitting with several radios.

After ten minutes it was time for us to get back to Camp Wright so the QRF could go back on standby. As we were rolling out I got a call on the radio, "Where is the water?" I told them we unloaded 20 cases of the 1.5 liter bottles. The reply was, "Are you sure you unloaded 20 cases because there are only two bottles here now?"

We drove over a short stretch of open country to avoid the crowds on the road, then popped back up on route Beaverton. SFC Natividad, who was gunning, pointed out that there were several herds being moved off the mountain toward the VetCap. For the next three and a half miles on Route Beaverton we saw the continuous parade of people walking their animals to the VetCap. I called back to LTC Velte and asked him if he wanted us to bring back more supplies. He said no he was going to cut things off at 3000 animals.

We named the emergency re-supply of meds a Hair Ball in honor of Tripod our cat and to give it the same ring as an emergency re-supply of ammo, "Speed Ball." At the end of the day the Ag section treated 3011 animals.

The Woch Now Village was coming up on our radar screen again. We still needed to inspect the water pipe project that we supplied the materials for. It was decided that we should fly to the top of the ridge line and walk down to the spring rather than walk up from the village. LTC Velte and I voiced our opposition to the plan stating that it was safer to hike up from the village. However someone convinced our commander based on imagery that air insertion was the best approach.

On March 14th SSG Valenzuela held a half-day training session on air insertion and rappelling. While at the same time SSG Tyner was training ten men from Woch Now Village on how to assemble re-bar cages. Our space was limited so we parked a MRAP in the yard to separate the two classes.

I had made 15 plywood triangles for the Woch Now men to use as framing squares. The re-bar cages required some parts to be tied at 45 degrees and others at 90 degrees. When SSG Tyner's class was finished he used the triangles as diplomas. Since all of the men were literate, Sam our interpreter, wrote their names on each triangle and SSG Tyner signed the back of each one. When we took the graduation photo all of them held up their triangles with pride. The village elder, SSG Tyner and I knelt down in the middle with some of the other re-bar creations. With that we loaded a dump truck with re-bar cut to the proper length, stirrups, wire, tools and several bags of hay to send up to Woch Now.

Woch Now graduation at Camp Wright March 14th 2010. Front row left LTC Kelly, Laj Bar the village elder and SSG Tyner on the right.

I told them I would pay $1.00 for every assembly with the speed they were assembling them. That equates to $16.00 a day per man. The average wage in Kunar for unskilled labor is $3.00 to $5.00 and skilled labor is $7.00 to $10.00.

Ground breaking for the Woch Now Co-Op crib wall manufacturing facility at Woch Now village. LTC Kelly and LTC Velte center the elders and men of Woch Now line the back row.

On the morning of March 15th, the Ides of March, the whole ADT assembled on the flight line. There would be two chalks flying up to the ridge and the remainder of our troops would wait on the flight line as a QRF. The QA/QC patrol consisted of SSG Arnold's security team, LTC

Velte, SPC Larson our medic, Sgt Percival our geologist, Spc Lopez our irrigation specialist, Sgt Olson our FO, and me. The other chalk would serve as our mountain top security, our over watch.

At 7:00 A.M. two Black Hawks landed at Camp Wright and shut down their engines. The crew chiefs and pilots gave us a quick class on bailing out of a UH-60 and told us what to expect with the anticipated difficult landing. The term landing is a courtesy word they were not landing on the HLZ. We were cautioned about the tail swinging and chopping us to bits, and going too far forward of the aircraft when we bailed out because of the gunner's position. Basically we were told to become one with the earth and watch out for dipping rotor blades.

Flight brief at the Camp Wright Air Field, March 15th 2010

We loaded up and did one practice run with all of the signals from the crew chiefs who also served as port and starboard gunners. By 7:20 two Apaches were on station over the Kala Kowchano valley and the rotors started turning on the Black Hawks. The lead Black Hawk took off with the main SecFor and circled to the east over the Kunar and then south. Once they were out of sight we took off. The Kunar River Valley was a bright emerald green still covered in winter wheat. Unfortunately due to dust and haze

I wasn't able to take a good photo. After flying south for a few miles we made a hard turn to the west and headed north. In the distance we could see miles of snow-capped mountains in the north, which is the finger that extends over Pakistan. Our UH-60 started hugging the mountaintops and flying through the canyons. On one side we were staring at vertical walls of rock and on the other the Kunar River Valley.

We were given the one-minute signal, a single index finger, then the thirty-second signal, which was the thumb and index finger closing together. I was sitting on the door and would be the first one out. I leaned forward, popped my seat belt off and hung on to the seat frame next to me. We weren't quite over the HLZ yet. I was looking at the canyon 3000 feet below when we came on the HLZ. I could see the tail hanging off the spur of the ridge line and the nose of the UH-60 protruding over the other side. The pilot made several attempts to get the front two wheels on the ground. I felt the wheels hit and the crew chief gave me the signal to jump. I threw my ruck out as far as I could and jumped just as the Black Hawk went back up in the air. We were told that this would happen and that the pilot would have to readjust as each pair jumped out of the bird. One person jumps from each side simultaneously. I grabbed my ruck and saw the rotor blades dip down. I held on to my ruck and rolled into a nook I spotted.

We quickly regrouped, orientated ourselves to the map and started moving out. The over watch, SecFor, set up a perimeter on the spur and we scouted out a route to the spring. SSG Arnold took the lead as we worked our way up to the ridgeline. The other direction was almost a sheer drop. The only possible route down was to work our way down the draw to the valley. From this area of the ridge is where the insurgents prefer to fire at Camp Wright. While SSG Arnold was scouting a trail we took up a hasty defense. SSG Arnold called back that he had found a Soviet mortar fuze. Sgt Percival and I both had our GPS systems so we locked in the grid. SSG Arnold came back and said the route was no good and we needed to find another trail. A few minutes later he found one. We were still in our hasty defense position, which was a narrow ledge in the rock. SSG Arnold stared down the trail he found; he was followed by LTC Velte, JW our interpreter, and SPC Rivera, SPC Coleman, Spc Arechiga. They got to a point where they had to slide off the ledge into the mountain side of loose gravel and shale. I was the assistant patrol leader, aka "Tail end Charlie."

I could see Sgt Olson getting ready to follow behind Spc Rivera when a boulder the size of half a footlocker broke free from above and tumbled down the mountainside. He yelled out "rock" and the team below quickly moved out of its path only to slide down after it. I worked down off the ledge I was on to another ledge about six feet below to move closer to the drop-off point. The whole trail was giving way. I radioed down to LTC Velte that the trail was giving way and I was sending back the rest of the squad. He concurred. We had to fire line some of the equipment back up the trail. The rucks made it impossible to turn around on the trail so each person took them off and handed them back. I was able to throw them up to Sgt Percival and he helped everyone back up top. I wanted to take Sgt Percival with me because he was an experienced rock climber and a good geologist. LTC Velte decided not to risk more people. I moved to the drop off point, called down to JW who was about 40 feet below and told him to catch my ruck. Then I carefully stepped off to the mountain side and slid as if I were on a water slide past JW. Several large rocks raced past me. One bounced off my thigh, which left a large bruise. I gracefully recovered and asked JW for my ruck. He said "I threw it down to the bottom of the hill." Sama Da Fra nock cree (okay no problem) it only had 300 feet of rappel rope.

Once we made the drop off the ledge, there was no turning back. The mountainside was so unstable: the more you attempted to climb up the more gravel and shale you brought down. The rope was useless because there was nothing to anchor it to. Any rock out cropping would give way with the slightest amount of force, and there wasn't sufficient space on the ledge for people to brace themselves as human anchors.

The point of no return to the HLZ. Once the rock formation was cleared, the shale was too unstable to climb back up. One half of the patrol was turned back at this point.

The next three and a half hours would be very tiring and slow. I recovered my ruck about 75 meters below where JW had hurled it, and was glad to have it back on my back; and that's where it stayed for the remainder of the hike. There were several times as we worked our way down the 60 degree incline that the earth just gave out from under us and we would slide 10 to 20 feet. SSG Arnold did a complete summersault and luckily landed on his feet in the upright position. After three hours, we finally made it to the crest of the canyon that led to the Woch Now spring. The vibration from the Apaches' rotors would knock rocks loose from above as they circled overhead watching for insurgents.

Once in the canyon we were obscured from the view of our over watch back on the HLZ. We were in the one section of the canyon that couldn't be seen from either Camp Wright or the ridge line. We all agreed there was no longer a need for the over watch or the Apaches to remain. The Apaches remained until the two UH-60s returned to pick up our troops. The recovery turned out to be more hazardous than the insertion due to the diurnal winds that had picked up.

Back on the crest of the canyon, SSG Arnold found a goat trail that we followed to a point that over looked the spring. The trail had taken us deep into the canyon, which protected us from the rocks that continued to fall down the mountainside. The ground above the spring was much more stable, but we still had to descend down the rock formations to get to the trough of the canyon. We carefully worked our way down the rocks to the spring. It had been 95 degrees since 8:00 A.M. We were wearing our full battle rattle and carrying our rucks loaded with extra ammo and equipment too. I had perspired to the point that my uniform was soaked down to my knees. I had consumed almost two quarts of water and LTC Velte had consumed all of his. The spring was situated between two vertical rock walls, which were nice and cool. The spring was overflowing enough that it filled a small pond below it, which was trickling down the canyon. LTC Velte asked, "Dave do you think this water is safe to drink?"

"Sure you're right at the source." As he took his first long sip of water I spotted a dead lizard behind him. It was about fourteen inches long and missing its tail. Hmmm I wonder, did the lizard die on the way to the spring or after drinking at the spring?

We waited at the spring for half an hour for Laj Bar, the village elder, to show up. During that time SSG Arnold scouted for an easier route to the camp and I documented the repair work on the pipe system. We finally decided that we needed to move on and headed down the only trail that we were sure led to Woch Now.

We worked our way out of the canyon to the backside of the Witch's Teton where the abandoned Gujer houses were. We inspected the old rock homes for signs of occupation or stock piles of munitions when Laj Bar arrived.

We didn't want to tell Laj Bar in advance about our trip, for security reasons. We called him in the morning when the helicopters lifted off. Laj Bar saw the two UH-60s land up on the ridge line and ran back to Camp Wright from his village to tell our TOC that the helicopters landed on the wrong ridge.

Laj Bar knew that it would take us a long time to reach the spring from where we were dropped off. His timing was very good. Had he started his hike an hour earlier he would have met us at the spring. Instead we found the only tree that offered shade by one of the abandoned rock house foundations and discussed the greater things in life. Laj Bar asked:

"Why did you start at the ridge?"

LTC Velte responded, "Because we're stupid, that's why."

Laj Bar became very concerned about our safety and told us to promise him that we would never visit the spring again. We were just 75 yards from where his cousin fell from the cliff face, that we just crossed, to his death a few weeks ago. One of the reasons we came up was to show our respects for the man's work. Given the limited tools that we provided the village, his cousin did a phenomenal job rebuilding the pipe system. He had driven the old pipes into the rock to support the new pipe. He had stacked two to three hundred yards of rocks along the mountainside where he could for more support. We even walked on the rock support he built, it was so stable.

Laj Bar told us again that he was at the spring just a few days earlier when some of the insurgents were above him and demanded that he climb up to their location. He refused and they pelted him with rocks.

We asked him about all of the abandoned rock houses that were built on the mountainside. Laj Bar said that is where he grew up. After the Soviets pulled out of Afghanistan the Taliban started harassing their mountainside village. One of the reasons they settled on the mountain was to be away from the Pashtos. Up on the mountainside with their spring they were self sufficient. The Taliban's harassment became so intense they abandoned their dwellings and moved to the valley below and lived in tents for a few years. After things stabilized they started building homes in the draw they call Woch Now. Within a few years the family became too big for the draw so Laj Bar's uncle took his family farther back into the Kala Kowchano Valley and settled the village of Arga Del. Later we learned his uncle moved because of a family fight and that the land that Arga Del was built on belonged to someone else. They were squatters.

Woch Now's main source of income is rock harvesting from the mountainside. The village charges $20.00 (in Pakistani rupees) for every truckload of rock that people harvest from the mountains around their village. We are still trying to determine what there other sources of income are. Laj Bar has one wife and ten children: five boys and five girls. They all looked fairly healthy.

After listening to Laj Bar's family history we followed him back to his village. He stopped us about 100 yards short of the mosque and apologized that he couldn't receive us at the mosque because some men were working there. We found a nice spot by a terrace and he called out to his children to bring us water and tea. The day before we had given every man who attended our re-bar class, a case of water to take home. We never thought we would be drinking that water. I had just finished sucking my camel back dry and a bottle of cool water was very refreshing. Then came piping hot tea! I was soaked with sweat and could feel the steam rise off my head when I took my Kevlar off and then I was being treated to a cup of hot tea.

I could see farther down the valley, two of my section's MRAPs were providing over watch for us at the end of the road. There was no way the MRAPs could make it up to Woch Now or Arga Del Villages over open country. A few months later I would have the roads built to accommodate our MRAPs up into each village.

We finished our tea with Laj Bar and headed down to the road below. We planned to walk past the mosque without looking. We didn't know what kind of work was going on and we wanted to respect the privacy of the mosque. As we approached, seven men came running around to the front of the mosque. "Come look. Please come look" one of them shouted out in English. Oh no what are we getting into now. To my surprise the villagers had assembled 75 re-bar cages to a very high standard. All of the ties were made tightly and at exactly 45 or 90 degrees. We hit the jackpot with these guys! I had gone through over 30 contractors trying to get the same product with no luck. Here in our own backyard with just a half-day's worth of training I was getting a quality product.

We said our good byes and moved down to the road. SFC Medina was there motioning us to climb on the MRAPs, but we declined his offer. It wasn't a matter of pride. We needed a semi level piece of road to walk on for a while and besides we were afraid if we got in the trucks we would stiffen up and couldn't get back out, after all Moogu Zor Askers (we are old soldiers).

Once we got back to the barracks we lost no time in dropping our gear and hitting the shower. Our colonel asked LTC Velte and me how it went. LTC Velte pulled out his pants and showed that the seat had been worn through and he had a pair of under shorts to match. I noted that I also had a pair of pants just like LTC Velte's along with some good size bruises from where the rocks hit me and a few places where the skin wore through to match the holes in my pants.

When I started cleaning my weapons, I noticed the side of my 9mm was badly marred from where we worked our way down the ledges and crevices. The heel of my left boot was chamfered from sliding down the mountain too. We both felt pretty good that evening but by bedtime the muscle spasms kicked in, and by morning the whole team was a bit stiff. At breakfast one of the troops asked me how I was doing and I gave him an honest answer. He was relieved to hear he wasn't the only one a tad bit on the sore side. SSG Arnold's team made it a point to work out and stay in shape and so do I. I couldn't imagine any troop who wasn't in shape completing that hike.

On March 17th we hosted another VetCap, this time on the other side of the Kunar River in Marah Warah. Since it was just on the other side of the river we could SP at 7:00 A.M. and have plenty of time to set up. It was the usual deal. SFC Hanlin rounded up 20 able bodied men to work the VetCap, JW our interpreter set up and ran the humanitarian assistance table (the give-away table) with the help of the local ANP (Afghan National Police). The first thing that happened was one of the men working for us ran up to SFC Hanlin and demanded to be paid for all of the people walking on his farm. SFC Hanlin gave him the choice: he could quit his job and keep people off his farm or he could work. Turns out the people were not on his farm. Later the man pulled a few more stunts to get himself fired.

The VetCap had been running for less than an hour when the ANP who was helping JW called a crowd over and started giving away all of our supplies to his friends. When J.W. tried to stop him he assaulted J.W. SFC Hanlin saw it and was about to draw his weapon in defense of JW when LTC Velte came over and ordered all the supplies back in the LMTV and declared that the give-a-way table was closed.

The day was finally over. We had set a record for firing local nationals and giving bonuses for outstanding performances. We had both extremes in the workforce and nothing in between.

That evening Laj Bar showed up at the gate and announced that he was out of tie wire and needed some new tools. I brought him back to the barn and SFC Fulton brought out the cash. With the help of Ralfi, one of our interpreters, we confused the daylights out of poor Laj Bar. He told me that his village finished half of all the re-bar cages. Half was 125 out of 250. He also needed more wire, and asked for some shade cloth and a few tools. I told him I'd pay him now for 125 re-bar cages, and to use that money to buy what he needed in town and to bring me the receipt. I would reimburse him for everything he bought. The rules were that I must have a receipt before I could hand out money. Laj Bar agreed and we paid him for 125 re-bar assemblies. Then he displayed a number on his wrist: 190. He told us they assembled 190 re-bar cages and asked me if I could pay for 190 re-bar cages then. We spent about an hour trying to explain money to Laj Bar. He finally agreed to go buy what he needed and come back with a receipt. I don't think he ever understood the transaction.

Chapter Thirty-Three

THE RETURN TO CHOWKAY
AND ONE SHARP LIEUTENANT

The last of the major VetCaps was over it was time to start planning the booster VetCaps. Every village that hosted a VetCap required a follow-up booster shot VetCap. We had used the attendance numbers from each of the VetCaps to plan for the follow-up booster shot program and were caught off guard. The locals believed that their animals would die if the veterinarians de-wormed or vaccinated them. They allowed their neighbors to test out the VetCap system first, the brave souls they were. This meant there would be a 30% increase in animals arriving at the booster VetCaps. One third of the animals wouldn't have received the initial vaccination nor have been de-wormed. We quickly adjusted our numbers only to be caught off guard again. By late spring a large number of families started migrating with their animals to different regions of the country. So, when we were showing up we had too much.

The Kunar ADT continued to offer a wide range of services to the battle space owners; these included flood and erosion control. The civil affairs teams was all for us coming out and building flood control structures, as long as we did 100% of the work, which included continuous meetings with the villages–something we didn't have the personnel to do.

Our crib wall enterprise with the Woch Now Village was progressing nicely. I had developed a business plan for the village's co-op, which included the minimum amount of equipment required. The first piece of equipment to arrive was a $5,000.00 concrete mixer, which was crudely made in Pakistan with a crank start engine made in China. When I fired it up, the hopper cables jumped their pulleys and the main drive chain popped off the sprocket. It took me the better part of the afternoon to put it all back together with the help of Sgt Carter. Turns out it was a two-person job.

The same company that sold me the concrete mixer also sold me four water tanks. I had asked for 1200 liter tanks. When they arrive I told the merchant that they were very small for 1200 liter tanks. "Oh sir these are 1500 liter tanks, the very best." The snow job was on! I told him that at the very best they were 600 liter tanks, but he insisted that they were 1500 liter tanks. I pulled out my tape measure and calculator and showed him that indeed they were 600-liter tanks, yet he was intent on charging me for 1200-liter tanks. He came back with the correct tanks the following day. He was instructed to deliver them up to Woch Now Village, but he only went half way and dumped them off the side of the road.

We were planning to go up to Woch Now Village on March 21st, Islamic New Year's Day to talk about women's health and building a construction yard for the village. The artillery had been firing at targets over in the Pech Valley sending rounds over the Kala Kowchano Valley, and standing by if their assistance was needed again. Everything was all set for our walk to Woch Now: our QRF was standing by at the barracks, the PRT was getting ready to leave with their convoy, and LTC Velte and I were staged with our security detachment. The next thing we heard over the radio was OP Bull Run is taking fire. The insurgents were spotted on the mountainside in direct line of fire of our artillery. The cannoneers could see their targets firing at OP Bull Run when the call for fire came in. Another group of insurgents appeared on a ridge line closer to the FOB once again in direct line of fire of two guard towers. The fifties struck up a lively conversation with a few loud interruptions by our twin 155s. It didn't take long to put the situation to rest. I'll admit hearing the crew serve weapons open up over head got my attention. My post was outside where I could hear everything.

The Laj Bar decided that it would be best if we visited another day so we rescheduled for March 27th the day after we would pay another visit to the Chow Kay valley.

March 26th would be our fourth visit to the villages of Seray and Karboray in the Chow Kay Valley. We loaded up bright and early on Friday morning and headed out to the Chow Kay district center to pick up the district Ag director. The district Ag director had no desire to go up into the valley out of fear for his life. He went anyway. When we arrived at Seray, our colonel and the Chow Kay district Ag director walked up to the clinic for a KLE with the village elders. We were expecting to sit in the trucks for at least an hour while the village elders addressed their concerns with the Ag director. This was the first time that the Chow Kay Ag director ever visited the villages so we were sure they would have lots to talk about. We had just finished turning the trucks around when they came walking back down the road. There would be no KLE in Seray. LTC Velte and I along with SSG Arnold and his team dismounted and followed them to Karboray.

The Karboray Village elders greeted us as we entered the village. We received permission from the village elder to go down to the river and check out their micro hydro electric plant. They agreed and gave us an escort. LTC Velte took the lead with SSG Arnold. I had the rear with SFC Hanlin and Sgt Johanson's team. The guide took us through the villages and wheat fields. We crossed the river a few times and finally ended up on a trail below the aqueduct that fed the micro hydro. The aqueduct was spilling over creating several waterfalls along the way, which fed a lot of greenery. The micro hydro plant was built on top of a flourmill, constructed of stacked stone.

The micro-hydro power plant and mill in the Chowkay Valley. SecFor checking out the structure for insurgents.

SSG Arnold's team took up security positions above the micro hydro. SFC Hanlin and I along with SGT Johanson's team secured the riverbed up to a large retaining wall. The micro hydro plant was not functioning, but the mill was in operation. Behind the retaining wall I could see several lush green poppy fields dotted with pink and purple blooms. I had found a nice big rock for cover from which I could see the firing positions that the insurgents used during our last visit. I made sure I was on the correct side of my big beautiful rock. There were two Kiowas flying security for us circling back and forth over the valley. I continued to scan the hills, but the only movement I saw was a group of people walking down a mountain trail. It was at that moment I heard a boom! I yelled to SFC Hanlin, "Hit the Dirt! In coming." I could see the smoke rising from the same location the insurgents fired at us before, but the cloud of smoke continued to grow. I was scanning the ridgeline for movement and held my breath for the impact explosion, but there was nothing. Then I heard SGT Johanson's radio traffic with the announcement that the Kiowas had fired. That would also explain the lack of the second boom. What I heard was the rocket impacting the mountain. So someone was up there, maybe. Less than a minute later the other Kiowa lit up the second insurgent position. Oh great now I'm on the wrong side on my precious rock.

I could hear Sgt Johanson's radio again. The traffic stated that they were just hitting all of the known insurgent firing locations in an attempt to smoke them out. I carried a radio for local control, while SSG Arnold and SGT Johanson carried an additional radio for support. During the ten to fifteen minutes LTC Velte was checking out the micro-hydro plant, the Kiowas hit all five of the insurgent's firing points one on each point of the compass from our position. LTC Velte is an electrician by trade, which is why he inspected the micro hydro plant. I was there to look the river over. Yes I verified that it still had water in it and any erosion control solution I could come up with would cost several farmers their poppy fields.

With the inspection complete, we returned to the village of Karboray by way of the poppy fields. We had some guests with us who wanted to get a better perspective of the diversity of agriculture. The poppy fields really stand out against the winter wheat. Even the fields that haven't bloomed, stand out. When we drove up to Seray the whole valley was green, but visually the wheat fields had a nice soft texture while the poppy fields looked course. The poppies stood out even when mixed with the wheat crop or weeds.

The opium harvest was about two to three weeks away. The poppy petals must fall first, then the bulb develops to the size of a golf ball. Workers then score the bulbs on four sides and wait for the sap to ooze out. They scrap off the sap, scratch the bulb again and come back one last time to harvest the last of the sap.

One of many poppy fields in the Chow Kay Valley

We loaded back up into the trucks still waiting to be attacked. Our convoy drove half way down the valley and stopped for the KLE scheduled for Seray. The district Ag director was scared for his life up at Seray; he felt that this was a better location for his sake. The KLE went on for little over an hour. During that time the bright sunny sky turned dark. We were being treated to an unexpected thunder storm for our trip home.

Saturday morning, we loaded up one 1151 with a trailer in tow for Woch Now Village. SFC Hanlin and I loaded up a balance beam scale that we built for concrete production, a catwalk for the water tanks, and two re-bar cages for phase two of our plan. LTC Velte threw in a case of children's shoes, and SFC Natividad added several boxes of school supplies that a Boy Scout troop back home donated.

As we left the back gate we could see some of the children from Arga Del and Woch Now walking to school. The men of the village had all assembled at the mosque waiting for us. Three hundred yards behind us was the 1151 struggling to get up the hill. It wasn't the grade that made it difficult; it was the children all wanting to help. The kids stood right in front of the 1151 pointing to the edge of the road. Spc Lopez was driving and was in the process of giving the 1151 some gas to get up the hill when the kids decided to help. It was obvious that it would be some time before Spc Lopez arrived at the mosque.

LTC Velte and I took off our battle rattle and sat down with the men for tea while Spc Lopez continued his quest to conquer the mountain without running over any of his little helpers. The 1151 finally arrived and I excused myself to direct unloading the supplies. The catwalk for the water tanks was in kit form so I had a few of the men assemble it on the road, while the others unloaded the trailer.

I handed SFC Hanlin the two re-bar cages that he made, then climbed up to the mosque. The mosque had a set of slate steps jutting out from the stacked rock retaining wall. The slate was at most three inches thick and we weighed between 220 to 300 pounds with our entire battle rattle on. It was a wonder the steps didn't snap in two.

SFC Hanlin introduced himself in Pashto, then started telling the men how to make the new re-bar cages. They told him, "We know how to tie the re-bar together. Look at what we did." SFC Hanlin, the "ham" that he was, pulled out his magnifying glasses and studied all of the tires. You could have heard a pin drop. All eyes were transfixed on SFC Hanlin. Then SFC Hanlin looked up and in Pashto, said "Excellent Job." The cheers went up and all of the men clapped their hands.

Now it was time for our little diversion. We wanted to help the women and young girls in the village. The last several times we attempted to do so they were pushed to the back and only the boys could get shoes or school supplies. SFC Hanlin and I were the main distraction and led the boys and men away while our SPC Larson with the help of Ahmad helped the women. Ahmad was one of our interpreters who had a grandfatherly appearance. While I played the part of the pied piper they walked over to where the women were. The next thing we knew, one of the village men appeared in the middle of them. Turns out the Gujer women do not speak Pashto, which is why one of the village men went to translate Pashto to Gujer. Ahmad who is ever alert heard one of the women talk to another in Urdu. Ahmad was fluent in Urdu. The women stayed together for thirty minutes sizing shoes and talking about women's health and hygiene.

In the mean time LTC Velte SFC Hanlin and I were looking over real estate to build a construction yard on. Laj Bar the village elder showed us a place that was very unsuitable, but we couldn't talk him into another location. Laj Bar was worried that the ADT was nothing more than a camel trying to get its nose into his tent. He asked if there was a chance that this yard would become the Army's construction yard. We reassured him that it would never be our yard. I used a piece of 550 cord and some stakes to mark out the site for the backhoe operator. The Army still refused to buy me any survey equipment and my GPS system was only accurate up to 27 feet. With that much error there is no way I could stake out the road or the lot.

I decided that I would have to come back with the backhoe and mark things out as the land was excavated. The road up to Woch Now was only seven feet wide so I'm was limited on the type of equipment I could use. SFC Fulton, who was my heavy equipment operator, and I decided that we'd just use a string line with some survey tape for working the final elevation of the road and the lot.

On Tuesday March 30th the men of Woch Now came down to Camp Wright for a class on the use of the concrete mixer we bought for them. SFC Hanlin and I taught Sam and Rafi how to service and operate the machine the day before so they could teach the men from Woch Now. There were eleven men. Each man was allowed to start the mixer and operate all of the handles. It became a competition of who was strong enough to crank start the "Clampherdown." A few good cranks and the release of the clutch, the Clampherdown would belch blue smoke, water would blast out of its radiator, the gears would grind and the hopper would slam down on the ground. The Clampherdown would sputter to a stop and the next man would step up to the helm and give it his best shot. After a few quarts of water and a hardy crank we would all choke from the blue smoke once again. A quick jerk on the hopper lever and the two pivot pins flew out from both sides and the hopper dove into the earth. I yelled at SFC Hanlin, "Shutter down!" It was too late. The main drive chain jumped the sprocket while the hopper cables broke free of their pulleys. The Clampherdown came to rest with a sputter and a hiss. All eyes were on me as if to say, "What now Colonel?"

"Lunch!"

Lunch is the magic word for any situation with Gujers.

SFC Hanlin and I led the parade to the Afghan café on post where we met up with LTC Velte and the Iowa ADT pre-deployment survey team. Iowa had sent a small team to see firsthand what our mission was. Iowa was scheduled to replace us in August of 2010. I gave LTC Velte, Laj Bar and company, and I took the folks from Iowa for a tour of the FOB.

I was bringing the Iowa ADT out of the balloon yard when I saw Laj Bar and company walking down to our mosque. SFC Hanlin told me they heard the call for prayer and left their lunch. "That's odd. They never pass up a meal."

"Oh sir they said to pray at our mosque is something very special."

"It must be to walk away from a free meal."

I called NATC up and told them to come get their bucket of bolts, "the Clampherdown" and to give me my money back. They arrived the next day to look at it, and told me that it was the finest piece of equipment available at the best price. I pointed out some of the many quality problems and told them that I paid two thousand dollars more for a piece of junk from Pakistan, than I would have paid in the States for something of quality made in China. They didn't believe me so I pulled up one from the Internet and sure enough one made in the United States was $3000.00, two thousand dollars less than what I paid. They told me that they would bring me a better one that had more capacity for just a little more. "OK, but first take back this one and give me my money back. Then we'll talk about another model." Hmmm they didn't like that response. I already had J.W. working on getting me a good mixer from Jalalabad, always planning ahead!

Planning ahead for contracts is a bit more challenging. You can't always see the hidden dragons that are lurking in the shadows. We had submitted ten projects for approval back in early February. So far only four had been approved. On three of the contracts I decided to become my own general contractor because I couldn't find a contractor to do the work. I thought this would be a good solution since the guidance had been to steer clear of contractors whenever possible. Turns out the powers to be would not allow me to be my own general contractor. I approached the PRT and our Civil Affairs on a teaming concept to complete the projects. The PRT agreed to supply the heavy equipment and operators, Civil Affairs came back empty handed for funding the labor.

The most important project to us was the Para Vet training, which was rejected by the brigade commander. This blindsided us. Our first VetCap in Baraki Baraki we hired some local veterinarians who were incompetent and a bunch of thieves. The folks at the American Embassy in Kabul directed us to Dr. Sofie, the head of the Afghan Veterinarian Association (AVA). This introduction was one of our VetCap's foundation stones of success. The AVA supplied competent well-trained personnel who didn't play tribal favorites nor did they loot our supplies and equipment. Together with the AVA we hosted 21 VetCaps in the Kunar Providence.

With this proven relationship and the endorsement from the American Embassy we thought the approval of the Para Vet program was assured. What we didn't see was USAID working in the background with a French NGO "Madera" and the Nangarhar School of Agriculture. They were fully aware of our work and plans to train one Para Vet for each district in Kunar. We had made the mistake of including Mr. USAID in one of our briefs.

LTC Velte had met with Madera before the Khas Kunar VetCap and Madera demanded that we purchase French manufactured pharmaceuticals or they would attempt to halt or discredit our program. Madera even went as far as to tell us that they were the only organization authorized to host VetCaps in Kunar. The problem was they weren't doing anything. When Madera first started their attacks I was puzzled. I had met with several of their Afghan representatives a few months earlier and was impressed with their accomplishments. I decided to verify their claims with the help of our USDA rep and his employees at the Kunar government center. Madera was nothing more than a paper façade. We couldn't verify any of their claims made months earlier. I even attempted to pay a visit at the Madera nursery compound just south of Camp Wright on my way to a government tea farm. The Madera compound looked more like an estate than the nursery that it was advertised to be. There was no sign of activity at their compound other than evidence that someone lived there.

We were copied on an email from another Lt Colonel who stated that the AVA was bad and had grave concerns about their program and storage of pharmaceuticals. LTC Velte made a surprise visit to the AVA with the Iowa ADT pre-deployment team to check out the claims made. Sure enough the AVA was still setting the standard for excellence. Dr. Sofie just happened to be there checking on the course of instruction. The classrooms were filled to capacity. There were locals with their livestock being treated, and the pharmaceuticals were all properly stored in refrigerators with temperature logs posted at each cooler. The facility was a show place!

Now we had a problem. We promised the Kunar Chief of Veterinary that we would train one Para Vet for each district in Kunar. We wouldn't have made the promise if we didn't have a verbal agreement from higher. This isn't the first time USAID has pulled the flying carpet out from under us. Just recently 1Lt Eidemiller caught a major fraud operation and USAID's name was involved. The governor of Kunar made a public announcement of a twenty-nine million dollar construction project to line both sides of the Kunar River with rock and concrete. USAID and the PRT were there when the announcement was made, but the PRT didn't endorse the project. Soon a fake "Notice To Proceed" letter was circulated about the project. The giveaway was the American eagle was flying upside down. Lt Eidemiller saw the letter and proceeded to question the main contractor, but didn't get permission to arrest him. Once the Army confirmed what was going on, the command put out a warrant for the arrest of two contractors. Things moved pretty fast because the Army's reputation was at stake. There was a lot of back peddling by Mr. USAID when all of the soft earth tone matter hit the fan. All of this coincided with Mr. USAID's urgent need to build flood control projects within sight of Route California, which overlooks the Kunar River. The sight in the lower Chowkay River Valley that feeds into the Kunar River was the location that Mr. USAID wanted us to survey and develop engineering plans for. That's when we discovered that Idea New and the PRT were already running multimillion dollar projects there. The main contractors were soliciting bid deposits from small contractors for the right to work on the project. What they were doing was referencing current projects as part of the big 29 million dollar project.

The governor was finally forced to make a public statement about the project. Mr. USAID continually boasted that he had a direct line with the governor.

LTC Velte decided to hold a Shura for the AVA and the major elders in the area to address the issue of animal health and just to let folks get to know each other. He scheduled the Shura for the same day as the Kala Kowchano Valley VetCap so all of the key people would be there.

The Kala Kowchano Valley VetCap would be our last VetCap for a while.

The goal of the VetCap was to give the needed booster shots to the animals that we serviced a few months earlier. Laj Bar, the village elder of Woch Now, said that more people would be coming this time. He told us that the last time people stayed away because they were afraid their animals would die. Now they have seen that all of the animals that went are healthier than theirs so they want to bring their animals. He was right! We checked the numbers. Our first VetCap for the villages serviced under 700 animals; this time we serviced 1100+ animals.

A few weeks earlier we had a visit from a LTC Owens who was excited about helping the villages, but couldn't do so because of the location she worked at. However she took my photos and a short story LTC Velte wrote and posted it on the "Spirit of America" web site. We received over $10,000.00 in donations. People sent us new lead ropes, shoes, school supplies, socks and coloring books. We asked our Civil Affairs team to come out with us to fit the children with shoes. The Civil Affairs team didn't have enough people so we tapped the PRT supply officer to come out as well. Soon we had a representative from just about every unit on post.

On Thursday morning April 1st our SECFOR headed out for the hills to secure the area followed by a parade of troops from Camp Wright. The village elder from Woch Now was standing by with 30 men from Woch Now and Arga Del Villages. Within 30 minutes the whole site was set up and ready for the first customers. The animals and kids flowed continuously until lunch.

While we were tending to the children and animals Wadat and Ahmad were busy cooking lunch for the Shura. They had been saving all of the Styrofoam packing boards to use as cushions, which they laid on the ground and covered with some of the green shade cloth we use for animal fencing. The two of them fed 250 people in an hour. The first group came in and sat down for lunch; our interpreters were the servers. Then they started delivering lunch to all of the troops working the VetCap that weren't invited to the Shura. The first group got up and went back to work at the VetCap as the second group arrived. The second group included some very influential people. We had one retired Afghan brigadier general, two colonels from the Soviet Afghan Army, some local Mujahideen commanders and other village elders.

LTC Velte stood up with Tahs Mohamed, greeted everyone and told them that there was no agenda for the Shura, that we just wanted to get to know everyone using the old three cups of tea concept. These guys preferred the three sips of tea concept and let's talk business. The main concern on their minds was animal health and the shortage of trained veterinarians and facilities in the area. The Shura went on for another hour while the VetCap was in full swing behind them.

I was pleasantly surprised with the reaction on post to the VetCap. All of a sudden it was no longer the ADT's VetCap. It was Camp Wright's VetCap, something that everyone could be a part of. We had a new PRT and several other units. The day's event really unified us into one community. Camp Wright has always been a friendly FOB with units that supported each other, but then there was just a different feeling. It was almost like an old-fashioned barn-raising event.

Chapter Thirty-Four

BLESS THE BEASTS AND THE CHILDREN

VetCaps, "Veterinary Civic Assistance Programs," are a health fair for farm animals. Originally in past conflicts and national building operations U.S. Army veterinarians would arrive at a village, vaccinate the farm animals and tend to the sick ones. That system worked in small villages that kept all of their animals nearby. In Afghanistan very few people own land so their animals are left to graze up on the hillsides.

LTC Velte had the opportunity to meet with a few people at the U.S. Embassy in Kabul in late October 2009 about VetCaps. This meeting led to our first VetCap in Baraki Rajan where we supported another unit. LTC Velte flew down with a small group of our junior NCOs a few days before the event. This would be the first VetCap for the Kunar ADT and the host unit. The host was surprised to learn that the local veterinarians stated that they would only show up and administer the vaccines. They had no intentions of setting up the operation. The host unit moved quickly to purchase all of the supplies and equipment while our team built a series of cattle chutes.

On November 13th the two units vaccinated 352 animals at the high school soccer field. This was a major event for the community. People were sitting on top of the walls and rooftops to witness the event. The local veterinarians turned out to be a pack of thieves.

A few days later we received a visit from Doctor Sofi the head of the Afghan Veterinary Association. He informed us that he had a clinic near the site of the Baraki Rajan VetCap that had a whole set of steel cattle chutes. He also pointed out the problems of using many of the local veterinarians. It was better to use veterinarians from outside the province or district and that the VetCap was in to ensure impartiality. With that we set out to run our own VetCaps. The unit we supported at COP Baraki Barak sent us all of their left over supplies because they decided not to host any more VetCaps.

The overall short-term gains from a VetCap were significant when it came to building relationships between the U.S. military and the communities where the FOBs and COPs were located. Our first VetCap was up at the small village of Tarey Kalay just outside Camp Wright. Everything went smoothly except the larger landowners thought that we should have set up inside his compound and serviced his animals only. We vaccinated only 74 animals but it provided an excellent learning opportunity.

The village of Naray near FOB Bostick provided even more valuable lessons. We vaccinated and de-wormed 461 animals in one day. We learned about employee accountability and the tricks the locals would play in an attempt to receive extra supplies, and what they would try to steal. We validated what a solid working relationship would require a civil affairs team and the work flow of animals. After the Naray VetCap we required all of our local hire employees to wear a bright orange safety vest with a number on the back. At the end of the day if you do not have a vest you're not getting paid. At the end of the day in Naray when it was time to pay our ten employees, nearly the entire village lined up. We had no way of sorting out the flock.

Another benefit of having numbered vests is keeping track of good employees and the bad. It is very easy to get rid of the bad employee and hire another out of the crowd. Employee numbers also eliminate problems at mealtime. We issued a HALA meal by employee number so individuals were not eating everyone else's meals or coming back for seconds. The HALA meals are meals without any pork products for Muslims and any other group that can't consume pork. We also learned that the locals would respect boundaries as simple as a white ribbon of engineer tape. Pashtos have no problem screaming and yelling in your face, but put a piece of engineer tape up and they don't cross it.

We hadn't received any feedback from the VetCap at Baraki Rajan or from Tarey Kalay so we had no idea of what the impact was on the community. A few days after the Naray VetCap, Captain Pittard gave us a call and told us the impact was phenomenal. The one day effort generated enough goodwill to last three or four months, just what he needed to develop other stabilizing projects. This positive feedback was echoed after each VetCap we conducted.

What we were not aware of was the rumors being spread among the villagers. Most villagers were under the impression that the United States was trying to kill their farm animals and the VetCaps were the mechanism to do so. The result was very few people brought their animals to the VetCaps. The other rumor that was going around was the VetCaps were a ruse to capture insurgents or people the Afghan government didn't like. The villagers countered this by sending their children to the VetCaps.

Baraki Rajan and Naray were isolated from the Pech and the Central Kunar River Valleys. Baraki Rajan was socially isolated and Naray was isolated by lack of roads and telecommunication, which prevented positive feedback from reaching other villages.

The State Department and the U.S. command continually stresses that we put an Afghan face on any operation that supports the community. The thought behind this is to make the people believe that their government is looking out for their welfare and that the government is capable of governing. The Afghan people are smart enough to understand that any help is coming from the U.S. What is really occurring is the Afghan government is being forced to be responsible. They may not be held accountable for the planning and budgeting, but they must give up some of their free time to meet with the public.

There is a secondary reason for the Afghan face and that is to buffer the U.S. from liability. The locals have learned to show up at the front gate of any FOB with dead animal parts and demand compensation claiming that their animal was killed by U.S. artillery or small arms fire during a TIC. It is odd that they don't approach the insurgents first. Depending on the ethics of the village there can be as many as 15 claims after an engagement with the insurgents for dead animals. Out of 20 VetCaps the Kunar ADT has only had one claim for a dead animal out of 13708 animals serviced. That individual couldn't produce the dead animal.

The Kunar ADT buffers itself by using AVA (Afghan Veterinary Association) veterinarians and technicians and the AVA prescriptions for administering the vaccinations. The Kunar ADT doesn't vaccinate animals. This protects the ADT from liability. When a farmer wants to make a claim his is directed to the AVA. The one claim against the Kunar ADT was from a farmer who stated that his cow was in perfect health and walked to and from the VetCap, only to be found dead the following morning. When asked where the corpse was, the farmer stated that he threw it in the river. He couldn't even tell us how old the cow was. We knew that no farmer would throw a dead animal into the river. They would butcher it up and sell it hide and all.

One of the challenges during a VetCap was to prevent people from bringing the same animal through twice in order to receive more free items at the Human Assistance (HA) table. We graded all of the animals coming through the VetCap and most were underweight and weak due to malnourishment. Farmers would walk their animals several miles to the VetCap, which placed a weak and sick animal under stress. Multiple times through the vaccination line increased that stress even more. To control this, the animal was painted with oxytetracycline, an antibiotic purple dye, and the individual's hand was marked with a permanent marker. It is standard practice for an individual to make several trips bringing a few animals at a time to the VetCap, which isn't a problem. That is the intent of the VetCap, but some people would just get back in line for another free radio, diet supplement or anything else that looked good.

There are several communities that stood out of the first 19 VetCaps we conducted during the winter of 2009 / 2010. The village of Woch Now stood out as the best. The Kunar ADT had already built a good working relationship with the village elder prior to the VetCap. This strong relationship and the inherent discipline of the Gujers made all the difference in the world. Laj Bar, the village elder, was at the VetCap site for the setup and talked to the veterinarians about each of the diet supplements, which were to be given out, then he asked how he could support the VetCap. We decided the best thing for Laj Bar to do was organize the flow of animals. This was a very prudent decision because the villagers recognized his authority and did as instructed. When things looked like they were running smoothly at the entrance, Laj Bar would support the goat and sheep pen operation, and then would work the Humanitarian Assistance table. That evening Laj Bar had the village men meet at the mosque and they went over what each of the diet supplements were for and how to use them.

Two weeks later, Laj Bar told us that he was worried when he saw piles of worms in the excrement of his animals. Then he noticed that his animals had more energy and were climbing higher up the mountains to food. Laj Bar also noted that his cows were giving more milk. Three months later when we held a booster shot VetCap for Woch Now we had over 900 animals show up. When we asked Laj Bar where the additional animals came from he reported that some of the people were afraid that we would kill their animals, so they let their neighbors go first. When their neighbor's animals didn't die they decided to bring their own.

This VetCap substantially increased the relationship between the villages of Woch Now and Arga Del, which guard the back door to Camp Wright. Soon whenever the villagers spotted insurgents in the mountains behind the FOB they promptly came down and reported the activity. It cost the Kunar ADT ten dollars an animal to treat all of the animals in Woch Now and Arga Del villages. The return on the investment was priceless. Camp Wright now has two villages that link their prosperity to the safety of the FOB.

The majority of the villages that received VetCaps respond by just relaxing their opposition of U.S. forces and became more willing to talk about issues that affect their community. Conducting VetCaps for specific villages provides the best results because the reputation of the village is at risk. When multiple villages show up, only the villagers know who belongs to which village. So when individuals misbehave it can't be directly linked to their village and subsequently affect the aid their village is receiving. When just one village is being serviced the village elders are present to ensure that everyone acts in a proper manner befitting their village.

We had noticed that the size of each VetCap was increasing as we moved the program up and down the Pech and Kunar Rivers. The Pech and Central Kunar River Valleys have cell phone coverage and paved roads that facilitate communication. Our VetCaps started with an average of 500 animals. The Khas Kunar VetCap had over 3000 animals with the remaining VetCaps averaging 1500 to 2000 animals. The fear that the U.S. was going to kill their animals was quickly extinguished when people saw their animals increase in weight and agility.

The nomadic tribes have a structure of elders. They don't call any location home nor do they have as much pride in their reputation. Villagers lobby for infrastructure improvements to their community so their reputation is important. The nomads live in tents and have no desire to settle in a village or build a village. This means only their animals have any value to them. The biggest gain in conducting a VetCap for nomads is to prevent the spread of disease among herds. The nomads in the Kunar province migrate from the mountains of Kabul in the summer to the mountains and upper valleys of Kunar in the winter.

The Kunar ADT conducted a 1500+ animal VetCap for nomads of the Patan Valley in the Noor Gul district. The nomads were extremely unruly and knew our Rules Of Engagement better than we did. I had to break up several fights between our workers and the nomads. To add salt to the injury the supporting Civil Affairs team decided to start their own give-a-way table in the middle of the exit corridor of the VetCap where the animals were being pushed through. At one point a Civil Affairs lieutenant called all of the people watching from the sideline over to get a free radio. We had a small riot that shut down the operation for fifteen minutes until the fighting stopped. The same lieutenant decided that he would give away blankets and jackets at the exit feed lot, which resulted in more fights among the nomads.

Later at the Sarkani VetCap the same Civil Affairs lieutenant arrived and started going door to door with a state department woman who claimed to be ex-FBI; that was her excuse for carrying a firearm. This woman didn't have a clue that carrying a firearm while wearing civilian clothes puts all of the other civilians at risk. She was then a combatant because she was carrying a firearm. Soon the Civil Affairs lieutenant started grabbing our medic to provide medical services to the local residents. It took some effort to get the Civil Affairs lieutenant and Ms. State department to knock it off.

This taught us some valuable lessons. First off the ADT runs the VetCap from start to finish and the host unit conducts outer cordon security. There are no joint activities going on. It is either a 100% VetCap or nothing.

The VetCap at Watahpur, which was conducted at the mosque outside COP Honaker Miracle, provided the greatest counter insurgent gain of the season. The villages above the 70 nothering line are very kinetic with entrenched opposition and distrust toward outsiders, especially Christians. The troops at COP Honaker Miracle had made many attempts to initiate friendship with the villagers. Their efforts weren't completely rebuffed, and were not welcomed into the villages. The day of the VetCap, the village elders of Sadar Village walked seven kilometers down the Watahpur Valley to Route Rhode Island where COP Honaker Miracle is located. They stopped to observe what was taking place at the mosque and asked a lot of questions of the villagers. That afternoon the village elders had a Shura with the leadership of COP Honaker Miracle; they were invited to come visit their village. The VetCap was the key to the village. The wealth of a village is determined by the health of their animals. In a society where barter is still the main form of commerce there is no greater service than to provide veterinary care for the animals.

With all of the success of the VetCaps, the Kunar ADT was receiving pressure to hand the operation over to the Afghan government. The corruption inside the government is so great it is impossible to hand over any program and see it survive. Most officials know that their time in power is limited so they feel they must steal as much as they can before they are fired. This mentality coupled with the Afghans' inherent inability to organize, plan and execute an operations means the ADT will always be involved in VetCaps. However, this doesn't mean the ADT must run the whole show.

We had been trying to get a private Afghan company to give us a bid for running VetCaps for us, with no success. After two months of assisting a company to develop a business plan and price structure we turned to the Gujers of Woch Now and Arga Del. The village of Arga Del still had a booster VetCap required for 130 animals that didn't receive their booster vaccines. We used this as a practice VetCap and hired an Afghani truck driver and the village elders of Woch Now and Arga Del to run the operation. With a minimal amount of effort on our part the two elders with their crews set up the VetCap and ran the animals through the chutes. The operations went very smoothly.

By late spring, the Afghan government decided to privatize all of the veterinary service programs. This, in theory, placed the ADT's VetCaps in direct competition with the private sector. What had occurred was an organization called Vet Clinic was able to successfully lobby the Afghan government to privatize all veterinary services so they could contract without competition with the U.S. and U.N. to provide veterinary services. Their first act was to strike out at the AVA, their main source of competition.

Chapter Thirty-Five

PULLING OUT OF THE KORENGAL VALLEY

The Kunar ADT was at Camp Atterbury preparing for movement to Afghanistan when FOB Keating and FOB Fritsche were attacked by the insurgents on October 3rd, 2009. These two FOBs were located in the Kamdesh District, a very remote part of the Nuristan Provence. Both FOBs had to be completely supplied by air; there were no serviceable roads. The next closest FOB that had could provide support with access to a semi-improved road was FOB Bostick. Semi-improved roads are not high-speed avenues of approach for the military. The thirty-mile stretch of road from FOB Bostick to Asmar requires almost five hours to drive safely. Constructing roads to villages in Nuristan has been challenging. One contractor found four of his superintendents beheaded along the side of the road. Another road contractor worked for the insurgents and started the construction project at the distant end so that it was next to impossible for the project to be inspected.

The Kamdesh District is extremely isolated to the point that it was one of the last areas in Afghanistan to be converted to Islam. Some of the villages made the conversation as recently as 2000 according to some of the locals. Over all, the residents just want to be left alone. They understand that if a road is constructed, more people will come to their villages and more outside influences will penetrate their culture.

The region is also a smuggling highway from Pakistan. There are few natural mountain passes in the north that facilitate foot travel. The village of Arandu where the Kunar River enters Afghanistan from Pakistan in one of the last major passes. There are more passes but farther north the mountains are capped with snow and glaciers.

Logistically it was very difficult and expensive to support FOB Keaton and Fritsche. The return on investment was extremely low when compared to areas with larger population density. The U.S. command in Afghanistan reviewed many of these lone outposts and decided to systematically shut them down. The sequence would coincide with the construction of barracks and other support facilities elsewhere.

FOB Keating and Fritsche used Afghan forces such as the ANA, ASG, and ANP to protect American troops. I had the chance to talk to several NCOs and company grade officers who had experience at these two FOBs and all of them stated that relying on Afghans to protect Americans was the fatal flaw in their security plan. The insurgents had, and have, fully penetrated all of the Afghan military and police organizations. Both FOB Keating and Fritsche had a fifth column of insurgents in their camps.

On October 3rd, 2009 a group of 200+ Pakistan Taliban rallied in the dark at a mosque with RPGs and rocket launchers. The provincial police chief, Muhammad Qasim Jangulbagh, thought that there were approximately 300 insurgents. Very few of the insurgent fighters were Afghans, but they had good communication with the villagers who knew the exact date when the FOBs would be closed down. It was this line of communication with the local villagers that allowed the insurgents time to stage ammunition and supplies in the ridgelines above the FOBs. The logistical aspect of the attacks required several days if not several weeks to hike all of the supplies into position. The terrain is such that a man is limited to what he can carry on his back. The insurgents knew that the U.S. is well armed and that they must be well prepared if they are going to sustain a long battle.

The insurgents had gained enough intelligence by watching the air movement of troops to know when the FOBs would be at their lowest level of troops. Their goal was not to take the FOBs, but to kill Americans for their own information operations. The insurgents knew that if they waited 24 hours they could just walk into the abandoned FOBs without a shot being fired.

At 5:00 A.M. Saturday October 3rd, the insurgents attached the local ANP stations, then moved forward to attack the FOBs. The ASG and ANA security guards killed their supervisors and joined the insurgent attack on the FOBs. During the next seven hours the fighting was intense and eight U.S. soldiers were killed. There was quick air support from Apache gunships that were on station in thirty minutes. The battle over the two FOBs lasted twelve hours. The U.S. had planned to destroy both FOBs upon exiting that morning so just about everything was rigged with explosives.

When the troops finally were able to withdraw, the insurgents swarmed the FOBs to loot whatever they could find. While the insurgents were busy looting the FOBs, American F-15s started dropping multiple GBUs. There is no account of any insurgents surviving the attacks on the FOBs.

The old saying, "Those who fail to read history, are doomed to repeat it," holds true. The FOBs and OPs located in the Korengal Valley were scheduled to be closed once quarters could be constructed for the troops. April 7th was the kickoff day for pulling out of the Korengal Valley. There were three FOBs in the valley, the biggest was FOB Korengal. It and two smaller FOBs were shared with Afghan forces, FOB Vimoto and Vegas. The U.S. ringed the valley with troops for extra security and made a deal with the local elders that if they could close down the FOBs in an orderly manner with no attacks, then the U.S. would not destroy the FOBs or equipment left behind.

The Korengal Valley is located a few terrain features behind Camp Wright. The Arga Del Valley is one of the more discrete avenues of approach for smugglers to the Korengal, which is located directly behind Camp Wright. Insurgents will walk on the northern ridgeline to smuggle weapons and drugs into the Pech River Valley. The one thing an insurgent fears is another insurgent. The fastest route to the Korengal Valley is to follow the Pech River from Asadabad. Some of the insurgents obtain their weapons in Pakistan, then bring them across the mountains entering Afghanistan through Ghaki pass and Maraware. The insurgents must make a decision to either move up the Pech River Valley quickly and hope they are not robbed of their weapons by other insurgents or work their way through the village of Yargul to the ridgeline above the Arga Del Valley then to the Korengal.

My section was supervising a road construction project in Woch Now, which was the perfect location to watch the ridgeline. We had two O.P.s, but there are a few spots that they couldn't see or effectively suppress. The insurgents know these locations. For the next five days my section along with SSG Arnold's squad spent eight to nine hours a day watching the road and the ridgeline.

The road construction project was entertainment alone. The first day, I asked for a backhoe because the road was so narrow I didn't think anything else could make it up to Woch Now. We lucked out with a great operator. Having a backhoe in Woch Now was bigger than the circus coming to town. The people were amazed at how fast the operator could widen their road and work the hillside. The main focus of the project was to build a construction yard to cast crib wall components. The land was owned by Laj bar, and still had its winter wheat crop on it. He had several of his girls out harvesting it by hand to ensure that not one grain of wheat was lost. By the end of the day there wasn't much else the backhoe could effectively accomplish. We had to bring up some bigger equipment. My problem was the road at its widest point was only seven feet. That meant that anything that would come up would have to make its own road.

I asked the PRT mayor for a bulldozer and explained the problem. He had one available and he could be on the job site at 7:30 the next morning.

The next morning, I had SGT Flynn standing by at the back gate with some supplies to load up on the bulldozer truck and trailer. He called me on the radio and asked where the bulldozer was. He had expected the bulldozer between 7:00 and 7:30, but it 8:00 A.M. when I walked up to the flight line where I had seen the bulldozer the night before, but it wasn't there. For a moment I thought I saw a flying red truck leap through the air. I decided I was seeing things because of the long night before. Then I heard a big crash. It turns out our bulldozer operator failed to chock the dozer on the truck. When the truck started to drive up the hill the dozer rolled off lifting the cab of the truck in the air.

Sgt Flynn and I met with the bulldozer operator and gave him some instructions as he went out the gate. LTC Velte and I had to meet with another contractor that morning so we pushed our start time back to 10:00 A.M. We staggered our departures to keep everyone off guard anyway.

As we were leaving the back gate LTC Velte asked me if that was my bulldozer sitting at the range. Naw it couldn't be mine; mine is building a road. Turns out it was my bulldozer just sitting there loaded next to the truck. The operator stated that it was Thursday and they only work half a day on Thursday so we couldn't accomplish anything. I asked him why he had been sitting on the range for the last two hours and not working. He replied no one told us what to do. I had just talked to him a few hours before and he couldn't remember what I looked like. I told him "You have two hours left. Get to work." LTC Velte offered to pay him extra if he would work longer. The operator kept trying to get out of working. I said "I'll call the mayor and see if we can get another operator." That was all that needed to be said. The next thing we know the cab of the red truck was up in the air and the bulldozer was rolling off the back.

We walked up the road to the first work site and waited for the bulldozer. For some reason he was having a difficult time just driving down a halfway respectable dirt road. He finally made it up to where we were waiting for him. He started to work the road then stopped. "Sir this road is no good; it needs to be paved for us to work on it," he said as he pulled out a chunk of hashish and stuck it in his mouth.

"Look friend the reason you're up here is to cut the road so we can pave it." With that he went back to work fighting a big boulder in the road. After a few failed attempts to roll the bulldozer down the hillside I sent him back, and called for the excavator. The bulldozer would have made short work of the road, but it is the operator that makes the difference.

The bulldozer operator and his truck driver buddy drove back to the range and sat there until lunch. The mayor knew that they were cut loose from the job, and finally sent someone out to get them. The excavator operator was able to work half way up the road to Woch Now by 16:00. We stayed out at Woch Now village a little while longer, then returned to base.

Friday was the Islamic holy day (The Christian Sunday) and few if any Afghans worked. We went up to Woch Now again, but only to watch the ridge and talk to Laj Bar. The villagers served us all lunch, which consisted of long grain white rice mixed with carrots and raisins, a salad of tomatoes and onions, a small amount of beef, some flat bread and believe it or not American Mountain Dew, not the international variety. Thankfully their food was very good. The one unforgivable sin in Afghanistan is to waste food. People think that Afghans are offended if you do not accept the food

303

they offer you; they are not, they are just saddened. What offends them is if you take their food and waste it. If you refuse their food someone else can eat it. Even the children will chastise you for throwing bread on the ground to feed the birds.

On Saturday, SSG Tyner was hosting equipment training for the men of Woch Now and LTC Velte had another KLE in town. This meant our SecFor wouldn't be available, but the PRT had the mission to patrol the back valley. I linked up with PRT's operations officer and he said I could use his SecFor for my mission. Sgt Flynn was at the back gate with the daily supplies as the excavator rolled out followed by a dump truck, which we loaded with water and other supplies. I briefed up the PRT's SECFOR about the history of the valley and what the mission was. We launched out the back gate at 8:00 and headed up to Woch Now. I stopped the patrol several times to point out the insurgent's favorite firing locations and other points of interest. We saw Laj Bar and his merry men riding in the back of a dump truck filled with rock. We stopped at the mosque and I pointed out some of the better positions for observation of the ridgeline, then we moved farther up the valley to the village cisterns.

I stopped by a big rock that was used as an anchor for the one-inch water pipe that hung over the dry river and waited for the patrol to assemble. From my perspective it looked like a well-spaced patrol. Slowly the troops rallied at the rock and started lying down. Some asked how much farther. Others had heard me point out the trail up the Witch's Teton and Lucifer's staircase and thought we were going up. I quickly put their fears to rest that I just wanted them to see the boxed canyon and the trailhead to the spring. I pointed out the insurgent's mortar site on the ridge above the box canyon.

It was about this time I realized all of the troops were specialists; the most senior ranking NCO was a newly promoted E-5. These were young kids and all out of shape. Here I am a diabetic and closer to fifty than forty and I was in better shape.

After everyone recovered, we went back to the mosque where I asked the kids to bring us some of the water we had stashed for the troops. Many of the troops didn't bring a camel back. I let the troops recover again while I watched the excavator work on the yard, then I signaled that it was time to return to base.

Just as soon as we started down the road the dump truck operator ran after me telling me if we left the insurgents would kill them. Then he pointed to the far ridge and that there were four. The PRT SecFor commander called up to the OP and asked for them to check out the ridge. Sure enough there were four people on top of the ridge, two men and two women. The report came back a white burka. In Kunar the women wear blue burkas. Then the report changed; it was one red and one green burka. You will not see a red or green burka in Afghanistan. With that, I told the SecFor commander to prepare to spend a few hours in Woch Now.

I was aware that there were no men in the village when we came up, but I discounted it to all of the men being down at the camp training with SSG Tyner. Then it dawned on me there were no men at all not even the men who quarried rock from the hillside. Soon the children of the village started bringing us bread and tea. For some reason the women of the village wanted us to stay. The possible problem with the insurgents didn't bother me; there was only a one in thirty chance that something would happen. Besides, I was in heaven being around some construction. I asked the PRT SecFor NCO if his troops brought food with them, and he said no. With that I decided we had been out in the valley long enough and I told the excavator operator to knock off for the day. I gave several of the boys who brought us bread, a U.S. dollar and told them to give it to their mothers for the bread they gave us, and I radioed down to the Camp to pay Laj bar a little extra for the women's efforts before we headed home.

When we got back inside the gate the SecFor commander decided to hold an after action review of the day's events. The first thing his NCO said was, "The ADT might be hiking those mountains everyday but this should have been a mounted mission." Then he asked everyone to raise their hand if they got whooped going up to the village cisterns, half of the hands went up. He turned to me and said, "Sir this was a real wake up experience for us. We were not prepared to stay more than a few hours and we are fooling ourselves if we thing we're in shape. They all took the day to heart. It will take more than a few days to get into shape, but they can at least prepare for an extended patrol."

There are a few tricks of the trade that we use when hiking in the mountains. We have climbed the mountains in the back of the camp enough to know how long it takes to get from one place to another and how much water we'll consume. We also know that there is a possibility of staying out more than eight or nine hours. We have developed a very good relationship with the Gujers and that has allowed us to store supplies in their village. I had a cache of water and MREs in the village. On long hikes I'd ask Laj Bar to have the children meet us with water. If we had to stay an defend the camp I could feed the troops. As much as we don't like to carry extra weight we all carried food, night vision equipment, GPS, field glasses, and a compass at a minimum.

By Friday night all of the troops from B Company 2-12 Infantry had pulled out of the Korengal Valley and were living at Camp Wright. I met up with their first sergeant and invited several of his troops to come out with us to Arga Del. He accepted my invitation. In the last three years over 150 troops had been killed in the Korengal Valley. The FOBs in the valley didn't have running water or electricity for creature comforts. These troops were living the same way we were in Honduras back in 1995. When they pulled out of the FOBs they took only what they could carry and burned the rest with the exception of a few pieces of equipment and fuel.

On Saturday April 17th we walked down to the government tea farm to check on a chain link fence, which was being installed. I was having a lot of problems with the Kunar Ag minister who was trying to shake down my contractor. The contractor wasn't going to pay him a bribe of 20% of the job so the Ag minister was making life difficult by continually kicking him off the job site. The Ag minister also wanted to extend the fence around some private property. When we got there, SSG Tyner and I inspected the work and it all looked first rate for Afghan. There are many things they do differently because of lack of experience or equipment. That evening LTC Velte and I hosted two platoon leaders and two scouts to a rehearsal brief for the walk up to Arga Del. We ended the brief with a salute to "Baker" company as they prefer to be called.

On Sunday April 18th we formed up behind our TOC and headed up to the back gate. The lead element departed, then one by one we exited the back gate in two staggered columns. Once the back gate rolled shut the lead man looked back then crossed to the other side of the road. Then right on queue everyone criss-crossed on the road just in case there was a sniper. The lower part of the valley is called Kala Kowchano; once you pass the Woch Now Valley you're in the Arga Del Valley. The Arga Del Valley is very narrow and the road fades into the river bottom. Walking on the Arga Del dry river is a bit of a challenge. There are large boulders to climb over and plenty of small round rocks to break your neck on. Arga Del has more water than Woch Now, but there are some water rights issues that prevent them from using it for agriculture. We tried to understand what the agreement was, but we couldn't get a straight answer from the villagers. Later we learned that they were squatting on the land and had no water rights at all. Arga Del is also home to a waterfall that dissipates into the floor of the valley leaving only a shallow pool about five feet in diameter. The earth just sucks it up. The waterfall is seasonal and only flows right after a rainstorm so it is not a dependable source of water.

The village of Arga Del is built on the mountainside much in the same way as the cliff dwelling Indians in Colorado. We met with the village elders and had tea sitting up against a stacked rock building trying to find some shade. We had a nice little Shura with the two platoon leaders from Baker Company. During the discussion, the elder's father came and everyone stood up to greet him. Once we were all seated again he stated that his father had broken his leg and asked us to look at him. We told him that there wasn't much we could do for a broken leg; he should take his father to the hospital. The elder's father then yelled something and a group of young men left for a house in the distance.

I kept an eye on the young men while LTC Velte talked about poultry and other great global topics with the elders. A few minutes had gone by and the men were carrying an elderly man on his bed to us. Just like in the Bible where a group of men ripped off the roof to lower their friend down to Jesus to be healed, these men thought we could do something for the elderly man. LTC Velte called for the medic to come up and I met the men. The first thing I noticed was that man had had surgery on his broken leg. His leg had steel bars on both sides and a set of screws holding them together. I gave a quick pinch to each of his toes and saw that the circulation was good. About that time our medic, SPC Gonsalves, made it up to our location. He was quick to note the green discoloration around the screws, which meant infection. The elderly man looked like he just wanted God to take him. He couldn't walk on his own; he was completely bedridden. LTC Velte asked where he had the surgery as if we didn't know. The village elder, Del Bar, stated at the camp and that he was supposed to go to another hospital for more care but it was too far away. LTC Velte pulled out 1000 Afs and the elderly man's eyes lit up with the fire of his youth again. On the way back I said, "That may not have been the best move; they just might break the old man's other leg for another twenty bucks."

From Agra Del, we took the back route to Woch Now being led by Laj Bar. Laj Bar keeping with tradition took us down a nice little trail that turned into a three-inch ledge on a rock face. SPC Gonsalves was ahead of me and started using three points of contract on the rock face. I had no choice but to follow suit. We came out on top of Woch Now Village and took a small path to the mosque. Sgt Stevens, Flynn and Percival started laying out the new orchard. Sgt Percival was testing the PH at various locations while Sgt Stevens and Flynn worked out tree and irrigation locations. Once again we sat and had tea with the platoon leaders from Baker Company along with SFC Medina, SSG Arnold, LTC Velte and myself.

The two platoon leaders from Baker Company were very impressed; it was the first time an elder had ever provided them with tea on the first visit.

After that SFC Hanlin and I marked out the road up to the village cisterns with spray paint for the excavator to follow. Laj Bar wanted us to continue the road up to his quarry. I told Laj Bar that he gets four days of excavator service and to use it wisely. We passed the cisterns to a point where we could see the back of the box canyon below the spring. I pointed out all of the important features to our guest from Baker Company and answered a few questions before we headed back down to the orchard site.

I didn't realize it but we had spent a lot of time outside the wire and dusk was setting in. We took up some comfortable positions along a rock wall while Sgt Stevens told Laj Bar about the orchard plan. At dusk everything is pretty peaceful; the thunder storms push a cool wind up into the valley, which is a welcome relief from the 97 degree heat. The best part is it is quiet, no generators or trucks.

Just as life couldn't be more relaxing SPC Gonsalves said, "Hey look at that lizard." The lizard shot over LTC Velte's boot followed closely behind by a cobra. The cobra shot right past me and stood up in the middle of the road then continued his pursuit of the lizard. The cobra stopped again on top of a small boulder on the side of the road. Laj Bar saw the snake, grabbed a bunch of rocks and started pelting the cobra. The cobra slipped under some rocks and Laj Bar quickly started flipping over every rock trying to find the cobra. The cobra moved so fast I couldn't track his movement until he stopped. Laj Bar turned to us and said, "If he bites you, you'll be dead before you get to the doctor or your skin will fall off."

On Sunday our mail showed up unexpectedly on schedule and I received several care packages from the Blue Star Mothers of Ohio and the Shepherd of the Valley Lutheran Church of Maple Valley Washington. Their arrival couldn't have come at a better time. I took them all over to Baker Company; their troops were still waiting for their mail to show up and were short toiletries. God's timing is perfect.

On April 20th we headed out to Woch Now with two contractors and one Afghan doctor in tow. We passed Baker Company as if we were two high-speed freight trains. They yelled over, "Hey we left you some tea up at Woch Now."

Chapter Thirty-Six

HANDS ACROSS THE KUNAR

The evening of Saturday, April 24th, twelve days after we closed down our bases in the Korengal Valley, a call came in for a GPS guided 155mm artillery shell. The camp's PA system told everyone to get indoors as the countdown started. The drawback with the GPS artillery shell is a five-pound ring that flies off right after they pull the lanyard. There is just no predicting where it will land. The next day, Sunday April 25th, either some insurgents dressed as ANP or some ANP attacked a squad of dismounted troops in Marawara where the mountain pass to Pakistan was. The attack started from the village of Daridam. One U.S. soldier was injured and medivaced off the top of the mountain. We could see the action from Camp Wright. The troops had the insurgents cornered in some caves, were keeping eyes on them and calling in F-15 air strikes with additional support of four Apache gunships. Over the next few months we would have more and more problems developing from the Ghaki pass where the villages of Daridam and Chinar were located.

Monday evening a major thunder storm moved in and the balloon team had a very difficult time reeling Willie the Whale back down to earth. At one point the tether almost snapped from the wind force. The lightning storm was a sight to see, but we didn't receive any rain until well after sunset. I had been walking out in the Kala Kowchano Valley most of the day in 90-degree heat so the evening showers and wind were welcome treats that facilitated a good night's sleep.

I wasn't the only one who thought it was good sleeping weather. South east of Camp Wright in the mountains overlooking the Kunar River is O.P. Nevada. O.P. Nevada is completely staffed by ASG and can be seen from both Camp Wright and FOB Joyce. This O.P. even has a small ammo depot not just a supply bunker like the other O.P.s. On Monday night, April 26, all twenty-two ASG soldiers at O.P. Nevada went to sleep except one, the one who worked for the Taliban.

At one A.M. Tuesday morning the insurgents attacked O.P. Nevada and hit the ammo depot first. The ammo depot caught fire. I had just got out of bed to answer nature's call when I heard the ANP troops at Camp Wright open up with DShK and ZKM 14 mm fire on the insurgents who were on the north side of the O.P. while FOB Joyce opened fire on the insurgents on the south side. The insurgents were able to kill two of the ASG soldiers and wound four others at the O.P. Later in the day a third ASG soldier died from his wounds. The fight went on for about thirty minutes with American observers directing fire to the ANP. One by one the insurgents were located in the dark and eliminated at a range of 1500 meters. There are a few tricks to the trade that the insurgents hadn't figured out yet. The ASG soldiers at the O.P. folded and ran from the fight and didn't attempt to hold the O.P. This is something the U.S. anticipated, which is why supporting fire occurred within seconds of the initial assault.

Tuesday morning we went out the back gate to Arga Del Village to run a mini VetCap. We hired a local truck and the AVA to run the operation. This was going to be the first time that the AVA would run the whole operation. They ran 123 animals through the vaccination chute without a hitch. On our way back to Camp Wright there were two platoons of ANA infantry in the valley running some drills.

Projects in Woch Now and Arga Del were moving ahead nicely. I found a good contractor who worked quickly with the terracing for the new orchard and vineyard. I met this contractor at the Afghan hospital on Camp Wright. Most of the less than desirable contractors pay the interpreters on post to lobby for them. These same interpreters also screen information so we never use them.

I had gone to the Afghan hospital to drop off several boxes of stuffed animals for the children they operate on, when I met one of the doctors. They all had a contracting business going on the side and were very aggressive. This doctor was much more polished in his appearance and his mannerisms. We talked for a while about the women up in Woch Now who needed medical care and the one old man in Arga Del with the broken leg. He agreed to go to both of the villages if I would pay for the medications. He told me that his wife was also a doctor so there would be no problem examining the women. We continued to talk about the concrete project that the Gujers were doing on post and he said he was starting up a contracting business and was looking for small jobs not big ones to get started. I asked him if he had an excavator and he said he could get his hands on one. With that we made a deal to rework the road to Woch Now and terrace off the new orchard and vineyard. It turned out to be a very good arrangement.

Since the U.S. shut down operations in the Korengal Valley there had been a noticeable increase of attacks in the Pech River Valley. The FOBs and COPs were getting mortared or rocketed daily. IEDs were coming back on route Rhode Island, which was unusual because the route is paved. On Sunday May 2nd a rocket attack hit one of the 155 artillery crews at FOB Blessing; nine men were injured, five seriously and one became a hero. When an individual is killed the/she is called a hero. When a medivac flight becomes a hero flight that means the soldier died in route to the trauma center.

Losing troops in your AO (Area of Operations) is like losing a distant relative who lives across the country. You feel the void even if you weren't close to that person.

Camp Wright has two 155 gun crews and some alternates so one crew was sent to FOB Blessing. The artillery alternates were pulled off guard duty and put on the gun line. The ADT picked up the slack until another gun crew could be brought in from the U.S. or Germany.

On Wednesday May 5th LTC Velte was reassigned to Jalalabad to work in the ADT cell there. The U.S. AID has an eight hundred million dollar watershed and flood control project marked for Kunar. LTC Velte would be the LNO (Liaison Officer) for the project. He left at noon Thursday with a sendoff from the troops from the Ag and SecFor sections.

LTC Velte got the last flight going south for the day. Molson shut down due to weather and Willie the Whale was hauled in. Rain makes for good sleeping weather. Once again when the rain stopped O.P. Nevada was attacked at 2300 hrs on Thursday night. The DShK and ZKM were firing across the Kunar at targets. The camp alarms when off. I took my traditional location by the bunker and saw the balloon crew release Willie the Whale. They just kicked the winch loose and Willie flew into the sky like Shamu breaching the surface for a leap into the stands. About this time, my colonel called for me to come into the TOC. I was, at that time, the deputy commander and the Ag OIC. The advantage of being in the TOC is you get to watch the live feed from Willie. We could see the tracers impacting from our weapons and the troops at O.P. Nevada firing their RPGs, but we couldn't see any enemy troops. Then we saw something moving very fast across the hills. A dog was having the time of his life running back and forth just enjoying himself. By midnight there was no sign of insurgency so the all clear was sounded and we went back to bed. At 3:00 A.M. Friday morning the DShK went off again. This time I told myself *I'm not getting out of bed unless the incoming alarm goes off.* It didn't.

Chapter Thirty-Seven

CONSTRUCTION AT WOCH NOW

On Sunday morning May 9th at 3:00 A.M. I was awakened with a start, fully alert to the sound of a shriek. I flew out of bed and hit the floor. I thought for sure we were under a rocket attack, and then the shriek turned into a roar of the afterburners of an F-15 flying the map of the earth through the Kunar River Valley. My next thought was *he is going to drop a GBU* and held my breath for the impact. The roar of the jet diminished finally, with no earth shaking. I dusted myself off and noted two bruised kneecaps; then I went back to bed. SGT Carter was in the ECP tower at the time. All he saw was the after burners as the F-15 flew south and banked east over FOB Joyce followed by the deafening roar. What a way to start the week.

The insurgents had increased their attacks on the outposts in the Pech River Valley to several times a day with mortars, rockets, recoilless rifles, IEDs and anything else they could find. We were set to go up to FOB Blessing to see USAID's number two man, Mr. USAID Jr., about some projects. I was never impressed with this man's judgment or ability to plan projects. As we were working our way up the Pech, each COP was being attacked just before we arrived on site, and once again after we passed through the area. We arrived at FOB Blessing with no contact and were under the impression that we had to walk around in full battle rattle because of the frequency of mortar attacks. Turns out we got the wrong information.

We linked up with a captain from the FOB Blessing HQ and USAID's number two Mr. USAID Jr. and had a pre meeting. I asked Mr. USAID Jr., "Do you have title to the land for each of these projects?" He said we can get it at the meeting. "So you do not have title now; is that correct?" I could see void behind his eyes; there was no land for any of the projects. I was very clear with him that we were not going to pay for the projects or run them, and I would not allocate the time or the resources to develop the projects if he didn't have a signed Co-Op and the land rights. He was really upset.

We assembled with SGT Stevens, Sgt Percival and SFC Fair and walked to the Naglam District center to meet with the community business leaders about the projects. Mr. USAID Jr. didn't have an agenda for the meeting and it quickly became a free for all. I put the meeting back in order several times. The final outcome was they didn't have the land. They thought they could rent it for a butcher shop, and cold storage. The demonstration farm was still in the idea stage. I asked what they wanted to use the cold storage for. They argued back and forth and finally agreed upon using it for produce.

From the district center we walked downtown to see the proposed sites. As we approached route Rhode Island, Mr. USAID Jr. said, "Here is the site you proposed for the hydro electric dam." I was quick to respond that I didn't propose any site for a hydro electric dam, but he insisted that the whole concept was my idea. I was about to boot him into the Pech when the district sub governor walked up. I greeted him in Pashto and we carried on a short conversation. Mr. USAID Jr. decided that he couldn't be part of the conversation and hit the road. The sub governor was ecstatic that I could speak Pashto. What he didn't realize was that it was a canned speech and package of questions I had memorized that made me look smart.

The site for the butcher shop and cold storage was a pit and a pile of rubble mixed with animal remains. We went to the experimental farm by way of an "orchard" that Mr. USAID Jr. wanted us to QA/QC. We arrived at a weed patch with six trees somewhere in the mix. Mr. USAID Jr. was very proud of his orchard establishment project. This was the largest of seven orchards that he established. I guess two trees in a row equals an orchard. The proposed site for the demonstration farm was also a bust.

We loaded up and took on additional passengers who needed a ride back to FOB Wright, which included the battery commander and the 1SGT of our big guns. We pulled out onto Route Rhode Island and passed a CLIP (Logistic convoy of civilian and military trucks) lined up on the side of the road for half a mile. Just as we passed the CLIP the last three jingle trucks in the convoy decided to latch on to the rear of our convoy instead of waiting for their CLIP to roll out. Every few miles we would pass a convoy set up in a defensive position along the Pech to secure Route Rhode Island for the CLIP. Just like our drive up the Pech, the COPs were being attacked before and after we passed by. The insurgents must have had a death wish on Monday with all of the guns and dismounts the U.S. had in the area.

On Tuesday May 11th we went up to Nawa Pass, which crosses over into Pakistan. The PRT had completed a road project through the three Nawa villages into Pakistan, but not without a lot of unpleasantness. The construction crews were plagued with IEDs and weekly ambushes by insurgents from Pakistan who didn't want the road. We were expecting to see some combat during our visit to the middle village. The three villages are just named low, middle and upper Nawa. The middle village had been receiving the lion's share of the support from the U.S. They had a new school that could be seen overlooking the highway and a lot of other small projects. The concern was that the other villages might become a little hostile toward the U.S. because of all the support we had given to the middle village. Our job was to verify a small watershed project that was proposed by a NGO from New York. At our pre-meeting at FOB Joyce the village elder stated that the environment was very dangerous for the villagers so we could expect that it would be dangerous for us. Then he said, "Please do not come looking for me when you arrive; I will come find you."

When we arrived at the middle village we were accompanied by the Afghan Border Police. There was a spot above the village suitable to turn our vehicles around as we dismounted. The Afghan border officer called us over and said there were no problems in this village or the other villages. Then he pointed down to Pakistan and said there was the problem. "You need to keep going and fight the problem in Pakistan."

317

While SecFor was setting up security on the road, SGT Percival, SGT Stevens and I worked our way up the draw with another team of SecFor to review the watershed proposal. The NGO knew what they were doing and had a very good plan. While I was there I checked out the road, which was already deteriorating. The contractor put on a slurry seal and sloped the road in the wrong direction. The contract called for four inches of ¾ base and a two-inch cap of 3/8 asphalt. Oh well what's American money when it's handed out like candy!

On May 12th the Army decided to swap out the satellite system that linked our computer systems to brigade. It took over a week for us to be back up and running, which meant many long nights for me catching up with all of our finances.

The week of the 16th was more to my liking with some concrete pours up in Woch Now. SFC Fulton and I had been up at the village several times instructing them on how to dig foundations and lay out the forms. No one can fault the villagers for a lack of a work ethic, but they are programmed for two things: harvesting rocks and building rock walls. When we arrived to inspect the forms, the foundation trenches were four-feet wide, not the 18 inches we asked for. It turns out that every time they found a big rock below they would dig it out, split it up and sell it. SFC Fulton and I realized that the moat they dug would hold the Missouri and consume all of our concrete. SFC Fulton told them to build a rock wall in the foundation to suck up some of the volume. A few days later they were still building the wall with a string line. They were building a precision wall, and they couldn't comprehend the concept of just dump some big rocks in the back of the trench. With that, SFC Fulton told them to use the concrete block that we were going to use for the retaining wall just to keep the project moving.

We arranged for a water truck to deliver 2000 gallons of treated water up to the village to fill up four of the 500-gallon tanks we had sitting up there. At the same time, SSG Tyner cut a deal for the use of a three CY mixer, which we hauled up to the village. The villagers were in awe of the mixer. They had never seen anything so big before. I don't think it occurred to them how all of the rock, sand and cement would be loaded or unloaded from the mixer that evening.

May 20th was show day. I stayed back at Camp Wright with a cell phone and a pile of cash just in case we were short materials up in Woch Now. SFC Fulton ran the show in the village, and the men of Woch Now were earning their keep the first day of the three-day pour. While I was waiting for a trouble call such as "we're out of rock or sand," Del Bar from Arga Del village showed up with ten of his men. Del Bar told me that his men came to work. I was caught a bit off guard with the announcement, so I told him again about the schedule that Wednesdays were his days to work on the FOB, but his concrete forms were not back from the shop yet so we had no work. Young Del Bar went on to tell me that his people were very poor and if they couldn't work every day at the FOB, they were not going to work at all. I told him that I understood his situation, escorted him back out the gate and wished him well. I could tell by the look on his face that this was not the reaction that he was expecting. What Del Bar had no way of understanding was I deal with contractors everyday back home who are extremely corrupt and play in the big league. Del Bar isn't even in the amateur league.

This came after Del Bar brought in one of his contractor friends a few weeks earlier and demanded I give him a contract for the road to Arga Del. The ultimatum was "either I build the road or no one builds the road."

"OK no skin off my nose; no one builds the road. Let me walk you to the front gate."

On Friday May 21st SFC Fulton was once again running the crew up at Woch Now when a few men from Arga Del came over to talk to Laj Bar, the village elder, about their situation. I had spies everywhere in a few minutes. I received a phone call telling me that there was a pending shakeup in the leadership at Arga Del Village.

On Saturday SFC Fulton called down and said they were finished with the foundation, and ready to start forming the slab. I couldn't believe it! That was a ton of concrete to mix in just three days. They were finished but the pour was not complete. We used about 300 to 500 gallons of water mixing and pouring concrete, but then we were out of water. I remember telling Laj Bar not to drink the water, it would make his teeth very white, but it would be hard on his kidneys. The villagers found a use for the water; it may have been a laundry and house cleaning festival. I can't imagine they drank 1500 gallons of water in five days.

We had about two weeks of work left up in Woch Now Village before we could plant the orchard and vineyard. I was standing on the new terracing with Laj Bar and I asked him how long it would have taken for his men to terrace off the land we just finished. He replied, "With all of the men, 30 years." I pointed up to the hillside and asked how long all of the terracing took above the village and he responded, "70 years." It took us $3000.00 and two weeks to terrace off five acres and notch out a 100-foot square construction yard. Land that had been dormant would soon be in production.

I had a chance to talk to the village elder from Yargadel, the village to the north of the FOB about the Arga Del Village. Young Del Bar had told me about this mean man who wouldn't give them water. That mean man was the village elder of Yargadel. Just like in proverbs one man sounds just until his neighbor tells the rest of the story. Some of the problems I was having with Arga Del were they couldn't come up with any land for an orchard or a concrete fabrication yard. The reason was they didn't own any land. They were squatting on land owned by people in Yargadel. The mean man was nice enough not to run them off and allowed them some water to live off. I didn't know if he was charging them rent or not.

Overall things were the same. We still received mortar attacks that missed the FOB and thunder storms in the mornings and afternoons. The 2-12 Infantry left and a new company from the 101st arrived. I had never seen so many privates before. The majority of the new unit was fresh out of basic training; the whole unit was very young. SFC Mosqueda set up some training for them on sighting some of the crew served weapons in the ASVs, which they would be using. These were air-assault troops. They were not accustomed to traveling around in vehicles. There we had to drive to the fight.

Chapter Thirty-Eight

THREE WISHES I GRANT YOU, BUT WISH A FOURTH WISH, YOU HAVE NO WISH AT ALL.

For awhile I didn't think anything noteworthy would happen in the Merry Month of May. I would soon be proven wrong. Wednesday afternoon May 26th I was counting up the number of crib wall components we had manufactured with the men from Woch Now and noted that we were running behind. Production had been ambushed during the last two pour days by heavy thunderstorms. I decided to call Laj Bar and see if his men wanted to pour some more components on Thursday May 27th. As usual the cell phone service to Woch Now was out of whack so I had Rafi wave down one of the sand trucks to deliver the message. The sand trucks were delivering sand and gravel to Woch Now for the slab pour. Laj Bar returned word via the sand truck that he would be at the gate with his men at 8:00 A.M.

Thursday was starting off well. We had SFC Hanlin back from leave, which would offset the loss of SSG Tyner who we sent up to Pertil King with SGT Stevens to teach about short corn. SFC Hanlin and I greeted the men from Woch Now and escorted them to the job site where SFC Fulton was waiting for them. I went to our Afghan café and ordered 15 lunches. By 9:00 A.M. concrete was beginning to pour and SFC Fair and I were receiving deliveries of pipe and water pumps and other items for a demonstration farm down in Chowkay, the friendliest village in all of Kunar. Their hospitality is second only to the humble residents of the Korengal Valley. I've yet to understand these people. They see nothing wrong with trying to kill you while at the same time demanding that you provide them with some type of service.

Things were really moving at Camp Wright, the airfield was seeing heavy traffic, Molson was flying their Sikorski loaded with passengers, there were Kiowas and Apaches reloading, a CH-47 stopped by and two Afghan Hips arrived with ammo. The Afghan Hip helicopters were painted in Afghan colors, but the pilots looked very Russian. There was something odd going on at the airfield. The two hips were being unloaded by a bunch of Afghan civilians, not the ANA or ASG troops. All of the men were wearing off-white manjamies (the typical Afghan clothing for men) and were unloading the helicopters as if they had done it so many times before. I didn't think much of it. I had plenty to do that morning. We were short handed and I was the support for my troops.

At 11:00 we had another delivery of some irrigation pipe. As I started down the stairs at the ECP gate (Entry Control Point) I heard one of the ASG (Afghan Security Guards) yell down to the ASG guards on the gate "Don't let the vehicle in." I asked Rafi if I heard the guard correctly and he said yes. My first thought was there must have been another attack at a FOB at their ECP gate. Just a week prior there was a suicide initiated attack at Bagram Air Base where 20 insurgents made it past the gate and three were able to make it back out alive. Americans are better marksmen than Pakistani insurgents give us credit for. The suicide bomber who was to initiate the attack wasn't able to detonate his vest at the prescribed time. Several well placed rounds from a very observant U.S. soldier spoiled his surprise. He blew up anyway.

I asked Rafi to ask the ASG guards if I could park the truck in the cool down yard and transfer the load to one of my trucks. A few minutes of discussion with Rafi told me that there was a labor dispute and the ASG guards were not letting in any vehicles. I had a 9mm pistol on me, there was one of our SecFor troops in the ECP tower with an SAW, and one Pennsylvania guardsmen at the vehicle gate with an M-4, but with five ASG guards armed with AK-47 and a PKM machinegun I was not in the position to press my luck.

I called for SFC Fair and SGT Percival to come out with a truck and we transferred about half of what was on the truck and sent the rest back because it was defective. I informed the PRT what was going on, then alerted the rest of the ADT. They had just received word that there might be a problem. At 12:00 noon we preempted their strike and replaced all of the ASG guards and disarmed them at the same time. SFC Medina and I decided to call off the concrete pour and send the men of Woch Now home. We made that decision just a little too late. The 12:30 Camp Wright Mosque call for prayer had been sounded. The Gujers were the first in the mosque and they were always the last out. It took 45 minutes for them to pray and wouldn't you know it one of them stubbed his toe and needed to see a doctor. SFC Hanlin took Laj Bar and eleven of the men to the yard to get their stuff and I took old sore toes to the Afghan hospital. We walked in just as the doctors were starting their prayers.

We finally got the Gujers off the FOB in time to start rounding up the weapons the ASG left at their post. They didn't have a choice in the matter. We put an RPG and several rounds in Major Leeney's office for safe keeping while the OGA started negotiating with the striking ASG members. There were four key ring leaders speaking for all of the ASG guards at Camp Wright and up at OP Nevada and our Ops.

The ASG (Asian Security Group) is a contracted security service just like ITT except ASG is almost exclusively Afghan. There are some retired Gurkhas working for them as well. The average unskilled daily wage in Afghanistan is $5.00. A highly skilled person will make $10.00. Under the old contract the ASG guards were making $175.00 a month about $5.80 a day. Under the new contract they were making $275.00 a month, about $9.00 a day. They received other benefits under the new contract, which included meals, uniforms, boots, equipment, and vacation. Only a few months earlier they were required to provide their own uniforms and equipment, less weapon. Now they were demanding that their pay be doubled to match what the ANA special operations teams were making: fewer hours on duty, more time off, severance pay, and be allowed to keep their weapons if they quit. They also didn't want to carry supplies up to O.P. Nevada.

This was another caper that was going on. The OGA had contracted for ten donkeys at $100 per donkey per month. The contractor only supplied six donkeys, but demanded the full $1000.00. One of the members of the

LTC David M. Kelly

ASG got involved and demanded $2000.00 per month and was going to sub out the work to the man already under contract.

O.P. Nevada, which was attacked the month prior, was fully manned by the ASG who never preformed their duty. When they were attacked, all of them were asleep except the one who worked for the insurgents. He was the one who let the insurgents in to the O.P. We were having a similar problem up at O.P. Shiloh where the lines to our claymore mines were being cut. We rotated out the ASG guard and the problem stopped.

The ASG went on to demand that they be treated like soldiers, but they didn't want to do physical training. I hate to tell them but physical training is part of being a soldier and so is humping your own gear up the mountain. If I haul 100+ pounds up the Witch's Teton and workout every night, so can these guys.

The OGA was buying some time and had all of the ASG guards put on their civilian clothes and sit out in the ASG volley ball court while they discussed the dispute. This explained why I saw the Afghan civilians unloading the Hips on the airfield. They were the soon to be striking ASG guards. By night fall the ASG members elected four men to represent them. The OGA said they were not giving into their demands, which prompted the striking ASG members to demand their pay. No problem! One by one they were paid and escorted off the FOB. Out of all the ASG guards we had on the FOB only one third said they wanted to stay when they got up to the paymaster. These men were quietly taken to another building for their own protection.

Meanwhile, the ex-ASG members were massing outside the front gate on route California and starting to get rowdy. SFC Medina was the NCOIC of the guard and was told to expect trouble. It is one thing to be stupid enough to bring a knife to a gun fight, but to think you would overrun a FOB empty handed against a bunch of well armed Americans who were pissed off after pulling a full day's duty and missing lunch and dinner along with having to wear their full battle rattle in 110 degree heat, was absurdity. SFC Medina wasn't all that concerned. There was no time like the present to have a conflict. The OGA went out to the ex-ASG guards and explained a few things to them and cooler minds prevailed. The men walked away stewing about what just happened because of their greed.

Turns out a local insurgent commander had orchestrated the whole thing to prep for a massive mortar attack, that didn't happen. TAO (Typical Afghan Operation).

Friday morning it was business as usual and we were loading up the convoy to Jalalabad. I made some quick rounds at 5:00 A.M. and all was quiet, not even a hint of trouble. We rolled out the gate at 7:00 and arrived at Jalalabad at 9:00, two hours right on schedule. SGT Palacios and SPC McCool were waiting for us. SGT Percival dropped me off at the ammo point while they loaded up the trailer and the rest of the convoy went over to the logistics yard where SGT Palacios loaded up our remaining trailers. Within the hour we were fully loaded up and ready to head back to Camp Wright. We still had some finance work to do to close out a few contracts and grab a bit to eat before heading back. I hadn't been to Jalalabad in several months and was shocked to see the changes at the post. The runway was completed and could handle a C-17, but they will never land one there. The reason is a C-17 would have to taxi to the end of the runway turn around and come back to the midway point where the tarmac is. The C-130s just slams on the brakes throw two engines in reverse and makes the turn.

The old civilian air terminal was being renovated with new vinyl windows; the interior was also being reconditioned. The Old Russian Mig that was out in front had been hauled off to the scrap yard. New sidewalks were crisscrossing the main camp and new pavilions at the PAX terminal and in front of coffee shop. They even expanded the bazaar of shops. It's an odd feeling to be coming from a forward deployed area where the artillery was going off every night to Jalalabad were people do not move with a purpose, nor does their IBA (Battle rattle) show any sign of wear, which is proudly on display in their offices. I looked at all of the troops at Jalalabad who paid close attention to their uniforms and wear reflective P.T. belts during the day. Then I saw our troops with patches on their uniforms, salt stains on their boots, the color on their uniforms have faded, and the soles of their boots well worn. I'd worn half of the soles off the new boots I had received two months earlier. Our troops were squared away when it came to appearance, but you could see the mileage.

I took care of some business mostly delivering items to different offices, then wished our troops a safe trip back to Wright. I was going to spend the night and meet with MG Curtis Scapurrotti the 82nd Division Commander the next morning to go over my Officer Evaluation Review. I was very impressed by him. This was the first division commander I met who took the time to meet with everyone he was evaluating. We had a short discussion about USAID, then about my career. He gave me a few pointers, then gave me an 82 Division coin. I wish we could have spent more time together; he was a very interesting man.

I grabbed a quick bit to eat and loaded up for my Molson flight back to Wright. I was told to wait at the runway crossing for the shuttle. A lot had changed since my last visit. I just assumed that there would be a shuttle bus coming by to pick me up. I watched the first Molson HU-1 rip down the runway and then shot over the mountains toward Bagram. Then another Molson flight started down the runway. I was standing at the shuttle stop with a young lady from Alberta Canada who was also the Molson PAX manager. She turned to me and said "this is your flight." I just assumed that I missed it since it was air born. The UH-1 turned sideways, hovered and stopped on the runway. The co-pilot jumped out and opened the side door for me. I threw him my ruck and jumped in to be greeted by a bunch of my civilian friends from Camp Wright. I had a great seat in the back next to the door looking straight ahead. The co-pilot was just closing his door when we lifted off. From my perspective we weren't that high off the deck and all I could see was the runway because we were tipped up on end going full throttle down the runway. I could see the end of the runway from the side window, then the pilot made a hard right while gaining some altitude. I compressed into my seat and we were over Jalalabad. The little airfield of FOB Fenty (Jalalabad) can be very busy. There is zero dwell time on the runway for aircraft.

We had been having some heavy winds the night before and it looked as if they returned that afternoon. The UH-1 was yawing all the way down the valley. I spotted FOB Joyce in the distance. After about 20 minutes of flight we made a hard turn circling around the FOB and made a quick landing for one PAX to jump out then headed out to Wright.

By the time I returned to Camp Wright, the OGA was able to bring in enough new ASG guards to free up half of my troops. I was handed an Intel report that the AAF (Anti Afghan Forces) didn't like us working with Woch Now Village and were planning a surprise for both of us if we were to go back out there. This concerned me because the last time the FOB was mortared, the insurgents also mortared Woch Now Village. The last thing I needed to do was to put the people of Woch Now at risk because we helped them establish an orchard. I couldn't help but wonder if it was our friends up at Arga Del who made the threat after their failed attempt to demand full time employment from me.

I pulled out our 30-day schedule and started to ponder how I could alter construction times to reduce the risk to the village. Then it hit me. Because we had the additional security duty I couldn't pull off the mission even if I wanted to; that is with my own troops. The almighty dollar would come to the rescue. I would just contract out the rest of the work. Problem solved!

I had just finished patting myself on the back when J.W., one of my interpreters, walked in with his sad story. "Sir I need to take 15 days off to get married."

I asked, "How much time do you have on the books?" (None, he used it all.) He told me that Lt Ko just didn't understand the culture and would only give him seven days off, but the interpreters were willing to give him some of their vacation so he could have a proper wedding.

" J.W. weddings take 30 minutes, just as long as a funeral. Why on earth do you need fifteen days to get married?"

"Sir, the wedding takes seven days but I'm expected to be with my wife for five days after we get married." (7+5 = 12 right?)

"J.W. I'm a bit puzzled here. Why do you need five days to accomplish what most people can accomplish on the wedding night?"

"It is our custom. The richer you are the longer the wedding."

"Well in that case J.W., why don't you just take the time off without pay? Your job will be here when you come back."

"Sir you don't understand. I'm poor. I can't afford to take time off without pay." (J.W. borrowed $10,000.00 for his wedding.)

"J.W. help me understand something. Last month the Gujers who are very poor, but eat well and are fully clothed held a wedding for one day, but you're so poor that you require 15 days to get married?"

"Sir this will be a onetime event in my life."

"J.W. this will be the first of four weddings in your life, if not more, if you divorce one of them along the way. Isn't this the girl you knew since you were a child? Besides you are going to see this woman for the rest of your life."

Young J.W. was our best snake oil salesmen but somehow he was just stumped trying to negotiate with me, a devout cynic who was keeping one eye on the project and leave schedules knowing that 15 days leave was a variable in the production equation that required an upper limit. Later I found out that he wanted to take off 20 days in June, four days in July and another four in August, but he wouldn't take off any time in September or October when the Iowa ADT would be on station. J.W. had spent all of his vacation time as he earned it and we even slipped him a few extra days to go home to buy some equipment for us. J.W. finally saw things our way and agreed not to take time off for several months in exchange for 15 days off in June.

On Sunday May 30th the PRT was coming back from Asmar and was ambushed from hill 1311. Hill 1311 overlooks the Kunar Construction College (aka the Taliban retirement center) and route California. This time the insurgent's aim had improved and they struck two MRAPs before being repelled. The first MRAP just received a few dents. The second had its 240 blown off the turret when the RPG penetrated the vehicle. The gunner received some minor wounds to his face but nothing serious. The PRT tried to recover their 240 but just couldn't find it. My guess it is somewhere in the bottom of the Kunar River. After seeing test results of what is in that river I wouldn't be too quick to wade around in the muddy water for any extended period of time. I was still fighting some type of fungus on my right foot that sprung up after multiple river crossings.

At about the same time the PRT was ambushed on Sunday a few insurgents attempted to infiltrate O.P. Shiloh, only to stop and rest in the direct line of sight of two 155mm artillery pieces. We were starting to see a pattern here. For some reason the insurgents enjoy looking down the bore of American artillery. After a while one would think they would get the idea not to set up a mortar or camp where the big guns can't see you. Hmmm that just might be the reason none of the insurgents left a note to others. "Warning DON'T Stop Here"

Monday was Memorial Day and there was no rest for the weary. I was up and about at 5:00 A.M. SSG Valenzuela and his team were running laps around the FOB in their IBA getting ready for a 5K run while my team was getting ready for casting concrete. We were expecting Laj Bar and his men first thing in the morning along with several material deliveries. Even though the OGA had received some replacement ASG guards they still required U.S. supervision. We still had extra towers and gates to man, which took away a lot of sack time and personnel. As luck would have it, everyone showed up at the same time while it was still cool. SFC Fulton and SGT Percival were running the Woch Now Co-Op. SFC Fair and I were receiving materials and paying vendors. SFC Medina and Hanlin had pulled guard shift after a full day's duty and were beat. I was still able to coax SFC Hanlin out of bed to practice his Pashto just before lunch. By mid-morning I was finally able to sit down and talk to Laj Bar about some of the threat reports we were receiving and what his nutty cousin Del Bar was up to.

Bottom line: the village of Woch Now is threatened by the insurgents all the time, and Laj Bar's nutty cousin didn't have the brains to work with the insurgents. Once again I asked Laj Bar, "Can you defend yourself against the insurgents?" I still didn't get a straight answer. Laj Bar once again said "We have no weapons to defend ourselves with and we don't need any weapons." The translation is *we have all the weapons we need and we know how to use them.* The older men in Woch Now were Mujahedeen and fought the Soviets in Asadabad. Laj Bar's father was one of the leaders and told me how they had captured large amounts of Soviet weapons and sold them in Pakistan. I don't believe they sold all of the weapons.

We ended the day by sending more equipment up to Woch Now and preparing for three more days of concrete pouring in the village. I could run the operation with just two NCOs and a squad of SecFor.

Fluor decorated the Mess Hall for Memorial Day and served a nice roast. We have been blessed so far with no injuries that cost a limb or any deaths from insurgents or accidents. Other units had not been so lucky.

Chapter Thirty-Nine

PSALM 24
THE KING OF GLORY
AND HIS KINGDOM

Afghanistan's farm fields are always in production. The winter wheat crop was harvested by the end of May and the farmers were preparing to plant feed corn. The harvest time of the feed corn coincides with the peak of insurgent activities along the major MSRs. The farmers plant corn on every available square inch of soil right up to the edge of the highways. This is ideal for insurgents to lie in their lair and wait for the right convoy to attack.

We had proposed to the battle space owners to pay farmers to grow seedlings for reforestation along the highways to reduce the amount of concealment for the insurgents, but that idea was rejected. The main reason was the amount of resources that would be required to monitor all of the individual contracts for the seedlings. Then a USDA rep arrived at FOB Bostick in Naray and presented the concept of growing short corn. The battle space owners liked the idea and proceeded to purchase $240,000.00 worth of short corn seed from Pakistan. At the last minute we were asked to validate the seed number and the concept of the project.

SGT Stevens hit the Internet and started making phone calls back to the States and Canada about the availability of short corn seed and its attributes. While he was researching the project, the new USDA rep was able to sell the concept to the outgoing and incoming brigade commanders. We were directed to buy enough short corn seed for the Central Kunar and Pech River Valleys. SGT Stevens learned from Monsanto that there was not enough hybrid short corn seed in the region to meet the demand of the brigade. He also learned that it wasn't all that short; it still stood five to six feet tall, enough to provide the insurgents adequate concealment to successfully attack our convoys. The short corn was developed for Canada and other regions that had a short growing season. The corn had a higher yield, a 90-day seed to harvest time, but required more water.

A few days after we were tasked to conduct the research, the USDA rep from FOB Bostick came down asking for help because the project was more than he could handle alone. We agreed to support him, and sent SSG Tyner, SGT Stevens and Sam, one of our interpreters, up to FOB Bostick. It quickly became evident that the USDA rep was only a bright idea man. There was no project planning or coordination. SSG Tyner and SGT Stevens summed up the situation and realized they had to take over if the project would fail. The two of them set up classes and sorted the seed for distribution to each of the villages that signed up for the short corn. At the direction of the USDA rep, Sam our interpreter, made radio announcements about when and where the seed would be distributed. Things were off to a good start. Sam knew how to handle a crowd based upon his experience working VetCaps; SGT Stevens handled the instruction while SSGT Tyner supervised the distribution of seed. The one person who was constantly missing was the USDA rep.

On Monday afternoon, May 31st a group of insurgents attacked the Bare Matal District center beheading two people and killing eight more. Bare Matal is located north of Fob Bostick in Nuristan. This had a very sudden impact on the short corn seed project. Because the route security to Naray was volatile the battle space owner decided to fly all of the short corn seed up to FOB Bostick on CH-47 helicopters. Moving 50 tons of corn seed required many flights. By Monday night, F-15 fighters were bombing the insurgent's operation center near Paprok, 12 kilometers away from Bare Matal. Soon all of the available air assets were redirected to support the ANA. Bare Matal is in a very remote location and difficult to support. The PRT had been building roads from Naray to Bare Matal with considerable violent opposition from the insurgents. Retaking Bare Matal couldn't be accomplished quickly by convoying ANA trucks up from Kabul; they would have to be flown. It appeared that American's success in pushing the insurgents out of Afghanistan in the south only pushed them into the far north by traveling through Pakistan.

By 1:00 A.M. Tuesday morning ANA Commandos and U.S. forces recaptured Bare Matal District center and cleared the area of insurgents. It was evident the insurgents were intent on using the district center as an operation base. They abandoned a large cache of bomb-making materials including IEDs ready to be placed, in their haste to return to Pakistan. By sunrise the ANA commandos found the bodies of over 70 insurgents and many more too wounded to flee. The majority of the insurgents were Pakistani. Col Shams of the 7th ABP (Afghan Border Police) made a press release stating the provenance was retaken without firing a shot.

His statement may have been altered a bit to support the atmosphere of the "Peace Jirga" that was scheduled to take place in Kabul on June 2nd. It is also possible that once the F-15s started prepping the battlefield, the insurgents decided to flee back to Pakistan before they were engaged by the ANA Commandos.

All of this activity put a halt on the future delivery of seed. The ANA with the support of the U.S. was set on sweeping Nuristan clean of insurgents before they could establish themselves. SGT Stevens attempted to explain the Army's logistic system to the USDA rep and how it would affect his seed delivery, to no avail. The USDA rep was certain that the seed would be delivered as scheduled and proceeded to place radio announcements telling each village when and where to pick up their seed. This nearly caused a riot when the seed wasn't delivered and people didn't get the late word not to show up. This soon became a cycle with the USDA rep that SGT Stevens and Sam had to deal with. Things went downhill from there with foot in mouth disease. While SGT Stevens was giving a class, the USDA rep announced though another interpreter, that the seed was guaranteed to grow if it didn't just bring the tag back and it would be replaced. Sam quickly told SGT Stevens about the announcement. Alarm bells were going off in the mind of SGT Stevens and the Battle Space owner. They knew what was going to happen next. The farmers would sell the seed as fast as they could and bring the tag back for more seed or demand financial compensation for the lost crop.

The reports from the field were not improving so I decided to recall my troops. The battle space owner was not amused with the USDA rep's performance either. There was a sign on the TOC door picturing a corn stalk with a line slashed through and the statement no corn discussion beyond this point. The battle space owner even directed the USAG rep to consolidate his office into his quarters, to limit his access to the command. Working out of quarters is not unusual. At Camp Wright all of the government civilians work out of their quarters. The USDA rep had been given luxury status by the last battle space owner. The 101st was not in Naray to play games; they were there to put an end to the insurgency.

On June 2nd SGT Martinez, our maintenance NCO, became a citizen of the United States of America. For years he had been putting the process off while all the time paying his dues to the United States. Soon he found that his military career had hit a ceiling and his opportunities to deploy diminished as well. He had reached a point in his career that in order to advance any further he needed a security clearance and that required citizenship. When we arrived at Camp Atterbury he decided to fill out all of the required paperwork to become a citizen and got the ball rolling. A citizenship ceremony is held twice a year in Afghanistan, once in November and again in June. We arrived in Afghanistan in mid October too late for his citizenship package to be processed in time for the November ceremony. SGT Martinez took his leave in February of 2010 and checked in with the legal office in Bagram when he returned on February 28th. Good fortune was on his side. He was asked to stay for a few days and complete the final requirements for citizenship. On March 3rd he was given a 100 question test where ten questions were selected at random for him to answer followed by a background interview. When the interview was completed he was told to watch his email for the ceremony date, which would be in June.

The afternoon of June 1st Sgt Martinez hopped on a Molson Air UH-1 for Bagram with a stop in Jalalabad. Wednesday morning June 2nd Sgt Martinez walked down Disney Blvd. to the post auditorium to join 80 other members of the U.S. military immigrants from 35 different countries to become U.S. citizens. The auditorium had the flags of all 50 states and territories displayed along the wall as they were given their oath of citizenship. Sgt Martinez handed over his Mexican passport and signed a statement renouncing his Mexican citizenship and was officially a U.S. citizen. His first act as a new U.S. citizen was to demand the delinquent 2404s on the vehicles, and fill out his security clearance request.

Another major event happened for us on Wednesday June 2nd. The change of command ceremony between the 82nd Airborne and the 101st Air Assault divisions took only a few minutes. It was official: the 101st Task Force Bastogne took over our AO. Col George the commander of Task Force Mountain Warrior handed the baton to Col. Popas. The real changeover in command occurred in the financial department, which took days, not minutes.

June has started out on a good footing; one of our troops was a new U.S. citizen and Camp Wright held its first 5k run. Back in May SPC Moreno got the idea to host a 5k run on Camp Wright. He bounced the idea off of SSG Valenzuela and SFC Mosqueda who in turn took it up to the PRT. SPC Moreno's idea was to raise some money for the Camp's MWR fund, which didn't exist. The run would be open to everyone for five bucks and if you wanted to compete for a prize the cost was ten bucks. Soon there were posters all over the camp proclaiming Camp Wright's first 5k run.

On the evening of June 3rd everything was all set; the trauma center would have a doctor at the finish line and medics stationed along the route with water. However things were not going well at the far end of the Pech River Valley at FOB Blessing. Once again the artillery at FOB Blessing received accurate mortar fire from the insurgents. Shortly after midnight when FOB Blessing's artillery was firing in support of some troops in contact with the insurgents, another group of insurgents fired a mortar at the gun crew. Five cannoneers were wounded. Some received shrapnel to the neck, others were a bit luckier and were only struck in the legs. The first groups of cannoneers to be medivaced came to Camp Wright for surgery at 3:30 A.M. and the rest were flown down to FOB Fenty in Jalalabad. Surgery at Camp Wright lasted until 5:30.

With the cannoneers resting and in stable condition the medical staff that volunteered for the 5k cleaned up, grabbed a bite to eat and supported Camp Wrights first ever 5k. Standing tall at the starting line was the entire ADT SecFor Platoon along with participants from all of the other units at Camp Wright. The race started on top of the hill by our barracks for a good downhill start. The real challenge of the 5k was not the distance but the route. The troops and sailors would run to the ECP gate then back past Willie the Whale along the back fence up to the flight line and back to the starting line three times, while dodging traffic and the down blast from helicopters. By 7:30 Camp Wright's first 5k ended in success with all of the competitors receiving a t-shirt.

The first report we received about the mortar attack at FOB Blessing stated that the mortar round struck in the same location as the previous rounds hade. No longer were the insurgents just firing random shots at the FOB that usually went astray and struck civilian targets in the community. There was someone up there coaching the insurgents. It is most likely the insurgents found a well concealed location for their mortar and marked out an aiming circle so they could set everything up exactly the same each time. The solution would be to find the insurgents' mortar pit or a new location for the artillery. Both were just a temporary solution. A trained mortar crew would be able to set up a new aiming circle and bracket the artillery again no matter where the guns were moved. The concern was one qualified instructor can train countless mortar crews that can attack more FOBs. The only limiting factor is the availability of mortar tubes and munitions.

A day later we learned that the 155's muzzle had blown apart leading to speculation that a shell detonated inside the tube during the mortar attack. The howitzer was destroyed, but the cause was unknown at the time. That afternoon a CH-47 sling loaded one of Camp Wright's howitzers to FOB Blessing along with its crew. The Army recovered the battle-damaged howitzer from FOB Blessing and sent it to a lab to determine what happened. It didn't take long to determine what had transpired that morning. During the mortar attack when the battery was firing in support of the troops, the insurgents fired a recoilless rifle at the howitzer. One recoilless round struck the muzzle of the tube at an oblique angle.

It was nice to have the answer, but the gravity of the situation was a bit unnerving. A recoilless rifle is a heavy piece of weaponry that requires considerable effort to move into position, and a trained crew to operate effectively. The smaller band of insurgents could not afford to train themselves on a recoilless rifle. This means an organization with financial resources and large amounts of land available for training was supporting the insurgents. The locals all pointed to the ISI of Pakistan.

Our projects continued to mount up and our troops were still pulling additional guard duty after the ASG went on strike. My preference was to have Americans on guard anyway. Preparation for our first orchard establishment was about ready even though it was a little late in the season. We had purchased an assortment of PVC pipe and fittings in Asadabad for the drip irrigation system that we were going to install in the orchard. I told Sgt Stevens to lay out all of the parts and make sure we had everything before we hauled it all up to Woch Now. We were in the barn and Sgt Stevens was showing me how he solved several of the problems connecting the drip system to the PVC pipe. I reached over and picked up a slip fitting and a section of PVC pipe during the conversation. I looked up at SGT Stevens and asked, "Can you tell me what is wrong with the pipe and the fitting?"

Without even looking, he said, "Oh no sir, we bought it all from the same shop. They've got to fit." Sure enough we had 25mm fittings made in India and ¾ inch pipe made in America. Back to the rubber hose and worm clamps.

SFC Fulton and Hanlin went up to Woch Now to check if they were pouring one slab for their construction yard and one for the orchard water tanks. There was no holding the Gujers back; they were going full bore mixing concrete. A few months earlier these men had only two skills: hewing rock from the hillside and stacking rock walls. Now they could bend and fabricate re-bar, set forms, cast concrete components, pour large slabs and screed them level. We still had more to teach them in our remaining 60 days.

On the 66th anniversary of D-Day a swarm of F-15s started engaging Qzr, an insurgent leader whose force took up residence in the Ghaki pass. The Ghaki pass runs from Pakistan to Mara Wara Afghanistan. For a good hour we watched F-15 after F-15 make the loop over Asadabad and back to Bagram. Usually we could hear the impact of GBUs and artillery in the distance, which sounded like a subdued thud, but not this time.

The insurgents were becoming active again with well placed IEDs in the Pech and northern Kunar River Valleys. On Monday, June 7th the insurgents placed a command wired IED on route California north of FOB Monti in Bar Kunar, Asmar. Five soldiers from A company 2/327 were riding in an 1151, an enhanced HMMWV, near Chapakoh Village when the IED was detonated. The results were catastrophic; two of the five were listed as missing. The blast was so powerful they couldn't be found. The insurgents used a fertilizer based bomb that cratered the road. Afghanistan has banned the importation and manufacturing of all fertilizers that can be used to make explosives. This means the CWIED was manufactured in Pakistan.

Further north on route California near Naray in the Ghaziabad District another CWIED detonated under an MRAP. The MRAP rolled over from the blast. There were no serious casualties but there was one broken arm and one broken foot. This crew was medivaced to FOB Fenty for additional care. SFC Fair flew back to Camp Wright with them. With the exception of broken bones and two missing front teeth, they were all right.

It didn't take long for a bunch of civilian know-it-alls to sound off about the use of the 1151 when they heard that the MRAP successfully protected its crew. People do not understand that you select equipment and vehicles based upon the mission and the risk. After being in Afghanistan nearly a year, rollovers are still the greatest threat, followed by RPGs then IEDs. Each vehicle has a different center of gravity and wheel base. An 1151 is better suited for rough roads and open country where MRAPs are better situated on improved roads. The new MATV (MRAP All Terrain Vehicle) can handle open terrain, but it has a higher center of gravity than the 1151, making it more susceptible to rolling over than an 1151.

This surge in the insurgency followed President Karzai's June 4th announcement to the Taliban "My dear Taliban, you are welcome in your own soil. Do not hurt this country or kill yourselves." One of the ideas proposed by the Peace Jirga was to pay the insurgents to stop fighting with make work jobs. The majority of the insurgents are foreign nationals recruited from Saudi Arabia, Yemen, Africa, Pakistan etc.

There seemed to be no end of conflicts on Monday. Dr. Sofi from the AVA sent up a load of chicken supplies to Woch Now Village. Laj Bar escorted him up to the village while the rest of the men from Woch Now worked on the FOB pouring crib wall parts. An hour later Laj Bar was back at the front gate wanting to talk to me. He said he gave me 28 names of people in Woch Now who wanted chickens, but the AVA only delivered 20 sets of chicken products. I reminded Laj Bar that you had to complete the training to receive the birds. Then he accused Taj Mohammad of stealing the other eight sets of chickens and giving them to another village. I stated that I instructed Dr. Dad from the AVA to give them to another village. Then Laj Bar told me that if he didn't get the other eight sets of chickens there would be problems between him and Taj and with me also. By this time there were two ASG guards standing on either side of Laj Bar and one Pennsylvania Guardsmen at the ready providing me over watch. I decided to sit down on the steps to soften my posture. Laj Bar and Dr. Dad continued to fight back and forth about the chickens. SFC Fulton was standing on top of the ECP stairs watching the whole show and staying alert for a fisticuffs to break out. We've learned to stand back and let the locals handle heated events with their own methods. I finally told Laj Bar I could solve the whole problem by giving his 20 sets of chickens to someone else. With that I offered Dr. Dad a cold soda and said goodbye to Laj Bar.

Somehow we were being drawn into a family feud between Laj Bar and Taj Mohammad. Since Taj worked for the AVA the AVA got sucked into the fire too. I had another idea, Dad. SFC Fulton and I went back to the concrete yard and I pulled Laj Bar's dad aside with the help of Amid, our interpreter from Dallas. I explained the problem. Laj Bar's dad said there would be a problem and he would talk to Laj Bar. Dad went on to tell me that he was the village elder and he was training Laj Bar to take over. The following morning Laj Bar arrived at the ECP gate and apologized for his behavior. Wow, thank you Dad!

Chapter Forty

A GAME OF CHECKERS

One evening, our chaplain decided to host a game night in the Camp Wright Chapel. The Camp Wright Chapel looks like a large non-descriptive shoebox with no exterior religious markings. People often mistake it for the carpenter's shop because of the large sign on the sign on the chapel, "PRT Carpenter Shop." I decided to relax and enjoy the evening up at the chapel. Only two other people showed up, the chaplain and Captain Huff. We played a few games of chess and checkers then called it a night. I could remember when my dad taught me how to play checkers up in the mountains one summer. My dad made it all sound so easy. The black checker moves on the black squares and the red checkers move on the red squares. If the other guy's checker is in your way jump his checker and keep going. When you get to the other end of the board your checker becomes a king and you can move back across the board. It didn't take too many moves before I realized that just because you knew the rules of the game it didn't mean you know how to play.

The same holds true for Afghanistan except the checkers are not solid colors. The black checkers (ISAF) fade from black to dapple grey; the red checkers (the insurgents) are a kaleidoscope of colors forever changing. Now stack seven checker boards on top of each other and play all seven games at the same time. That's Afghanistan.

Attempting to explain exactly what is going on in Afghanistan is not as easy as Alice in Wonderland's Cheshire Cat put it, "Start at the beginning and keeping going until you get to the end and stop." The trick is finding the beginning. The United Sates has been involved in Afghanistan for a long time. In the 1950s the United Sates sent Morris and Knudsen to Afghanistan to build irrigation systems in response to the Soviet Union's efforts. All that faded away until the Soviet Union invaded Afghanistan in the 1970s. Since the invasion one country has benefited from the continuous fighting in Afghanistan and that's Pakistan, a country that didn't exist until 1947.

During the years of the Soviet occupation of Afghanistan, Pakistan was America's conduit for sending aid, military equipment and money into Afghanistan. For some reason the United Sates didn't want to invest the resources to develop their own contacts inside Afghanistan. That left Pakistan in the position to determine who receives what in Afghanistan, and how much. Pakistan's ISI (Central Intelligent Agency) was the best organization inside Pakistan to facilitate support to Afghanistan. All of the information that the United States received about operatives and operations in Afghanistan was filtered through the ISI.

When the Soviets finally withdrew, Pakistan had skimmed enormous amounts of weapons and money off the top of the U.S. aid to Afghanistan. Pakistan decided to keep all of the training camps open for their own covert operations in India. These training camps were funded by the United States and Saudi Arabia. Saudi Arabia had their own objectives in central Asia: they were, and still are, religious control of the region and control of natural resources specifically oil and natural gas.

During the cold war the United Sates built its defense of the Middle East oil on two pillars, Saudi Arabia and Iran. These two countries have been historically at odds with one another for thousands of years. There is the religious difference of Sunni (Saudi Arabia) and Shia (Iran), and then there is the ethnic difference between Arabs and Persians. Saudi Arabia started instituting its own covert operations against Iran with the training bases where students are indoctrinated into the Wahabi sect of Islam, the official religion of Saudi Arabia. The Saudi's started building schools in western Pakistan and in Afghanistan to start putting pressure on Iran. This is a long-term goal to head off the construction of a pipeline from Iran to India and other projects.

Pakistan armed and trained an initial group of 10,000 Taliban fighters that they planned to send into India to attack government agencies in Kashmir. That plan was never fully achieved. Instead the Taliban moved into Afghanistan. During the time the Taliban was in control of Afghanistan, Saudi Arabia was funding a large number of Wahabi schools in the region while the Taliban negotiated with two oil companies to build pipelines.

Unocal from the United States and Bridas from Argentina both were making bids to construct several pipelines from Turkmenistan to Pakistan, India and to the Arabian Sea. This consortium became known as TAPI (Turkmenistan-Afghanistan-Pakistan-India). The TAPI pipeline would run from Turkmenistan south along the western provinces of Afghanistan to the Arabian Sea with two west to east lines cutting across the Kandahar province to Pakistan and India. One line would carry oil the other natural gas. This concept has fallen apart with Unocal and Bridas suing each other. Unocal was purchased by Chevron, and in 2010 Iran is looking at building a pipeline through Pakistan to India without going through Afghanistan.

Pakistan, who would have benefited from the TAPI pipeline, is the same key player who worked to stop it. Pakistan would benefit from the oil and gas pipelines and so would India. Pakistan would rather do without than let India benefit too.

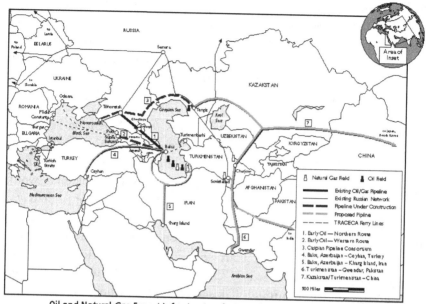

Oil and Natural Gas Export Infrastructure in Central Asia and the Caucasus

Source: U.S. Department of State.

The next problem:

If you look at the names of the Asian countries they all end in "Stan." Stan means kingdom of. India is also called Hindu-stan; the U.K is called either English-stan or British-stan. The word Afghan is another name for Pashtuns so Afghanistan could also be called Pashtun-stan. The last thing Pakistan wants is for Afghanistan to have a sense of National Pride with a modern military. Currently, Pakistan is building a fence on its border with Afghanistan. Pakistan states that this is to protect Afghanistan from armed insurgents who cross the border from Pakistan. The insurgents they are referring to are tribal Pashtuns. The Pashtuns do not recognize the border. As far as they are concerned the border crossed them; they didn't cross the border. There is a fear that the tribal Pashtuns may want to unify their kingdom, which would take a bite out of Pakistan. There has already been case precedence of this happening with Kosovo being cut out of Serbia with the support of the United States. The bigger fear is Afghanistan nationalism.

The national borders of Indian Pakistan and Afghanistan were created in1893 by Sir Henry Mortimer Durand. The Afghans call their border with Pakistan the "Durand Line." Great Britain drew up the borders of

India and Afghanistan with the agreement of the King of Afghanistan. The borders remained in effect until 1993. If you look at the outline of Afghanistan you'll notice a little finger of land in the upper northwest. This finger of land was deliberately created so that no part of the Russian Empire would touch the British Empire. The western border of India separated the two major Islamic groups, the Pashtuns and the five major tribes that created Pakistan in 1947. The original Afghanistan Empire included present day Pakistan with ports in the Arabian Sea.

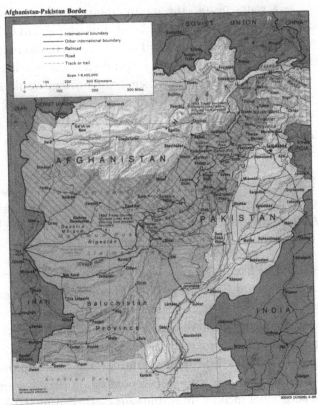

The outline of Pashtunstan shown against the current borders of Afghanistan. Map from the University of Texas at Austin.

When the United States invaded Afghanistan the Taliban fighters fled to Pakistan. The Pakistan border police, Army and ISI all knew they were in route to Pakistan but didn't arrest them or deny them entry. They were all welcomed back and took up safe refuge in Waziristan where the rest of the Pashtuns live. It wasn't long before the Taliban were able to regroup and take full control of Waziristan with the approval of the ISI who had designs on using them against the Army, and other government centers. This is when the fear of a "Pashtunstan" started to take on a physical reality.

This is also why Pakistan is against a strong Afghani military out of fear of either a new Pashtunstan or Afghanistan reclaiming their pre Durand Line Empire, which would mean the end of Pakistan. The media is quick to point out that Pakistan has nuclear weapons to defend itself against Afghanistan. Nuclear weapons against Afghanistan would be just as effective as a water pistol. The mountainous terrain in Afghanistan would funnel the nuclear blast straight up into the air and the fallout would spread all over Asia. If, "key word if," Afghanistan was to unify itself and decided to reclaim Pakistan they would do it covertly using the same tactic that Pakistan used to control them. Afghanistan would slowly eat Pakistan up, one tribal kingdom at a time until it was too late for Pakistan to react. Afghanistan wouldn't take all of Pakistan. They would leave part of Pakistan as a buffer between Afghanistan and India. India is one of Afghanistan's biggest trading partners.

Iran also has some concerns about a renewed Afghanistan military. There are parts of Iran's eastern territory that were once part of Afghanistan too. The Shaw of Iran was over thrown without the use of conventional military forces by the Ayatollah Khomeini who came out of exile from France.

Pakistan is built of five major tribes who view themselves as the "Pure" Islamic state. The word Paki means pure. There is no unification among these tribes; each is trying to build its own empire inside Pakistan. The Pakistan Army and the ISI have been locked in battle for over 30 years. They have been having a proxy civil war. The Army has been using the civilians to fight the ISI's Taliban. The families that make up the ISI and the Army are mafia families with deep-rooted ties in the government and they make additional income from smuggling. Their primary smuggling route to central Asia, southern Russia and Eastern Europe is through Afghanistan. If there is a strong government in Afghanistan, then their ability to freely move product through Afghanistan would be severally restricted.

Pakistan and India are two of the legal opium growing countries that sell to the pharmaceutical industry. Both countries have lobbied to keep Afghanistan out of the legal opium trade. This doesn't mean that all of the legal opium grown in Pakistan and India goes to legal markets; it just means that Afghanistan doesn't have access to legal markets. Pakistan moves their illegal opium through the northern regions of Afghanistan.

Pakistan's Continued Insurgency in Afghanistan

Pakistan is still in the money business. Pakistan is selling intelligence about the insurgency that they are sponsoring in Afghanistan. It is very easy to plan an attack, then sell the attack plan to the U.S. What is really happening is they are letting the U.S. do their dirty work. If a Taliban (Insurgent leader) doesn't play by their rules then they sell him out to the United States. If there is no insurgency then there is no need for intelligence, so Pakistan's ISI continues to pay the insurgents.

I refer to the enemy as insurgents because there is not a Taliban organization that fits the American org chart. The Taliban is really a creed that many of the insurgents subscribe to, not an organization. The organization is the ISI. There are at least two Taliban pods for a lack of a better description. There is the Pakistan Taliban and the Afghanistan Taliban. The difference is in family ties and the territory they call home. The Afghan Taliban insurgents are all Pashtuns while the Pakistan Taliban insurgents are recruited from the Middle East and Africa. Pakistan had two missions for the Taliban. One was control of Afghanistan and the second was to cause government instability in India. The Taliban hasn't embraced going into India; they are really focused on tribal warfare. Since the Taliban fighters were not motivated to attack India, Pakistan recruited another group of religious extremists know as Lashkar-e-Taiba, a derivative of Al Qaeda, a Wahabi (aka Saudi Arabia) backed group. There is a distinct difference between the two groups. Both are religious extremists but one is Afghan and the other is Arab. The Afghans do not like Arabs. An Afghan will die fighting you, but he will not commit suicide to kill you. An Arab will commit suicide to kill others so he can go to heaven. Suicide attacks in Afghanistan are almost always by Arabs who follow the Al Qaeda creed.

The Money Trail:

The ISI funds Afghan insurgent leaders based upon performance. Payment is made in cash, weapons, and supplies, or other support. For a major operation the ISI selects a proven leader and equips him. These are the high payoff operations. If an insurgent leader decides at the last minute to hit a soft target he runs the risk of losing future contracts or being sold out to the U.S. The ISI doesn't want to see the supplies they provided used on another target. All operations are filmed and the film is sent back to Pakistan as conformation that the operation was completed. One of the indicators troops watch for when driving on the highways or dismounted are cameramen. The observation of a cameraman is a good indicator that an ambush is imminent.

There are many "want to be leaders" in the world of insurgents. The only way to get noticed by the financers is to film an attack on ISAF. This means that there are many attacks that are not planned by the ISI, Al Qaeda or Taliban organizations. There is a market for video tapes, because selling a video tape requires access to the financer's front men. These video tapes are traded just like futures in the stock market. A small operative knows that blowing up an MRAP is worth "X" number of dollars if he can get the tape to the financer's front man. There are two types of operatives; one who just needs the money and another who is looking for a career. The individual who needs the money will sell the tape at a discount to a broker. The career man will do all that he can to get the tape into Pakistan for better exposure and money.

There are other groups that have been forced to be a part of the insurgency where their families are being held hostage. These fighters usually fire upon ISAF at ineffective distances just to say *I did it, now let my family go.* There are other groups that see a direct economic benefit to the war so they conduct a harassing fire just to bring about a response from the U.S. Areas that have a significant amount of insurgent action tend to receive more aid projects in order to win the hearts and minds of the locals. The peaceful areas are forgotten.

Pakistan's Opposition to Roads

Road construction projects are usually under constant insurgent fire, which is under the direction of the ISI. Roads are the last things Pakistan wants in Afghanistan. Currently Pakistan is the largest exporter to Afghanistan, and they do not want to lose that position. Roads mean that commerce can move freely inside of Afghanistan. Prior to the road from Jalalabad to Asadabad being completed the majority of the merchandise and produce sold in Asadabad was from Pakistan. After the road was built the travel time from Jalalabad to Asadabad decreased from six hours to two hours.

Additionally Asadabad's importation from Pakistan dropped, because they were now buying products from Jalalabad.

The road from Asmar to Naray, which is another 60 miles, comes under heavy attack. Asmar is 30 miles north of Asadabad. This road will link Naray to the government center in Asadabad. The highway will also be linked to several border crossings to Pakistan. Pakistan understands that there will be increased economic competition with Afghanistan. Open competition will harm Pakistan's economy, and the roads will hinder Pakistan's illegal smuggling operations through Afghanistan even more. A paved road means a nation can rapidly move its military and police forces to areas of conflict. No longer will insurgents be able to hold a community hostage. Paved roads that are used for border crossings are also easier to control, especially if you are trying to collect import taxes, and block illegal immigration. There are many Pakistanis who come over to Afghanistan to work on projects funded by the United States.

The United States is starting to improve ties with India and hinting at acknowledging the problems in Pakistan. Everything I've written came from the Associate Press, books available at public libraries and my interviews with the local Afghans.

During my deployment, I took advantage to interview many Afghans of different educational and cultural levels, along with government officials and private businessmen. Once a good solid relationship is established Afghans are very open and will talk candidly about politics, economics and religion. If you want to know the truth it is best to talk to an Afghan in private otherwise they are more likely to present the party line because they never trust another Afghani.

Chapter Forty-One

...A TIME TO BUILD A, A TIME TO PLANT...

One of my favorite verses in the Bible is Ecclesiastes 3, which reminds us that there is a purpose for everything that happens under heaven. For every sorrowful event there is something to celebrate. Once again, the week didn't start the month off well in Kunar. We were seeing a sudden surge in IEDs in the Pech and the central and northern Kunar River Valleys. Spc Larson was in the trauma center when an ANA soldier was brought in after his face was blown off. The ANA soldier was pulling up an insurgent aiming flag that was bobby trapped. The resulting explosion blew his face off with the only recognizable feature being his tongue. Soon there would be other problems associated with the planting of feed corn.

The Afghan government privatized the veterinary service industry during the April-May timeframe. This signaled the end of the traditional VetCaps. We had recently trained the Gujers to run VetCap operations with the AVA performing the actual service in preparation for the expected privatization.

Our last VetCap would be the first district sponsored VetCap in Khas Kunar. Once again the U.S. Army would pay 100% of the cost and the local Afghan government would look like they did it all. Planning for the event started in May with the final details being worked out in early June.

When we arrived at the final planning meeting, the new Battle Space owner had appointed the same junior NCO who months earlier told me that he didn't have time for VetCaps or agriculture-related projects; he had two kinetic valleys to worry about. His attitude and behavior had changed significantly. The Khas Kunar Ag director stated that he was against using the AVA or any other outside veterinarians. We agreed to use his veterinarians and to provide him with all of the equipment and supplies required to vaccinate 3000 animals. We would deliver most of the equipment prior to the VetCap and the medication the day of the VetCap. We needed to maintain the cold chain on the vaccinations. There was the high probability that if we delivered the vaccines in advance they wouldn't store them correctly and they would be rendered destroyed.

It had been raining IEDs in the Pech and Kunar River Valleys by mid June and we had our last VetCap scheduled for June 13th. Route Beaverton, which had recently been paved, had a large IED detonate near where the VetCap was to be hosted at a village near the Khas Kunar district center. Route Beaverton was known for IEDs the year prior when the road wasn't paved. Afghan insurgents will not place an IED on a paved road due to the risk of losing local support. Paved roads are the backbone of economic stability for any Afghan village and the villagers will not tolerate the destruction of their roads or bridges. IEDs on the paved roads mean foreign fighters were in the area, not just the indigenous local fighters.

On June 13th we loaded up and rolled out to our last VetCap. What the Khas Kunar district Ag director didn't know was I had his whole operation completely backed up with a full team of veterinarians from the AVA, additional vaccines and cash on hand to pay local workers. This VetCap would be an Afghan operation, but if it failed it would be America's fault. (Even if you're not at fault you are at fault if you're an American.) To our surprise the Khas Kunar veterinarians were AVA veterinarians who had participated in some of our other VetCaps and knew exactly what to do. We watched what was going on for a few minutes, then I dismissed the backup team of veterinarians and told them to make mini-village house calls to vaccinate the animals that couldn't make it to the VetCap. I had paid them for a day's service and the additional vaccinations were on hand. Later on I received a CD with photos showing the team in the smaller villages. We waited another hour and gave them a few pointers on crowd control and returned to base.

The Khas Kunar Afghani organizers made one small change in their operation. When we hosted the VetCap we stayed on site until the villagers stopped arriving. The Khas Kunar officials shut down operations at lunch as advertised.

Privatizing the veterinary industry in Afghanistan sounds good until you realize that the people don't have the money to pay for the veterinary services. What was really happening according to Dr. Sofi was that an NGO was sponsoring an Afghan company called "Vet Clinic." Vet Clinic was a private company and would be fully funded by U.S. and U.N. sources.

Late in the morning on June 15th one of our sister units lost a soldier near hill 1311 on route California, a place we had driven by many times on our way to Asmar and other points north. This time the 60-man insurgent force bit off more than they could handle when they intended to ambush a logistics convoy. They made the fatal mistake of stepping on the adder's tail when they opened fire on a mounted patrol from the 101st. This time the insurgents attacked from both sides of the Kunar River. Within minutes artillery fire was massing from B 3/321 Bulldogs of CP Wright and Monti, followed by Kiowa support and more troops being set up from other FOBs. Soon there was a swarm of F-15 holding above Camp Wright waiting for their queue to engage the insurgents. The fight finally ended late in the evening when the last of the insurgents abandoned their positions for a safer sanctuary.

That same afternoon an IED went off in the PECH lifting an MRAP up on its end before it returned to earth rolling on its side. Everyone inside survived with only minor injuries except the TC who suffered back and neck injuries. We received a call to escort the EOD with our QRF. SFC Mosqueda had his trucks lined up in five minutes waiting for EOD who was getting some last minute information before they rolled out. Our QRF stayed out until the MRAP was recovered and EOC cleared the route. The mess hall staff made sure that there would be hot meals for them when they returned.

There had been reports on the Afghan radio and from the Afghanis who worked on Camp Wright of the ABP (Afghan Border Police) capturing several Pakistani Army troops near Asmar a few days after a series of IEDs were detonated. Feedback from the field was the IEDs were made from

Pakistani military-grade explosives, not the cheep stuff the locals buy for quarry work. On June 15, the ABP captured another 40 Pakistani soldiers in Mitai, Sarkani District after a number of IEDs were detonated on routes California and Beaverton near Noorgul and Khas Kunar. The official news release was the Pakistanis were lost and the ABP was providing them food and water while they facilitated their return to Pakistan.

SFC Fair had made several dismounted trips up to the Pakistani border and he brought his GPS and a map and compass with him to make sure he stayed in Afghanistan. It is hard for me to believe that soldiers that were born and raised in the area were lost in their neighbor's country several terrain features from their border.

Things were heating up in the Ghaki Pass and in Marawara with the insurgents. The Ghaki Pass is Pakistan's covert gateway into Afghanistan's Pech River Valley. The Pech River Valley and the Muryagul Dry River converge across from each other in Asadabad. On June 16th the insurgents decided to flex their muscle near the village of Daridarn located in the Muryagul Dry River Valley (also known as the Daridarn-Mora Valley) east of Marawara. We could see the action from the blue gate on the ridge line across from Camp Wright as U.S. troops were inserted with fire support from our 155s. The battle lasted the full day.

The task force "No Slack" commander decided that a permanent fix to the problem was required. Both the Pech and Kunar River Valleys were crawling with insurgents who were multiplying like rabbits. During a 30-day period between May 15 and June 15 there had been over 1000 IED events in Afghanistan. That didn't include the increase in ambushes and attacks on the FOBs. We were briefed on operation Strong Eagle that was designed to clean the insurgents out of the Muryagul River Valley. Holding a rifle in one hand and yelling follow me is the easy part of an operation. The challenge is in the planning. Support is the key to success. The support plan would include the amount of ammunition, how to move it to the battle field, food and water support (Class 1) aviation support UH-60 for troop movement, Kiowas for close air support, F-15 and C-130 for additional support, medivac operations, rescue operations coordinated with the Air Force, alerting the trauma center so they can have the mass causality operation set up... the list goes on and on.

Our role was to come in right behind the combat troops with the "No

Slack" commander and provide stabilization services to demonstrate that the U.S. and the local government could support the villagers.

The operation was scheduled to take place before I went on leave, but was continually pushed back due to challenges with coordinating with the Afghan officials. We came up with a menu of quick support items that the Battle Space owner could offer to the village elders after the insurgents were cleaned out.

Taking leave was rapidly taking its toll on me making sure everything that I was responsible for would be taken care of before I left. The first order of business was to submit all of the awards for our troops. Our departure was just 60 days out and the brigade needed our awards without errors by the 17th of June. We had a good awards team. SFC Medina and I wrote up the awards for the Ag section, SFC Mosqueda took care of his troops and Major Leeney wrote headquarters and became the editor in chief of all the awards. SFC Graham burned the midnight oil getting everything perfect. Then it was my turn again to sign them all and put in the final comments. Our troops accomplished a lot during the year we were in Kunar, from construction projects, and orchard establishments, along with responding to calls for help with our QRF there was never any down time. Well-written awards are a fitting way of letting people know that their efforts were appreciated and didn't go unnoticed. I had kept a log of our soldiers' accomplishments and was astounded when I recounted their achievements and the quick thinking that occurred.

Our junior NCO brain trust continued to make great strides. SGT Flynn and Stevens were nearing completion on the Woch Now orchard and vineyard. The orchard establishment wasn't a simple project. The land that was offered to us by the village was on a steep hillside that needed to be terraced off. Water was the next problem that we solved. SPC Lopez who had experience with a family business installing drip irrigation systems in the central valley instructed the men of Woch Now how to install the drip system. Spc Lopez even solved our problem with the dissimilar PVC fitting by taking them all to the shop and drilling them out with a spade bit. Sgt Stevens purchased the trees and vines from NATC an Afghan company. SFC Hanlin and Fulton continued to coach the villages on concrete construction pouring the slabs for the water tanks and concrete yard. The whole project took several weeks to complete but it was worth it.

We turned a piece of dormant land into a productive orchard that within a few years would help meet the needs of the village's population boom.

Another project that we got saddled with was demonstration farms. There had been a briefing that the ADT had established 16 demonstration farms in the Kunar Province, which was false. When instructed to make the demonstration farms a reality I started asking questions. Where are these farms located and do we have land agreements? I was assured that everything was all ready to go, we just needed to get the water to the fields and provide the seeds. Our USDA rep gave me a list of districts with a blank line next to each for me to write in the demo farm location once we found someone to donate their land to the government. The concept of demonstration farms was just an idea and it would be up to Major Leeney and me to make it happen. The only district that was close to agreeing to operate a demonstration farm was Chowkay. I wrote up a land use agreement based upon a template brigade sent me and gave it to Major Leeney to get signed. Major Leeney came back with a signed land use agreement for a piece of property located behind the district center. I called Dr. Matiullah Mashwani of Sayiban Watan Construction Company, a contractor whose honesty and quality we could rely upon. Dr. Mashwani is a medical doctor at the Christopher J. Speer Medical Clinic, an Afghan hospital located on Camp Wright. He had been volunteering his medical services with us for some time, and decided to start a construction company to help make ends meet. He was doing a very good job at it. Dr. Mashwani went down to Chowkay the next morning to meet with the district extension manager about the project; two days later he had equipment on site. I handed the whole project off to SGT Stevens.

Managing the project was the easy part. The challenge was the conflict resolution issues that came up with the neighboring farmers, and our USDA rep. Shortly after breaking ground, our USDA rep who thought he was the co-commander of the ADT grabbed SGT Stevens and told him to cancel the project. His reasoning was the cistern that was being constructed would be a breeding ground for mosquitoes and the children might use it as a pool in the summer and drown. SFC Medina had a "come to Jesus" meeting with him similar to the one I had with the USDA rep up in Naray, put an end to his hysteria, and let him know that there were some new rules. The USDA reps all had access to USDA funding, but preferred to use U.S. Army funds by tapping into the ADTs, so they wouldn't be burdened with the responsibility. There are some sharp highly motivated USDA reps in Afghanistan, whom I have met in passing. The sharp USDA reps will take the time to fully develop a project to include cost analysis, scheduling, a training plan, current needs, future sustainment requirements, and will work with the local government to make sure the project is successful. Far too many of the government reps simply come up with an idea, make promises to local governments and villagers, then expect the U.S. Army to develop, fund and manage their idea to completion.

Our poultry projects were making great strides, but we were still having some challenges getting Afghani women involved in managing the program. Our biggest challenge was we were men not women and our interpreters were men as well. I was reviewing a poultry proposal for $85,000.00 with a long list of men who would be handsomely paid with no connection to women's poultry along with a list on remodeling items for their offices. The one item missing was chickens. What I needed was a woman with the support of a female interpreter. Sometimes the solution is right under your nose and you never see it. Spc Tanson came whizzing through the barn filling us in on all the latest events and mentioned a new female interpreter. Bingo! "Specialist Tanson congratulation you are now in charge of women's poultry." I handed her a stack of contracts and told her when her next meeting would be at the governor's compound, and she was off and running.

Spc Tanson's first meeting was a test of wills. Included in the meeting was our USDA rep and Jamaluddin, his Afghan assistant, who dominated the meeting. Finally the two of them had to leave for another meeting, which was the break Spc Tanson needed. Across the table from her was a woman named Naseema, a beautiful Afghan woman whose ring finger had been chopped off by the Taliban. Naseema didn't provide too many details about the event other than in 2005 the Taliban broke into her home and chopped off her finger. SPC Tanson was pretty astute about the politics and the hidden agendas that were going on. She quickly saw that there was a group of men including Jamaluddin using the guise of women's poultry to advance their own interests and feather their nest. The men in the group objected to having the AVA provide the training and chickens and made a series of unsubstantiated degrading accusations about the AVA. Each man had a friend or was in the business of selling chickens. The AVA's saving grace was the infighting among the men each wanting all of the pie not just a piece of it. Our USDA rep joined the anti-AVA chorus, and stated

357

he found a company that could do the job for less. Our USDA rep didn't even know what the scope of work was or how much we were paying.

Spc Tanson and Naseema agreed on initiating four poultry projects in the local villages and that the AVA would be the contractor. During the following weeks we received calls from men claiming to speak for Naseema stating that the AVA was not to provide the service. Each time Spc Tanson would have her interpreter call Naseema and make sure that nothing had changed. We had nine months of a solid honest working relationship with Dr. Sofi and Dr. Dad from the AVA and we were committed to continue that relationship. We had given other organizations an opportunity to provide services and they all quickly tried to cheat us.

On Thursday evening just a few days before my leave LTC Velte called me and said "Guess what? J.W. is down here at FOB Fenty to sell John Deer gators, and motorcycles."

I reminded LTC Velte that J.W. had just gotten married during the week to a young 15-year-old girl. This LTC Velte knew and was why he was surprised to see J.W. out hustling. J.W. had boasted to everyone that his wedding was going to cost $10,000.00, one third the cost of a new house in Afghanistan. Just maybe J.W. over committed his resources trying to prove to his neighbors that he was rich. J.W. had asked LTC Velte for a letter of reference because he needed to find a higher paying job. We had supported Waydots efforts to advance so it wasn't out of the question.

A week later while I was on leave I received an email from Major Leeney that J.W. walked into the contractor's office and claimed to be LTC Velte's personnel interpreter and was to transfer immediately to FOB Fenty Jalalabad. Major Leeney and Lt Ko straightened that mess out quickly. By mid week J.W. was working another angle for more time off. He recalled that when Waydot's family was victim to a rocket attack in Jalalabad we took up a collection for him and made arrangements with Mission Essential Personnel, the company he worked for so he could have some additional time off. Waydot lost a son in the attack and his wife had multiple injuries including a broken back, arm and leg.

J.W. called Lt Ko and announced that his wife was in the hospital and he needed more time off. By this time J.W's credibility had vanished and he was told to return to work as agreed. On June 30th J.W. arrived at Camp Wright and said "I quit." SFC Medina explained to J.W. that it wasn't that easy; he needed to turn in all of his equipment that we issued him and clear with Mission Essential Personnel. SFC Medina made sure that J.W. stayed around until he cleared supply and Lt Ko.

Three weeks later on July 21st I received an email from J.W. giving a slightly different account of events and asking for a letter of reference so he could get another job with the U.S. Bottom line. The great high-paying job J.W. had lined up fell through when he no longer had access to U.S. bases in Afghanistan. Greed can blind a person so that they only see the road before them not what is around the bend.

Chapter Forty-Two

LEAVE, JUST GETTING THERE IS HALF THE FUN

The U.S. Army introduced a new leave policy that was very beneficial to the troops. Before, when you deployed and took leave it was subtracted from your leave earned. The troops were putting off taking leave so they could take it when they got home and not have to worry about what was going on back in Iraq or Afghanistan. The result was the troops that were in the fight were not recharging themselves and having higher levels of stress. The new policy was two weeks of non-accruable non-chargeable leave if you served one year in country. Basically, a soldier could have his cake and eat it too.

I wasn't planning on taking leave because I wanted to tour the U.S. when I returned. When the new leave policy was announced and verified, I called my dad and asked him which country he would like to meet me in. He chose Scotland because it was an English-speaking country—at least that is what the travel guide said. My father, being prior service, understood that the Army could change its mind and cancel my leave if it desired so he put off purchasing a ticket. When my leave was officially approved my dad went to buy a ticket to Scotland but the price had gone through the roof, so he bought a ticket to Dublin instead. I didn't think it would be a problem because there were ferries and there should have been plenty of channel flights.

I was putting in a lot of early and late hours trying to get everything squared away before I left, especially the money. The 101ˢᵗ had taken over and was making daily changes to how they would process money requests and what information they wanted on the request. The S-9 shop sent a major up to brief us on how COIN (Counter Insurgency) should be reflected in the ADR request for CERP funds. Taking good notes I made sure my next funding request followed the new guidelines, and I had the correct signature blocks on all the documents.

There was a lot to worry about that needed funding, with about eight weeks left of our deployment and a bunch of project commitments that needed to be completed. We also had to look at our re-deployment requirements and the left seat, right seat with Iowa, our replacements. With the help of SSG Palacios and Major Leeney we developed a final day-by-day schedule up to the day we would salute and get on the bird out of the country. This plan also included the spending plan for the final three bulk fund draws.

I was scheduled to start traveling to my leave destination on June 20ᵗʰ. The local insurgents wanted to make sure I wouldn't forget them while on leave, and gave me a three-mortar salute on Friday June 18ᵗʰ. Their first round struck above Arga Del Village 180 degrees from the FOB; their second landed next to Laj Bar's house in Woch Now Village and the final round popped a hole in my cargo trailer, my first piece of battle-damaged equipment as commander. The mortar round lit the canvas tarp on fire, put a dent in the axel, and flattened the front tire of the 101ˢᵗ MRAP that was parked next to the trailer. Had the insurgents been better trained they could have taken out an Apache that had landed for lunch or one of our 155mm howitzers. We were lucky!

I continued to burn the midnight oil getting all of our funding requests sent up to brigade only to receive a late night email with a new signature block for the funding request. Just my luck our scanner was down and the only other one on post was locked up in the PRT Engineering office. I printed all of the corrections and gave them to Major Leeney with instructions on how to process them. I felt badly saddling Major Leeney with all of the responsibility for the ADT. We had split the responsibilities; now he had the whole wagon.

SFC Graham had gone over all of the special leave instructions with me while SFC Natividad continued to check the flight status to see if I was manifested for a flight to Bagram. Sunday morning June 20th came and brigade hadn't published a manifest, which meant I would just be a strap hanger and go space "A."

I waited with eight other hopeful travelers on the flight line watching the air show of Hips, Hinds, and UH-60s come and go. Finally the Molson flight was in view; it was a big bird, a Sikorsky S-61 painted in royal blue and white. We all stood and admired it come in, then in unison did an about face with the exception of one young lady. She suddenly understood the purpose of our close order drill and she was pelted with dust.

The Sikorsky 61 set down on the pad closest to us while the crew chief opened the cargo door, then the passenger door. Molson's policy is all seats need to be filled, unlike Embassy Air. The crew chief told everyone to get on and we would make three stops on the way to Bagram, first at Joyce and the second at Fenty to refuel, the third at FOB Marmon located on the Kabul River. I lucked out! The Sikorsky 61 has special memories for me. It was the first aircraft I flew on with my father from the Disneyland heliport to LAX. I spent my second grade summer in El Paso Texas with my grandmother.

It took 90 minutes to finally arrive at the Bagram Air Base. I missed the 09:00 departure brief at the fixed wing PAX terminal. I wasn't too worried; I made it to Bagram. The rotary wing PAX terminal is located at the far end of the runway while the fixed wing PAX terminal is located at the midway point. It was a bit of a walk with my battle rattle, ruck, and several boxes for the post office. My first stop was CIF (Central Issue Facility) to exchange my boots. Every soldier who is going home on leave can stop by CIF and exchange his/her uniform and boots so to go home in something clean and un-tattered. I only needed a new pair of boots, my third pair since arriving in Afghanistan. My luck was improving. CIF had my size and width; it was the first time I was able to get a pair that properly fit! What a difference it made.

My next stop was the post office, which was closed, so I checked in at the PAX terminal and was told to be back at 1600 for roll call and flight information. The next stop was to turn in my 9mm at our ALOC located at the other end of the runway. The NCO in charge of the ALOC was nice enough to let me leave my ruck and battle rattle in her supply room while I went back to the post office and grabbed lunch. When I checked in at the PAX terminal the desk sergeant warned me to keep a sharp eye on my gear; they had a major thief problem. This was just the opposite of Fenty, our other air base, where everyone watches out for each other.

After lunch, I walked back to the ALOC where the secret PX is located and purchased two history magazines and some food for the road just in case I had to miss a meal. I took the ALOC NCOIC up on a ride to the transition tents. I spotted SGT Flynn and SSG Carter coming back from leave along the way. We said hello and agreed to meet up back at the tents. I gave them both a rundown of all the events they missed and what lay ahead in Marawara.

The 1600 roll call finally commenced and terminated with the announcement that our flight turned around over Bagram and went back to Kuwait because of mechanical problems and to come back at 04:00 for the next roll call, but we could stay close to the PAX terminal for a chance at a space "A" to Bagram. The 04:00 roll call was just like the 16:00 roll call the day before, "NO PLANE" and I was now required to attend the 09:00 brief. At 09:00 we were told to be back at 16:00 for roll call. It was beginning to sound like Ground Hog Day. At 16:00 we were told that we all had a seat on the next flight out, "Torqe 67" not a "Moose" flight. The difference is a Torqe is a C-130 and a Moose is a C-17, which has a toilet. Each type of aircraft has its own name: Snap; dash; nome; grizz. Once again return at 01:45 for roll call. At 01:45 June 22 we presented ourselves for roll call along with forty other hopeful strap hangers all hoping to get on the flight.

The flight originated from Bagram meaning it was a pretty sure bet that we would take off. After roll call we sat in the briefing room until 0:300 when we were told to take our gear over to the pallet yard and load everything on a big 400-pound aluminum pallet. After that we were in lock down in the PAX terminal until we loaded the bus for the plane at 05:00. The bus took us out to where all of the C-130s were parked. I enjoyed reading all of the different state names on each of the planes. Our flight was courtesy of the Minnesota Air Guard. Soon we would all envy sardines with their spacious canned accommodations. For six hours we sat with our legs interlocked and our carryon bags in our laps. Fortunately for me I had the one ruck that was on the pallet.

We landed at Ali Al Salem air base in Kuwait and parked next to another

C-130. Two buses were waiting to take up to the LSA (Logistic (or Leave) Support Area) for in processing. When we arrived there was a large formation standing in front a mega tent of about 500 troops all waiting to in process. It was 127 degrees and the reflective heat off the desert hit us like a blowtorch every time a gust of wind belched off the earth. Within five minutes my uniform was soaked to the tops of my boots.

Once inside the first mega tent we were divided into CONUS and OCONUS leave groups. (CONUS = Continent United States, OCONUS = Outside the Continent United States.) We filled out our leave forms and passed them in, along with our ID cards, to be manifested for flights to Germany for the CONUS troops and for airline tickets for the OCONUS troops. The OCONUS troops were told that we would be leaving that night and to turn in our battle rattle and come back in 30 minutes.

Just a short walk from the mega tent was a warehouse where troops check in their body armor and Kevlar helmets. The warehouse team didn't want to be responsible for anything other than our body armor and Kevlars and instructed us to strip everything else off. SFC Graham had already given me a heads up so I left my first aid kit, extra ammo, knife, and other goodies at Camp Wright. The only thing left was my camel back and M-4 wolf strap to remove. We dropped our equipment into a big tri-wall and were given a call number so we could retrieve it when we returned. During our R and R, the warehouse team would systematically X-ray all of our plates and replace any of them that had been damaged.

We reassembled back at the mega tent and waited for the next block of instruction. A young spc-4 walked up to the podium and announced that there would be no commercial flights out of Kuwait that evening, then instructed us to get a room for the night. The transition area of Ali Al Salem LSA is composed of 216 insulated tents that sleep from ten to 20 troops depending on how many bunks are in the tent. I dropped off my ruck at the P-1 tent for safekeeping. After Bagram I wasn't so trusting anymore, and went to lunch.

I made an observation about the quantity, quality, and selection of food provided to the troops. The food provided in the FOBs nearest the fighting is the best and degrades with each stop toward Kuwait. The food in Kuwait is fine but nothing to rave about; it was still one or two steps above the cuisine provided in the United Kingdom.

I had plenty of time in Ali Al Salem to get a haircut, send an email, read both of my history magazines and buy two more. The LSA had everything for the soldier, which included a USO, two large MWR mega tents, McDonalds, Pizza Hut, a donut shop, coffee house, jewelry stores, and plenty of local vendors selling junk.

The lights at Ali Al Salem's LSA would turn on in midday because the dust was so thick it would trigger the photo switch. When the dust lifted I could see the concrete hangers that the French had build, which the U.S. destroyed during the first gulf war. These were huge A-frame concrete structures designed to protect their aircraft. The concrete was several feet thick with large holes blown through, but the structures were still standing. The Kuwaitis never repaired the structures for some reason.

The following day we reported at 10:00 for roll call in our civilian clothes at the mega tent. From there we walked over to the SATO travel office, made copies of our orders, verified our destinations, and were told to report back at 20:00 for a bus ride to the airport.

After dinner I saw no reason to sit in my tent. I could read in the mega tent and be ready to go at the same time. I was quietly waiting when a customs agent asked me if I was flying out because they were closing up the custom warehouse. I followed him over to the customs warehouse where my ruck was x-rayed and tagged. Once I had the custom's stamp on my leave orders I was allowed to pick up my itinerary from the Afghanistan LNO desk and move to the locked down area in another mega tent. Since OCONUS travelers were few, the chaplain's corner was used as the lock down area.

At 21:30, a security guard came over and told us that our bus was there and it would be a one-hour ride to the airport. The windows of the bus were all covered by curtains so I sat in the front to enjoy the sights. Taking the front seat earned me the prize of bus commander as I was proudly presented a radio to use in an emergency.

Our bus pulled out following an escort vehicle with its lights flashing that led us to the back side of Kuwait International Airport. We switched from the large luxury bus to a small minibus to be driven to the front of the airport. The driver dropped us off at the corner at 2300 Hrs and told us to just walk in and find the ticket counter.

The Kuwait International Airport is a small very clean terminal. All of the restaurants were full and the Kuwaitis were wearing traditional dress. Several hours were due to elapse before my flight would leave allowing me some time to look around. It was very easy to observe the different sects of Islam by looking at the apparel the women wore. American women stood out the most by wearing provocative clothing, but no one seemed to mind or take notice.

On June 24th at 0345 I departed Kuwait on Emirates Airline for Dubai. What a treat! The crew of Emirates was standing ready when the door of the aircraft was opened, unlike U.S. carriers where they are still busy getting things ready. Emirates also served full meals with real silverware and sold alcoholic beverages by the plenty to a flight filled with Muslims.

We touched down in Dubai at 6:20 A.M. Thursday June 24th with just enough time to race across the airport to catch the 7:50 flight to Glasgow. At 1300 I was solving the remaining piece of my leave in the Glasgow airport, "How to get to Dublin where my father was."

Aer Lingus was the only airline flying from Glasgow to Dublin with one seat open for $300.00. I recovered from the shock and purchased the ticket. After all what choice did I have unless I wanted to swim? The next shock was the $15.00 fish and fries I consumed at the airport, which still left me hungry.

A quick hop over the water and a six-Euro bus ride later I was at the Trinity Hotel, the perfect place to transition from the noise of the combat in Afghanistan. Our room overlooked a six-engine firehouse that was very busy at night. It was fairly late at this point, but I wanted to celebrate the reunion with my father with a steak dinner. We found the O'Neil Pub that was recommended by the hotel clerk in time to eat what was left over. It still tasted good. My leave had officially started.

Chapter Forty-Four

RETURN FROM LEAVE

July 10th finally arrived signaling the end of my leave. My Emirates flight boarded for Dubai at 1330, which gave me time to finish a book about the Irish in Afghanistan. They had the same problems we had with the Afghan forces. When the fighting broke out you had to lift up all the rocks and drag the ANA back into the fight. I spent the last of my pounds on lunch (fish and chips) and the rest on Cokes and cookies that came in handy later.

My Emirates flight took off at 14:15 from Glasgow to Dubai arriving in Dubai at 1:00 A.M. I moved quickly to the other terminal and boarded in time for a 1:45 take off to Kuwait. We pulled away from the gate on time, but had to hold on the tarmac because two passengers didn't make the flight but their luggage did. The luggage crews sorted through the bags until they located the couple's luggage. I thought it would have been easier to just leave them on the plane. All of the flights had close connections, but rules are rules.

One of the stories the Irish told about dealing with the Afghanis was there weren't any movies they could show them because all western movies are religiously offensive. From my seat on the plane filled with Muslims I could observe what people were watching on their personal in flight movie screens. The Arabs had no quarrel with watching the risqué movies. I did notice the preference was Walt Disney's "Jungle Book."

We landed in Kuwait at 2:25 A.M. The airport was packed with people greeting friends and family. The Kuwaiti women were making loud noises like a tribe of Indians whooping up a war cry in a spaghetti western. Some families threw confetti, which was quickly cleaned up by the Philippine service crew.

Security at the Kuwait International Airport was tight. All of the bags were X-rayed upon arrival; they don't take any chances. I greeted the immigration officer in Arabic and he started to address me in Arabic. I had to explain that I only spoke a little Pashto. He asked me for my visa, which I didn't have. He asked if I was military and for my I.D. card. He just put a sticker on the back of the card and directed me to the luggage area.

It was 3:00 A.M. Sunday July 11th and there was no U.S. reception in sight. I looked around for signs that would direct U.S. military to a waiting area, but there were none. As I walked through the terminal, taxi drivers came at me from all directions, "Sixty dollars to Ali Al Salem." I politely told them all no that I didn't have any money. I decided to walk over to the corner where I was dropped off two weeks earlier. There was bound to be a shuttle bus on the way. Another taxi driver greeted me with a sign he made for the troops and offered to take me to the base. I explained that I didn't have any money. He responded by telling me that there was an ATM machine in the terminal. I told him I didn't have an ATM card or cash because it wasn't used where I was stationed. With that he walked me over to the waiting area for the U.S. troops, the coffee house in the terminal.

Gradually more and more troops started to arrive. There was one pair who had been making daily trips to the airport to collect their luggage and equipment that was trickling in one piece at a time. Finally at 5:30 A.M., a U.S. airman dressed in civilian clothes came in and told us that the shuttle bus was at the corner and to hop on. We were driven to the back of the airport again to wait for another bus to the base. Even with having to wait for the next bus it was still faster than taking a taxi. What the taxi drivers fail to acknowledge is there is a long walk through the desert from the gate where they would drop the troops off.

We made it back to the base at 7:30 just in time to in process and to eat breakfast. When we arrived at the mess hall a Spc-4 who was part of the staff insisted that we show our orders to eat. What he wanted to do was close down the mess hall and not serve a bunch of troops who had been flying for 24 hours.

At the in processing tent we were told to come back at 1800 for roll call and flight information. That gave me time for a haircut, laundry, to finish up on some reading, and most importantly recover my battle rattle from the warehouse.

The warehouse was ready. All of the anticipated troops' equipment was laid out in rows for quick re-issue. When I put on my battle rattle it didn't fit quite right. The clerk at the desk told me that part of the service they provide is inspection of our plates. They take them out, X-ray them and replace them if damaged, which might account for the need for a few adjustments.

At 1800 we turned out with several hundred other troops under a large shed in front of a sign with our destination on it, something similar to the sorting corrals at a stockyard where they sort out the herds. "No flight, come back at 08:00 tomorrow for roll call."

On Monday morning July 12th the Bagram group was standing at the ready in from of a sign that said "Bagram." A Spc-4 came out and told us all to come back at 08:45 with all of our gear. I went back to my tent, put on my battle rattle, grabbed my ruck, stopped by billeting, signed out of my spacious tent and waited at the Bagram sign with 80 other troops.

At 08:45 another Spc-4 arrived and collected our I.D. cards to create the manifest and assured everyone that we would all be on the flight to Bagram. With that we moved into Mega tent three to wait for the next set of instructions. At 10:45 we were assembled and instructed to palletize our gear outside under one of the sheds. While we were palletizing our gear a civilian came out and announced that only 32 of us could go; the rest would go on the next flight in the afternoon. A group of U.S. VIP full birds loudly objected about the possibility of being bumped. After all they were NATO officers and there was not a speck of sweat or dirt on their custom battle rattle. They had come from a world where you break starch twice a day. It was bad enough that they had to be outside in the heat. They made enough noise to get on the flight. We were moved into Mega tent number one. We were officially in lock down. Our bird's call sign was Moose 84 a C-17 with a toilet! I was concerned that when it was announced that with only 32 PAX for the trip we would be flying on a C-130, the old work horse.

Mega tent one had the famous Jimmy Dean lunch packages, some muffins and a Pizza Hut order desk if you had the cash. The troops passed up the Jimmy Deans, which had never been a real hit. At 1300 we were called outside for one final roll call then loaded the bus for the air field.

We arrived on the tarmac, recovered the gear of the troops who would be flying on the afternoon flight to make way for the NATO VIPs, then waited on the bus for the plane to be refueled. We loaded up at 14:00 and took off at 14:15 for Bagram, a three and a half hour flight with a one and a half hour time change. When we entered Pakistani airspace the crew chief announced that it was time to put on our battle rattle. I noticed the flight crew didn't take the same precaution. An hour later we landed at Bagram. Since I had a ruck, I just picked it up off the tarmac. The rest of the troops had to wait until the freight crew delivered the pallet to the PAX terminal.

I had just enough time to make it to dinner before they closed the mess hall at 21:00. The food at Bagram was a step up from Kuwait. After dinner I collected my 9mm from the ALOC and attempted to get a flight to Jalalabad or Wright with no luck on either a fixed or rotary wing. I grabbed a bunk in the transition tent and tried to get some sleep. What a misconception that was. Every 30 minutes another group of troops would come in the tent hunting for a bunk. The F-15s were taking off all night long. Then to top it off the honey truck arrived to pump out the latrines. The honey truck was the only sound that could be heard over the roar of the F-15s.

I had miss-set my watch and showed up to breakfast an hour early, then returned to the tent for 45 minutes until the mess hall opened. After breakfast I went back to the PAX terminal to sign up for a space "A" flight to Bagram and was told it didn't look good. Maybe there would be a flight late in the evening. And, there was a long list of people who had been bumped the day before. I walked down to the rotary wing PAX terminal to try my luck there.

The ring flight would not be taking off until 23:30 and there were no other Mil air flights scheduled for the day. While I was talking to the private in charge of manifesting, a Molson crew chief stepped in the terminal and yelled out, "last call for JAF!" I broke contact with the private and raced out the door just as the crew chief gave the last seat away. The crew chief handed me the number for Molson and said they would be back.

I wish the airlines were like Molson. When you call you get a live person who knows what they are doing. The gal on the other end listed all of the departure times for Bagram to Jalalabad and to Wright. She said they were all booked, but there was always a seat, just show up.

I tried to get a ride on Embassy Air, but they said since I'd never flown with them before I couldn't be added to their manifest. They were coming to Bagram to pick up two people leaving several seats empty. I compared their service to Molson when asked if they could make a stop along the way to get a soldier back to his base. Molson doesn't hesitate for a second. The response is, "Hand me your ruck and get on. Aye."

The 1400 Molson Sikorsky 61 flight arrived loaded to the gills. The crew chief came over to the PAX terminal and yelled out, "Who needs to go to Jalalabad?" Eight people came forward. A few asked for special stops along the way once again, "No problem Aye." Upon arrival I was told that the flights to Camp Wright were cancelled due to thunderstorms, but the Mil air would be flying and to give them a try. Within a few minutes of our landing all of the Molson helicopters were tied down for the storm.

Chapter Forty-Five

WHILE YOU WERE AWAY

On Tuesday, July 13th I arrived back at FOB Fenty just in time for lunch while I continued my journey back to Camp Wright. My first task was to email Major Leeney and the rest of the crew from the MWR and inform them that I had arrived at FOB Fenty. On my way there, I ran into SGT Olson and SPC Mc Cool without their mule. FOB Fenty is a big base if you're working supply. Sgt Palacios was able to secure two Kawasaki mules, one for use at FOB Fenty and the other back at Wright. In the animal world a mule is a hybrid of a horse and a donkey; in Kawasaki's world a mule is a hybrid of a pickup truck and a golf cart. Sgt Palacios is affectionately known as the "Burro Meister." When you are surrounded by jackasses he is the man you want on your side. So a mule was the perfect vehicle for Sgt Palacios and his supply team. Sgt Mc Cool and Olson gave me a quick overview of the events of the past three weeks, then we parted.

After taking care of a few things, I met up with LTC Velte, my first step in getting caught up with the life in Afghanistan. We went over the brigade's timetable for our replacements and our exodus from Afghanistan. If everything went as planned we would have only two days of overlap with our replacements from Iowa. Two days would not be enough time for a thorough left seat right seat hand off. There were two places in the schedule that were prone to delays that potentially could mean we would miss Iowa.

We discussed some happier topics such as women's poultry, the AVA Para Vet project, and the multiple requests we had been given to stay. Life had been exciting while I was away both at FOB Fenty and back at Camp Wright.

Part of our redeployment required our troops to have everything inspected at the FOB Fenty customs office. The plan was for all of the troops to pack everything they didn't need, drive down to FOB Fenty, have it inspected, then sealed by customs in tri-walls to be shipped back to the states. This would require three trips starting with the first group going down on June 29th.

On Wednesday June 30th the Ag section convoy rolled out from Camp Wright at first light down route California for their turn at FOB Fenty customs. The insurgents were also rolling out at first light to FOB Fenty with a different objective.

While all of this was going on, Sgt Palacios and Jessie from the Kunar PRT were busy getting ready for the Ag section to process through customs and to haul back several loads of supplies. At 7:00 Sgt Palacios and Jessie were riding in their Kawasaki golf cart through the motor pool when a suicide bomber drove a car loaded with explosives along the back wall of the FOB passing several guard towers manned by ASG, then stopped at the old back gate behind the motor pool. Just as Sgt Palacios and Jessie rolled by, the suicide bomber detonated his VIED blowing the gates off their hinges.

Sgt Palacios pulled out his 9mm as he ditched his Kawasaki mule while more explosions erupted. One insurgent made it into the FOB and fired his RPG at a jingle fuel truck; this created a second explosion and burned. Sgt Palacios and Jessie made their way to the nearest bunker while Kiowas and Apaches took to the air and engaged the remaining 14 insurgents. The insurgents had been waiting in a farmer's field that was full of soft muddy soil, which restricted their movement. Sgt Palacios could see them working their way through a creek that ran near the back wall of the FOB. With only two clips, he couldn't afford to engage them at 100 yards. He would have to wait and make every shot count. The insurgents were concentrating their RPG fire on the guard towers. The insurgents knew if they could knock out the towers they had a chance of entering the FOB. Things weren't going well for the insurgents as troops raced to the perimeter to get a shot at them. The insurgents attempted a second assault on the

FOB further along the back wall, but only succeeded in lighting the FOB dump on fire. Sgt Palacios was stuck in the bunker for three and a half hours while hot brass rained down from the war birds above. Every now and then LTC Velte would give him a call on his cell phone to see how he was doing. When the assault was over five insurgents were dead, four were killed by the tower gunner and the fifth, who was the only insurgent who was successfully able to enter the FOB, was the suicide bomber. His body was broadcast over the FOB along with parts of his car.

Meanwhile the Ag section was making its way over the Bahsood Bridge. We received word that FOB Fenty was under attack and not to attempt to enter the base. They simply pulled into FOB Finley Shields to our sister Missouri ADT home and waited for the all clear.

When the all clear was sounded Sgt Palacios and Jessie gave their Kawasaki mule the once over, kicked the tires and continued to get ready for the Ag section's big day with customs, while the post engineers repaired the back entrance. Sgt Palacios had some difficulty releasing the brake. When the VIED went off he jammed on the brake with everything he had so he could jump clear. It took some doing to release the brake.

The Taliban immediately gave a press release about massive damage that they inflicted on the FOB. The local paper was already on the scene taking photos and nullified the Taliban's claims as just blowing smoke up their kilts. The only photo to make the press was of the smoke billowing up from the dump, with the caption, "Smoke rises up from FOB Fenty after attack."

For the ten days Sgt Palacios was traveling between FOB Fenty and Wright he was in the middle of hostilities each time. While waiting at the FOB Fenty PAX terminal with Sgt Fry an insurgent was able to lob an RPG over the south wall missing the mess hall; it landed in the earth next to the runway. Sgt Palacios heard the sound of the RPG firing and hit the dirt injuring his thumb in the process. Sgt Fry alerted Palacios that his thumb was bleeding and dislocated. With that Sgt Palacios was certain that the Taliban were tracking his cell phone or that he was just jinxed.

I parted with LTC Velte and tried to get manifested for the Pech Ring flight that would take off at midnight. I had arrived on the last Molson flight in or out of Jalalabad so my only option was to fly one of the ring flights. I did have another option and that was to ride back with the Bravo

377

Company of the 3-27th of the 101st that was down at Fenty for a supply run, but my back just wasn't up to riding four hours over open country in an MRAP.

The insurgents frequently attack targets of commerce and government centers in Jalalabad in an attempt to destabilize the area and keep in under the proxy control of a shadow government. On July 10th, the insurgents placed a large bomb in a rickshaw and stationed it on the Bahsood Bridge. Their goal was to attack a convoy while it crossed the bridge. The Bahsood Bridge is the main bridge in Jalalabad that crosses the Kunar River connecting the government centers of northeastern Afghanistan and Kabul. It is a key bridge to control. When the insurgents detonated their rickshaw bomb it damaged the bridge enough to require traffic to be re-routed onto an unimproved quarry road on the eastern side of the Kunar River. This detour increased the travel time from Asadabad to Jalalabad from two hours to four.

I made the PAX terminal my home for the rest of the afternoon while I waited for the midnight Pech Ring flight. At 23:00 I checked back in with Military Air to make sure the flight was still on when I was told that it would be staying at FOB Blessing for five hours, then would continue down the Pech stopping at Wright last. Wright would be a courtesy stop just for me. I realized I wouldn't be getting any sleep, and wouldn't be of any use when I finally arrived at Wright. I thanked the good captain, signed up for space "A" on Molson and found a tent to sleep in. The following morning SGT Olson, McCool and I waited with six other hopefuls for seats on the 8:00 Molson to Wright. It was a VIP flight and the VIPs didn't want to share the empty seats so we waited for the next flight at 10:30, which we all got on. Had we stayed a few more hours we could have watched the afternoon rocket attack. Once again the insurgents claimed they inflicted major damage on the base. The truth was their rockets were duds and didn't go off. Soviet quality control was never up to ISO 9000 standards. As we were getting on the bus for the Molson pad, Sgt Percival jumped off, greeted us and remarked that he would be back at Camp Wright that evening. We broke the bad news to him that we were on the last flight of the day to Wright. Oops! Sgt Percival thought it would be a quick trip and didn't bring his assault pack so he got to enjoy the night without the additional comforts of a sleeping bag or his shaving kit.

When I arrived back at Camp Wright the first thing I wanted to know about was the Marawara offensive, "Strong Eagle" and the follow up Ag Shura at the new Marawara District Center. The offensive was to have taken place before I went on leave, but Governor Wahidi who had to approved the offensive was in India. The operation was continually pushed back until Sunday June 27th the last night that the moon light would support operations.

As with any operation or project it must be made to look like the Afghans were leading the way. The ASG Tiger group led the attack against the insurgents while special operations troops were on either side of the Daridarn Valley. There were between 600 and 700 U.S. and Afghan troops and 200 insurgents locked in battle in the 1500 Km long Daridarn - Mora Valley (The Mora Valley feeds into the Daridarn Valley). One insurgent was able to hold off ten Tiger team members. "No Slack," the taskforce that was running the offensive, called in a C-130 gun ship when they heard that the Tiger team folded and ran. Shortly after that the special operations troops found themselves surrounded and called in for air support. The F-15s that were above in a holding pattern dropped several 500-pound bombs around the hilltop where the special operations troops were holding their ground. The blast was so intense it knocked the U.S. commander off the hilltop causing him to roll 150 feet down the hillside.

The U.S. wounded were being evacuated to the trauma center at Camp Wright where our medics SPC Gonzalvo and SPC Larson were supporting the surgical teams. Nineteen solders were flown in to the trauma center where two died of their wounds. The fighting continued in Marawara, Daridarn, Chenar, and Betaw-Darri for several days as the insurgents moved in from Kunar to join the fight.

The insurgents soon realized that CP Wright was playing an integral part in the offensive and started to increase their attacks on the FOB, which commenced on June 29th and repeated on July 1st 2nd 3rd and 5th. On Saturday July 3rd Governor Wahidi was promising to help residents returning to their homes in Shigal and Dangam Districts by repairing infrastructure while the insurgents where making a concentrated mortar and RPG attack on FOB Wright. This time the insurgents sent in a well-trained team, which consisted of a forward observer who would signal the mortar team when aircraft were on the flight line. The first attack started at noon with a mix of 82mm white phosphorus and high explosives. Seven troops and two civilians were injured on the flight line from the shrapnel, but were saved because the white phosphorus sealed their wounds at the same time. A total of eleven people were injured during the attack. The base returned direct 155 fire at the insurgents who had set up their mortar directly above Woch Now Village overlooking the Witch's Teton, not in their normal secluded location behind the abandoned Gurja Village near the spring. Every time a helicopter would land the mortar crew would fire. At the end of the day several vehicles and one building were damaged.

On July 4th, Governor Wahidi announced that the fighting had ended, but the fighting continued. The operation lasted one week and over 150 insurgents were killed. The insurgents decided not to attack the FOB on July 4th, but decided to lob a few more mortar rounds on the 5th of July so we wouldn't forget them. The base commander took all local national cell phones away on July 5th and the mortar attacks stopped.

Our SECFOR was staying busy with their QRF duty, and so were the insurgents on hill 1311. Another convoy was ambushed losing one MRAP. Once again the vehicle's design saved the crew. The RPG round struck the ground first and ricocheted into the belly of the vehicle lighting the hydraulics on fire, which in turn lit the tires on fire. The crew was able to exit the vehicle with no injuries as they watched their ride home go up in flames. The vehicle eventually extinguished itself with its onboard fire control system. Since the tires burned off the vehicle, it would require a lowboy and a wrecker to be returned to base. The recovery team from Camp Wright was called out and the Kunar ADT's SECFOR provided security while the other units continued to engage the insurgents.

Thursday July 1st was our big Ag Shura day held at the new Marawara District Center with Task Force No Slack. We had developed several quick response projects we could offer to show good faith to the villagers such as women's poultry, veterinary services with the AVA, seed, pipe system repair and installation. Just prior to operations, "Strong Eagle" the battle space owner showed the Ag section a photo of a large pipe that crossed over the Muryagul Dry River. The question they had was, "how fast could the pipe be repaired if we have to blow it in order to advance up the dry river?" A few days before the Shura the battle space had another photo showing the pipe with a few 40mm holes in it. One of the insurgents stationed his vehicle in front of the pipe to engage the 101st and lost.

Repairing a 12-inch pipe in the remote Daridam Village would be no easy task due to accessibility and the availability of the pipe. SSG Tyner, along with Sgt Flynn and Stevens put their heads together and came up with a few solutions. When the convoy was refueling, after its return from FOB Joyce where the Ag section looked over the photos of the leaking pipe, SSG Tyner spotted an old fuel bladder that had run the course of its life. He asked if he could have it and proceeded to cut it into several wide strips. He gave it to SGT Flynn and Stevens who took it with them to the July 1st Shura.

The Shura didn't go as planned. After a few minutes it was evident that the elders didn't want to talk about agriculture. Colonel Val, the battle space commander, dismissed the ADT to have a look around Daridarn Village and to fix the pipe that linked the larger section of the village to the smaller section over the Muryagul Dry River.

The Ag section departed after giving the elders a bunch of Pakistani tools that had been collecting dust, hay and feed supplements, and some seeds. The Ag section returned to Daridam on July 13th to check the pipe repair and see if there was any other service they could provide. The bottom line was the villagers didn't want anyone in their village: not the Taliban, the ANP, ANA, ANP or the Americans. They just wanted to be left alone. The U.S. had invested a lot of money in 2003 and the improvements were still in good repair, but the investment didn't win over any favoritism from the villagers.

By the end of my first day back at Camp Wright I was starting to feel the toils of travel, but just couldn't sleep. I went out to the blue gate where SFC Median and Hanlin were and shared a few stories about my leave and stayed until they were replaced by Sgt Flynn and Stevens. They used the time to brief me on the plan for a demonstration farm in Sarkani, and to share a few more stories about the Marawara offensive. We saw a few green meteors falling toward earth and the Apaches launching flares at the junction of the Pech and Kunar Rivers. That reminded Sgt Flynn and Stevens that a few nights earlier Pakistan was bombing the far side of the ridge while they were on duty. They could see the glow of the explosions breach the silhouette of the ridgeline with each drop; then the whole ridgeline was fully lit in a bright aurora when one of the bombs struck a weapons cache. The lack of moonlight made the sight even more eventful as the light of the explosion reflected off the Kunar. Before turning in for the night I noticed with the new moon the Milky Way was visible again.

Chapter Forty-Six

SUMMER STORMS

Nearly two weeks had passed since operation Strong Eagle One was completed. The results were a significant drop in IEDs and ambushes in the Pech and Kunar River Valleys along with attacks on the various FOBs. However insurgent activity was picking up in the lower Kunar River Valley just north of Jalalabad. Since the main bridge had been damaged, traffic was rerouted over semi-improved roads. The insurgents took note of the diversion and refocused their attacks on the bypass route in hopes of cutting off the population centers in the Pech and Kunar River Valleys from the government center in Jalalabad.

There were still some hot spots in the Daridarn-Mora Valley along with some suspected weapons caches and continued smuggling activities. Task Force No Slack had to continue their push farther east toward Pakistan to curb the insurgency in our A.O. On Sunday July 18th we received word that Task Force No Slack would be conducting a follow on offensive in the Daridarn-Mora Valley called Strong Eagle Two commencing that night at 2200. The task force commander had given the insurgents plenty of warning of what was going to happen if they didn't clear out.

At 0900, SPC Larson started making the rounds asking people to come in and get their blood type verified and to fill out the blood donor forms. Everyone is a walking blood bank. During the last offensive, 19 wounded troops were medivaced to Camp Wright. The trauma center was put on alert for Strong Eagle Two in preparations for a mass casualty event. A mass casualty event means this is a large number of wounded, which could be U.S. forces, ANA, ANP, or insurgents.

I went up to the trauma center at 10:00, had my blood typed again and renewed my blood donation forms. The troops trickled in all day to the trauma center to do the same. Giving blood is a privilege on the battlefield; no one has to be forced to donate. While I was having my blood type verified the trauma center medical staff was busy setting up for the expected mass casualties. Large triage boxes were set out on the back patio along with piles of litters; the chapel would double as the walking wounded overflow. While the medical staff was setting up it was missions as usual for the other units.

Camp Wright is home to a large number of special units and service providers that support programs and operations in the general area. While I was on leave, several of the units were required to send troops closer to their customers requiring the other units to cover down on their duties. The ADT drew the task of manning the ECP gate (Entry Control Point). We would share the responsibility with the PRT by swapping crews every other week. SSG (P) Tyner was assigned as the NCOIC of the ECP gate. The ECP can be a grueling task during peak periods such as the start and end of the workday, or when a CLIP arrives. I stopped by just to let SSG Tyner know that he was not forgotten and to see how the operation was going. SSG Tyner's response was, "Busy. That's how it's going sir!" SSG Tyner didn't seem to mind. He was in his element and enjoying all of the activity.

Over all, the day was relatively quiet. SFC Fair and I had our hands full trying to get our bulk funds from the new brigade, and SFC Fulton and Hanlin were preparing to build a crib wall. At 2000 hours the Bulldog Artillery started firing at selected targets in the Daridarn-Mora Valley; this concluded at 2100 only firing a few selected salvos. At 2200 the offensive kicked off and everyone held his breath waiting for intense 155 fire, or a mass casualty call on the PA, but it remained quiet. The next morning the big guns hadn't fired a shot since they went cold the night before, and the only medivac, which arrived at 05:30, was non-combat related from another location.

Monday morning we were off to Chowkay to conduct the final QA/QC of the Chowkay demonstration farm located behind the district center. Sgt Stevens ran the project from start to finish after I signed up a contractor. He would have a chance to see the fruits of his efforts. Our USDA rep had insisted on a specific seed supplier for the demonstration farm. His supplier would only sell in metric tons; we needed a few kilograms. Sgt Flynn called up our friends at NATC who delivered all of the required seed in the quantities we needed within 48 hours of the call. Sgt Stevens loaded the seed and the remaining tools. We had mostly shovel heads in the back of his MATV and we took off for Chowkay.

Our contractor SWCC was standing by to demonstrate the irrigation system along with the extension manager who had his hand out, upon our arrival. This was Sgt Steven's show so I stood back and supported security while Sgt Stevens worked on some conflict resolution topics.

The first thing the extension manager announced was that the pump we had installed at the irrigation canal was no good and that it needed to be bigger. SGT Stevens asked, "What's wrong with it?" Our contractor fired it up and it purred like a kitten. We hiked to the cistern and watched the water pour out of the three inch pipe at 1500 liters per minute. "So what is the problem?" The extension manager started rattling off a long list of problems that were all false. The bottom line was he promised his neighbors that the ADT would provide irrigation to their farms too. All he had to do was ask and we would have sized a different pump and contracted for a series of cisterns with float valves. We agreed to swap out the primary pump for one with greater capacity.

After that he didn't get very far. Thinking that he was on a roll he told SGT Stevens that he needed money for farm labor. When SGT Stevens worked up the agreement with the extension manager it was agreed that the ADT would handle the irrigation and earthwork and the extension office would handle the farming operations including the seed. We provided the first batch of seed to prime the operations. SGT Stevens turned the tables on the extension manager. The extension manager stated that it was past planting time. All of the labor had moved on to other jobs, and he would have to import the labor. SGT Stevens pointed out to him that before the ADT installed the irrigation system the land was dormant during the summer.

"What would you have planted if we hadn't made you wait for the earth work to be completed?"

The response: "Nothing."

"Whom do you hire to plant the fields during the planning season?"

"My family."

It went downhill from there.

The extension manager wasn't finished yet. After losing the last round with Sgt Stevens he recited a list of demands that he expected to be filled. "I need tools!"

SGT Steven asked, "What about all of the tools we just gave you?" He responded that they were no good and they needed handles. The expensive part of the tool is the iron piece; the handles are cheap. We had given him about 40 shovelheads for free. SGT Stevens told him that he could buy the handles out of his own money. Then he demanded 20 shovels and picks for every farmer located behind the district center. I was enjoying this amateur's show trying to outmaneuver SGT Stevens who wasn't budging. We finally agreed to do a few things for the good of the community and parted the demonstration farm.

While SGT Stevens and I were taking our final look at Chowkay, we hoped, SFC Fulton and Hanlin were having the ultimate gym experience assembling the crib wall. Since the month long delay of getting more bulk funds we couldn't pay the merry men of Woch Now to build it for us. SSG Tyner made arrangements to borrow an excavator and crane for the project with the mayor (BMCS Nunemaker). The excavator prepped the site, but broke down before it could be properly leveled, but all of the boulders were out of the way. SFC Fulton and Hanlin along with SPC Lopez each grabbed a shovel to finish leveling the site. Next came setting all of the crib wall pieces. A few days earlier SPC Lopez was complaining about being snookered into working out with SGT Stevens who worked through a deck of cards to determine his work out. Two hours later SPC Lopez was spent. He was moving 1000-pound concrete beams and using a pick and shovel while wearing his battle rattle. Looking back, two hours in the gym with Sgt Stevens wasn't all that bad compared with the tribulation of going through in 100+ degree heat. Together the three of them and Sam, our interpreter, placed half of the foundation before the crane operator quit.

The evening of July 19th SFC Fulton, SGT Flynn and I met with Laj Bar and his father to discuss the future with the new ADT from Iowa. We had Amid do the translating because he was the same age as Laj Bar's father whom we were really talking to. Laj Bar started off the conversation asking for 13 days pay for himself and eleven of his men. I told him we didn't ask him to work and we weren't going to pay for civic improvements that we didn't ask for. This had been a reoccurring subject during our seven-month relationship. Laj Bar would try again and again to have us pay for improvements to his village that his people should do on their own. From there we moved on to business operations and how he would have to sell his products at a competitive price, and he would have to set aside some of the money to buy materials, which led us to the topic of water.

Woch Now's water consumption constantly outpaced our projections for mixing concrete, and the orchard. Laj Bar told us the tanks were leaking, but not enough to suck down an additional 1500 gallons a week. Just prior to our meeting with Laj Bar, SGT Stevens sent a truckload of reclaimed water up to Woch Now for the orchard. Laj Bar rejected the water because of the odor. SFC Fulton explained to Laj Bar that he either accepts the free water or uses some of his profits to pay a trucker to deliver river water. We had suspected that the villagers were drinking the water and using it for cooking and laundry. We had told Laj Bar not to drink the water many times. The water that was delivered was potable water from a well, but the trucks that delivered it indiscriminately hauled river water and other liquids in their tanks. There was no telling what finally ended up in the water by the time it reached Woch Now. We had scheduled our meeting with Laj Bar and his father on the 18th, but Laj Bar called to cancel the meeting because the people in his village were sick and he had to take his son to the hospital. At that point we were pretty sure he was drinking the water. We went over the subject of water with Laj bar and his father in great detail making sure that he knew only to drink his spring water.

The hours of the afternoon were ticking away and nearly an hour had passed since the afternoon call for prayer had gone out. Muslims have one hour to respond to the call for prayer. We escorted them down to the mosque for their four-minute afternoon prayer. At lunchtime the prayer is 10 minutes long, but somehow they require 30 minutes. Upon exiting the mosque, Laj Bar told me that he lost some of his family in recent combat. His family was inside a friend's house when the Taliban attacked. His family was firing back when the U.S. started bombing the village. The result was several of his family members were killed. He made it sound as if it had happened in the past few weeks while I was gone. He wanted some financial compensation for the loss of the family members. He said he had gone to the governor's office and a scribe wrote up the claim, but the governor rejected it. I told him I would call around and see if there was a program that could help him. He handed me the papers from the governor's office as he departed. Amid looked at the papers and told me that they were over two years old and they didn't match the story Laj Bar had just told me. When I relayed the story at dinner SFC Median and Fulton responded, "Oh he tried the same story with us. Laj Bar was well aware that the gravy train was getting ready to pull out so he was working every angle he could for more fat little dollars.

Tuesday morning July 20th, I went with SFC Fulton and Hanlin to lend a hand with the crib wall. Once again lots of pick and shovel work. I told Laj Bar that we could provide work for three men and him. He arrived when he saw the crane show up. SFC Fulton took the men aside and trained them on hand and arm signals, how to rig a load, and basic safety. The men learned quickly, but Laj Bar just didn't get the concept. We tried to have him direct the crane while we worked the loads, but he was more interested in getting a close look at the operations. He quickly forgot the signals and started making up his own, but never repeating them twice. He became frustrated and yelled at the crane operator to do as he said. SFC Fulton took over directing the crane, but let Laj Bar think he was doing it. The crane operator knew whom to watch. Our backs were beginning to tire. As the day progressed we had just misplaced a 12-foot stretcher, and SFC Hanlin asked "Do you think we could just wedge it over with the bar?" I told him maybe two hours ago, but at this point we needed the crane. By 1300 we finished placing all of the remaining pieces. There were still 84 more pieces up at Woch Now Village that had to be recovered and installed, but we had no money.

That evening I sat down with Doctor Mashwani from SWCC and talked to him about finishing the crib wall job. With the additional security responsibilities we had and our replacements on the way we just didn't have the manpower to do the job ourselves. The doctor parted from me and went up to the job site, then to Woch Now to look over the stock. He was met by Laj Bar who said it was his job to build the crib wall, not SWCC's. I met with the doctor in the morning; we both agreed that Laj Bar was nuts if he thought his men could stack the 1000 pound pieces eight feet on top of each other without a crane. The doctor gave me a very attractive price for the job and I gave him the go ahead.

Wednesday was a day of surprises. At 6:00 A.M. SFC Natividad called me on the radio stating that the ECP called because someone was trying to take an excavator off post. I went to the ECP gate and it was Dr. Mashwani with an excavator wanting access to Woch Now Village. I told the ASG guards that it was OK and to let him pass. Dr. Mashwani has a different approach to work compared to the Afghans who work at Camp Wright. Dr. Mashwani believes in "come early and stay late," and you better be tired when the day is over.

SFC Fair and Stevens jumped on a Molson flight to Jalalabad to grab our next bulk draw traveling as straphangers. SFC Fair returned with $50,000 and current Stars and Stripes newspapers that we devoured.

SFC Fair and I hit the books paying off all of our outstanding debits and promises to clear our books before we TOAed (Transfer OF Authority) with Iowa. We were expecting Iowa's Advon that afternoon, but they got bumped and spent another day waiting for a plane.

Friday was going to be a light day for us. One group would convoy up to FOB Blessing in the Western Pech River Valley while SSG Tyner prepared for a concrete pour in the balloon yard, with the remaining Ag and SecFor troops on QRF duty.

IED attacks had stopped in the Pech and Kunar River Valleys since Task Force No Slack pushed through the Daridarn-Mora Valley. Ambushes were still a problem, but nowhere nearly as destructive as IEDs. At mid morning, Major Leeney and SFC Mosqueda, the convoy commander, rolled out of Camp Wright for Blessing to attend a targeting meeting. SGT Flynn was pulled from the Ag section to gun for one of the trucks. Things were going smoothly until the convoy crossed over the Pech River onto route Rhode Island. The ANP was busy handling a large traffic accident that blocked the highway. SFC Mosqueda told SGT Johanson to dismount and ask the ANP if it would be all right if they pulled off the highway and used a road that bisected a cemetery. The ANP said, "Yes please do. It would help relieve some of the congestion." Following closely behind the ADT was a caravan of jingle trucks.

The first glitch of the convoy was over, but there were still several known ambush points they had to cross. After passing the ANP station near FOB Honiker Miracle they noticed a man sitting on the hill overlooking the ANP station dressed in white manjamies with a cell phone. He was a lookout for someone. As they came up on the Tantil ANP station, the location of our first TIC, SGT Contreras heard the first RPG round fire. SPC Tropeano spotted two more insurgents and opened up with 50 rounds of MK 19 fire. The ambush occurred from both sides of the road, SAF from one side and RPGs from the other. The big guns at FOB Michigan fired several rounds of HE at the insurgents as the convoy cleared the kill zone. Then all was quiet. These were a new group of insurgents much bolder than the ones who were active during the winter and early spring. These insurgents were engaging the convoy from 100 to 400 meters, where the other insurgents in the Pech wouldn't engage closer than 500 meters.

The meeting at Blessing went as expected; no more projects period. The battle space owner was now focusing his efforts on kinetic operations. It was evident that the relationship between the villagers and the U.S. troops had changed. Months earlier when we would drive by a village the kids all would give us the thumbs up and wave; at this point they were throwing rocks; one even struck SPC Robledo.

The convoy back was also eventful. SSG Arnold switched places with SFC Mosqueda as the convoy commander and waited their turn to move down route Rhode Island. Mad Dog had the next convoy slot following closely behind the ADT. As the convoy approached Tantil Village Major Leeney announced over the radio that the villagers were running. SPC Robledo spotted the insurgents on the hill facing them and engaged with 200 rounds of .50 cal as small arms fire opened up from the village, followed by RPGs fired from just above the village rooftops. One RPG landed five meters away from SSG Arnolds MRAP. SFC Graham witnessed the smoke from two RPGs being fired on the hillside above the village where the insurgents had dug in. He attempted to engage them but the insurgents had moved too close to the village to safely open up on them. Mad Dog heard the announcement of the ambush and closed in on the ADT to provide supporting fire. Closing with the ADT would also deny the insurgents time to reload in preparation for another ambush.

Within a few minutes the ambush was over. SSG Johanson noted that the ANP station didn't have any bullet holes in it as the convoy moved out of the kill zone. The village of Tantil was the site of many ambushes with the

ANP station set in the middle of the action. Amazingly there was no battle damage to the building. Major Leeney spotted the same villagers he saw flee from Tantil lingering about the next village waiting to return home.

Friday was a day of celebration. Our convoy survived two ambushes with no injuries, and four members of the Iowa ADT arrived: Captain Birgy, 1LT McNaul, CSM Collins, and SFC Nelson. Several of us met them at the flight line with a truck for their gear just before dinner. SFC Medina squared them away with rooms, while Lt Ko and I linked up with our counterparts and started giving base tours. We went over the reaction to indirect and direct fire procedures and told them not to worry; "we usually get attacked every four weeks." The four of them called it a night and were looking forward to sleeping in after several days of traveling.

Saturday morning I was working early because of network problems. I figured out that fewer people would be on the network in the morning and things should be faster. SGT Palacios arrived on the nine o'clock Molson flight after pushing out two CONEXs worth of triwalls to the States. Captain Birgy and Sergeant Major Collins from the Iowa ADT arrived at the barn at the same time to go over how the CERP process worked. There was a lull in the conversation when I thought I heard an explosion, but discounted it because of some heavy equipment work going on. SPC Larson was on duty at the blue gate at the time. She witnessed the smoke from the mortar and the first impact in Woch Now Village. She called the attack in on the radio. SFC Medina came into the barn and announced that we were taking incoming. The indirect alarm sounded as we stood up; just as we exited the barn a mortar round struck one of the barracks buildings above us. SFC Medina directed the Iowa troops into the bunker while I grabbed my gear and reported to the TOC. SGT Palacios was a minute behind me when another mortar round impacted near the TOC. He came in the TOC and proclaimed, "I'm going to stomp on this phone if the insurgents keep this up." Sgt Palacios was certain that the Taliban were tracking his cell phone.

A total of six rounds were fired at the FOB; two fell in Woch Now Village, another 100 meters west of the back gate as the mortar team walked their rounds into the camp. Our ASV crew spotted the insurgents above the Witch's Teton on O.P. Rachel. O.P. Shiloh confirmed the sighting in time for two Apaches to start their hunt. It quickly turned into a game of cat and mouse with the insurgents moving back to the Korengal Valley without their mortar tube.

The insurgents had transformed the old U.S. COPs Vimoto and Vegas in the Korengal into a base of their own shortly after the U.S. pulled out of the valley. The U.S. made an agreement with the villagers that if the U.S. could pull out without a firefight, then the villagers could have the crane and all of the diesel fuel that was to be left behind. Attacks on U.S. forces, convoys, CLPs, (Combat Logistic Patrol pronounced Clip) and FOBs steadily increased since the U.S. pulled out of the Korengal, including attacks on Camp Wright. The 101st was now looking at going back into the Korengal the same way they did in the Daridarn-Mora Valley.

Insurgent attacks are not the only danger to the local population. Natural disasters pose an even greater threat that cost more lives than the insurgents. Summer brings monsoon storms to India and Pakistan, which spin off major thunder storms to northeastern Afghanistan. This was the case when a major storm system struck Pakistan during the week of July 25th. The storm steadily increased in intensity causing major flooding in Afghanistan. In Laghman Province homes and farms were washed away. The ANA launched their Russian Hip helicopters and rescued close to 2000 people in Nangarhar from floodwaters on Wednesday July 28th. What was impressive was the Afghanis had both the training and will to respond to a national crisis. This occurred the same day a Pakistani air carrier Airblue Airbus A321 crashed in the hills near Islamabad. Search and rescue efforts were hampered by the heavy rains. The following day after the mountains in northern Pakistan and Afghanistan shed their flood waters, the Kunar River began to swell increasing the havoc in the Kunar River Valley. Trees and timber were washed down the river, while the riverbanks gave way causing the stacked rock homes to collapse into the river. Lumberyards that were 20 feet above the normal river's surface were flooded with their smuggled timer floating down the river.

In Asadabad, the Kunar River swelled spilling over its banks flooding the university that occupied the low ground and parts of downtown. People flocked to the river casting fishing poles toward the floating lumber and logs, while others waded out into the torrent in chest deep water to grab wood. The Bella Sarkani pedestrian suspension bridge just south of Sarkani that crosses the Kunar River was loaded with people standing nearly shoulder-to-shoulder as the water lapped over the bridge grabbing at timbers that were passing under the bridge. Lt Commander Edwards (The PRT commander) and I observed the people on the bridge at 10:30. Then at 10:45 the southern suspension cable snapped and the entire bridge platform let loose like a mass gallows instantaneously dumping the people into the surging Kunar River. Only one person was seen cresting the surface of the river less than a minute later a half mile downstream. People were risking their lives to gather firewood. Ralphi, our interpreter, told me that the bridge was built by one of five construction companies owned by Governor Wahidi. The eastern approach road to the Marawara Bridge also washed out due to no erosion control structures. The Marawara Bridge was said to have been constructed by one of the governor's companies too.

July 29th was not entirely filled with tragedy. That evening we formed up in the balloon yard to promote SSG Palacios to Sergeant First Class.

Chapter Forty-Seven

IOWA ARRIVES WITH RAMADAN

Sunday August 1st our last air freight load was flown out of Camp Wright to FOB Fenty where SFC Natividad, SGT Olson, and SPC Lopez moved it to the fixed wing cargo area. I took a series of photos for SFC Palacios to document the cargo in the event it was lost along the way. SFC Palacios and SPC Fry flew out on an earlier Molson flight to push all of the cargo out to Bagram and onward to Camp Atterbury.

Before going back to the balloon yard to check on the Gujers and the team of SFC Hanlin and Fulton, I took the opportunity to tour some of the route clearing equipment. Many times we called upon the services of the 3/D/1-377 IN Route Clearing Patrol (RCP) to clear the way for us, or we sent our QRF with them when an IED or land mine was discovered. The route clearance teams have some unique and unusual equipment. The first piece that will catch your eye is the husky. The husky looks like a road grader except it has a small engine and the single seat operator's cabin is mounted high in the air. The husky can be equipped with a variety of attachments such as ground penetrating radar, a set of rollers to either safely push objects off the road or set something off. Then there is the buffalo, a massive MRAP vehicle equipped with a folding arm that can be extended a far distance out to dig up any suspected explosive device. They even have a camera system mounted on a telescoping column for getting a better look at things.

Route clearing is very dangerous and strenuous work. While I was admiring their equipment they were preparing for another mission up by Asmar. Asmar is located at the convergence of the Kunar River Valley and Dangam Valley with headwaters at the Loegran Pass. The Loegran Pass is a high speed avenue of approach for insurgents from Pakistan, which is used to support ambushes at hill 1311. Hill 1311 is located south of Asmar next to the Kunar Construction College, a USAID institution operated out of Kabul. The KCCs have many ex-insurgent students. South of hill 1311 is Mora where the Shigal and the Sholton Valleys converge. The Sholton Valley leads to the Kaga Pass, another smuggling route. The insurgents have a base of operations in the Shigal Valley, which is one terrain feature behind hill 1311.

During the first few months of our deployment, ambushes from hill 1311 came from one firing position, which usually consisted of no more than three RPG rounds randomly fired at a convoy. Since the 101st took over the battle space, the ambushes at hill 1311 have become more complex and intense. SFC Fair and crew were in two ambushes in the Shigal Valley early on in our deployment.

The RCP 8 had put in a very long day clearing roads checking for possible IEDs, mines and other UXOs. They had been supporting the engineers inspecting bridges for flood damage from the recent monsoon flooding from Pakistan. Many of the bridges over the Kunar suffered substantial structural damage from the storm. All of the bridges required inspection to ensure they were safe for military traffic or to develop a scope of work for contractors to make the require repairs. By late afternoon the engineers called it a day due to lack of sun light. They proceeded back to Camp Wright.

The journey home took them past hill 1311 where the insurgents had all day to set up their ambush. As RCP 8 came down Route California, the insurgents fired RPGs at their convoy singling the start of the ambush followed by two DSHKA gunners opening up on them. There were thirty-five to forty insurgents firing from both sides of the Kunar River firing over 30 RPGs. Some of the insurgents were as close as 35 meters firing PKMs and AK-47s. Soon the sound of a mortar could be heard firing at them from the eastern side of the Kunar. RCP 8 came to a halt and the insurgents emerged. The RCP 8 TOW gunner spotted one three-man DSHKA team and eliminated them while the other gun crews engaged other insurgent teams. Two RPG rounds struck the back of one of RCP 8's MRAPS blowing the toolbox off the back door and penetrating the armor causing minor wounds to their medic and one other soldier. The other RPG round damaged a small rear window. The insurgents broke contact and RCP 8 left the kill zone passing through Shin Kowrak Village when five insurgents started firing their AK-47s from the road and other insurgents started firing from residences. The rules of engagement didn't leave RCP 8 any choice other than to push through the second ambush and return to Camp Wright.

Members of RCP 8 train on a TOW system at Camp Wright the day after they repelled the ambush at hill 1311.

I was giving a courtesy call to SFC Medina and Hanlin at the blue gate to see if they wanted me to get them a cold Gatorade when the call came in to expect RCP 8 to be passing through with wounded. Things were starting to get very busy. During the afternoon we started hearing rumors that the insurgents had occupied two houses in the Daridarn-Mora Valley and had posted some guards for security on several other houses during the week. It didn't take long before the rumors were verified and Task Force No Slack responded as promised. The insurgents were told if they came back they would be attacked, and they were.

Shortly after RCP 8 came home, we could see the troops from No Slack passing by with their air support just a few minutes behind. U.S. troops moved from compound to compound evacuating residences until they isolated the two suspected strong holds. The insurgents decided to take hostile action toward the U.S. troops and by morning three insurgents were dead. No Slack found two more insurgents who went into hiding after a local national gave them a tip. The two remaining insurgents decided that they would be better off surrendering to the U.S. verses returning to Pakistan.

I welcomed Colonel Bargfrede, the incoming ADT commander, Friday afternoon as he stepped off one of Molson's UH-1. He still had plenty of energy and was excited about getting down to business. Meanwhile it was business as usual for us planning for Laj Bar and the rest of the Gujers. Friday night would be our last official night of guard duty. Saturday morning the Gujers arrived on time and Laj Bar was starting to make last minute demands. The lesson learned is *the more you give the Afghanis the more they demand.* Laj Bar presented me with the solar powered cell phone charger that we gave him several months ago. He said it didn't work. I explained that it wouldn't in this stormy weather because of the cloud cover. He thought it was our responsibility to give him a new one. I pointed out that we had paid him handsomely for his services over the last few months and surely he had saved enough money to get it repaired.

We assembled the Gujers near the balloon yard and SFC Hanlin demonstrated to the Gujers what to do if the FOB was attacked. He simulated taking his shoes off and diving into the mosque. SFC Median's replacement, MSG Sheasley, witnessed the demonstration and asked, "Do you get attacked often?"

I told her, "No usually just mortared," and pointed out the insurgents' favorite locations. SFC Hanlin and SSG Tyner put the Gujers to work at the balloon yard while SFC Fulton retrieved a triwall of shoes and blankets that were donated to us by people back home. We had made arrangements to give it to a girl's high school in Asadabad before we departed. The rest of our troops started packing their gear for the flight home. The plan called for two chalks on CH-47s; the first group would be the SecFor platoon on Saturday followed by HQ and Ag on Sunday. The two chalks would meet up at Jalalabad then fly on to Bagram, then home. The next thing we heard was no CH-47; we were flying Molson. That was music to our troops' ears.

Things were progressing quite well at the balloon yard when the big guns started firing in support for troops in the Pech. A few minutes later an F-15 flew up the Kunar and banked into the Pech followed by a medivac and its Apache escort. The big guns went cold as another pair of Apaches flew up the Kunar and into the Pech. Soon we saw the medivac UH-60 circling around the FOB to land at our trauma center. The U.S. troops rescued a young teenage boy who was wounded when the insurgents initiated their ambush. Spc Larson saw the boy come in with wounds to his head and said it looked as if he was already posturing for death. The insurgents don't care who they maim or kill when they attack.

SFC Median came down to the balloon yard just as it was starting to sprinkle. There was an announced that everyone was leaving today on Molson. There was another major storm front coming in and Molson was kicking it in high gear to get two days worth of flying into one. SFC Fair and I took over with the Gujers while the rest of the troops turned in weapons and ammo. I went up to the flight line at 09:45 to see the SecFor section off. The big guns went hot again and starting pounding the Pech while the ANA was firing at the range. In the mists of the roar from the weaponry we heard a distinct boom followed by the incoming alarms. I ran back down to the balloon yard to check on the Gujers, but Ralphi, our interpreter, had already evacuated them into the mosque and was about to enter our bunker. He gave me a quick head count and I went into the TOC. Colonel Bargfrede was there with his team running the show as our sections called in head counts.

The first chalk of the Kunar ADT leaving Camp Wright for Jalalabad, the first leg of their journey home on a Molson Air Sikorsky S-61.

The all clear was given very quickly; we thought it must have been a false alarm. One of the teenage boys from Yarga Del found a part of an RPG and struck it with a rock causing it to detonate. The detonation is what caused the PRT to sound the incoming alarm. The boy was rushed to our trauma center for treatment. Spc Larson saw him on the way to surgery and noted that his knees looked like hamburgers.

I made sure the Gujers were okay as they came out of the mosque with the rest of the local nationals who sought refuge with them. The sprinkling turned into a heavy mist and then to very humid vapor. I returned to the flight line to see the SecFor off as the rain returned. Ten members of SecFor loaded up onto Molson's Sikorsky and took off for a two-night stay in Jalalabad.

I went back to the balloon yard and told the Gujers to clean up the job site and call it a day. We provided them with an early lunch in the Afghan Café and paid them their wages for the day. Laj Bar hit SFC Fair up for a second paycheck, then asked if he could bring more of his men down to work. We both told Laj Bar that he had been paid once and he needed to talk to Iowa if he wanted to alter our agreement. Both SFC Fair and I made it clear to Iowa that the U.S. doesn't owe Laj Bar or anyone from Woch Now any money and we haven't promised them anything more that Iowa needs to deliver. Iowa was already onto Laj Bar's game.

Just before SFC Hanlin and SSG Tyner left, the older men Hakim, Musafer, and Rasol from Woch Now said they would pray for their safe return home and thanked them for all that they had done for their village. Laj Bar didn't even say good bye. When I walked the twelve men from Woch Now to the gate the older men all shook my hand and said good bye. Laj bar wanted to know when I would replace is solar cell phone charger. I told him I wasn't going to do so and he walked away.

I went back up to the flight line to find the Ag section standing by for their Molson flight, which had been delayed due to bad weather in Jalalabad. It would be our last time together since we were all going back to Camp Atterbury at different times. SFC Hanlin called out "Name all of the famous people who died in plane crashes."

That was the game we played in the dark at FOB Fenty airfield in October waiting for our CH-47 flight to Camp Wright. We could still remember the night we arrived when we dog piled on top of our gear to keep it from blowing away. A year ago Camp Wright was all dirt roads and old bee huts. Now all of the roads on the FOB were paved solving the flooding and mud problems. We had a new sidewalk running around the back side of the FOB that doubled as a running trail, and new two story brick barracks. We even speculated, "whatever happened to Snoopy." Snoopy was one of our unofficial camp mascots. Tripod, the cat, was the other. Snoopy was a short haired dog of a caliber that had his own story.

Snoopy was found half dead trying to die because he was severely beaten by some Afghanis. The Special Forces that were assigned to the FOB found him while out on mission one night back in 2003. They brought him back to the base, gave him food and water. He continued to bleed out of his mouth for several days, then suddenly recovered.

Snoopy was quick to discern between Afghanis and Americans. He could spot an Afghani day or night before anyone else could. Soon Snoopy was going out on missions with the Special Forces and earning his keep. His greatest joy was riding on a four wheel ATV around post.

As the years progressed, troops came and went but snoopy remained. He was taken in by the "big gun" boys for a while. Snoopy loved being around the 155s when they were firing; he also liked going out to the range and being with the troops.

Not all Americans are good and Snoopy learned that the hard way one afternoon. There was a unit out at the range firing AT-4s and Snoopy was watching from the firing line. One soldier picked up an AT-4 and yelled out, "Watch this." He made sure Snoopy was in the back blast of the AT-4 and fired it. Snoopy let out a big yelp and ran back to base. Both of his ear drums were ruptured from the blast. Snoopy is now deaf, but we think some hearing has returned. It didn't take long for the boys at the big guns to bypass the UCMJ and commence judgment on Snoopy's attacker.

Snoopy recovered, but there were other Americans he had to worry about. There is a team in the Army that goes from post to post trapping animals and then shooting them. Snoopy's sponsors feared that with all of Snoopy's prowling around, he just might end up in one of the many traps. So they found a foster home for him down at FOB Fenty in Jalalabad. For Snoopy, Camp Wright was home not Jalalabad. Then before anyone knew what happened, Snoopy escaped from FOB Fenty and started for home. It took him four days to walk the 60 miles from Jalalabad to Camp Wright. It was an amazing little journey; the highway is very dangerous. The Kunar River that flows next to the highway is unforgiving in many places, and on top of it all, *how did he know the way home?*

Snoopy arrived at Camp Wright and a new group of Special Operations folks took him in. The animal trappers were not allowed inside their compound so Snoopy was safe just as long as he didn't try to escape. Snoopy was given an ID card just like an ANA (Afghan National Army) soldier. An ANA soldier's ID card has his photo and reads Name: Unescorted with weapon. That means the individual can go where ever he or she wants with a weapon. Snoopy's ID has his photo and reads: Name Snoopy; Unescorted with teeth.

Snoopy on the trial to OP Bull Run. October 2009, OP Shiloh can be seen in the distance. Photo by 1Lt Ko.

Snoopy would instantly attack any Afghani especially if there were Americans present. He feels an obligation to protect Americans. We were ordered to protect the Afghanis from Snoopy even if that meant shooting Snoopy. In the evening, Snoopy would come out to the blue gate when all of the Afghanis were off post and curl up on a chair to slumber the night away until he caught the whiff of an Afghani. Snoopy would be up with a start racing down the road to rid the camp of the unwelcomed interloper.

The Special Operations Forces came and went and Snoopy was adopted by another special group that decided to keep him locked up on the back side of the camp where there was a small green pasture and several other unofficial dogs. Snoopy was an escape artist and would frequently get loose. During one escape attempt, Snoopy was walking on Route California and was struck by a car. He was lying on the side of the road when a couple of Afghanis saw him and were attempting to pick him up. Snoopy took one look at the Afghanis and took off running. He had had enough of Afghan aid.

Somehow we lost Snoopy and Tripod during the summer 2010. Snoopy, who had escaped several times and was recaptured, finally got off post and was never seen again. Tripod started losing weight and refused to eat cat food. Troops started to set out chicken and tuna, but she refused that too. Finally one day she crawled under Bee Hut 20, her favorite hiding spot, and went to sleep.

Molson's Sikorsky finally arrived and we loaded up everyone's gear and they were off to Jalalabad lifting off at 1500. Col Bargfrede came up to the airfield to wish everyone safe travels home with me.

SFC Velasco was the last member of the ADT to leave on Saturday and would be arriving at 1600. I came back to the flight line at 15:45 to find SFC Mosqueda and SFC Velasco waiting for Molson. We heard the two set rotors working their way up the Kunar thinking it was Molson's Sikorsky, but instead it was a UH-60 medivac with its escort coming into Camp Wright. The young boy from Yarga Del had come out of surgery and was being sent to another facility for additional treatment. The two UH-60 landed and the a team from the trauma center came out carrying the boy on a stretcher with Chaplin Anderson at the front left and the surgeon at the front right. There was one ASG guard with them as they loaded the boy on the UH-60. The boy's father was escorted around the front of the helicopter and entered from the far side. Once again insurgent munitions caused harm to an innocent child.

Molson's Sikorsky was approaching just as the two UH-60s were preparing to take off. Molson swung our over the Kunar and flew a figure eight while the UH-60s took off for Jalalabad. Molson landed and shut off the engines to allow a forklift to safely remove several triwalls of mail before SFC Velasco would board. Soon the rotors were turning and the Sikorsky lifted off as a few of us assembled on the flight line to wave goodbye.

Sunday morning, the thick clouds completely covered the mountains as they were drawn down into the valley by the up draft of the warmer air coming off the Kunar. The weather didn't look good for Molson flights, but we stood at the airfield with great hopes. Flights from Jalalabad to Bagram were turned back in midstride due to foul weather and the flights north to Wright were postponed every thirty minutes. Finally at 11:40 Molson's Sikorsky landed and Spc Tanson loaded up to join the rest of the Ag section at FOB Fenty.

The fourteen of us left would help Iowa get up to speed with a left seat right seat ride of the battle space. The week of August 8th was their turn in the driver's seat with their troops expected to start arriving on Monday August 9th. Ramadan started on August 11 and concluded on September 10th. Ramadan occurs in the 9th month of the Islamic calendar from new moon to new moon. During this time people of the Islamic faith fast from sunrise to sunset; the fasting includes not drinking water. The purpose of Ramadan is to remind people what it feels like to be poor and hungry. However, the locals do cheat and eat and party time starts at sundown and ends at sunrise. No one is starving. This religious demand put the temperament of the locals on edge, putting it mildly. During the 2009 Ramadan, an Afghani police officer shot and killed a U.S. serviceman because he observed him drinking from his camel back during a patrol. The police officer was neutralized by the other U.S. troops in the area before he could kill any more Americans.

Chapter Forty-Eight

THE LEFT SEAT RIGHT
SEAT RIDE

Things were not going well for the rotation of both our sister ADT from Missouri and us. There was a major finger-pointing contest going on between Camp Atterbury and Brigade as to who was responsible for moving the replacement to Afghanistan. The bottom line: the main bodies of the ADT would not overlap as planned reducing the amount of historical information that could be passed along. Brigade came up with a plan that the main bodies would leave Afghanistan as scheduled and each ADT would leave behind a cadre to mentor the new ADTs

On July 26th, all of Iowa's Advon finally arrived at Camp Wright with each Molson flight. We had already given CSM Collins and Captain Birgy a hardy welcome by including them in a fire line of 100 sacks of cement. One of our remaining projects was to build a brick and mortar building in the balloon yard. This would be a learning project for the Gujers. Part of the project included pouring vertical concrete walls for a septic tank, the same construction techniques that would be required for a future cold storage project. The project doubled as part of the left seat right seat orientation for Iowa's Advon.

The concept of a left seat right seat is similar to riding in the front seat of a car while the driver shows you around town. After a while you trade places with the driver and the driver coaches you from the passenger seat. With the construction project in the balloon yard we showed the Iowa team how to receive deliveries, in-process local day labor through the gate, and everyone's favorite activity, payday.

We made everything look easy. SFC Fulton and SSG Tyner spent a fair amount of time planning the project with the support of Ralphi, our interpreter. When Monday morning came around, everything was in place waiting for the Gujers to arrive. SFC Hanlin supervised and coordinated the labor and SSG Tyner ran the job. SSG Tyner expected the Gujers to work at an American pace and led by example in 110-degree heat. At the end of the day it was time to pay the Gujers. We owed the Gujers a lot of money for casting 80 crib wall components, which Laj Bar asked me to keep a secret. I told Laj Bar that we had to tell all of the men how much we were paying and what it was for.

On the way out, LTC Stockfleth accompanied us to the ECP to say good-bye to the Gujers. He was expecting us to take all of them out of the personnel office and was surprised that we took them out the vehicle gate–just a little trick of the trade for safety. If we were to take the Gujers out the personnel office they would be searched twice by the Afghan ASG guards who would take note of thousands in Afghan currency then call their friends. By going through the vehicle gate they would be searched by a Pennsylvania guardsman who wouldn't draw attention to their payroll.

All payments must be conducted in private away from other Afghanis. Crime is a problem in Afghanistan as well as the Western world. Afghanistan doesn't lop off hands for crimes; they have prisons just like the rest of the world for the criminals they catch.

While we were showing LTC Stockfleth the ropes, the rest of the Iowa Advon was loaded up in our trucks for a trip to FOB Joyce. Major Leeney and SGT Martinez decided it was the perfect opportunity for the LMTV sea trials. During our VetCap era we were continually borrowing the PRT's LMTV with the big green box on the back, our rolling barn. Major Leeney found a LMTV that had sat idle for over a year and instructed SGT Martinez, our maintenance NCO, to bring it back to life. Soon SFC Fulton, SGT Stevens and Percival would join in the fun. At one point the LMTV was completely disassembled, spread across the shop and the welding yard blocked up on cribbing. A contract crew was brought in to rebuild the transmission, replace the windows, and the list went on and on. Several times it was driven around the FOB only to be returned to the shop. On July 26th we thought it was ready for a real road test. SFC Fulton and crew put it in line for the convoy to FOB Joyce. I watched it roll out the gate onto Route California at a whopping five mph. It didn't go much faster than that. The air system that kept the cab suspended above the motor went out so the cab rested on the motor the entire trip causing it to limp all the way to FOB Joyce and back.

While Iowa's Advon was making their way in to Camp Wright we were sending a team down range to handle shipping our equipment home. Monday at noon a Molson flight took SFC Natividad, SGT Olson and SPC Lopez down to FOB Fenty where they made sure our equipment was safe guarded and transferred to the fixed wing for a flight home. The next team to leave was SFC Graham and Major Leeney who set everything up for our arrival at Camp Atterbury. They flew out on August 1st.

Jamaluddin, an Afghan national who is on the USDA payroll, stopped by to talk about the Chowkay demo farm. Our friend, the Chowkay agricultural extension manager, was not giving up on having us pay for planting his farm. Jamaluddin pleaded his case, stating that he only needed 20 people one day to plant the demonstration farm in Chowkay. SFC Median and I didn't want to leave Iowa any open issues to deal with, so SFC Fair and I checked the books and we had some funds left. We agreed to pay 20 people one day's wage to plant the field. I asked Jamaluddin if there was anything else he needed to complete the project; the response was no. I left him to talk to LTC Stockfleth for a few minutes when SFC Medina called me back.

"Sir, Jamaluddin says it will take him two days to plant the field."

"Okay we'll pay two days." It didn't stop there. Two days turned into a request for three followed by "we need fertilizer." The USDA trained this guy right: keep asking for other people's money. I told Jamaluddin that he would receive a lump sum for the labor and it would be up to him to get the field planted.

"Oh sir what about the fertilizer?"

"Jamaluddin, how much do you need and how much will it cost me?" Jamaluddin thought for a moment and said, "2500 Afghanis per 50Kg sack." I told him I needed to make some phone calls and then grabbed SGT Flynn and had him call NATC to get a price delivered. I came back to Jamaluddin and asked if the price he quoted me was delivered to Chowkay; it wasn't. I knew it wasn't because the price he quoted me was less than half the going rate for fertilizer. I told him that we would purchase the fertilizer and deliver it to the demo farm. Jamaluddin looked heartbroken. I was certain that he would have just taken the money and put it in his pocket.

Earlier in the year we had given him a bicycle to get around town. He would still attempt to give me receipts for taxi trips to the FOB. When I'd tell him "no" he would give the receipts to our USDA rep who would attempt to get me to pay them. The answer was still no!

SFC Medina received word that the farmers in the upper Kunar River Valley started selling the Hybrid short corn seed on the local market for feed. The farmers planted the corn seed they were familiar with and sold the seed they were given. This was exactly what SGT Stevens said would happen. USDA strikes again. With that, farmers were once again paid by the battle space owners not to grow crops along the roadside.

On July 31st we took the Advon team from Iowa down to the demonstration farm in Chowkay. We showed them the basics and delivered the fertilizer to the extension manager's son. We decided not to have the fertilizer delivered directly to the extension manager because we couldn't trust him. By delivering the fertilizer ourselves; we could ensure it got to the farm. Unless we supervised the planting of the seed we couldn't guarantee that the fertilizer was ever applied. There was still a high probability that it would be sold, but at least the extension manager couldn't claim we never gave him any fertilizer.

August 1st 0805 Hrs Major Leeney, SFC Graham SFC Teso boarded Molson Air's Sikorsky 61 for Fob Fenty where they would link up with SFC Natividad and SPC Lopez. Spc Lopez would return to Camp Wright while Major Leeney would take the three NCOs back to Camp Atterbury to prepare for our return. After a few days travel they found themselves stuck at the Indianapolis airport for twelve hours waiting for someone from Camp Atterbury to pick them up.

Meanwhile we were starting to have problems with Laj Bar. On his last visit he asked us again to pay for nine days wages for his men because they worked on his property. We told him "no" in front of all of his men. Laj Bar then told his men that he would pay them all because it was his decision to have them work on his property, but all of the Co-Op equipment was his. I quickly axed that proposal and told the men that per the Co-Op agreement if the equipment belonged to the village and if the Co-Op was ever to go out of business then all of the equipment was to be sold and the money was to be given to the mosque. Then one of the men said well if the equipment belongs to us then let's sell it and get our wages out of it!

Oh boy, did we set up Iowa with a monster. I explained to the men that they would make a lot of money running the Co-Op. They just needed to run the business. We had lined up buyers for their product. The response was we don't want to run a business; we just want to show up for work and get paid. Then once again the subject of the nine days pay came up. I explained to them that they were to only build the retaining wall to five feet in height and the rest of the block we sent them was to build a second retaining wall to protect the road and their mosque. Laj Bar had the men build the concrete yard's retaining wall to a height of eight feet so he could convert it into a house fitting his stature as the up and coming village elder. Wow, Laj Bar learns quickly; using public funds to pay for personnel expenses–the anthem of a true socialist.

At this point I was no longer focused of trying to save the Co-Op. We invested months of our time and energy to make sure Iowa didn't have any lingering problems. I also wanted to reclaim the equipment and metal forms we had sent up to Woch Now. I presented a counter proposal to the men. "Gentlemen how about we go back to the old way of doing business? I will pay you for the nine days' work you did, and you bring the equipment back here." Everyone agreed and Laj Bar looked dumbfounded. During this heated debate, his father had taken him outside several times to straighten him out, to no avail. I went on to tell them that they would continue to make re-bar cages at their village in the concrete yard and we would take care of all equipment maintenance. They could expect several blue trucks to arrive at their village in the next few days for the equipment. When it was over, Laj Bar's father shook my hand, thanked me and breathed a sigh of relief. I asked Akim if it would be alright if I brought Iowa up for a visit and he suggested Thursday August 5th.

On Wednesday night Major Parmenter, Iowa's S-3, held Iowa's first operation brief for the trip to Woch Now Village. I suggested that they start early in the morning and the earlier the better. They took my advice.

During Major Parmenter's brief, LTC Lewis stated that we were just going to look at the crib wall and the orchard and come back. I piped up and said, "Sorry you're having a KLE with Laj Bar like it or not." LTC Lewis was under the impression that we could sneak into the orchard and leave because the orchard was short of the village. I explained that once you reach the crib wall the village will know you're on the way; when you step into the orchard the village will come to you and escort you to the mosque for tea. I could tell there was some frustration in the room.

Then Iowa's response came, "That's not what we were told would happen at Camp Atterbury." Sure enough the same group of Afghani nationals provided misleading information because Kunar was in the Pashto tribal area.

SFC Mosqueda started assembling his troops at 05:00 Thursday morning for a 6:30 departure. The trip to Woch Now was routine for us, but the left seat right seat ride required considerable instruction. There were many details that we learned to do second nature, such as movements, dealing with the locals, where to pay extra close attention for insurgents, etc. Iowa elected to drive up to Woch Now on the same road that Laj Bar said was impassable. I had already checked the road out and it looked good to me. Laj Bar was just trying to get out of returning our equipment.

The first stop was the crib wall check dam. It had held during two major rain storms and had successfully protected the road to Woch Now. The storms had made a cut through a large island in the dry river bed and deposited massive amounts of rock against the check dam. The check dame was under construction, but it still held. The large boulders we placed on the downstream side did a beautiful job at distributing the force of the water. The next stop was the orchard.

We walked from the check dam to the orchard while the trucks moved forward to take up over watch. Sure enough just as we entered the orchard Laj Bar arrived to greet Iowa. The next thing LTC Lewis knew he was being escorted up to the village for tea and cake. Instead of going to the mosque, LTC Lewis elected to go to the concrete yard across from the mosque. Laj Bar gave him a quick tour, then asked me if he could keep one concrete mixer so he could continue to work on the mosque. I told him that I needed both mixers back at Camp Wright and he reluctantly agreed.

Two blue trucks arrived while we were meeting with Laj Bar, once again demonstrating that the road was still trafficable. We parted from Laj Bar and the rest of the men from Woch Now and went back to Camp Wright. LTC Lewis had another meeting to attend at FOB Joyce. It took three trips to collect all of the equipment from Woch Now Village. Each time a load came down we would load the trucks with scrap lumber for the village. They could use the lumber for fuel and we could clean up a few more fire hazards around the FOB at the same time. The last truck arrived with Laj Bar and his men. We invited them in and paid them all for their labor while they ate lunch. It cost me just a few hundred dollars to recover $30,000.00 worth of forms and equipment. I never saw a group of men so happy to give back a lucrative enterprise. The forms and mixers were the result of several other crib-wall projects conducted with other FOBs. The other FOBs never had any real success getting their villagers to cast crib wall components so the equipment and forms were returned to us. We just used them for Woch Now Village. The problem the other FOBs ran into was lack of trained U.S. personnel who knew anything about concrete coupled with the fact that their villages wanted a magic wand solution and dollars to fall from the sky. At least we got some work out of Woch Now.

Chapter Forty-Nine

CERP AND MAAWS

Our left seat right seat ride was progressing at a good pace, until we hit the topic of finances. There were basically two types of funds the ADT would use: FOO (Field Ordering Officer) and CERP (Commander's Emergency Response Program). The ADT is a combat multiplier for the battle space owner's COIN (Counter Insurgency) fight. The ADT's primary weapons system uses CERP funds as ammo.

The concept of Money As A Weapon System (MAAWS) has been around for generations. If you can win the hearts and minds of the people over with a few dollars, then you have saved lives. There are many agencies that have MAAWS; they include the U.S. combat forces, State Department, USAID, USDA, and many non-governmental agencies that are funded by the United States tax payer either directly from the U.S. government or filtered through the United Nations.

CERP funds are used by the battle space owner, PRTs and the ADTs. These are ready cash funds that a commander can use to change the dynamics of the COIN. There are two distinct financial operations going on in Afghanistan, development and COIN. On the surface they appear to be the same but each has a specific goal. Electrical power can be either a development project or a COIN project depending on why it is implemented. For example, the 350 KW hydroelectric power plant uses water from an irrigation canal to power a small village. From a development prospective this 350 KW power generator will allow the village to run a small canning plant that purchases crops from local farmers. The results is lower food imports from Pakistan and the potential to export the product or meet off-season nutritional needs of the Afghanis. From a COIN perspective the same 350 KW power generator would allow the villagers to install floodlights to illuminate their village and hillsides increasing their security and reducing their chance of being targeted by the insurgents.

Another example would be paying farmers to grow timber seedlings along the roadside. The development project goal would be reforestation and a renewed timber industry. From a COIN standpoint it reduces the concealment available to the insurgents to initiate close ambushes on convoys.

Both COIN and development projects if properly orchestrated will improve the local and regional economy reducing Afghanistan's dependence on Pakistan. This is something Pakistan is against for many reasons including, ethnic control, unifying the pre 1895 Islamic empire, and the balance of trade.

Quick reaction CERP projects are usually under $5,000.00. For projects over $5000.00 there is a lengthy process for securing the funds. Typical quick reaction projects include installing piping for a water system, village poultry, veterinary services, and a small-scale irrigation system. Midscale projects that are supervised at the battle space owner level may include building a veterinary clinic, village flood control, and establishing a new business such as crib wall manufacturing. Large scale projects at the PRT level can be a school but tend to be transportation orientated such as roads and bridges. Roads and bridges can be both a development and a COIN project. Roads and bridges improve the economy, but they also allow the government to rapidly move troops and resources to defend the border and to react to insurgent attacks.

The challenge to all projects is to make sure the project remains the property of the community. Afghanis will sign any agreement if they think it will get them what they want. Under their moral absolutes it is acceptable to lie to an infidel, aka Christian. Under the rules of CERP money can't be used to directly benefit an individual. We were careful to establish small co-ops for orchards and to make sure that landowners signed written agreements with the Afghan government's agriculture extension manager about the use of their land, before starting a project. Unfortunately even with the best safeguards in place dishonest people can still prevail.

The first case of fraud we heard about was with cold storage projects. Typically a land owner would agree in writing to donate a section of his land for a community cold storage project. After the project was completed the landowner would announce that the cold storage unit was his property not the village's knowing full well that it would be next to impossible to repossess the subterranean cold storage unit. In another case a village wanted a community slaughterhouse that was built on donated land. The slaughterhouse was converted into a carwash and people continue to butcher their animals on the street.

There is a massive amount of U.S. tax payer money flowing into Afghanistan. The U.S. Army maintains very tight control and oversight of the funds used in the battlefield. When something goes wrong such as a dishonest contractor, word is quickly put out so the same people can't swindle the American public a second time. Usually the only recourse when a contractor takes off with the money is to prevent them for doing any future business with the U.S.

From time to time the news media will do a piece on military spending in Afghanistan that is askew from the truth. The U.S. Army foots the bill for many of the other government agencies, a fact the media fails to observe. One example: a State Department rep has a meeting to attend at a district center. The U.S. Army provides the transportation and security for the meeting. At a minimum, there would be four MRAPS and a security detachment. From a business stand point the MRAPS and troops are a sunk cost of the operations, however the personnel and transportation assets could be used for something else such as providing security for the construction of a key bridge. Then the sunk cost is offset by the lost construction time and the additional costs charged by the contractor to the U.S. for having personnel and equipment on standby.

The USDA sends contract employees to the FOBs to either run their own programs or to support battle space owners. When there is an ADT in the area they will often partner with the ADTs. Some USDA contractors become part of the ADT staff; others attempt to make the ADT subservient to their desires. When we first arrived in Afghanistan we were told that the USDA didn't resource their personnel with funding, equipment, or other materials and that they were on their own. Later after LTC Velte moved to the brigade we learned that the USDA did resource their personnel with funding and their reps needed to do the proper paper work to access the funds. Some of these USDA reps prided themselves by stating they had established several orchards without expending any funds. What occurred: the ADT established an orchard and demonstration farm with CERP funds and the USDA rep took credit for it.

The USAID rep attempted several times to have the Kunar ADT engineer, fund, and manage construction projects within view of Route California strictly for the photo opportunity. It is very difficult for the general public to know who funded and managed a project from a photo. The most heavily guarded secrets are the contracts the NGOs are given by U.S. government organizations. Even searching the Internet doesn't reveal much other than the title of the contract. The titles are very deceiving.

At one meeting, the USAID rep bragged that his jobs program had created over 300 jobs in Asadabad. These jobs were sweeping the streets in the morning with tree branches. By the next morning the process started all over. When the PRT or ADT commits to a project they must show tangible results, such as 25 miles of road constructed and paved; construction of a flood water retention dam with a holding capacity of three-acre feet.

For COIN and development projects to be successful they must be sustainable by the Afghanis after the U.S. departs. A temporary jobs program may keep 300 would-be insurgents occupied for 90 days, but it does nothing to advance the local economy. Since 90% of the insurgents are foreign fighters, the argument of keeping insurgents off the battlefield with "make work" jobs is void. The construction of a citrus packing house coupled with the planting of two sections of citrus would employ more people annually and create a demand for other services such as machinery mechanics, which would be sustainable with the revenue generated by product sales.

The Afghanis know that the U.S. will not stay forever and are just looking to grab as much cash as they can to meet immediate needs and desires. For the most part Afghanis do not plan for the future. The Enshalla (Allah willing) mentality dominates their thinking. We witnessed it first hand with the village of Woch Now. After setting them up with all the equipment and training to manufacture and build crib walls they walked away from the enterprise. The Gujers were so indoctrinated with communism and living hand to mouth they were blind to the greater opportunity of running their own company. They could have made more money managing their own business, but they preferred to work for someone else at a lower wage.

President Obama has stated that the U.S. will be pulling out of Afghanistan in the near future. If Afghanistan is going to become an active participant in the global marketplace then some key major infrastructure projects must get underway while U.S. forces are in the region providing stability and actively fighting a counter insurgency. Short-term COIN projects are the keys to maintaining local security while major projects are constructed.

Some of the major NGOs refuse to work with the military on major development projects stating that people die if the military shows up. This argument doesn't hold any water. I've researched these claims and have found very few reports of targeted violence against people working for NGOs. Violence is usually connected with an Afghan government official who has failed to receive a demanded kick back from a contract. In which case these corrupt government officials reach out to their insurgent friends to inflict violence. The real reason NGOs and other government agencies don't want the military near their project is accountability. The U.S. military is a disinterested third party, which writes daily reports on their observations during patrols and KLEs. If a project was never completed it will be reported, not something you want if you're in the process of deceiving the public.

After several NGOs declined to take on an irrigation canal project from Marawara to Sarkani, I was asked to look at the project. The easy part of the project was the route of the canal the challenge was too many organizations wanting to be involved. The USAID rep at Camp Wright was extremely opposed to the project stating it required blasting. I checked the route out with my geologist and there weren't any locations that required blasting. Even if blasting was required it is a very simple process. The State Department contract representative wanted the whole project constructed by hand to create the most jobs. The Kunar Ag minister wanted 20% of any contract associated with the canal. What stopped the project was the people couldn't agree on land issues and water rights. This canal was not a simple trenching project. There were over 28 natural dry creeks that had to be crossed with elevated structures, which would require abutments and other structural requirements. I was even told that heavy construction equipment was not available in Kunar.

The lack of heavy construction equipment is another myth presented by the media, U.S. government organizations and NGOs. There is an abundance of heavy construction equipment and trained operators. It only took a few weeks of getting orientated to the Kunar area for me to make all of the right heavy equipment contacts. Just about any piece of equipment can be on a job site in 24 hours.

Finding trained equipment operators is not difficult, but finding qualified engineers is. In Afghanistan anyone who walks across the border and can operate a computer is an engineer. Most people who call themselves engineers in Afghanistan only know how to build rock and concrete walls.

Major infrastructure projects would best be constructed by U.S. or Western European firms if they are to be successful.

Chapter Fifty

ENGINEERING PROCUREMENT AND CONSTRUCTION & ENGINEERING ETHICS

An engineer shall hold paramount the safety, health, and welfare of the public in the performance of his professional duties.

During my final week in Afghanistan with Iowa we went out to the Kala Kowchano Valley to look at the check dam that was under construction. Two storm systems had just passed through the area pushing an enormous amount of water down the valley. The check dam held even though it was under construction. It even protected the road to Woch Now, which surprised me. Another surprise was the amount of rock that had moved down the dry river during the storm. My replacements started asking questions about the project and construction techniques. I had to keep explaining that we were in Afghanistan, not the U.S. and designs and construction operations must be developed with local technology and materials in mind.

There are many challenges to building projects in Afghanistan. The key is to always keep in mind the standards and ethics that American engineers adhere to. The problems and obstacles encountered in Afghanistan are the same in nature that are found anywhere else but they are more flagrant with increased intensity.

I started in Engineering Procurement and Construction (EPC) in Mexico working in the citrus industry. We had the best structural designs available, but maintaining quality construction was very challenging due to the level of craftsmanship and the graft. The same holds true in Afghanistan, in fact there is very little difference between Mexico and Afghanistan. Both countries have a major insurgency going on, same work ethic and government corruption.

After working with Afghan contractors, the U.S. State Department, U.S. Aid for International Development, U.S. Department of Agriculture and several non-governmental agencies, I have decided never to release a drawing of any type. When structures fail, investigators will look at the engineer for accountability, not the people who circumvented the engineer's authority, which ultimately caused the structural failure.

The security environment of Afghanistan prevents sudden unexpected inspections or continuous monitoring of a construction site without committing large amounts of resources at great expense. The contractors know this and take full advantage of it, just like in the United States, when a contractor will make a major pour on a weekend without telling the engineer and then provide questionable test cylinders. In the States, it's no problem. I'll just core the pour and make my own cylinders or make them demo the slab.

In Afghanistan concrete is a premium product and the Afghans use it sparingly. This is why they prefer rock and concrete walls. Rocks are cheap and so is sand. The sand that is available in Afghanistan will not come close to meeting any ACI standards. It's all dug out of the river full of silt. In some cases they dig it out of the mountainside, which is mixed with earth. On one job site the contractor mixed ten parts of sand to one part cement and sprinkled some rocks in the mix. When SSG Tyner scooped up a handful of two-day-old concrete in his hand the contractor told us to come back in a week because it was slow cure concrete. I told him to dig it all out and re-pour it with the mix design I specified in the contract. He responded, "If Allah wills it, it will be done."

" Then if Allah wills it I'll pay you, but right now I'm not paying you."

The quality of cement that is available in Afghanistan is always suspect. I specify "Lucky" concrete, which is supposed to be the best. However not all Lucky concrete is the same. The fine print on the bag says it all.

"Made in Pakistan," means it meets Pakistan's standards.

"Made in Pakistan for export," means it shouldn't be used in Pakistan because it didn't meet the standard.

"Made in Pakistan for export to Afghanistan only," means something went very wrong with this batch.

Elephant brand cement is the lowest quality cement that is exported to Afghanistan.

On important jobs I will provide the cement and spray paint the bags. I will issue the bags out based upon the construction schedule. I use a modified version of RSMeans (a 30-city national average reference manual for construction cost in the United States) to project construction time, which includes the Afghan factor of, "Pray, socialize, rest" five times a day if the Americans are watching. I require the empty bags to be returned before I issue more cement. This is far from being a foolproof system for QA, but it makes it just a little more difficult for contractors to be dishonest. When we drive through town I can spot concrete bags with our paint marks on them. That means that the contractors either reduced the amount of cement in the mix and sold the excess, or exchanged the higher quality cement for elephant cement and pocketed the difference. With this system, the contractor would have to trade un-bagged cement, which would be a mess. The other trick is to reduce the amount of concrete in total by dropping large rocks and boulders into the pour. This trick is usually easy to catch. Few contractors will vibrate their pour, and when they throw large rocks into the pour they are usually the nice round river rocks. The end result is voids around the rocks that are easily spotted even if they fill in the voids with mortar. The other give away is the nice round rocks just don't grab the concrete so large chunks will break free when the pour is slightly stressed.

If properly supervised concrete pours can be made of adequate quality even when using river sand. The key is to make sure they follow the mix design. I wouldn't trust the concrete for any major structure, but for 90% of the projects it holds up just fine. We cast some concrete beams using low-grade Pakistani re-bar that held up under the weight of an MRAP after curing for 28 days. We selected an MRAP as our test fixture because the crib wall components were going to be used as part of a road that would be supporting MRAPs.

Humble thievery doesn't stop at the sleight of hand tricks with concrete. The Afghanis are just as adapt at performing disappearing magic tricks with re-bar as they are with concrete. My team of Sgt Flynn, Stevens and Percival had completed several watershed and flood control engineering studies. USAID decided that they would fund the flood and erosion control aspect of one water shed project and sent a contractor to me for the engineering. USAID was using this contractor for a minor public make-work job of sweeping the streets of Asadabad with tree branches every day. Now this same firm was going to tackle a large construction project.

I met with three men who all introduced themselves as civil engineers. Most engineers in Afghanistan have only a 12th grade education at best. Some have received formal training in India or Pakistan. These are usually men from prominent families. Formal engineering education has no bearing on the competency of the individual. In the United States we require a P.E. license to weed out the graduates from the diploma mills. I met some self-taught engineers in Afghanistan who were very astute in horizontal construction, and I've met engineers with formal training who couldn't use a can opener if they were starving to death.

My meeting with the three civil engineers that USAID had contracted to build 78 flood control structures in the Kala Kowchano Valley didn't start well. I pulled out the master plan showing the whole valley and walked them over to a point where I had painted 3+00 on a rock wall. I told them this is where the last structure in the survey starts at the road 0+00. They looked at me as if I was from Mars. One of them reached into his pocket and pulled out a GPS and said we wanted to give us this. I told them that their GPS was only good up to 27 feet; they needed to use a tape. That discussion didn't go far. The next topic was the construction of the check dams. I showed them a drawing with the re-bar details, which included the size of each re-bar, and the foundation depth. I took the time to go over the drawing with them. They asked if they could build the check dam out of rock and concrete. I asked them, "Will you use re-bar?" I couldn't get a straight answer out of any of them. I told them the design would change if they were not going to use re-bar. I knew they were not going to use re-bar. The typical Afghan approach for building a rock and concrete wall is to build it in four-foot lifts with a smooth cap of cement mortar with one rock sticking up every ten feet to key into the next lift. They understand that the wet mortar can only support so much weight so they stop at four feet of elevation.

Usually on the job site they will have a pile of #4 re-bar, but nothing in the pour. It is all for show, just like contractors in the U.S. who will pull the re-bar out of a slab if the owner isn't around right after the inspector leaves. The Afghans don't even bother installing it in the first place. Changing of the re-bar size is another common trick. Smaller re-bar will be used at the bottom of the pour with the large size on top. The same technique is used in concrete; water and sand are used on the bottom and concrete is used for the top three inches. The quality of the re-bar is always in question. It is next to impossible to trace from where it originated. Afghanistan doesn't make re-bar; the bulk of it comes from Pakistan. Every now and then there might be a load from Russia, which is pretty good. The re-bar from Pakistan is not consistent. Some have a high carbon content and others are contaminated with other recycled metals. Some of the re-bar can be bent by hand, others must be bent using hydraulics and often will fracture.

The Afghan contractor is not the only entity that raises concerns for an engineer. The State Department and USAID will also attempt to dictate design and construction techniques for their own agenda. USAID and its NGO contractor IDEA New wanted all of the check dams that would be installed to be made out of gabions. Gabions are just wire baskets that hold rocks. Both had their own reason. IDEA New wanted to start a backyard gabion business for local women and saw erosion control projects as an ideal market. USAID wanted to use gabions because it would create the most manual labor jobs and take a very long time to complete. USAID stated that they would not fund any flood control or erosion control project that wasn't 100% gabion. This was one of the reasons they backed out of the Kala Kowchano Valley project.

Gabions are one of many tools in the flood and erosion control toolbox. Concrete and rock retaining walls have their place, just like crib walls, earth dykes, and riprap; each have a specific place and purpose. I showed Mr. USAID photos of gabion baskets still intact, which were orientated with the flow of a dry river and more than 300 meters from their original location. This didn't change the position of USAID. Bottom line: government and non-government agencies could care less about flood or erosion control. They only want their programs to continue.

Most of the watersheds I have surveyed can only make used of a few gabion structures; the rest must be built of reinforced concrete in order to deal with the forces encountered with heavy flooding.

Changing of priorities is just as damaging to a project as alternate political and business agendas. Even if the contractor is above board using the highest quality materials available there is still the possibility that funding for the project will be terminated. Projects can be abruptly terminated for several reasons. The most legitimate is the security in the area has diminished to the point where the contractor's life and the lives to the community members near the job site are in danger. The usual cause is the contractor's refusal to pay off the insurgents or government officials. Many of the government officials are friends with both sides and make good use of insurgents to do their dirty work. The deal is, pay for protection. A bribe to the district sub-governor will ensure that the police will not rob the job site. Refuse to pay the bribe? Then expect an attack by the insurgents, or expect harassment by the police. This is a very predictable scenario because this has been the norm in Afghanistan for centuries.

Projects that are taken over by U.S. government agencies such as USAID are more likely to be terminated after a career or political goal is reached. USAID had agreed to contract three flood control project sites in the central Kunar River Valley of their choosing if the ADT would do the engineering. All of the project sites that were selected by USAID were located along the main highway where they could be photographed. Our USAID's representative's plan was to start the project at the road working both up and downstream, take some project photos, then stop the project. The funding agency, not the engineer, has final control over the contract development, which includes the sequence of work. The funding agency can dictate in the contract where the contractor will break ground. This sets up any village, farm or people for disaster. It would be safer never to build the structures in the first place. Flood control structures need to be started at the headwaters where the flow is the smallest.

The only time an engineer should design a flood control system is when he will have direct control of the design and construction of the project from start to finish.

Changes in leadership also affect projects. Usually when leadership changes priorities there is plenty of notice to prepare. Leaders who are making rational calculated decisions will listen to what the second and third order affects are to cancelling a project in midstream. Unless there is a major degradation in the level of security or a sudden shift in the local Afghan government the command will let a project be completed as planned. The problem comes from commanders who panic over the scale of the project and fear that if the project fails it could adversely affect their career, or they cannot see past their ego. These types of commanders not only cause accounting and contract problems, but they also put the public safety at risk from uncompleted flood control projects.

Land ownership is another hidden dragon that will raise its head when least expected. Before a project is undertaken all of the stakeholders must sign an agreement. Since most people in Afghanistan are illiterate; they put their thumbprint on any document if they think they will get an instant reward. Once they understand the project they will attempt to renegotiate the terms. A landowner downstream may refuse to let construction personnel cross his property, or another may refuse to let a structure be built on his property. This also impacts the safety of the project by not completing the structures in the correct location or in a timely manner before the next rainy season.

Theft is another factor the engineer has no control over. Structures must be designed to be theft proof. Gabion baskets and riprap are ready sources of rock for market. When construction is complete and all of the flood control structures are in place along with 500 gallon water tanks to provide water to erosion control trees, it will only stay in place as long as all of the property is in the sights of a rifle. Small rocks are sold to rock crushing plants, larger rocks are sold for wall construction etc. Gabions should only be used to protect personal property because the property owner has a vested interest in maintaining the gabions. Setting gabions and riprap in concrete to prevent theft defeats the purpose of having a porous structure.

For an ADT to run any type of major construction project would be counterproductive to its mission. It would also be in poor judgment to hand over an engineering package to any other agency and expect that it would be properly constructed. The best approach is to focus on small flood and erosion control projects that can benefit villages of 25 families or less. Small-scale projects that are undertaken by villagers have the highest chance of success because the villagers have a vested interested in maintaining the structures.

When projects reach the district level there is less community buy in and oversight. The bridges that have been built are of questionable integrity and in many cases their location inaccessible. There is no eminent domain in Afghanistan. Irrigation canals, roads and bridges are placed according to property rights not where they would best serve the general welfare of the public. Bridge projects are usually constructed by firms from Pakistan using labor from Pakistan. If the local villagers can't be employed working on a project they will not support it. It is the villagers who provide the QA/QC on projects. Since there is so much corruption with major contracts, usually the poorest materials and construction practices are used. The quality of concrete is a given, but contractors will not sink caissons down to the bedrock or to a depth that is not affected by scouring and can withstand the overturning movement of the force of the river.

I was asked to evaluate the structural integrity of a bridge from Chowkay to Klas Kunar that spans the Kunar River. I was handed the blue prints for the Klas Kunar Bridge that spans over the Kunar River. The plans were very basic and left a fair amount of design to the contractor. The blue prints provided the overall dimensions of the bridge structure, but not the re-bar details, the concrete mix or anything else. There was no documentation or photos taken during construction that I could use. The only thing I have observed is units send one MRAP over the bridge at a time and the bridge was still standing. I told everyone since the bridge is built there is no way I could evaluate the plans or really determine the quality of construction.

I've learned that the Afghans can't read even simple drawings; everything must be a template. I asked our civil affairs folks how the contractors were able to build schools if they couldn't read blue prints. The answer was they keep using the same group of contractors and they don't change the design. The first school was a learning project build with a lot of mentoring by U.S. forces. For new projects you are only going to get what the contractor knows how to build. If you ask for a chain link fence you are going to get a rock and concrete wall.

The Kunar ADT selected the villages of Woch Now and Arga Del to be the demonstration sites for flood, and erosion control. This will allow us the opportunity to set up a Co-Op to manufacture crib wall components, construct various types of flood and erosion control structures and most of all improve the quality of life for two villages. The Afghan people will only attempt something new when they see it being successful.

Chapter Fifty-One

NOT ALL WHO WANDER ARE LOST

When I first read the Hobbit, the quote, "Not all who wander are lost," forever stayed in the back of my mind. Our deployment was drawing to an end with fewer and fewer missions to deal with as we completed our open projects. Our replacements from Iowa were slowly finding their way to Camp Wright. They joined us one evening in the barn while we recalled some of our adventures. In ten months we had managed to wander all over the Pech and Kunar River Valleys for one reason or another.

SFC Fair was our first vagabond to wonder about and get a look at Pakistan. SFC Fair had been loaded out to Task Force Chosen's 1-32nd Infantry several times, and never knew just what he was getting into each time he fell in with Chosen. During his first trip with an MRAP crew from our SecFor, he served as a subject matter expert for highway construction, a subject far away from his area of expertise. He was expecting a long uncomfortable ride in an MRAP over open country, but instead he was air inserted into the Mollagur Valley, along with SPC Coffman, due to inaccessibility by vehicle.

Task Force Chosen's mission was to get all seven villages in the Mollagur Valley to agree upon a road construction project that would link their villages to the government center in Jalalabad in Afghanistan and to the community of Shaunkai in Pakistan. The Shaunkai pass is a trade route used by smugglers and insurgents. Shaunkai Pass is the gateway to the Mollagur Valley, which converges with the Chowkay Valley at the Kunar River. The Chowkay Valley shares the headwaters with the Korengal Valley. The Korengal Valley is a tributary to the Pech River. When we first arrived both the Chowkay and Korengal Valleys were hot beds of insurgent activity. After the U.S. pulled out of the Korengal Valley it became an operation base for the insurgents.

There were several reasons for building a two-lane highway through the Mollagur Valley. The first was to head off weapons smuggling. With a two-lane highway, an ABP station could be stationed and supported there. The secondary effect would be a reduction of traffic on Afghan Highway One from Jalalabad to Pakistan.

Task Force Chosen and SFC Fair hiked a circuit of 20 km during the course of the day to convince all of the villages to sign an agreement to allow the road to be built. The villagers were extremely hesitant to sign the agreement. They knew that roads meant access in both directions, their people could travel faster to other regions, but outsiders could invade, rob, and loot their villages faster too.

Seven shuras and several pots of tea later, the team was finally looking over the Shaunkai Pass down at the community of Shaunkai in Pakistan, their turn around point to move back to the LZ. Construction of the road would take place once the bridges over the Kunar were in place.

A shura with village elders and Afghan Border Police on the Duran line. Photo SFC Fair collection

The next time SFC Fair was OPCONed to task force Chosen he had his own 1151 HMMWV and crew. The morning of December 8th SFC Fair and crew waited at the entrance road of Camp Wright for Charlie Company 3rd Bn. 1-32 Infantry 10th Mountain Division to drive by on Route California on their way up to the village of Lachay. Lachay is located in the Snigal Valley north west of Asmar. The crew of SPC Tanson-Driver, SFC Fair TC, SFC Natividad Gunner, SSG Tyner Left rear, SGT Percival right rear fell in as the third vehicle with Charlie Company as they passed the entrance of Camp Wright. SFC Natividad was swinging in the gunner's seat. It was a trapeze swing that works well on a smooth paved road but quickly becomes a hindrance when having to traverse the turret in combat. On either side of the gunner's seat is a red tab that a crew member can pull to release the seat to either clear it from the gunner or drop the gunner down into the vehicle if wounded.

Thirty minutes later the convoy turned off route California at Mora for the Snigal Valley. They passed five villages on their way to Lachay for the Shura. Along the route were several known ambush sites. At 1455 hrs. near the village of Ghanikac the insurgents commenced their ambush on the convoy. SFC Natividad called out the first contact, "RPG 50 meters 8 O' Clock!" The next RPG was fired at a distance of 100 meters accompanied by SAF (Small Arms Fire) from both the front and rear of the convoy. The first RPG flew over the vehicle behind them and impacted on the road rocking their 1151. SFC Natividad swung his .50 cal turret around to the rear where the two closest insurgents were, one standing who had just fired an RPG, the other prone firing his RPK, at the Charlie Company's MRAP behind them, who engaged his .50 cal and eliminated them both.

SFC Fair reported the contact up to Chosen 3 (Major Horrigan) on the radio and told SPC Tanson to continue to move forward slowly so they would not bunch up. SSG Tyner started handing ammo up to SFC Natividad while SGT Percival pulled the gunner's seat out and started clearing the hot brass and links away from SFC Natividad's feet. SFC Fair was calling out distance and direction of more insurgents firing RPGs at the MRAP in front of them. The RPGs missed striking the road seven meters in front of their vehicle.

Events were happening fast. In just 200 meters of travel the insurgents were raining the convoy with RPGs and SAF. The insurgents were firing indiscriminately at the moving vehicles. The convoy commander called a short halt so the gunners could better engage the insurgents. SFC Natividad started to engage the target 200 meters away that the led vehicle had engaged before. They went around the bend in the road. More RPGs were being fired from the hillside in front of them, which skipped down the slope impacting the outcropped boulders near the road. SFC Fair called out, "RPGs again," while SGT Percival untangled SFC Natividad's headset. SFC Natividad swung around to engage when an RPG round whizzed over his head and impacted the rock face 20 meters beside him. He could barely breathe when he heard SFC Fair yell to get the 50 back in action. SGT Percival pulled his gloves off and started checking SFC Natividad for wounds. SFC Natividad pulled the empty ammo can off. While hanging the next box of ammo he spotted another insurgent charging his RPK, taking aim at him and opening fire on SFC Natividad. In one continuous movement SFC Natividad ducked into the turret, pulled out his M-4 and shot the insurgent. The MRAP gunner to their rear, followed SFC Natividad's traces and opened up with his M-240 ensuring that the insurgent was out of the fight.

If time were measured in heartbeats, then the short halt of a few seconds lasted hours. SFC Fair called back to SSG Tyner and SGT Percival and had them check SFC Natividad again for wounds. The convoy started rolling again. The road made a turn through a draw, then a left hand turn climbing up a visually obscuring rise. SFC Natividad still holding his M-4 spotted several more insurgents and opened fire on them at a range of 75 meters. SFC Natividad finished reloading the .50 cal as the convoy finally broke contact and moved out of the kill zone. SFC Fair conducted a LACE (Liquids-Ammo-Causalities-Equipment) review and called it up to Chosen Three. They were blessed with no injuries.

An hour later the convoy arrived at the village of Lachay for their scheduled Shura. SFC Fair, SSG Tyner and SGT Percival dismounted with the Chosen KLE (Key Leader Engagement) team and started their two kilometer hike to the village leaving SPC Tanson, and SFC Natividad with the 1151. While the dismounts were moving to the village, the convoy commander started turning the vehicles around in preparation for their return to base. SFC Fair and SSG Tyner each carried M-14s with 3.5X10 power scopes. The M-14s were pulled from the state's honor guard, but then looked like EBRs with their extensive modification. The M-14 is a very good weapon compared to the M-4, which is prone to double feeding. My M-4 must be cycled by pulling back the charging handle after each round is fired even after the bolt was rebuilt. Other units have the new M1-10 or the proven M-1 Grand for the extra distance.

By 1630 the Shura was over and the KLE team was preparing to return to the trucks. The KLE team was moving in the dry riverbed when the boom of RPGs echoed down the valley followed by the sound of SAF. SFC Fair, SSG Tyner and SGT Percival took up positions behind some boulders in the riverbed. The insurgents were well outside the range of their weapons, but with the scopes on the M-14s they could observe and track the insurgents. SFC Fair and SSG Tyner would call out their sighting and SGT Percival would relay the information to the convoy commander MSG Roome for fire support. The insurgents were firing a recoilless rifle at the parked vehicles.

SFC Natividad noted that the fire was coming from the convoy's rear in the northwestern hill tops about 1000 meters across the valley from them. There were more explosions to the south of the convoy as the gunners started to scan the high ground. Six RPGs volleys came streaming across the sky toward the convoy from multiple positions across the valley to their north. Three of the RPGs landed around the convoy while the other three RPGs rained upon the ANA vehicles that were staged behind the convoy to the west. The MRAP gunners engaged the launch positions individually while SFC Natividad engaged the dismounted insurgents who were getting ready to fire RPGs from the valley below.

SPC Tanson started calling out distance and direction while moving the vehicle back and forth. The attack suddenly stopped for a moment. SFC Natividad placed his binoculars on top of the .50 cal and started scanning the northern terrain features. He saw a flash and yelled out "RPG! RPG! Coming our way, brace yourself!" He fired back with a long 20-round burst at the firing position. The RPG that was coming directly at them fell short and detonated on the cliff face supporting the road. The other MRAP gunners keyed in on the RPG gunner and engaged him at 1000 meters.

SFC Fair, SSG Tyner and SGT Percival were still in the riverbed with the KLE team calling in the locations of the insurgents. The Task Force Chosen's NCOIC, MSG Roome was adjusting fire based upon the information they were providing. Soon two OH-58s Kiowas who had joined the fight suppressed the insurgents with .50cal and 2.75 inch rockets. Insurgents often exclaim that it is very "unfair" for us to use the Kiowas.

The insurgents cut their losses and broke contact as the shades of nautical sunset were darkened by the western mountain shadows that impeded the remaining daylight. The insurgents knew that that darkness didn't favor them as the U.S. troops started preparing for night operations. The insurgents had at the most fifteen minutes of useable daylight left. The moon was in its last quarter, which meant near complete darkness in the hills. The Kiowas continued to orbit the battlefield while the KLE team moved the two kilometers through the dry riverbed to the trucks.

With everyone accounted for, the convoy moved out in total darkness. The remaining insurgents returned later to treat their wounded and collect their dead, a task they would complete by first light. It was not by chance the insurgents selected the date and location of their ambush. When the Shura was scheduled someone among the village elders or government officials informed the insurgents.

Chapter Fifty-Two

SILVER WINGS TO CAMP ATTERBURY

Our main body was still at FOB Fenty Jalalabad going nowhere fast, including our cargo and pallet riders, SFC Natividad and Sgt Olson. Getting home isn't that easy; there are many parts that must move like a Swiss watch. Our Swiss watch came in a do-it-yourself kit with no instructions.

SFC Fair and I left SFC Medina and SFC Mosqueda at Camp Wright with a small selection of SecFor to finish off the left seat right seat ride with Iowa. SFC Medina continued to assist the senior staff while SFC Mosqueda worked with the SecFor. Our sister ADT from Missouri were doing the same down at Jalalabad.

The morning of our flight the big guns were laid on for the Badel valley near Chowkay just sitting idly waiting for the call for fire. The 101st was going to clean out some of the insurgents who had been attacking one of the O.P.s and had all of the big guns in the area at the ready for support. Within the hour the big guns of Camp Wright were lobbing 155 rounds down on Badel in support of the troops. Soon a convoy pulled in with wounded from an ambush just north of FOB Fortress.

While we were assembling our main body of troops down at FOB Fenty, the Missouri ADT was doing the same from FOB Finley Shields for their flight to Bagram. For the first time in almost three years the insurgents made a direct attack on FOB Finley Shields. None of the Missouri ADT troops were hurt. Since they had just arrived at FOB Fenty once again they missed out on their CABs. There was a running joke between the two ADTs that if you wanted your CAB, go visit the Kunar ADT. One Missouri soldier even joked that he would reenlist if he could stay with the Kunar ADT so he could win his CAB. At the time of our departure only two members of the Missouri ADT had received their CAB, which they won when visiting another unit. Kunar was branded the Wild, Wild West for a reason: lots of hot lead.

SFC Fair and I arrived at FOB Fenty, unloaded our gear at the PAX terminal and signed up for Space A (Available) to Bagram. The PAX terminal is the hub of activity for all of the non-residents; wait there long enough you'll meet everyone. The PAX terminal had been expanded since we first arrived in October '09 with the addition of several large ramadas and cargo bins. The beheos were packed so SFC Fair and I camped out in the cargo bin with our gear. SFC Fulton was the first to arrive and announced that Laj Bar was still calling him every morning asking if there was any work. SFC Natividad showed up next. He felt like a resident of FOB Fenty since he had been stuck there for two weeks trying to get our cargo out.

Molson made a roll call announcement for the 1300 flight to Bagram. SFC Fair went into the PAX terminal to vouch for us, while I watched the weapons. He came back with the sad news that we had been bumped, but we were on the 1400 flight. Our challenge was the fixed wing flight to Bagram. Our main body was full so we couldn't travel with our main body.

Since we had some more time I decided to check in with LTC Velte who would be the last member of our unit to come home. The brigade commander asked him to stay and help with the September elections. I missed LTC Velte. He had flown out that morning to FOB Michigan to conduct a commanders 15-6 investigation for the brigade commander. LTC Velte said he would return via Camp Wright and meet one final time with Iowa.

I came back from the Brigade TOC just as Molson announced our flight. SFC Fair and I loaded our gear in the back of the shuttle bus and took off for the Molson heliport. The bus was full of gear and seven passengers. I had assumed we were flying on the Sikorski, but I was wrong. We were all flying on the HU-1 packed to the gills. We made a stop at one FOB along the way to swap passengers.

We landed at the rotary wing terminal at the end of the runway, but we needed to be at the fixed wing terminal at the midway point to meet our troops. We spotted a bunch of troops loading up on a bus and asked for a ride down to the fixed wing terminal. The driver said, "Sure, hop on." When he saw the gear we started throwing on the bus he was beginning to have second thoughts. SFC Fair and I wasted no time loading the bus. Any open window had a ruck or duffel bag pushed through it onto the lap of an unsuspecting passenger.

Iowa's LNO met us at the fixed wing terminal, took our ammo and wished us luck. It would be a while before our main body and pallet riders arrived so we racked out on some wood pallets outside the terminal.

At 2:20 A.M. Wednesday morning I greeted SFC Natividad and SGT Olson as they swiped into the PAX terminal. SGT Olson and I talked for a few minutes while SFC Natividad coordinated a place for them to sleep. He thought he could do better than the R & R holdover tents, but his bad luck had returned as he was given two bunks in the holdover tents. The two of them called the R&R tent home until August 19th, and finally arrived at Camp Atterbury the night of August 20th.

At 5:05 Wednesday morning the main body of the Kunar ADT walked into the fixed wing PAX terminal from Jalalabad. We loaded all of our gear into a panel truck and jumped on a bus to Camp Warrior. The changes to Camp Warrior since our arrival in October were staggering. The tent city that we stayed in still existed but was dwarfed by the rows of clamshell tents. There was a new consolidated mess hall nearing completion and one clamshell was being converted into a laundromat for the troops.

Back at Camp Wright our SecFor was waiting to take Iowa to the range on Wednesday, the last task to complete for their left seat right seat ride. That morning SFC Medina, SGT Fry, SPC Brumley moved their equipment up to the flight line for their movement to Bagram. SGT Fry had already ensured that all of Iowa's radios were set to the new comsec and that their radio folks knew all of the little tricks with the Harris radios and TACSAT.

The morning was theirs to do as they pleased. At 08:45 SFC Medina was walking from the flight line to the TOC when he heard the first RPG round take flight. He looked back and saw the gunner half way up the hillside below Shiloh then he heard the impact near the CP Wright Mosque where a dust cloud was billowing up. SGT Fry was walking up from the TOC when he heard the round impact. He started moving up to the mess hall, a hardened structure, while SFC Medina ran down to the TOC to sound the alarm for Iowa. SGT Fry made it to the last set of barracks before the mess hall and was about to run into the mess hall for cover when an RPG round struck ten feet from him impacting the last barracks building. SGT Fry made a quick left and ran into the USO MWR building instead.

When SFC Medina entered the TOC it was vacant. The lights were all off and the projection screens were blank. Iowa's plan was to let the troops relax for the morning and go to the range just before lunch so there was no need to staff the TOC. SFC Medina started going through the bee huts telling everyone to get in the bunker. SFC Media saw S-3 Major Parmeter in the bunker and told her, "You need to get accountability. Go in the TOC and get on the radio," as more RPG rounds impacted the FOB. This was the first attack on the FOB where Iowa had to be in the driver's seat with no one to coach them. It usually takes one attack or TIC for that tiny switch in the human brain to flip from training to combat. This was the event to do it. Col. Barfreed was the only member of the staff who was up and around at the time dining in the mess hall with some of his troops.

SFC Mosqueda and SPC Brumley were eating a late breakfast in the mess hall when they heard the low thud of the first two rounds go off followed by the deafening blast from the round that missed SGT Fry. The old residents of the FOB remained at the tables finishing their breakfast while the new troops from Iowa dove for cover. The Iowa troops had already been briefed to stay inside hardened structures in the event of an attack. The concussion from the round that missed SGT Fry was loud enough to cause some temporary damage to his hearing. A third RPG round took out one of the interior gates with a fourth striking near our old troop barracks before the attack was over.

Things went back to normal at Camp Wright very quickly. SFC Mosqueda and the remainder of SecFor continued to work with Iowa, but eventually called off the range day in lieu of more training on the FOB. SFC Medina

SGT Fry and SPC Brumly flew to Bagram arriving at 1900 on Wednesday August 11th with a group of marines from the 15th Expeditionary force that was in route to Pakistan. They were on a humanitarian mission to assist with the flooding caused by the monsoons. Their orders were, "No weapons of any kind!" The area where they were going was opposite the Kunar River Valley, the source of insurgent support. This is the same area the U.S. was running UAV missions, firing 155 missions and providing F-15 support.

Thursday August 12th started the same. SFC Palacios and I were up just before 05:00 followed by SFC Medina and SGT Eden. Some traditions never change. The day dragged on while we waited for the last of our troops to arrive. Molson announced that they had to pull maintenance on a few of their helicopters and canceled a large number of flights, which meant the rest of our troops wouldn't be arriving until the 13th. Later in the afternoon while a group of us were writing letters and swapping photos I received a phone call from Captain Birgy stating that brigade claimed that we hadn't closed out two contracts. I told him where to find the project folders and that we had attempted several times to close them out but the database continually reverted their status back to committed from completed, but if they pulled up the file and actually looked at it, it read completed with all of the supporting documents. I was more frustrated than concerned. I knew we properly closed the contracts out several months ago before the change of command between the 4th ID and the 101st, so I wasn't worried.

By evening, thunderclouds returned as they did the night before causing the whole camp to cool off in a few minutes. The temperature suddenly dropped followed by a strong wind. SGT Flynn called out, "It's going to rain in about five minutes." Sure enough our clamshell tent started to get pounded by the rain. Within fifteen minutes we had two feet of water outside and rain was coming through the roof vents soaking our bunks. Water started to pour over the sandbags at the north end of the tent. Everyone came to, started picking up gear and moving bunks away from the roof leaks. The bunks could only be moved a foot in any direction because there were so many of them stuffed in the clamshell. The storm lasted an hour flooding most of the clamshell.

Our flight with the Missouri ADT from Bagram to Kuwait was canceled again Friday night which meant another wonderful fun filled day in

Bagram for all of us, except for our rear detachment. There weren't enough seats on the plane home for all of us so the rear det. would have to fly commercial. Saturday morning 0:800 SFC Mosqueda arrived with the rear det at the Bagram fixed PAX terminal. I found a flight going to Qatar for all of them leaving at 9:15 on a C-17; they were flying deluxe. During the five minutes I was outside the terminal explaining their travel arrangements, the flight was canceled. The only other flight out was on a C-130 leaving at 14:15 to Qatar, which they were able to get booked on. Just to be on the safe side they left us their weapons. Even though the rules allowed for weapons to be transported on commercial aircraft in a locked box in cargo its best not to chance it. SFC Mosqueda, SSG Arnold, SSG Vensula, Moreno, SPC McCool, and Spc Robleos with any luck would arrive at Camp Atterbury ahead of us. Qatar offered two direct flights a day to Baltimore, Maryland followed by a short hop to Indianapolis. However, their flight took a very different route when one of the pilots took ill. They landed in Germany, switched aircraft, then flew to Maine, then to Detroit, and then finally to Indianapolis.

On Saturday evening August 14th Missouri came over and announced that our flight was being called early and to get ready to move. The Army was no longer tracking the Kunar ADT and the Missouri ADT as two separate units. We were now all Missouri ADT, which simplified things and reduced the confusion. The PAX terminal sent over two buses and two cargo trucks for both ATDs to load up on. The trucks were allowed to drive straight out to the pallet yard, which was a blessing for the troops. Otherwise we would have had to unload the trucks and move all of the gear 200 yards to the pallet yard, then build the pallets.

With the pallets loaded the flight coordinator came out and collected everyone's ID cards and put us in lock down. SFC Hanlin and I swapped history magazines during the course of the evening. Some of the troops broke out the cards and started a few games around the terminal while others slept. We lined up at the door to terminal one when our flight "Moose 55" was announced at 23:30. We were told that there would be a 30-minute delay before we could load. We returned to our seats while twelve working dogs passed through the terminal at 0:15 hrs and out to the field to be loaded on an aircraft. SSG Tyner and I were admiring the dogs when SSG Tyner said "Did you hear something?"

"Yes it sounded like a thud." SSG Tyner thought about the thud again and decided that they must have dropped off a stack of pallets next to the PAX terminal.

Less than a minute later Spc McCool walked over to SFC Fair who was standing behind us and announced that he heard the security net call out "IDF (Indirect Fire) on the field." That would explain the thud SSG Tyner heard. At 0:30 the all clear was sounded, not that anyone took evasive action to begin with. The next announcement was our C-17 was being converted to an air ambulance for a medevac flight to Germany, the one reason for a flight delay that no one had any heartburn about. An hour and a half went by and our flight was restored. We were marching across the tarmac to our C-17. The interior was configured with civilian style seats in the middle and regular military bench seats along both sides. The civilian style seats had seen a lot of service over the years and were mounted on cargo pallets. There was about an inch of play in the supporting rollers so every time the plane stopped or started the seats shifted back and forth.

We landed four hours later at Ali Al Salem Air Base and were quickly whisked off the field to the R&R reception center. There was a two-hour wait for our buses from Camp Virginia and cargo truck to arrive. That was enough time for the troops to eat breakfast and email or call home.

Camp Virginia was just that, a big camp with tents that covered half a square mile and provisions for even more. Camp Virginia had it all, McDonalds, a pizza parlor, several huge MWR centers, coffee houses, you name it, they had it. Unfortunately laundry service was similar to Bagram. At Bagram laundry service required a seven-day turnaround. Camp Virginia claimed they could have laundry back in 24 hours. We didn't have a lot of confidence in that claim since we were down to two uniforms and both needed to be laundered. We set out to find an alternative laundry facility and we did. "Permanent Party only," that was us. It didn't take long for the troops from both ADTs to start arriving at the little laundry oasis. It gave us the chance to start comparing notes of what took place in the course of the year.

Monday August 16th was a down day at Camp Virginia. Troops stayed busy watching movies at the MWR or calling home. Most tried unsuccessfully to get some sleep in the afternoon in preparation for our final journey, which was to commence at 0:200 Tuesday morning when we would go through customs.

The customs office was the true start of our journey home. They selected 25% of the troops at random for a full 100% inspection of every item they packed. The rest of us went through x-ray screening similar to what the airlines use except a little more thorough. After that we were locked down until it was time to go to Kuwait International Airport (KCIA). This time we were really locked down inside a fenced compound with no contact with the outside. We were given a tent with cots and chairs where the troops either slept or played cards until 10:00 A.M.

At 10 o'clock we formed up one platoon of baggage handlers, another for security and the main body. The buses arrived and we were off to Kuwait International Airport for our final flight home. We arrived on the backside of the terminal and drove down a military tarmac with a mix of military and civilian aircraft with one Boeing 737 standing out of the crowd, our "freedom bird" from Miami Air International.

The baggage team slithered into the belly of the plane to stuff our gear underneath. There wasn't enough room for a man to stand up in the cargo hold, just enough to crawl in and stuff rucks. Wheels were up at 14:00 and our first stop was at Bucharest Romania for a crew change at 1750 Kuwait time. When we landed in Romania the airport looked identical to Manas, the same terminal design of the Soviet era. Keflavik Iceland was our next landing at 23:40 Kuwait time, 9:40 local time. In Keselvick we were allowed to deplane leaving our weapons onboard to walk the terminal. It was still daylight with a beautiful view of the tundra and the mountains in the distance. We had time to buy a few chocolates at the duty free store. The store manager gladly took our American dollars. We had one more crew stop before reaching Indianapolis.

At 10:50 P.M. local time our 737 touched down at Portsmouth, New Hampshire. The pilot cracked the PA system and said "Let me be the first to welcome you back on U.S. soil." Cheers went up with elation. We were given an hour on the ground to stretch our legs so I decided to grab my razor and use the time to shave. One customs agent came on board to collect a few customs forms while I pulled my razor out. I departed the plane, handed my customs form to the officer in the terminal and was greeted by a man with a clipboard who welcomed me home. The customs area was deserted as I worked my way around to the main corridor. I heard the music first then saw the people of Portsmouth lined shoulder to shoulder on either side of the corridor welcoming us home. It was a rather moving experience to be greeted by WWII vets, Korean War vets and the general public. At the distant end of the terminal hung a series of signal flags from the USS Constitution, the oldest warship in the Navy spelling out welcome home. Out in the main lobby cell phones were handed out for troops to call home. There were donuts, ice cream, stuffed animals, and a pastor handing out bibles. People brought their dogs in for the troops to pet and just about everyone did pet them. Outside there were more people welcoming us home in the dark asking us about our deployment. The hour was ticking by quickly. Before we knew it we were all called back to the main part of the terminal for a ceremony and group photo. I hadn't noticed that the walls of the terminal were lined with the photos of all the troops who had returned through New Hampshire. Ours would soon be added to the wall of fame. The two ADTs stood together for a few photos, then several older veterans unfurled old glory and presented the colors to us. A lady stepped forward and sung the national anthem and we all joined in to sing. Another veteran came forward with a bag of stars cut from the field of the flags that the VFW and Legion retired. He presented one star to each of the troops to carry with him.

The Missouri and Kunar sister ADTs at the Welcome home ceremony in New Hampshire on U.S. soil again. Photo courtesy of JoAnne and Fred Schottler of the Pease Greeters. (WWW.peasegreeters.org)

Over the course of the years, over 75,000 troops had returned home through Portsmouth and each had received a star. Then the master of ceremonies asked both commanders to come forward to accept an autographed sweatshirt from all of the people from "Pease Greeters." LTC Jackson and I stepped forward and were greeted by two ladies who had the sweatshirts draped over their backs. This tradition started during a trip to the Whitehouse when President Bush invited a delegation of the "Pease Greeters" to be honored in Washington. They presented the president with an autographed sweatshirt. The master of ceremonies said, "We want to give you the shirts off our backs in thanks for your service." Each lady gave us a hug and a sweatshirt. Then we were each given the microphone to say a few words of thanks and we were off.

LTC Jackson and LTC Kelly receiving autographed sweatshirts from the citizens of New Hampshire. Photo courtesy of JoAnne and Fred Schottler of the Pease Greeters. (WWW.peasegreeters.org)

The people of New Hampshire were still showering us with gifts as we boarded the plane-chocolate bunnies, large bars of white chocolate, boxes of girl scouts cookies. As we taxied away the pilot called to our attention that our greeters were out on the tarmac waving flags for our final send off. The New Hampshire welcome was a far cry from the one we received in 2006 at Los Al where we were promptly marched off the airfield bypassing our families and well wishers to the post auditorium for several speeches.

Wheels were up at midnight for the final leg of our journey. At 2:20 A.M. we touched down in Indianapolis. The plane taxied back to the old abandoned international terminal sporting a banner, *warehouse space available*. We were greeted by Brigadier General Johnson and CSM Roman of the 40th Infantry Division along with soldiers from Missouri and Camp Atterbury. Our baggage detail quickly went to work pulling our gear out of the belly of the plane while the rest of us were sequestered in the terminal. It was announced that coffee and pastries were available in the parking lot. The first troops who tried to indulge were told they couldn't leave the terminal. I attempted to see what was going on and was told weapons were not allowed outside the terminal. I passed the word along and SFC Hanlin decided to get a cup of coffee. The attendant at the truck said he only had one cup for the coffee. SFC Hanlin decided that since he was the only one outside he would have the honors of the only cup of coffee. The welcome we received from Indianapolis was a sharp contrast to that from Portsmouth. Odd that the American public had no problems with us carrying weapons into combat and entrusting us to clear our weapons every time we returned inside the wire, but in our own country we couldn't be trusted to carry an empty weapon. The trip from Kuwait to Indianapolis took us 19 hours and 20 minutes, from wheels up in Kuwait to touchdown in Indianapolis.

We headed south on Hwy 65 with only a few street lamps. The highway frontage was a dark abyss until we came upon a Christian church. The church was the only thing lit up bright as day. That's when it hit me that we were really home. I had walked by many vacant churches and cathedrals in Ireland and England during my leave that looked cold and deserted. This small community church struck me as being full of life even in the predawn darkness. During our deployment it was the small community organizations and hometown churches and temples that supported us, not the multi-national corporations, or the city-states of America.

Chapter Fifty-Three

THE LAUNDRY ROOM

The slow road home allowed for the soldiers of the Kunar and the Missouri ADT time to decompress and to just relax. The laundry room at Camp Virginia was an ideal place for the troops to compare notes. In Afghanistan we were not subject to the same media filters that American people are in the United States. Having access to news coverage from Asia, Pakistan, Iran, and input from educated Afghans put a different light on events.

The one topic everyone talked about was the major covert war going on between the Shiite and Sunni Muslims with Iran and Saudi Arabia being the two dominant players. Saudi Arabia currently has the upper hand in the war. The difference between the two is Saudi Arabia is waging a global war where Iran is fighting a defensive regional war. Saudi Arabia is funding the construction of mosques and Islamic Centers in the United States, Western Europe, Pakistan and Eastern Afghanistan to spread their brand of Islam called Wahabism. This is the violent sect of Islam that advocates killing infidels. Infidels are anyone who is not a Wahabi.

Saudi Arabia has been successful in obtaining the backing of the United States and the United Nations to invoke sanctions again Iran by playing up Israel's fears of an Iranian nuclear bomb. Saudi Arabia's goal is to prevent the land locked Asian countries from exporting their petroleum reserves to the Western market so that Saudi Arabia can continue to exert its influence on the world's economy. This has led Iran to seek an alliance with Russia for nuclear power development and trade.

Iran was once one of American's two main pillars of strategic defense of the Middle East oil fields against the Soviet Union. It has now aligned itself with Russia the Bear, which has raised itself up on one side. This alliance includes Turkey, another unlikely ally given the past centuries of armed conflict with Russia. Iran and Turkey provide access for Russian and Central Asian oil and gas to western markets. China is already developing pipeline access to Central Asian energy, which will reduce their demand on Middle East energy.

If you can control the flow and distribution of oil you can control the market and impact the global economy. Central Asian pipelines that route through Iran or Turkey to market can't be controlled by Saudi Arabia or the United States, but pipelines that run through Afghanistan to the Indian Ocean can't be controlled by Russia or Iran, Saudi Arabia's primary nemesis religiously, politically, and economically.

The construction of oil and gas pipelines through Afghanistan has been stymied again and again by Pakistan, which is heavily influenced by Saudi Arabia. The educated Afghans with whom I talked about Iran's nuclear ambitions believe that it is in response to Pakistan's nuclear capability, not for a preemptive strike against Israel. Politically, Iran couldn't state that they are developing a nuclear bomb to counter the threat from a fellow Islamic Republic, but it is politically acceptable in the Islamic world to state that it is being developed to counter Israel's implied nuclear threat. The Afghans believe that Pakistan's nuclear arsenal is controlled by Saudi Arabia even though the warheads are in Pakistan. Saudi Arabia has no need to develop a nuclear bomb if they can control Pakistan's. The great game is alive and well, but this time the stakes are higher.

There is a second covert Islamic war going on with Saudi Arabia's support in the shadows. This covert war is being conducted with no planning or organization on the part of Saudi Arabia, just passive financial support. The birth rate of third world Islam is skyrocketing. In Afghanistan the lower class males each have four wives and each is expected to give birth to four sons before they can use birth control. If each wife only has four sons then every man would father sixteen children. But, not every baby is a male; some are females increasing the number of children even more. Afghanistan is not the only Muslim country with an exponential birth rate. When the carrying capacity of a country is exceeded, that country must export its population. The carrying capacity can be either economic or basic life supporting requirements such as food. Europe, the United Kingdom, and Australia are experiencing a tidal surge of Muslim immigration which includes legal, illegal, refugees and asylum seekers. The United States is seeing an influx of Muslim immigration along with a second third-world invasion from Mexico. The events in Mexico are extremely similar to what is happening in Afghanistan; both countries have a drug cartel problem.

The convert invasion of the west is starting to organize and demand that Shura law be practiced. Once a country falls to Islam there is no turning back. Death or exile is the only ways out of Islam. Even the now Wahabi sects of Islam preach violence toward infidels and specifically Christians. At FOB Finley Shields the FOB Eiman was preaching death to the Americans, the same Americans who were providing jobs, and building Afghanistan. Our interpreter Sam was almost assaulted when he walked into a mosque on FOB Bostick just for wearing an American uniform. It didn't matter that he was an Afghani and a Muslim, he wasn't welcome in the mosque because the Eiman was preaching violence against the U.S. and they feared he would report what he heard.

Many women's groups in the States believe that if Afghan women are enlightened about western ways and the rights women have in the west they will stand up and demand their rights. Even if there was no opposition to Afghan women they would not depart from their strict Islamic culture. These women know no other life; they are confused and perplexed when they see western women in authority or in control of their own lives. The Afghan women have no way of relating to western women; even eastern European women of Muslim faith are a world away from them.

There were a series of cold war era experiments conducted on dogs to test theories of suppressive behavior. The dogs were placed in a divided pen where they received electrical shocks from the floor pad. The dogs would quickly jump over the partition to escape the pain. The dogs were then tied to one side so they couldn't escape and repeatedly shocked. Later the dogs were untied and shocked again but the dogs' minds were conditioned to the concept that there was no escape. They remained in the pen and endured the pain of the electrical shocks. This is exactly what takes place in Afghanistan with women starting from childhood. The only difference is the pen has been replaced with an adobe compound.

Had it not been for the Christian Reconquista of Iberia during the Granada War of 1492 when the Moors of the Nasrid Dynasty made their last stand of a five hundred year war, the western world would be bowing to Mecca today.

Chapter fifty-four

HOBBITS, FOBBITS AND OTHER CREATURES OF MENTION

Back in 1937, Ronald Reuel Tolkien, a WWI veteran wrote a series of stories that have stayed popular over the years. Most notable was the Lord of the Rings, which started with a book called the Hobbit. The main character was Mr. Bilbo Baggins, a Hobbit and the reluctant hero of the story. Mr. Bilbo was not your average Hobbit who would stay put on his farm and refuse to go out and see the world. With the nudging of a wizard, Mr. Bilbo found himself in one contest after another for the lives of his friends and his own. Mr. Bilbo wouldn't return home any richer or more famous than he was when he embarked on his adventure.

The story of the Hobbit has been a favorite among the troops for years. Every FOB I've been on has at least one of J.R.R. Tolkien's books on his library shelf. From the description of a typical Hobbit came the term FOBbit, a term given to soldiers who refuse to leave the safety of the FOB but still want the glory that comes with the deployment. These FOBbits are also known as, "Glory Hounds," the first to stand in front of the camera, or coordinate interviews with a webcam in their quarters and lay claim to accomplishments that they hindered from start to finish.

FOBbits stand out from the rest of the soldiers. They are usually obese, continually in the MWR on the Internet or the phone with their families,

451

or glued to the TV. They may have gone outside the wire once to get their CAB (Combat Action Badge), but refused to go out again. These are also the troops who complain bitterly about pulling guard duty or lending a hand when it is time to work in 100+ degree heat. They are first in line at the mess hall, and take thirty-minute showers using up all of the hot water just before the troops return from an eight-hour mission. FOBbits are found on all installations, every unit and at all levels of the officers and NCO corps.

There are soldiers who have no business going outside the wire. Their job is to be at the ready on the FOB in times of need such as a surgical team, or aircraft mechanics. These are the tireless soldiers who keep on working until the job in completed, who roll out of the rack in the middle of the night and race to their duty station, miss meals and hot showers along with hours of solid rest never to be confused with a FOBbits.

The Kunar ADT SecFor missed meals and many a good night's sleep responding to the call for help. Usually they responded with the Explosive Ordnance Disposal or Route Clearance Patrol after an ambush rendered a vehicle disabled or a second IED was discovered that had to be disposed of. The rules are once you find an IED you own it until EOD arrives. For EOD and route clearance patrol to safely do their job they must be protected. EOD and route clearance operations move very slowly. One of the route clearance teams was nicked named the "Kunar Creeper" because of the snail's pace they moved. When the Ag section would conduct a VetCap or watershed survey their safety depended upon the SecFor remaining ever vigilant. VetCaps could last as long as nine hours while SecFor soldiers remained in the field continuously scanning their sectors. Scanning a sector isn't glamorous work; it means remaining alert at all times fighting fatigue, heat and dust.

The Ag section was the main focus of the Kunar ADT because of the unit's mission. The Ag section wouldn't have succeeded without the SecFor. Over the course of the year, I kept an ear to the ground for stories about the SecFor troops. The stories were few because they did their job as professionals. Stories come from adversity when things go wrong. I included the names of the SecFor troops to thank them for their support and service to the Ag section.

There is an old proverb "All boats rise with the tide." It holds true with any organization. The accomplishments of a few people can carry the weight of many. I was reminded of this proverb by SFC Hanlin when the brigade downgraded awards and stated awards must correspond with the individual's rank not leadership, accomplishment and responsibility. This means that gifted junior NCOs with strong leadership and organizational skills would carry the weight of obese couch potatoes who would come home with a bronze star while the junior NCO received a hand shake and a pretty piece of paper. There are others who claimed to participate in half of a unit's missions. When reviewed, those missions were to the safe areas close to home. Bottom line: we didn't go to Afghanistan for flashy awards; we went to make a difference.

God has blessed our nation a thousand times. The members of the Kunar ADT come from a military linage dating back to the Mayflower Compact, the first legal document to be written in what would become the United States of American. The first line gives honor to the lord God that created us, "In the name of God Amen." Since that time, God has continuously blessed and tested our nation. The freedoms we enjoy are a result of eternal vigilance of the citizen soldier, the minuteman, a farmer who stays ready and waits for the call to arms. A reluctant warrior when called holds nothing back for the defense of his home and nation. Just like Mr. Bilbo Baggins, the lead character in J.R.R. Tolkien's Hobbit, the humble hero when the mission was accomplished and order was restored, he quietly returned home.

There were other people to thank who supported us in our time of need. The Brigade Chaplin Mejia and Camp Wright's Chaplin Anderson of the U.S. Air Force were always there when our troops needed guidance and support for things that went wrong at home and for the unit when we had some trying personnel changes. Like every unit we had our problems but on one wants to remember the problems when you are bouncing your grandchild on your knee. I left those stories and their causes out.

On Sunday August 22nd our sister ADT from Missouri loaded up a bus for home at 05:00 while the Kunar ADT was shuttled throughout the day to the airport for flights to the closest airports to home. Some of the troops knew that their jobs wouldn't be there when they returned and had already started the process of finding new employment prior to our redeployment. My current and former supervisors had taken care of me and found me a position of greater responsibility with another agency.

Ag

SFC Medina (Platoon Sergeant) SGT Bently, SFC Fair, SGT Flynn, SFC Fulton, SFC Hanlin, SFC, PFC Lopez, SSG Lucas, SFC Natividad, SGT Percival, SGT Stevens, SPC Tanson, SSG Tyner

SecFor

SFC Mosqueda (Platoon Sergeant); SFC Mead (1st Squad Leader) SGT Contreras, SGT Eden, SPC Garcia, PFC Mercado, SPC Rojas, SPC Tropeano, SPC Ybarra; SSG Arnold (2nd Squad Leader Dismounted) SPC Derouen, SGT Johanson, SPC Batucan, SPC Mills, SPC Coffman, SPC Clements, SPC Rivera, SPC Wong-Arceso; SSG Valenzuela (3rd Squad Leader) SSG Carter, SGT DeGeorge, SPC Arechiga, PFC Borbon, PFC Mc Gee, SPC Moreno, SPC Robledo, SPC Votava; SGT Wareham, SGT Diaz.

Special Troops

PFC Molina our cartographer and illustrator, SGT Brumley IT specialist, SPC Fry communications NCO, SPC Gonsalves Medic, SFC Graham Adjuant, SPC Larson Medic, SGT Olson Forward Observer and supply clerk, SSG Palacios Supply sergeant, SFC Teso Operations, SFC Velasco Intel.

GLOSSARY

Word	Definition
155	Artillery
1151	An up armored HMMWV
A-10	Thunderbolt II close support aircraft "Warthog"
A1-c	An A1C blood test shows an individual's average blood sugar level over the past 60 to 90 days. Used for monitoring and controlling diabetes
AAFES	Army Air Force Exchange Services, provides merchandise and services to active duty military, Guard and Reserve members, military retirees, and family members
A-bag	A duffle bag that contains basic items a soldier will need to live in a forward area
ABP	Afghan Border Police
Absolute Air	Air cargo company that uses Hip helicopters
ACM	Anti-Coalition Militia

ACU	Army combat uniform
ADT	Agricultural Development Team
AGS-17	A Soviet manufactured, tripod mounted, automatic grenade launcher, which fires 30mm grenades from a thirty-round drum magazine. The maximum range of the AGS-17 is 1700 meters
AK-47	Kalashnikov 7.62 mm assault rifle
Allah Akbar	God is greatest
ANA	Afghan National Army
Angel Flares	A (decoy) flare is an aerial infrared countermeasure to counter an infrared homing surface-to-air missile or air-to-air missile
ANP	Afghanistan National Police
AO	Area of Operations
AOR	Area Of Responsibility
Apache	A Boeing AH-64 is a four-blade, twin-engine attack helicopter used as an Advanced Attack Helicopter
Arbab	Local Chief
Aerostat	A balloon system that remains aloft primarily through the use of buoyant lighter-than-air gases that is used as an observation and radio communication platform
ASG	Asian Security Group
ASR	Alternate Supply Route
ASV	Armored Security Vehicle

AT-4	Shoulder launched Anti-Tank weapon
ATTA	Afghan Transit Trade Agreement
AVA	Afghan Veterinary Association. The Afghanistan Veterinary Association was established in 1996 in order to meet an urgent need for the reliable delivery of animal health care services. Its 1020 members include veterinarians, assistant veterinarians and para-vets.
Bernau	Czechoslovak M26 light machine gun, which fires from a top loading 20-round magazine. This 7.9mm weapon was developed between World War I and II and was sold abroad as the M30 to China, Yugoslavia and Romania. The British Bren gun is based on the M26 design. The Mujahedeen called them 20 shooters.
BFT	Blue Force Tracker is a system that integrates GPS tracking and text messaging.
BHO	Battle Hand Off
Black ammo	Running out of ammo
Black Hawk	A Sikorsky UH-60 is a four-bladed, twin-engine, medium-lift utility helicopter, also used as a gun ship
BM-1	Single barrel 107 rocket launcher
BM-12	An outdated Soviet multiple rocket launcher. The Chinese improved and manufactured it as the type 63. Most Mujahedeen BM-12s were actually Chinese Type 63s. It is ground mounted, has twelve barrels and fires 107mm rockets to a distance of 8500 meters. It weighs 661 kilograms.
Boomerang	An acoustic gunshot shooter detection system that pinpoints the direction of the origin of incoming small arms fire

BSB	Brigade support battalion
Burqa	Loose garment with gauze patch over eyes, completely covering woman's body
BX	Base Exchange
CAD	Computer Aided Design
CCA	Close Combat Air
CCP	Casualty Collection Point
CERP	Commander's Emergency Response Program. Funds that provide tactical commanders a means to conduct multiple stability tasks, which include purchasing equipment, building materials, and service contracts. Usually used for items under $5,000.00, but with appropriate approval can be used for items as much as $200,000.00
CET	Convoy Escort Team
CF	Coalition Forces
CH	Chaplin
Chalk	A group of passengers manifested for a military flight that will travel together.
Charahi	Road junction
CLP	Combat Logistic Patrol
CLS	Combat Lifesaver Bag – emergency medical supplies
CMA	Afghan National Army Central Movement Agency
CO	Commanding Officer

COL	Colonel
COP	Combat Out Post
CP	Check Point
CWIED	Command Wire Improvised Explosive Device
Dari	The language spoken by the educated people in Afghanistan
Day of Ashura	Massacre of the prophet Mohammad's grandson Hussein and his 72 followers at Karbala in Iraq
DFAC	Dining facility run by a civilian contractor. Mess halls are run by military personnel.
DShK	Soviet manufactured 12.7mm heavy machine gun. It is a primary armament on Soviet manufactured armored vehicles and is effective against ground and air targets. It has a wheeled carriage, tripod and mountain mount for ground and air defense firing. It has a rate of fire of 540 - 600 rounds per minute with a maximum range of 7000 meters and an effective range of 1500 meters against ground targets and 1000 meters against air targets.
DUKES	The CREW Duke system is a vehicle-mounted electronic jammer designed to prevent the remote detonation of IEDs
ECP	Entry Control Point
Eid al Adha	Feast of sacrifice. The Islamic holiday that marks the end of Ramadan, the month of fasting
EKIA	Enemy Killed in Action

| Enfield | British manufactured .303 bolt action rifle, which was the standard British infantry weapon from 1895 through the Korean War. It saw wide service on the North-West frontier and its long range and powerful cartridge made it a favorite in India and Afghanistan. It has a maximum range of 2550 meters, and an effective range of 800 meters. It has a 10-round magazine and can carry an additional round in the chamber, so the Mujahedeen called them 11 shooters. |

| EOD | Explosive Ordnance Disposal |

| EOM | End Of Mission |

| ETT | Embedded training team |

| Evac | Medical evacuation (also medevac) |

| EWIA | Enemy Wounded in Action |

| Exfil | Exfiltration (getting out of there) |

| FOB | Forward Operating Base |

| FOO | Field ordering officer (FOO) funds are primarily used by units to purchase mission critical requirements that cannot be obtained through the higher headquarters' logistical air- or ground-delivery resupply plan or through the regional contracting center's (RCC's) existing, local contracts |

| FRAGO | Fragmentary order, provides changes to existing operations orders. |

| GBU | The Guided Bomb Unit is a 250 to 5,000-pound laser-guided bomb. It is designed to be used with F-15E and F-111F aircraft. |

Ghar	Mountain in Pashto
Goryunov	Heavy machine gun. The SGM Stankovy Goryunov Modernizovanniy M-49 was adopted by the Soviet Army during World War II; modernized versions are in service with the Russian Army today. It is a gas operated, air cooled, company level 7.62 weapon that has vehicle and ground mounts. It has a rate of fire of 650 rounds per minute and a maximum range of 2500 meters and an effective range of 1000 meters.
Green zone	An agricultural region of gardens, orchards, fields and vineyards bisected by a network of irrigation ditches. They normally border rivers and some sections of highway and most are practically impassible for vehicles.
Haj	Muslim pilgrimage
Haji	The title given to a person who has made the pilgrimage to Mecca
Harbakai	A Pashtu Tribal policeman or regulator
Hawala	Customary system of money transfers
HESCO Barrier	A wire basket used for erosion control produced by the HESCO company, which the U.S. army adapted to use to build defensive walls filled with earth and rock
Hind	A large helicopter gunship and low-capacity troop transport, also known as a Mil Mi-24
Hip	Soviet designed cargo helicopter
HLZ	Helicopter Landing Zone
HMWVV	Modified Hum Vee – also known as the 1114 and 1151 for up-armored variants

HUEY	A Bell UH-1N Twin engine medium utility helicopter
IBA	Interceptor Body Armor ballistic protective vest system
ID	Infantry Division
Idea New	A None Government Agency that contracts with the State Department or USAID for construction and agriculture projects
IED	Improvised Explosive Device
Infil	Infiltrate
IOTV	Improved Outer Tactical Vest
IR	Infrared light
ISI	Inter-Service Intelligence (Pakistan Intelligence Service)
Jerib	A measure of land about .195 hectares
Jihad	Holy war
Jirga	Tribal council (Pashtun)
Jui	Water channel
Kalashnikov	Soviet automatic assault rifle. The AK-47 and the AKM Kalashnikovs fire a 7.62mm round while the AK-74 fires a 5.45mm round.
Karez	Hand dug underground water channel
KBR	Kellogg Brown and Root
KE	Letters assigned to the central Kunar River Valley Battle space for pre plotted artillery

Khan	Originally a title customarily used for landed elite
Khan	Nomad
KIA	Killed in Action
Kinetic	A term used to describe hot, sporadic activity by insurgents
Kiowa	A Bell OH-58 helicopter - a single-engine, single-rotor, military helicopters used for observation, utility, and direct fire support
KLE	Key Leader Engagement - a meeting between U.S. or ISAF leaders and Afghan community / government leaders to discuss topics that are relevant to the stability of the village, city or region
Km	Kilometer. Approximately 0.6 of a mile (slang "clicks")
Kochi	Kochi are nomadic tribesman of Afghanistan. They live primarily by herding and trading sheep, goats and camels.
Kyarizy	Afghan system of underground tunnels
LACE	Liquid Ammo Causalities Equipment
LED	Light Emitting Diode
LMTV	Light Medium Tactical Vehicle - a large flatbed cargo truck
Loya Jirga	Grand assembly or counsel
LTC	Lieutenant Colonel
LZ	Landing Zone

M1-10	A semi-automatic rifle that is chambered for the 7.62x51mm NATO round
M-14	Rifle that shoots 7.62 (.30 caliber) cartridges. Derived from the WW-II M-1 Garand
M4	Carbine version of the M-16 rifle
M-4	A carbine version of the M-16
M72A2 LAW	Light Anti-Armor Weapon is a portable one-shot 66 mm unguided anti-tank weapon
Madrasa	Koranic school
Malik	Local leader
MEDEVAC	Evacuation of personnel requiring immediate medical attention, usually on a UH-60 helicopter
MG	Machine Gun
MI	Military Intelligence
MIA	Missing In Action
MK-19	A 40 mm belt-fed automatic grenade launcher or grenade machine gun
Model 1938 Mortar	The Soviet model 1938 107mm mortar was originally the standard regimental mortar for mountain units. It is a reduced size version of the 120mm mortar suitable for transport on a pack animal. It can fire 15 rounds per minute and has a maximum range of 5150 meters firing heavy rounds and 6300 meters firing light rounds
Molson Air	A Canadian helicopter company providing rotary wing services in Afghanistan

MRAP	Mine Resistant Ambush Protection
MRE	Meal Ready to Eat
MSR	Main Supply Route
Muezzin	One who calls the faithful to prayer
Mujahid	One who leads the faithful in holy war, or takes part in a holy war; also known as mujahedeen
Mullah	Islamic religious leader
MWR	Morale Welfare Recreation
NCO	Non-commissioned Officer
NCOIC	Non-commissioned Officer In Charge
NGO	Non-governmental Organization
NIPR Net	Non-classified Internet Protocol Router Network (NIPRNet), basic commercial Internet access
ODA	Operational Detachment Alpha, a type of special forces team
OEF	Operation Enduring Freedom
OGA	Other Government Agencies
OIC	Officer In Charge
OP	Observation post
OP Order	Operations Order - used to describe the situation, the mission, and what activities the unit will conduct
OPORD	Operation Order

OPS	Operation
Outside the wire	Out of the FOB, or COP
Pashtun	The dominant Afghan tribe; approximately 50% of the country is Pashtun
Pashtunwali	Pashtun tribal code, which is still followed in mountainous villages
PAX	Passenger Air Terminal. The term PAX is also used as a reference to passengers.
PFC	Private First Class
PID	Positive Identification referring to a target
PK	Soviet 7.62mm company machine gun, which replaced the Goryunov machine gun. It weighs 16.5 kilograms and has an effective range of 1000 meters. The Mujahedeen called them 100 shooters since they fire out of 100-round box linked ammunition.
PKC	Soviet light machine gun
PKM	Soviet machine gun
POL	Petroleum, Oil and Lubricants
POO	Point Of Origin - referring to the location from where shots are coming
PQ-2	Infrared sighting device
PRT	Provincial Reconstruction Team
Pashtun	The dominant ethnic group (nearly 50%) of Afghanistan who speak Pashtu. The British referred to these people as Pathans

PX/BX	Post Exchange / Base Exchange is a small store
Qawm	A kinship group; can be used at the level of family, extended family, tribe, sub-tribe, etc.
QRF	Quick Reaction Force
Ramadan	The Islamic holy month of fasting; the 9th month of the Islamic year
RCP	Route Clearance Patrol - a team of engineers that clears roads of land mines and other IEDs
Rhino	An electrical device mounted on the front of the vehicle that protrudes like a giant rhino horn; it is designed to detonate roadside bombs along a route before the convoy reaches them
Roots of Peace	A Non Government Organization dedicated to the removal of landmines and the subsequent planting or replanting of vineyards and orchards
RPG	Rocket Propelled Grenade
RPG-18	Soviet manufactured single shot, shoulder fired antitank weapon, which fires a 66mm shaped-charged rocket. The rocket is stored in an extendable storage tube, which also functions as a launcher. The launcher is thrown away after use. It has an effective range of 135 meters and is a copy of the USM72A2 LAW
RPG-7	Soviet manufactured shoulder-fired antitank weapon that fires a shaped-charged rocket. It has an effective range of 300 meters
RPK	Soviet 7.62 mm light machine gun
RTB	Return To Base

S/G section	A staff section with the letter "S" is for battalion or Brigade level staff; the letter "G" is for Division level staff.
S/G-1	The Adjutant responsible for the personnel and administration center
S/G-2	Intelligence staff responsible for preparing and developing intelligence estimates, and situational awareness
S/G-3	Operations staff responsible for planning and coordinating operations, and training
S/G-4	Logistics staff responsible for planning, coordinating and supervising supplies, services, and equipment and vehicle maintenance, and the transportation of equipment
S/G-6	Communications staff responsible for computer and radio systems
S/G-9	Civil Military affairs
SAW	Squad Automatic Weapon, M-249 5.56mm
SAW	Squad Automatic Weapon - light machine gun, 5.56 mm
Sayyid	Descendant of the prophet
SFC	Sergeant First Class
SGT	Sergeant
Shabnama	Night letter - a letter placed on a resident's door at night threatening death or harm if the occupants doesn't do as the letter directs.
Shari'a	Islamic law

Shura	Village council (similar, though often not as formal in its construction, to the jirga)
Shura e Nazar	Supervisory council of the north
SIPR Net	Secret Internet Protocol Router Network (SIPRNet) - an Internet system used to transmit classified information
SKS	Samozaryadiy Karabin Simonoval gas operated semi-automatic Soviet carbine with a folding bayonet. It has a ten-shot magazine and fires the 7.62x39 cartridge to a maximum range of 1000 meters with a 400 meter effective range. The first models were fielded during World War II through the early 1950s. The Mujahedeen simply call them carbines.
SOP	Standard Operating Procedures
SP	Start Point
Sufi	A mystic branch of Islam with considerable influence in Afghanistan. Sufis are more widespread among Sunnis
Sunnis	The majority Islamic community in Afghanistan. Over two thirds of the populace are Sunnis, followers of the Hanafi School
T wall	Precast concrete barrier
Tadjik	Ethnic Afghans from the northeastern regions of Afghanistan who make up about 25% of the population
Talib	A religious student

TC	Tank commander, truck commander
TCP	Traffic Control Point
TIC	Troops In Contact with enemy forces
TO&E	Table of Organization and Equipment
TOC	Tactical Operations Center is a command post that includes a small group of specially trained personnel who provide guidance and support to troops in the field during a mission
Tsadar	All purpose cloth that Afghans carry and wear. It serves as a ground cloth, sleep bag, camouflage, bundle wrap and shroud
TTP	Tactics, techniques and procedures
UAV	Unmanned aerial vehicle
Ulema	Religious scholars or leaders
Uluswal	District administrator
Uluswali	District - subdivision of a province
USAID	United States Agency for International Development
USDA	United States Department of Agriculture
Usher	Islamic tax, one tenth of crop

USPFO	The United States Property and Fiscal Office for each state handles the Federal property and funds for the state's National Guard, both Army and Air Guard
Uzbek	Ethnic Afghans primarily in the north central part of Afghanistan who make up 10% of the population and speak Turkic
VBIED	Vehicle Borne Improvised Explosive Device
VETCAP	Veterinary Civil Assistance Program
VS-17	Marker panel used to signal friendly aircraft
Wahabi	Wahabi or Wahabism is a conservative Sunni Islamic sect based on the teachings of Muhammad ibn Abd-al-Wahhab. It is associated with radical Islam
WIA	Wounded In Action